POLITICAL HEBRAISM

Political Hebraism

Judaic Sources in
Early Modern Political Thought

———⚬⚬⚬———

EDITED BY

Gordon Schochet, Fania Oz-Salzberger,
and Meirav Jones

SHALEM PRESS
JERUSALEM AND NEW YORK

Book and cover design: Erica Halivni
Cover pictures: Copyright © VISUALPHOTOS
Geographical Map of Europe by Pietro de Cortona

Printed in Israel

ISBN 965-7052-44-0
       978-965-7052-45-7

∞ The paper used in this publication meets the minimum requirements of the
American National Standard for Information Sciences—Permanence of Paper
for Printed Library Materials, ANSI Z39.48-1992

CONTENTS

Introduction

―――⇒∘∘⇐―――

Meirav Jones

1. The Question

Key political thinkers at the onset of modernity—those who formulated
ideas such as national sovereignty, the modern social contract, international law, and republicanism—often extensively referred to the Hebrew
Bible and later Jewish sources. Incidences of such citations have been
noted by scholars of political history and early modern political thought.
In the absence of a framework such as that provided in this volume,
however, the scope of these uses of Hebraic sources could hardly be
appreciated.

A brief survey of previously acknowledged examples reveals the following: in Holland in 1617, the chair of politics at Leiden University—later
noted by Bayle as one of the greatest thinkers of his time—wrote a semi-
nal work of political theory entitled *De Republica Hebraeorum* (On the
Polity of the Hebrews).[1] In 1651 Jacob Cats opened the Great Assembly
of the States of the Netherlands with the words "Ye Children of Israel,"[2]
and in the same period the painting chosen for Holland's senate building
was Ferdinand Bol's *Moses with the Tablets of the Law*, representing the
victory of the rule of law over the rule of the church.[3] Even Hugo Grotius,
the Dutch scholar condemned in his time for atheism and hailed to this
day as the father of modern international law, invoked the authority of
"the Jews Philo and Josephus" and of Maimonides throughout his major
work, *On the Laws of War and Peace*.[4] In the same years in England, the

writings of such important thinkers as Bacon, Milton, Hobbes, Harrington, and Locke were permeated with Old Testament models and examples that often met or exceeded these authors' similar dependence on the Greco-Roman legacy.[5] Throughout the English Civil War, sermons and parliamentary discussions were shot through with the image of Israel,[6] and Cromwell justified his actions by analogizing himself to Old Testament figures.[7] England's most remarkable legal thinker, John Selden, scattered hundreds of rabbinic—and mostly talmudic—references throughout his major work, *Of the Laws of Nature and of Nations According to the Teachings of the Hebrews*.[8] The French theorist Jean Bodin was absorbed in both Testaments and included in his works scores of citations from Philo, Josephus, the Talmud, the Zohar, Rashi, Maimonides, Gersonides, the Aramaic paraphrasts (targums), David Kimhi, and Abraham ibn Ezra.[9] In Catholic Italy, in his list of ideal founders of states, Machiavelli included Moses alongside Cyrus, Romulus, and Theseus. In Germany, radical Anabaptists transformed Münster into a quasi-Utopian city, dubbed "the New Jerusalem,"[10] and in secular political thought, Althusius found the earliest application of the federalist model, which he advocated, in the federation of biblical tribes.[11]

The conference that produced this volume, which took place in Jerusalem in August 2004, was the first-ever concentrated effort by scholars from across the globe to recover the meaning and extent of Hebraism in the politics and political thought of early modernity.

In December 2003, when the Shalem Center contemplated holding an international colloquium on political Hebraism, cautious optimism surrounded the effort. The goal would be to gather scholars from around the world who had researched or reflected on the Hebraic foundations of such works as John Selden's *De Jure Naturali et Gentium Juxta Disciplinam Hebraeorum Libri Septem* and others described above, and to explore together the various roles played by Jewish sources in early modern political thought. The target was to reach between seven and twenty scholars from different countries. When the initial call for papers produced over sixty proposals representing scholars from seven countries and from a range of fields including literature, political science, history, philosophy, Jewish studies, and more, it seemed that the subject at hand, which had received relatively little concerted scholarly attention, was waiting to be addressed.

But why had the role of Hebrew sources in the history of political thought never before been the subject of concentrated scholarly inquiry?

Perhaps the fact that the most obvious sources of early modern political Hebraism were never translated from Latin should be considered. More important, though, is probably that modern scholarship, having been shaped by the Enlightenment, tends to relegate religious texts to separate "religious" fields and is uncomfortable with their integration into "rational disciplines." This may even explain why the texts were not translated: as part of an effort to "hide the evidence" of Hebraism in early modern political thought. One striking example of this is that many editions of Hobbes' *Leviathan*—as early as the eighteenth century and as late as the twenty-first—contain only the first two books of the work, ignoring the third and fourth, which lean on traditional religious sources.[12] This is particularly pronounced in the State of Israel, where to date there is still no full edition of *Leviathan* in Hebrew. Rather than considering the Old Testamentism of the second half of *Leviathan* as placing Hobbes within a mode of seventeenth-century political discourse that read religious and especially Hebraic sources in a certain way, scholarship has for the most part isolated the more "religious" books of *Leviathan* from his political theory. Not only is much of the evidence for Hobbes' reliance on Hebraic sources and images thereby lost, and his argument in *Leviathan* left incomplete, but some of his critique of the religious politics of his time is lost as well, together with aspects of his connection to Harrington, Selden, and arguably even Puritans who also relied on Hebraic models.

While *Leviathan* may have an irrefutable connection to the Old Testament, would it be correct to call the Bible as Hobbes conceived of it a "Jewish" text? Should we really consider a thinker such as Hobbes, who may not have known any Hebrew at all,[13] a Hebraist? More than it intended to answer questions such as these, the conference that yielded the papers in this compilation sought to place them on the table and to encourage debate and discussion among scholars. The standard histories of political thought would have no such debate.[14] If ancient sources of secular political ideas were to be found, they would be discovered in Greece and Rome. Religion, and certainly Christianity, contains ideas about how people are to live, but it was never intended to be the foundation of nations or sovereign states. Christianity was to overcome considerations of politics and nationality and to work, sometimes through politics, toward salvation. But did all Christians read their tradition this way? Certainly in the sixteenth and seventeenth centuries, in the aftermath of the Reformation, it seems not. There was a variety of readings: some read into the eschatological concept of the "new Israel" ideas that were explicitly political, and others—without necessarily eschatological or even theological motivations—looked back to ancient Israel for a political model. Post-biblical Jewish writings shed light on Hebrew political models, as did the Hebrew language itself, which allowed firsthand access to the original text. The Reformation recovered the Hebrew Bible from the control of the church, and, just as had happened when Aristotle was recovered three centuries before, the newly available body of work served as a source of humanism for some, whereas for others it corroborated and enriched existing theological positions.

And so the question of this compilation, which was also that posed at the conference "Political Hebraism: Judaic Sources in Early Modern Political Thought," is: What were the Hebrew language, Old Testament images, rabbinic sources, and Jewish themes doing in the political thought of early modern Europe? And it seems, as the papers in this compilation demonstrate, that there is no simple answer.

2. The Answers in this Compilation (and the Questions They Raise)

We begin with anecdotes from the earliest years of the period under consideration. The first of these papers, by Professor Wilhelm Schmidt-Biggemann of the Free University of Berlin, depicts a brand of sixteenth-century Christian political theology in which Hebrew learning and close readings and interpretations of Jewish texts were used by Christian thinkers to advance their theology and to justify employing political means to that end. This piece also illustrates the intricate relationship between Jews and Christians in the context of early modern German Hebraism and political theology: while Hebrew learning and Hebrew books were highly valued by Christians, some of whom fought to preserve the Talmud, the Kabbala, and other Jewish or quasi-Jewish books, at the same time, the attitude toward contemporary Jews was anti-Semitic. This tension was found elsewhere in Europe in this period to a greater or lesser degree. Schmidt-Biggemann's essay stands apart from others in this compilation for its focus on a political theology where the direction of the thinkers at hand, in writing and in endorsing political action, is Christian and eschatological. The paper raises a methodological issue that lingers as the field of political Hebraism continues to be defined

and entered into: is all Hebraism associated with politics in a single period to be studied under the same banner, or should Hebraism that has a
clearly defined Christian theological end somehow be separated out from
Hebraism directed toward the worldly and political? Then again, are these
strands of thought at all separable?

In the article that follows, Christopher Lynch identifies a strikingly different application of Hebrew sources in the political context. Machiavelli's
use of the Bible is not messianic, theological, or religious at all. Rather, he
reads the Bible as one of the histories, where ancient histories are held in
high esteem. Hence, while in the past historians of political thought tended to ignore Machiavelli's treatment of biblical events and figures, Lynch
suggests that the author both took the Bible seriously as a source of ideas
and wisdom and recommended that others read it in a similarly serious
and "judicious" way. The idea that a serious reading of the Bible may in
a certain sense be "secular"—in this case meaning "worldly"—even in its
ends, persisted into the seventeenth century, when readings of the Bible
and later Hebrew and Jewish sources for political purposes took place
within largely religious societies.

The next section of the book transports us to Reformation Europe.
The increased accessibility of the Hebrew Bible, and the humanist political thought that still dominated the republic of letters and relied upon
ancient models, facilitated the biblical text itself's being viewed as one
such model and arguably the best of them. Kalman Neuman takes us into
this world, looking at the genre of writing termed "the literature of the
Respublica Hebraeorum." In this genre, which developed from the late sixteenth until the late seventeenth centuries and spread throughout Europe,
antiquarians and others set out to reconstruct the constitutional history
of the Hebrews by interpreting the biblical text with the increasing array
of tools available to them. In their studies of the political institutions of
the Hebrews, writers in this genre anticipated Hobbes, Spinoza, and later
thinkers, who would draw on them.

Emile Perreau-Saussine's article on Bossuet's thought illustrates an interesting extension of—or deviation from—the predominantly Protestant
tradition of reading the Bible for politics. *Politics Drawn from the Very
Words of Holy Scripture* is a work by a Catholic thinker in which the Old
Testament, or Hebrew Bible, very much in the spirit of *sola scriptura*, was
employed to construct a political alternative to the traditional Catholic
relationship between church and state. This was not an antiquarian reading but a deeply political one. What motivated Bossuet—a Catholic

bishop—to break with traditional readings of the Bible and to find in the Old Testament a polity in which church and state are a single power and pope and church seem humiliated? Ennobling the state through Hebraic imagery, Bossuet comes to far-reaching and contentious conclusions that place him comfortably within the context of early modern political thought and show him to have employed a brand of Hebraism in which one might least expect to find bishops taking part.

The Calvinist bastion of Reformation Holland and the heart of seventeenth-century England are the next sites for our analysis of political Hebraism. Although English and Dutch societies differed significantly in their attitudes toward contemporary Jewry—the Netherlands' being home to an open Jewish community that interacted with Christian society, while England prohibited Jews from entering until the late seventeenth century—both societies displayed similar respect for biblical Hebrews and Hebrew learning. A self-identification as the "new Israel" pervaded both English and Dutch national consciousness, and while this "new Israel" identity was for the most part associated with Christian eschatology and salvation theology, the image of Israel in its simplest form and other Hebraic images entered every aspect of social life, politics, and even political thought and philosophy.

By the seventeenth century, post-biblical Jewish authors had gained legitimacy in the minds of various classes of writers and thinkers and were widely read. Jews were thought to have privileged access to the biblical text due to their knowledge of Hebrew, and for some thinkers the post-biblical Jewish tradition was itself a model, with certain rabbis and institutions revered. Maimonides' *Guide*, already known to medieval Christian philosophers, appeared in new translations in this period, and numerous other accessible editions—including tractates from the Mishna and from Maimonides' code of Jewish law, the *Mishneh Torah*—found their way into the hands of scholars, theologians, and politically aware individuals seeking relevant meanings in Jewish texts.[15] Sometimes these meanings were used to inform Christian theology and millenarianism, sometimes they informed political thought, and they even served as sources of political ideas with lasting import in the modern world.

On the Dutch scene, the key political players on whom new light can be shed by focusing on their Hebraism are no doubt Hugo Grotius and Petrus Cunaeus. The former is dealt with extensively though not exhaustively in Arthur Eyffinger's article in this volume, whereas the latter is more extensively treated in introductions to the English and Italian translations of *De Republica Hebraeorum*.[16] Eyffinger portrays the extent to which certain Dutch thinkers turned to Hebraic sources in search of long-term resolutions of urgent political crises, focusing on Hugo Grotius and on an aspect of his thought and works often neglected by scholars of international law, namely his intense interest in the parallel between the Hebrew and Dutch peoples, which so captured the Dutch popular imagination of his period.[17] Grotius' biblical plays and political writings both attest to this interest, and Eyffinger finds Grotius' Hebraism in both these genres to be in response to pressing political issues. For Grotius, the Hebrew example was not an ancient model of antiquarian interest but a close-to-home source of viable political ideas for which there was a dire need in the United Provinces.

Miriam Bodian's article returns us to the tensions between European—in this case, Dutch—identification with the people of Israel and attitudes toward contemporary Jews. Bodian shows the way in which different Hebraisms—some of which were more humanist and political, others more Calvinist and theological—incorporated different attitudes toward Jews, the former being more tolerant, whereas the latter were less so. For the most part, the Jews of the Dutch Republic did not respond to the Hebraism of the time, but Bodian focuses on an exception: the ex-*converso* litterateur Daniel Levi de Barrios, who, in the introduction to his *Triumpho del govierno popular* (1684), refuted some of the Hebraists' claims regarding Jewish political organization and sought to re-possess the tradition, there being no "new Israel" but only a continuation of the old or ancient Israel—the Jews.

In the context of widespread political Hebraism, Spinoza may be seen as arguing with and responding to not only a Jewish tradition but a Hebraic trend. Indeed, in his contribution, Menachem Lorberbaum identifies Spinoza's main interlocutors as Maimonides, Machiavelli, and Hobbes, all of whom are significant participants in the discursive setting presented in this volume. Moreover, Spinoza advocates a rational reading of the Bible reminiscent of Machiavelli's "judicious" reading, as expounded earlier in the volume by Lynch. In his *Theological Political Treatise*, however, Spinoza goes beyond Machiavelli and Hobbes and into political theology, as Lorberbaum terms it. Politics for Spinoza is a science learned from experience. As such, it must find a way to deal with religion, the permanent form of human response to fortune. Politics, therefore, if it is to hold, has a permanent need for political theology.

English Hebraism has been far less acknowledged than Dutch, yet the idea of England as the "new Israel" is pronounced already in John Foxe's *Acts and Monuments (Book of Martyrs)*, first published in 1563 and in its eighth edition in 1641. More famous, perhaps, is the Hebraism of the Puritans who landed on American soil, as is the incorporation of Hebrew in emblems of American universities, in curriculums, and in the résumés of university founders.[18] Our study of English political Hebraism takes us a generation earlier to the time of Hobbes, Selden, Harrington, and Locke—when the theoretical foundations of America, England, and much of the modern West were laid.

The section on England begins with an essay by Jason Rosenblatt, presented at this conference as work in progress on his book, *Renaissance England's Chief Rabbi: John Selden*, since published by Oxford University Press. John Selden was widely acclaimed in his own time as the most learned man in seventeenth-century England, highly regarded even by Hobbes, who rarely quoted his contemporaries favorably.[19] Selden's impact on contemporary politics was considerable: he was blamed for preventing Presbyterian government in Scotland;[20] famous for his parliamentary orations criticizing the Puritan version of the Hebrew Bible;[21] co-participant with Hugo Grotius in the founding debates of modern international law;[22] and chosen by Cromwell to draft England's constitution. Inseparable from Selden's political activity, and noted as such by his allies as well as his critics, was his Hebraism. Israel's first chief rabbi, Isaac Herzog, published an evaluation of Selden's talmudic scholarship and concluded that while Selden largely misinterpreted the Talmud, it was astonishing that a non-talmudist—and moreover, a non-Jew—could have arrived at such insights and erudition.[23] Rosenblatt focuses on Selden's masterpiece, *De Jure Naturali*, in which the author accepts the validity of the Noahide laws, which serve for him as universal natural law and, though found in the Talmud, date back to God's utterance in the Bible. Selden cites dozens of rabbinic sources, including the Talmud and such *Rishonim* and *Aharonim* as Rashi, Maimonides, Radak (R. David Kimhi), Abravanel, and many others. Selden sees continuity from a pre-Israel Noahide state, where natural law presided over the Jews and all men, through the revelation at Sinai to the Jews as a people, right down to contemporary Jewry. Moreover, he sees the development of Jewish law from principles of natural law to particular *halachot* as a model that the English can and should follow in their own legislation and understanding of their common law.

Gary Remer's contribution focuses on another English Civil War thinker, James Harrington, and his *Commonwealth of Oceana*. Making the case that this work should be read in the light of Machiavelli's and Hobbes' readings of the Bible for political ideas, Remer shows where Harrington differs from both these thinkers yet participates in the same discourse and employs the same approach to the Bible and Hebrew sources. Harrington's unique and somewhat critical attitude toward the biblical Hebrews does not prevent him from drawing what he considers to be most valuable political lessons from their experiences.

Fania Oz-Salzberger, co-editor of this volume, ends the section on England with an essay on John Locke's political thought in the context of early modern European political Hebraism. This was one of the keynote lectures at the 2004 conference. Oz-Salzberger acknowledges that, for the last three decades, scholarship has taken Locke's use of biblical references quite seriously but has attributed them to his Christianity or to the fact that these served as common ground in his debates with Robert Filmer. Oz-Salzberger suggests that New Testamentism should be seen rather as theism, and highlights the fact that in Locke's *Two Treatises on Government*, neither Jesus nor Paul is mentioned, whereas Old Testament figures such as Aaron, Abel, Abimelech, Abraham, Adam, Adonizedek, Ahaz, Cain, Esau, Eve, Isaac, Ishmael, Jephtah, Moses, and others not only appear but are discussed at length. For Locke, the Bible is a historical record of a people in history—the Israelites—with a constitution and in many senses a model system of law and governance. Locke famously stated that "in the beginning all the World was America," yet it is far less well-known that Locke's America is actually Genesis-like and that the Old Testament actually informs his ideas of natural and early society as well as the positive statements of political morality in the *Two Treatises*.

The compilation ends with a state-of-the-field analysis by coeditor Gordon Schochet, who, in an elaboration of the other conference keynote address, revisits the notion of the "Judeo-Christian" tradition said to lie at the foundation of the modern West. Schochet uses the history of political thought and autobiographical narrative to attack the notion of Judeo-Christianity. The papers in this volume, and the area of political Hebraism introduced by them, challenge this notion by pointing out that political thinkers at the onset of modernity conceived of Judaism as distinct from Christianity. They consciously borrowed and appropriated from Jewish tradition *rather than* from Christian traditions, though the latter would have been more accessible to them. "Judeo-Christianity" would do away with this distinction and, in a single construct, distort the history of ideas. Our challenge, as we work to uncover political Hebraism and its significance, is twofold: To remain conscious of how a reader's Christianity affects his reading of Jewish sources and of the fact that learning from Jewish sources does not imply tolerating Jews or even respecting contemporary Judaism; and to re-insert the reliance upon Jewish sources and its significance for the modern West into the history of political thought.

3. The Larger Project

Each of the articles in this volume is the result of the independent research of an individual scholar. The fact that these essays, conceived by thinkers isolated from one another and from others studying Jewish sources in early modern political thought, could come together into a single coherent volume, says something for the field waiting to be born.

In retrospect, it is difficult to pinpoint the "founding moment" of political Hebraism. And yet the field has certainly been founded. It has produced a peer-reviewed quarterly journal, *Hebraic Political Studies*, as well as a subsequent conference entitled "Political Hebraism: Jewish Sources in the History of Political Thought" in December 2006, and it will go on to produce further articles, books, conferences, courses, and more.

Part of the project of political Hebraism is the defining and redefining of the field. We have no need to arrive at conclusive definitions, but we hope to continue to ask and argue about key questions: What is a Jewish source? What is Hebraic? When is something to be considered political thought? Is the shift in perspective to the Hebraic a meaningful exercise? Does the discursive context of political Hebraism add anything to our understanding, and if so, what? Does the field add to each of the disciplines from which it borrows, or does it dilute them?

As we embark on the next chapter in the story of the field of political Hebraism, we once again invite our readers to join us on what we believe will be an exciting adventure, a quest for a new old world. We do not know just what we will find there, but we are confident that it will be refreshing and important.[24]

Notes

I would like to thank my coeditors Gordon Schochet and Fania Oz-Salzberger; my mentors and colleagues at the Shalem Center, Yoram Hazony and Ofir Haivry; and Gadi Weber for his comments on a draft of this introduction.

1. Lea Campos Boralevi, "Introduzione," in Petrus Cunaeus, *De Republica Hebraeorum (The Commonwealth of the Hebrews)* (1617; in English, 1653) (Florence: Centro Editoriale Toscano, 1996), pp. vii–viii. See also Richard Tuck, *Philosophy and Government 1572–1651* (Cambridge: Cambridge University Press, 1993). Tuck considers Cunaeus' work to be "one of the most remarkable pieces of political theory to come out of the early-seventeenth-century United Provinces" (p. 167).

2. Simon Schama, *The Embarrassment of Riches: An Interpretation of Dutch Culture in the Golden Age* (New York: Alfred A. Knopf, 1987), p. 100.

3. Ibid., pp. 117–121.

4. See Hugo Grotius, *De Jure Belli ac Pacis; Book 1: The Translation*, trans. Francis Kelley (Oxford: Clarendon Press, 1925), in which the index cites Maimonides 26 times and Philo 114 (pp. 913, 917–918). The use of Maimonides and other rabbinic authors by Cunaeus and Grotius has been considered by scholars. For example, see Phyllis S. Lachs, "Hugo Grotius' Use of Jewish Sources in On the Law of War and Peace," *Renaissance Quarterly* 30:2 (1977), pp. 181–200; Arthur Eyffinger, "Introduction," in Petrus Cunaeus, *The Hebrew Republic*, trans. Peter Wyetzner (Jerusalem: Shalem Press, 2007), p. lv n. 43; Aaron Katchen, *Christian Hebraists and Dutch Rabbis: Seventeenth-Century Apologetics and the Study of Maimonides' 'Mishneh Torah'* (Cambridge, Mass.: Harvard University Press, 1984), pp. 39–65. The employment of Philo, on the other hand, has not yet been studied. In fact, while the text refers to "the Jews Philo and Josephus" (Grotius, *De Jure Belli*, p. 450), the footnote heading is "Philo Judeaus, Greek Philosopher" (Grotius, *De Jure Belli*, p. 917). On the Hebrew sources of Dutch Republican discourse, see Eco Haitsma Mulier, "The Language of Seventeenth-Century Republicanism in the United Provinces: Dutch or European?" in Anthony Pagden, ed., *The Languages of Political Theory in Early Modern Europe* (Cambridge: Cambridge University Press, 1987), pp. 179–195.

5. Fania Oz-Salzberger, "The Jewish Roots of the Modern Republic," *Azure* 13 (2002), pp. 88–132 (esp. p. 103); J.G.A. Pocock, "Time, History, and Eschatology in the Thought of Thomas Hobbes," in Pocock, *Politics, Language, and Time* (Chicago: University of Chicago Press), pp. 148–201 (esp. p. 153). It is notable that Pocock makes this point about Hobbes but not about Harrington. Cf. Mark Goldie, "The Civil Religion of James Harrington," in Pagden, *The Languages of Political Theory*, pp. 197–222, where Harrington's thought is labeled "Hebraic civic humanism" (p. 211).

6. Adam Sutcliffe, *Judaism and Enlightenment* (Cambridge: Cambridge University Press, 2003), p. 46. William Haller comments that "the life and poetry of Israel were easier to naturalize in common English life than those of Greece and Rome." Haller, *The Rise of Puritanism* (New York: Columbia University Press, 1938), p. 133.

7. John Morrill and Philip Baker, "Oliver Cromwell, the Regicide, and the Sons of Zeruiah," in Jason Peacey, ed., *The Regicides and the Execution of Charles I* (Basingstoke, England: Palgrave, 2001).

8. See Richard Tuck, "The Ancient Law of Freedom: John Selden and the Civil War," in John Morril, ed., *Reactions to the English Civil War 1642–1649* (Oxford: Macmillan, 1982); Jason P. Rosenblatt, *Renaissance England's Chief Rabbi: John Selden* (Oxford: Oxford University Press, 2006). As noted later in this introduction, work in progress on Rosenblatt's book appears in this volume.

9. Frank E. Manuel, *The Broken Staff: Judaism Through Christian Eyes* (Cambridge, Mass.: Harvard University Press, 1992), pp. 55–56.

10. Similarly, Thomas Muentzer set up a covenanted community of the elect patterned after the Old Testament model. On this and on Luther's criticism of these readings of the Bible, see John M. Headley, "Luther and the Problem of Secularization," *Journal of the American Academy of Religion* 55:1 (1987), pp. 21–37.

11. Daniel J. Elazar, "Althusius and Federalism as Grand Design," in Karl Engisch, H.L.A. Hart, Hans Kelsen, Ulrich Klus, and Sir Karl R. Popper, eds., *Rechtstheorie* 14:16 (Berlin: Duncker & Humblot, 1997).

12. See Goldie, "The Civil Religion," p. 300: "Who now reads the third and fourth books of *Leviathan*?" Goldie notes Pocock as an exception. Cf. Pocock, "Time, History, and Eschatology."

13. Fania Oz-Salzberger has claimed that Hobbes was a "dedicated Hebraist," basing this claim on the fact that "two of *Leviathan*'s four books rely heavily on the ancient Israelite model." Oz-Salzberger, "The Jewish Roots," p. 97. Menachem Lorberbaum has since claimed that "Leviathan does not reflect knowledge of Hebrew." Lorberbaum, "Making Space for Leviathan," *Hebraic Political Studies* 2:1 (2007), p. 80. At the same time, it is clear that Hobbes was influenced by Selden's Hebrew scholarship. On this see Rosenblatt, *Renaissance England's Chief Rabbi*, p. 169. Standard curriculums in English schools and universities during Hobbes' period included some Hebrew, but actual programs of study varied widely. See Roger Kimball, *Orators and Philosophers: A History of the Idea of Liberal Education* (New York: Teachers' College Press, 1986), pp. 99–102.

14. For a survey of standard histories of political thought and the extent of their acknowledgment of the role of Hebraic sources in the history of ideas, see Yoram Hazony, "Judaism and the Modern State," *Azure* 21 (2005), pp. 33–51.

15. Katchen, *Christian Hebraists and Dutch Rabbis*, esp. pp. 11–13, 95.

16. See note 1, above. See also Eyffinger, "Introduction."

17. For more on the Dutch popular imagination, see Schama, *The Embarrassment of Riches*.

18. Conrad Cherry, *God's New Israel* (Chapel Hill: University of North Carolina Press, 1998); Shalom Goldman, ed., *Hebrew and the Bible in America: The First Two Centuries* (Hanover, Mass.: University Press of New England, 1993).

19. According to Pocock, Selden's *Titles of Honor* (1614 and 1631) is almost the only contemporary work mentioned with respect in *Leviathan*. Pocock, "Time, History, and Eschatology," p. 149 n. 3. Cf. *Leviathan*, book 1, ch. 10.

20. On Baillie's attack of Selden and his Hebrew learning as preventing Presbyterian government in England, see William Haller, *Liberty and Reformation in the Puritan Revolution* (New York: Columbia University Press, 1963), p. 222.

21. One famous anecdote from Selden in the Westminster Assembly (1643) is his "perhaps in your little pocket-bibles with gilt leaves the translation may be thus, but the Greek or the Hebrew signifies thus and thus." Cited in Tuck, *Philosophy and Government*, p. 218.

22. Abraham Berkowitz, "John Selden and the Biblical Origins of the Modern International Political System," *Jewish Political Studies Review* 6:1-2 (1993), pp. 27-47.

23. Isaac Herzog, "John Selden and Jewish Law," *Journal of Comparative Legislation and International Law*, 3rd ser. 13:4 (1931), pp. 236-245.

24. This invitation first appeared in "From the Editors," *Hebraic Political Studies* 1:1 (2005).

I. EARLY YEARS

Political Theology in Renaissance Christian Kabbala: Petrus Galatinus and Guillaume Postel

Wilhelm Schmidt-Biggemann

1. The Sixteenth-Century Controversy over Jewish Books in the Holy Roman Empire

In the year 1518, the famous Jewish printer Gershom Soncino from Ortona, Italy, printed a book subtitled *A Work Most Useful for the Christian Republic on the Secrets of the Catholic Truth, against the Hard-Hearted Wickedness of Our Contemporary Jews, Newly Excerpted from the Talmud and Other Hebrew Books, and in Four Languages Elegantly Composed.*[1]

At first glance it seems odd that a Jewish publisher—the most famous of his time—would decide to publish a book which so overtly features itself as anti-Jewish. This tension may be reconciled, however, by understanding the relevant historical context, that of the early sixteenth-century debate as to whether postbiblical Jewish literature should remain the preserve of Jewish communities in the Holy Roman Empire.

The Cologne convert Johannes Pfefferkorn, intent on convincing his erstwhile brothers in faith to convert, with violence if necessary, had been publishing anti-Jewish pamphlets since 1507. In his *Judenspiegel* (*Jewish Mirror*, published in Latin and German in 1507), he had reported on subversive and highly treasonous plans of the Jews. He continued his anti-Jewish propaganda in subsequent pamphlets, namely, *Judenbeicht* (*Jewish Confession*, 1508), *Osterbüchlein* (*Easter Booklet*, 1509), and *Judenfeind* (*Jewish Enemy*, 1509). Pfefferkorn argued that the authorities should confiscate all Jewish books, aside from the Old Testament, in order to deprive the Jews of access to most of their traditional texts and thereby to make it easier to convert them. He turned to Johannes Reuchlin with his plan; however, the latter refused to be involved. Pfefferkorn then turned to the Cologne Dominican Jacob Hoogstraeten,[2] who supported his plans and furnished the support necessary to earn political endorsement for the convert's redemptive ambitions. On August 19, 1509, Hoogstraeten obtained a mandate from the emperor ordering the confiscation of Jewish books by authorized agents. In his capacity as a Frankfurt agent, Pfefferkorn immediately began carrying out the order. However, others put up such a degree of resistance that the emperor had to rescind it: in July 1510, he decreed the return of the confiscated books and instructed the universities of Cologne, Mainz, Erfurt, and Heidelberg, as well as the papal inquisitor Jacob Hoogstraeten OP, Johannes Reuchlin, and the Jewish convert and cleric Victor von Karben, to draw up expert opinions on the matter. The ensuing legal battle over the Jewish books provoked, among other things, a debate on the *Epistolae virorum obscurorum* (*Letters of Obscure Men* 1515/17) that was to accompany Reuchlin for the rest of his life.[3]

Throughout his life, Reuchlin was convinced that Christian truth was hidden in kabbalistic sources. Kabbala, for Reuchlin, included large parts of the talmudic tradition, and this understanding of Christian truth provided him with a compelling argument in favor of leaving the Hebrew books to the Jews.[4] He defended this thesis with conviction in his *Augenspiegel* (*Eye-Mirror*, 1511). The legal debate lasted nine years, beginning in Mainz with an unpleasant trial: Reuchlin was first up against the Cologne Dominicans, and later against the entire Dominican order, since the debate eventually came under the papal justice system at the court in Rome. It was against the backdrop of this lawsuit that Reuchlin published his most important text on Christian Kabbala, *De Arte Cabalistica*, in 1517, but the case had by then already caused him much trouble, and it was to cause even more.

Despite the fact that the emperor and most judges, including Pope Leo X, were inclined toward Reuchlin's position, too many others were disinclined, including the entire Dominican order and the French king.

As a result, after ten years of cases from Mainz to Rome, Reuchlin finally lost the lawsuit.

Reuchlin's *Augenspiegel* was condemned on June 23, 1520, in Rome: "The aforementioned *Speculum Oculare* [*Eye-Mirror*] is scandalous and offensive to the pious ears of Christian believers. It is also favorable to the impious Jews; and therefore must be removed from the hands and usage of Christian believers. Johannes [Reuchlin] is sentenced to perpetual silence and condemned to pay the expenses of this cause."[5]

Although Reuchlin was disappointed by this outcome, condemnation of him seems to have been contained within certain circles. Over the course of these same years he had become a professor in Tübingen, and his standing was undiminished.[6] He died during a stay at a health resort on June 30, 1522, in Bad Liebenzell, long before the violence of the great theological-political event of the sixteenth century, the Reformation, unfolded. As the Reformation gained momentum, it attracted widespread intellectual, political, and religious attention, and indeed the fervor it aroused difused interest in this conflict over Jewish texts.

This is the environment into which Petrus Galatinus' *De Arcana Catholicae veritatis* was published, subtitled *A Work Most Useful for the Christian Republic on the Secrets of the Catholic Truth, against the Hard-Hearted Wickedness of our Contemporary Jews, Newly Excerpted from the Talmud and Other Hebrew Books, and in Four Languages Elegantly Composed.* In the context of the debate over Jewish books, it may now be obvious that excerpts from the Talmud as well as from other "Jewish" books brought in Galatinus' work could be used to support Reuchlin's case. If the Talmud and other books of the Jewish tradition did in fact contain hints and secrets pertaining to the Christian Doctrines, it was not only useless but counterproductive for the authorities to confiscate them, since they could effectively serve Christian missionary purposes so long as they were left in the hands of the Jews. It was in this specific historical situation that it seemed useful, even for a Jewish printer, to publish a book replete with attacks on his own religion.

It was, nevertheless, a risky endeavor for Gershom Soncino.[7] In order to defend the Jews from the Dominicans and their missionary imputations, he chose to support the Franciscans, who had unsuccessfully tried to defend Reuchlin in his trial at the papal court. But the Franciscans were also interested in the conversion of the Jews. The final conversion of the Jews was predicted in Saint Paul's letter to the Romans[8] as the event which immediately preceded the final state of eschatology, and Petrus Galatinus was one of the most ardent eschatologists of his Franciscan order. An adherent of the twelfth-century eschatologist Joachim de Fiore, Galatinus shared De Fiore's political theology, which anticipated the imminent coming of a third age characterized by the reign of the Spirit.[9] Petrus Galatinus even saw himself as a representative of the "angelic pope," perhaps even as the "pastor angelicus" and the "good shepherd,"[10] who was predicted to introduce that third age of the Spirit which often was identified with the last thousand years' reign before the final judgment. So although the Jews stood to benefit politically from Galatinus' book, Gershom Soncino's decision to publish it was not at all without political and intellectual risk.

2. Petrus Galatinus and 'De Arcana Catholicae Veritatis'

So who was Petrus Galatinus?[11] He was born in Lecce in the south of Italy, with the secular name Pietro Colonna in 1460, and later named himself after Galatina in the diocese of Otranto, in southern Italy, where he witnessed the plundering of the village by the Turks. He studied ancient languages, including Hebrew, with Elias Levita, and was a professor of Greek, philosophy, and theology in Rome. He held major offices, and especially noteworthy is his position as papal "Poenitentiarius." We also know that he corresponded with crowned heads, including the emperor Maximilian, and with the renowned Johannes Reuchlin. We know for certain that he died sometime after 1539, perhaps in 1540.

Whereas other major works remained in manuscript, we have already seen that Galatinus' chief work, *De Arcana Catholicae Veritatis*, appeared in print. The work encompasses twelve books, and is written as a trialogue between Galatinus himself, Capnion or Reuchlin, and Hoogstraeten. Galatinus is cast as a Christian who knows everything about Jews, and in this way resembles a convert. Reuchlin represents a Christian kabbalist, whereas Hoogstraeten is featured as an anti-Jewish Christian. The twelve books are titled:

   i. *On the Talmud, and Its Content*
   ii. *On the Trinity of Divine Persons, on the Unity of Divine Essence, and on the Divine Names, Through Which the Divine Trinity Together with Its Unity and Its Perfections Are Perfectly Indicated*

iii. On the Incarnation of God's Son, That the Messiah Is God and That His Names Indicate His Divine Nature, on the Connection, Participation, and Equalization of God and Men

iv. On the First Coming of the Messiah

v. Refutation of the Endeavors of Contemporary Jews to Prove That the Messiah Has Not Yet Come

vi. The Redemption and Salvation of the Human Race for the Sake of Which the Messiah Will Come

vii. On the Most Holy Mother of the Messiah

viii. On the Mysteries of the Messiah Which Are Completely Fulfilled in Our Lord Jesus Christ

ix. On the Eternal Damnation of the Jews and of the Vocation and Salvation of the Gentiles

x. On the New Institution of the Law Which Will Be Founded by the Messiah

xi. On the Cessation of the Old Law When the New One Arrives

xii. On the Coming of the Second Messiah, and of the Future in Him

A careful study of the work reveals that it relies most heavily on three sources: The first is the *Pugio fidei*, a large anti-Judaic treatise by the Spanish Dominican Raimundus Martini (1220–1285); the second is a fifteenth-century forgery by Paulus de Heredia, a Jewish convert, entitled *Gale razeya*, גלי רזיה; the third is the *Apokalypsis Nova* by pseudonym Beatus Amadeus, who has been identified as Giorgio Benigno Salviati (Juraij Dragišić).[12] I will characterize each of these sources below and will then try to show, briefly, how Galatinus arranged these in his opus *De Arcana Catholicae Veritatis*. Finally, I will attempt to identify the kind of apocalyptic thought in which Galatinus took part, and how this was transformed in his political theology.

Pugio Fidei

Raimundus (Raymond) Martini published his *Pugio fidei* in 1278,[13] fifteen years after the famous religious disputation of 1263 between Christian inquisitors and a group of Jewish rabbis, including Nachmanides, in Barcelona. The end result was discussed by the Christian and Jewish commentators of the event; both flattered themselves to have been victorious. Be that as it may, the outcome provoked Raimundus Martini to write his large treatise, *Pugio Fidei* (Dagger of Faith).[14]

The book is composed of three parts: The first (pp. 191–258) is entitled "Of God, and of the Science of God, of the Highest Good, the Creation of the World, the Immortality of the Soul, and of the Resurrection of the Dead," and is written against the Saracenes. The second (pp. 259–478) is written against the Jews and entitled "About the Twelve Tribes, on the Division of the Jews into Christians and Jews, the Christian Doctrine of the Messiah and the Prophecies Concerning Christ as Found in the Old Testament: In the Book Daniel, in the Book of Genesis; That the Destruction of Jerusalem Is the Punishment for the Jews' Disbelief, the Prophetic Dicta of Malachi." In this part, Martini claims that Jesus is the *Nuncius foederis*, the messenger of the covenant. Refuting the Jews' objections that the Messiah has not yet arrived, he asserts that Jesus is the rock of faith.[15] The third and longest part (pp. 479–960) is further divided into three subsections. The first subsection, "On Doctrines of Trinity and Divine Predicates; *Sapientia Divina*," discusses whether the Torah or law is identical with divine wisdom and offers "Proofs of the Holy Trinity to Be Found in the Old Testament." The second subsection is called "On the Original Fall and the Punishment for the Sins." And the final subsection is entitled "On the Redemption of Humankind and the Reprobation of the Jews." This last part encompasses the Christian doctrine of the Messiah, who came to redeem the sons of Adam; the doctrine of the sacraments: baptism, confession, Eucharist; the dogmas of Christ's passion, his descent to the underworld or hell, his ascension, and the New Law of the Messiah, a doctrine following Saint Paul's notion that the law is suspended by the Evangel.

The last two chapters of Martini's book, chapters 21 and 22, are explicitly anti-Jewish. Chapter 21 (*De Iudaeorum reprobatione*) is about the reprobation of the Jews, since they failed to recognize the Lord. Chapter 22, moreover, brings citations, allegedly from the *Midrash Mechilta*,[16] containing *foetida* (infamies) attesting to Jews being permitted to kill Christians ("*quod possunt & debent occidere Christianos*").

As a whole, the book features the standard topics of Christian anti-Jewish polemic, but these specific attacks feature exceptional force and nuance, since Raymundus Martini was a trained Hebraist and knew the Talmud by his own readings. There were at least two important arguments for the irrelevance of Judaism to Christianity expounded in the *Pugio Fidei*. The first argument stems from a sentence in the talmudic tractate Nidda 61b, "That in the coming (world) the law will be suspended,"[17] which was drawn on by Paul in his dialectics of law and evangile.[18] The second argument consists of the suspicion that when Ezra and his colleagues redacted the biblical canon (*tikkun sofrim*), they extinguished all hints from these texts concerning Jesus Christ. This is, of course, a circular argument born of the logic of suspicion, which reinforces its own prejudices.

Gale Razeya

Galatinus' second source is a fifteenth-century forgery of Paulus de Heredia, a Jewish convert.[19] Heredia's booklet, *Gale Razeya*,[20] was evidently part of the Franciscan propaganda for the dogma of the immaculate conception of Christ's virgin mother, Mary.[21] Aside from having been used by Petrus Galatinus,[22] this book was also featured in Agostini Guistiniani's (Justinianus') commentary to the Polyglot Psalter of 1516. The full title of the Vatican manuscript is *The Opusculum of Nahumia the Son of Hakana Concerning Secret Messages before the Coming of the Messiah, Excerpted around the Year 50 from the Book Gale Razeya of Rabbenu Hakadosh.*[23] Rabbenu Hakadosh is one of the known titles of R. Yehuda Hanasi, editor of the Mishna dated to the second century CE; however, in this booklet Rabbenu Hakadosh is set into the second century BC.[24]

Gale Razeya is composed of two epistolary parts. The first part is a "letter" written by Rabbi Neumia Hakana[25] (the father) to his son, about a dialogue that took place in the second century BC between Rabbenu Hakadosh (R. Yehuda Hanasi) and Antonius, a Roman consul. The second part consists of a letter by Hakana (the son) about the biography of Jesus.

(i) The first letter, from father to son, claims to have been written about the year 50 BC, and prophesizes that according to the book *Gale Razeya* (which he is going to reveal), "the coming of God and his revealed justice are near and will come in fifty years."[26] He is now seventy-five years old, and hopes that his son Hakana will witness the Messiah. Nahumia Hakana "decided to gather a few profound sayings and secrets from those I discovered in that same book, *Gale Razeya*, concerning certain petitions which Antonius, consul of the city of Rome, sought from Rabbenu Hakadosh,"[27] and write them down in an "Epistle of Secrets."

Antonius asks eight questions that provide the opportunity for exercises in Christian Kabbala and anagogical exegesis. Of these eight questions, some are more pertinent to political theology than others, and they will be more extensively explicated below.

The first question asks for the "meaning of the name of four letters, that is, the tetragrammaton, and the name of twelve and of forty-two letters." The result is a Christianized form of the *shem hamephorash* (explicit name of God), in which the tetragrammaton is interpreted as a symbol of the trinity and of the sophia. The name with twelve letters is the Hebrew version of father, son, and holy spirit, because together these Hebrew words consist of exactly twelve letters; the name of forty-two letters is again a trinitarian one: forty-two Hebrew letters spell out "God father, God son, God spirit, three in one, and one in three."

The second and third questions deal with Mariology[28] and the virgin mother. The core is an interpretation of Isaiah 8:3: "And I went to the prophetess, and she conceived, and bore a son." This prophetess is interpreted as the mother of the king Messiah, and "she is called prophetess because she knows in her prophecy all things from the beginning to the end, including things which not one of the prophets has ever been able to know."[29] In other words, the author of *Gale Razeya* identifies the *topos* of the divine *Sophia* with Christ's mother. In this context, verses from Proverbs, Isaiah, and Micah[30] are also quoted and claimed to be further proofs.[31]

The specific kabbalistic exegesis, however, is the interpretation of Genesis 2:7, where God formed Adam's body from the dust of the earth. The word "and formed" (*vayetzer*, וייצר) "is written with two Yods, although it ought certainly to be written only with one. And it is written with two so as to show us that two human bodies were formed by the word of God: Adam and the King Messiah who is to come."[32] Thus, it is obvious to the Christian reader that the Messiah was originally created by God's word that existed before all time, and that he parallels Adam, who became flesh in Paradise.

Of less immediate importance to the present discussion of political theology, the fourth question enfolds a typology of the cross, and the fifth one consists of a vision of the celestial Jerusalem, where Elijah and the patriarchs pray to God to send his son, singing the "Holy Holy Holy" recorded in Isaiah 6:3.

The sixth question presents another Old Testament allegory for Christ and Mary. The question, Why is Israel called God's own people? is answered with an exegesis of the verse in Daniel 2:34. It deals with Nebuchadnezzar's dream of a statue of gold, silver, brass, and iron and the feet of iron and part clay. "Thus thou sawest, till a stone was cut out of a mountain without hands, and it struck the statue upon the feet thereof that they were of iron and clay, and broke them in pieces." This stone is interpreted as the people of Israel, from which the Messiah comes. Israel will not fulfill its tasks; it will torture and kill the Messiah. This interpretation is particularly Christian. It connects Psalm 117:22, "The stone which the builders rejected; the same has become the head of the corner," which is frequently interpreted in the New Testament as an image of Christ,[33] with Isaiah 8:14, "and he will become a sanctuarium, and a stone of offense, and a rock of stumbling to both houses of Israel."[34] This corresponds exactly to Saint Peter's first letter (I Peter, 2:6-8): "Wherefore it is said in the scripture: Behold, I lay in Zion a chief corner stone, elect, precious. And he that shall believe in him, shall not be confounded. To you therefore that believe, he is honor, but to them that believe not, the stone which the builders rejected, the same is made the head of the corner: And a stone of stumbling, and a rock of scandal, to them who stumble at the word."

Paulus de Heredia continues: He (the Messiah) will descend to hell and resolve the saints, and then after three days his soul will return into his body and will leave the stone. The exegetical proof for this prophecy is a passage beginning Exodus 33:21: "Behold there is a place with me, and thou shalt stand upon the rock. And when my glory shall pass, I will set thee in a hole of the rock..."

The allegorical argument of the whole passage can be summarized as follows: The stone cut without hands which will offend Israel represents both the Jewish people and Mary bearing Jesus.[35] Since Israel had a covenant with God, which is also allegorically represented by the rock, Mary, Christ, and Israel belong secretly together. The proof is a *gematria*:[36] the numerical values of *brit* (covenant) and *Miriam veYeshu* (Mary and Jesus) are equivalent, and each equal 612. The meaning of the allegory is again Mariological: Mary is the *Sophia* and Matrix through whom the divine seed is made real in time and space.

The seventh question is an exegesis of a verse from Psalm 80:9. The Vulgate text Paulus de Heredia uses translates as: "Thou hast brought a vineyard out of Egypt"; the vine is interpreted as Jesus' returning from the flight to Egypt. Psalm 80:16: "And perfect the abacus which your right hand had planted"[37] is interpreted as a symbol of Mary again: "The mother of God is compared to a cupboard inasmuch as she is like an armarium [treasury] which princes construct to bring together gold and silver vessels so that their wealth and glory may be displayed to all. Thus the mother of the King Messiah will be an armarium which God made for the Messiah himself to sit in order to show the glory of his majesty to all mortals."[38]

The eighth and final question brings the exegesis of Isaiah 7:14: "Behold, a virgin shall conceive," which was, according to Paulus de Heredia, predicted six hundred years before the Messiah's coming in order to create an account of biblical chronology in sections of forty years.

These eight questions and ensuing interpretations comprise the first part of the prophecy which Hakana the father reported from a meeting between the Roman Consul Antonius and Rabbenu Hakadosh that supposedly took place around 120 BC–100 BC.

(ii) The second part of Paulus de Heredia's *Gale Razeya* is a letter of Hakana the younger, whose father had hoped his son would witness the Messiah with his own eyes and ears. The letter pretends to having been written immediately after Jesus' resurrection, and its purpose is to demonstrate to the unbelieving Jewish people that Jesus was the Christ. The letter reports the history of Christ's birth in Bethlehem, the flight to Egypt, and most importantly, it describes the biblical account of Jesus among the sages in the Temple. It reports that Jesus demonstrated so much wisdom that the wise judges decided to incorporate him into their community after he had reached the age of eighteen. After he had been accepted, Jesus told the story of his birth by the virgin mother. Aside from this core, the rest of the son's letter is a short summary of Jesus' death and resurrection. Hakana the younger reveals his purpose in writing: "And since those who hate him write devilish things about him and tell many lies so as not to follow sacred faith, I have rattled my quiver to make the truth known to all who read this epistle, and to perform a great benefaction for them and for myself."[39]

Apocalypsis Nova

Galatinus' third source is the *Apocalypsis Nova* of the so-called Beatus Amadeus, a popular Franciscan vision-book. Its origin is not quite clear, but the author is most problably Giorgio Benigno Salviati.[40] We know that Giorgio Benigno Salviati was close to Petrus Galatinus, since he wrote a letter of dedication that was printed in the first edition of Galatinus' *Arcana Catholicae Veritatis* but was omitted from later editions.[41]

Giorgio Benigno Salviati was born in Srebrenica (Bosnia) about 1450 under his Croatian name, Juraj Dagišić, and, in 1463, fled from the Turks to Ragusa (Dubrovnik), where he became a Franciscan. He later studied in France and England, finally settling for thirty years in Santa Croce, Florence, where he served as a professor of exegesis in the Franciscan convent. In 1507 he became bishop of Cagli in Umbria, and Pope Leo X made him titular bishop of Nazareth. Benigno was a member of the commission that defended Reuchlin in his case on the *Augenspiegel* at the papal court. In 1515 he wrote a defense of Reuchlin, *Defensio Praestantissimi Viri Johannis Reuchlin*, which was printed in Cologne in 1517.

Salviati was presumably the author, and certainly the redactor, of the *Apocalypsis Nova*. The text basically consists of two parts: a short treatise on the *Pastor Angelicus* (Angelic Shepherd)[42] and eight celestial visions. Whether Salviati considered himself to be the Joachimite eschatological *Pastor Angelicus* who was to open the third reign of the divine spirit in the history of salvation is not quite clear,[43] but it is obvious that he belonged to a circle of Franciscan apocalyptic thinkers who preserved the eschatological ideas of Savonarola, burnt in Florence in 1498. The *Apocalypsis Nova*[44] is not merely a prophetic work encompassing many subjects similar to those discussed in other contemporary documents such as the coming of the angelic pope as responsible for the instauration of a universal spiritual unity and one Christian kingdom, the end of the "sects" of the Muslims and of the Turkish empire, and the establishment of an everlasting era of peace and the reign of the Holy Spirit. Rather, the *Apocalypsis Nova* distinguishes itself as a theological treatise which in many codices is divided into eight *raptus* (prophecies), alluding to the *raptus Pauli* in Saint Paul's second letter to the Corinthians:[45]

1. The creation of the angels.
2. The fall of the angels, the creation of Adam and Eve and their sin.[46]
3. The time of the creation of the world and the era of Adam and Eve in paradise, God's prescience, which allowed men to commit sin, the character of the original sin, the first "happy" stage and the second "unhappy" one.
4. The double quality of Adam, how and why the virgin (that is, primordial Eve) was saved from the original sin, how Christ was incarnated in the first primordial Adam, who did not commit sin. The perfection of the earthly Mary's soul and her vote for virginity. The heavenly paradise and the beatitude of the vision consisting in the delight of God.

5. Mary's engaging and the Annunciation; the formation of the divine word in Mary's womb, that the angels knew from the beginning the coming incarnation of Christ, Jesus' nativity and his life.

6. The Eucharist and of what the transmutation consists.

7. The science of the Trinity: God alone is *res absolutissimus*. The divine persons are coexistent, but they are truly *sola deitas in relationibus absolutis*. The three persons constitute one *sola res* from where the power of creation derives. They are three *creantes* but not *creatores*. There is a second filiation, that is, a second son from which one can speak as the substance of the trinitarian image. This is the archetype after which angels and men are created.

8. Eulogy for Mary who did not commit sin and who knows all wisdom; Joseph's death, Mary's death, resurrection, and assumption.

The *Apocalypsis Nova* and Paulus de Heredia's *Gale Razeya* clearly share the same ideas concerning the speculations of cosmic Mariology and of Christ's virgin birth. This coincides perfectly with the seventh book of Galatinus' *Arcana Catholicae Vertitatis* and its Mariological purposes.

3. Galatinus' Mariology, Eschatology, and Christianization of Hebrew Political and Theological Concepts

Galatinus deals with cosmic Mariology in the seventh book of his *Aracana Catholicae Veritatis*. This book can be interpreted as part of the Franciscan Mariology and should be connected to Galatinus' desire to represent the angelic Pope. In book 7 he first quotes the *gematria* of the names of Jesus and Mary as being equivalent to the *gematria* of brit. This *gematria* was already extant in the sixth question of *Gale Razeya*.[47] With this interpretation, the core political and theological concept of the Jewish religion becomes Christianized because, as based on this argument, whenever the word "brit" appears in the Bible, it can be replaced by "Mary and Jesus." This interpretation was also used when the question of theodicy, or why God created the world, arose: he created the world for the sake of Jesus and Mary.[48]

Herewith, for the Christian kabbalist, it becomes obvious that the creation took place because of God's love for Mary and Christ. The whole enterprise of creation can be legitimated by the argument that God had foreseen Adam's sin, but that he conceded this fact because of his love for Mary and Jesus. *Targum Onkelos* is quoted as an authoritative Hebraic source for the fact that God created the world because of his wisdom—and Mary is identified with that wisdom.[49] This citation and the association it contains proves to the Christian kabbalist that Mary is the divine wisdom through which the sinless world is created. She gives the divine ideas their space, their time, and thus their reality. She is the worldly matrix in which God's ideas become reality; she grants God's grace, which lets the world subsist.[50]

In the same sense Galatinus quotes and interprets the seventh question of Paulus de Heredia's *Gale Razeya*; here Mary, interpreted as the cupboard of God, features as the vessel and showcase through which God's son is to be brought into apparition. She is the matrix of the divine Jesus, who was conceived at the beginning of the world. Christ remains hidden as long as he is inside, so to speak, of the Trinity. But when he becomes apparent as God's begotten word, he is "outside" and therefore spatial. This space is the Word's matrix, and that is why the Word becomes somehow materialized (this is the meaning of the Latin *materia, matrix*). The matter is the mother, represented by spiritual Mary, and thus, for the Christian kabbalist it becomes obvious that Christ's mother Mary has been conceived together with the beginning of the Word, insofar as it became visible. This heavenly matter was part of the eternal Adam, the first primordial Adam not yet touched by sin.[51]

For Galatinus, the families of Adam's pious descendants participated in this pure spiritual matter despite original sin, and Mary's father, Joaquim, was descended from this holy stem.[52] Moreover, this divine fertile matter is the matrix of the divine seed Jesus,[53] so that Mary does not in any way partake in original sin.

What do these speculations have in common with political theology? The first point is that Galatinus intended that his knowledge of Hebrew should serve his eschatological endeavors. He thought that the second coming of Christ was instant, recalling Saint Paul's prophecy: "For I would not have you ignorant, brethren, of this mystery (lest you should be wise in your own conceits), that blindness in part has happened in Israel, until the fullness of Gentiles should come in. And so all Israel should be saved."[54] There can be no doubt that Galatinus subordinated his knowledge of Hebrew and Kabbala to his political-eschatological interests. When the gentiles, the Turks in Galatinus' case, are defeated, which was the hope of the pious Franciscans concerning the endeavors of the emperor, then the conversion of the Jews was extant. With that conversion the final coming of Christ the Messiah was nearly granted.

Since Galatinus was convinced that the final events were imminent, he wrote a commentary on the book of Apocalypse in the New Testament. This commentary was not printed, but the manuscript still exists in the Vatican library. Galatinus finds the Turks foreseen in the book of Apocalypse,[55] but he considers himself as the prophet of the Apocalypse, since he knows himself endowed by the Holy Spirit with the wisdom of the secret book, which the author of the book of Apocalypse in the New Testament devours. The text of the commentary makes clear that Galatinus oscillates between prophecy and exegesis. He saw himself as one of the spiritual men whom the Holy Spirit was to send in order to interpret the Holy Scriptures in the sense in which they were written, and to witness them in the convents of the elect.[56] As such, Galatinus must have seen himself as prophet and witness of the imminent Apocalypse.

4. Postel as an Apocalyptic Figure

The person who made a sincere political theology out of all these speculations was Guillaume Postel. He tried to bring the French king and the German emperor to agree to his apocalyptic ideas and to make them part of their politics. Such politics should accelerate Christ's last coming by supporting the ideal of the universal concord of all earthly reigns throughout the world, and so contribute to the idea of a single religion uniting Christians, Muslims, and Jews, as was prophesied in Saint Paul's Letter to the Romans.

Postel was born in 1510 into a rather poor family; he must have achieved much of his philological knowledge as an autodidact. He continued and perfected his studies in ancient and new languages, theology, and medicine at the Collège Sainte-Barbe and at the court of Cardinal Lemoine.[57] His career began brilliantly: in 1535 he became a member of a royal delegation, which was sent under the leadership of the French diplomat and philologist Jean de la Forest to the Court of Soliman II in Istanbul. In 1536 or 1537, he returned to Paris via Venice, where he contacted the Christian printer Daniel Bomberg, who printed the first

Hebrew Bible and the Talmud. In 1537 the French king donated 225 écus to Postel so he could purchase books and prepare lectures at the Collège Royal in Greek, Hebrew, and Arabic. Postel, however, not only prepared philological lectures, but also unsuccessfully tried to convince the French nobility of the practical importance of his political eschatology. On account of these failed attempts, the royal court severed its connection with Postel.

Between 1540 and 1542 Postel seems to have suffered from a severe spiritual crisis.[58] It is at least clear that from around this time his interests turned increasingly to spiritual and speculative matters. Perhaps he would be most accurately termed a speculative philologist, writing books advocating the unification of all religions in order to accelerate the Messiah's last coming. His most important books printed in that period[59] are Panthenosia ΠΑΝΘΕΝΩΣΙΑ Compositio Omnivm Dissidiorum circa aeternam ueritatem s.d. s. l. (Alliance of all Dissidents Around the Eternal Truth, published in Paris in 1547) and De orbis terrae concordia (Concord of the Earth, Paris; published in Basel by Johannes Oporinus in 1643). In the Paris edition of De orbis terrae concordia, which is dedicated to François I and his sister Margarete of Navara, the cardinals of Lorraine and Turneau, the bishops and the French nobility, he makes plans for the universal mission for the unifying of all religions. His idea is that the philosophia Christiana (including Christian Kabbala) will convince all people of one philosophical, historical, and Christian truth, and convert them through this truth. He promises to write a succinct introduction to this Christian philology-philosophy and argues for completely new translations of the Bible into Arabic and of the New Testament into Hebrew. This program implements the political theology of Saint Paul's prophecy, and Guillaume Postel declares it to be the duty of the French kingdom to contribute to the history of salvation, facilitating the coming of the Kingdom of Eternal Peace.

It is not at all surprising that the French king and the nobility did not take Postel's plans, which involved the abolition of their offices, seriously. This caused Postel to break with the French court, and the court with him. The emperor, who stood not only to retain his position of power with the implementation of Postel's political theology, but even to take on the greater role of a spiritual power, was also not really interested when Postel offered him his apocalyptic plans in 1543–1544.

So Postel went to Rome in 1544, where he joined the circle of the first Jesuits around Ignatius of Loyola. However, he broke off his novitiate in the spring of 1545 because of difficulties he had with his brethren, especially concerning the interpretation of the Apocalypse. Evidently, the *Apocalypsis Nova* and Postel's kabbalistic and eschatological-political ideas were at odds with the Jesuits' ecclesiastical aims.

After his departure from the Jesuits, which we know not to have been hostile, Postel became chaplain at the Ospedale di San Giovanni e Paolo in Venice. Here it happened that Postel acknowledged the Cosmic Mary, the *Sophia* who should spiritually give birth to the last coming judge—the Christ, the Messiah. Postel was then thirty-five years of age, more or less the age when Jesus died. His cosmic eschatological Mary was Mother Jeanne (Madre Zuana, 1497–1549), a charitable Venetian woman who had dedicated a hospital, cared for invalids, and was nurse to them. It seems that he identified her as the divine woman by her physical similarity to Mary in a picture in Saint Marco in Venice.[60] However this came to be, she became his Virgin Mary, *Sophia*, and *Shechina*, and—unwillingly and perhaps even unknowingly—his spiritual mother. For his cosmic Mariology, Postel relied on the visions of Pseudo-Amadeus[61] and on the theories of Petrus Galatinus and Paulus de Heredia.[62] He shared their understanding of the cosmic mother, who brings the divine ideas, the first male seeds, into reality. For him, since the father is the beginning, in the Godhead, of the Son, "the divine nature of passivity is intermingled with activity." It is then through the work of *potentia passiva* (female receptivity) that the *Sapience créée* (created wisdom) can be distinguished from God and that the separate world comes into existence.[63]

Postel saw this truth incarnated in his *Madre Zuana*. In other words, he saw *himself* as the prophet of the coming Messiah, and he was willing to prove it on the funeral pyre.[64]

The core of Postel's kabbalistic and eschatological ideas can be found in a short "Censure," which he wrote at the beginning of his *Commentaire sur l'Apocalypse*.[65] Obviously he had seen himself as the anti-type of Cain, but here he becomes the announcer of Christ, the Elias Pandocheta, and a new John the Baptist. His spiritual father is Adam or Christ, his mother Eve, Mary, or Madre Zuana. The argument is as follows: Just as Christ, according to Saint Paul's exegesis, was the anti-type of the fleshly Adam,[66] so too is Postel the anti-type of Cain. He overcomes Cain's sin like the historical Jesus overcame Adam's. In his present role, Postel prepares the way for the primordial Adam (whom he terms spiritual Christ or the divine *Nous*) to bring about the final redemption of the universe. In this task, Postel-anti-Cain, is also the reborn John the Baptist, who says, according to the beginning of Saint Mark's Gospel, "I send my angel before thy face, who shall prepare the way before thee"[67] and prepares the way for the final redeemer. In this meaning, John the Baptist is also the anti-type of Cain reincarnated by Postel. As the prophet of the last judgment, he is also the typological representative of the prophet Elijah, who, according to Jewish and Christian traditions, is the prophet of the Messiah's last coming.

In this typological puzzle Madre Zuana is the new Eve. She has spiritually conceived the divine Christ, who is the spiritual Adam, and she gives birth to Postel, the new Cain. She represents also Christ's mother Mary, who was the anti-type of the fallen Eve. As the anti-type of the female part of the spiritual nature, Mary and Madre Zuana participate in the female part of divine wisdom. In that role, the new Eve, Madre Zuana, is the nourishing ground for Postel's spiritual existence as Elias Pandocheta, the new Cain, and the reincarnation of Saint John the Baptist. Madre Zuana represents the matrix Dei and is, as female wisdom, the *intellectus possibilis* for the divine *intellectus agens*, and the child she conceives is the newly reborn prophet of the last reconciliation.[68] This is how Postel becomes a prophetic witness to God's final revelations.

It is not at all surprising that, with these eschatological speculations, Postel was to encounter troubles with his Roman Catholic Church. Like many prophets, Postel lived an unquiet life. From 1547 to 1549 he was occupied with the affair of his cosmic Eve. His Madre Zuana died in 1549, but even her death did not abate his enthusiasm. He felt himself gifted by her with an immortal body, the heavenly matter of the matrix Dei. He thought that dark forces hindered it from coming into apparition. Postel left Venice for Jerusalem in 1549—a real and not merely spiritual journey.[69] Postel, traveling without sufficient money, had difficulty buying the manuscripts he was interested in and organizing the Syrian translation of the New Testament. But by chance he met the French ambassador Gabriel de Luetz, Baron of Aramon, who supported him financially and offered him the opportunity to buy Hebrew and Arabic manuscripts (which, when in urgent need of money, he later had to sell to the Pfalzgraf Ottheinrich in Heidelberg).

After returning to Venice, Postel ran into difficulties with the Venetian inquisition as well as with the French king. In 1553, François I demanded that the Venetian authorities arrest Postel, but the prophet fled to the emperor in Vienna, where he was immediately appointed professor of Greek. He nonetheless returned to Venice six months later, in 1554, only to find himself trapped: since some of his books were on the Venetian Index of prohibited books, Postel saw no other way to escape than to present himself to the Inquisition. The Venetian inquisition was mild with him, merely classifying him as "*insanis, demens, et delirans.*"[70] He lost his office as a priest, and was forbidden to write anything on theological subjects. After another six years of fleeing, troubles, irritation, and confusion, he was arrested in a cloister in Paris, where he died in 1581.

5. Conclusion

Were Petrus Galatinus and Guillaume Postel political theologians? If political theology is defined by the key notions of politics playing a fundamental role in theology, they clearly were. In the tradition of Western eschatology, they represented the tradition of Joachim of Fiore, connecting this Christian eschatological tradition with speculations concerning Mariology and kabbalistic ideas deriving from their knowledge of Hebrew. They strove to convince the authorities in their lands that the last days of mankind were imminent. As Christian syncretists, they sought their speculative truths in every theological, historical, and philosophical source available. These apocalyptic authors were fascinated by the idea that the primordial world of the divine *Sophia*, who they identified with the spiritually impregnated Mary, will return as the celestial Jerusalem at the end of days. They all tried to accelerate this process, evidently in vain.

The only result for their own standing was that they dangerously approached the borders of heretic theology. When, in the process of sharpening the dogma of the Protestant and Roman Catholic churches, Neoplatonic speculations became theologically suspect, Christian kabbala was increasingly considered heretical, and was consequently condemned as "enthusiasm." This was specifically the case with the "apocalyptic Mariology" of our authors. Apocalyptic Mariology, which was originally part of a specific Franciscan pious tradition, was considered as heresy both in Trinitarian, especially Christological and in Mariological, respects, and the eschatological theology deriving from it was suppressed as directed against the official theological doctrine.

Notes

1. The original Latin reads: *Opus toti christianae Reipublicae maxime utilis, de arcanis catholicae ueritatis, contra obstinantissima Iudaeorum nostrae tempestatis perfidiam ex Talmud, aliis hebraicis libris nuper excerptum; & quadruplici linguarum genere eleganter congestum.* Translations from the Latin are generally my own.

2. Also known as Hochstraten, Hooghstraten etc. On Hoogstraeten, see Horst Ulrich, "Jacobus Hoogstraeten OP" (ca. 1460–1527), in Erwin Iserloh, ed., *Katholische Theologen der Reformationszeit*, vol. 4 (Münster: Aschendorff, 1987), pp. 7–14; Johannes Marinus Peterse, "Causa Invidiae? De strijd van Jacobus Hoogstraeten tegen Johannes Reuchlin (1510–1520)," dissertation (Leiden: Leiden University, 1993), also appearing in a German edition, published as Johannes Marinus Peterse, *Jacobus Hoogstraeten gegen Johannes Reuchlin: Ein Beitrag zur Geschichte des Antijudaismus im 16. Jahrhundert* (Mainz: von Zabern, 1995).

3. Friedrich Lotter, "Der Rechtsstatus der Juden in den Schriften Reuchlins zum Pfefferkornstreit," in Arno Herzig and Julius H. Schoeps, eds., *Reuchlin und die Juden* (Pforzheimer Reuchlinschriften Bd. 3) (Sigmaringen: Thorbecke, 1993), pp. 65–88; Winfried Trusen, "Die Prozesse gegen Reuchlins Augenspiegel," in Stefan Rhein, ed., *Reuchlin und die politischen Kräfte seiner Zeit* (Pforzheimer Reuchlinschriften Bd. 5) (Sigmaringen: Thorbecke, 1998), pp. 87–131.

4. This aside from the *Toldot Jeshu* and the *Nizachon* that Reuchlin would not have left to the Jews.

5. "Speculum Oculare nuncupatum fuisse et scandalosum, ac piarum aurium Christi fidelium offensivum, ac non parum impiis Judaeis favorabilem, et propterea ab usu et de manibus Christi fidelium tollendum usumque ius inhibendum etc. cum impositione perpetui silentii eidem Johanni et condemnationem eiusdem in expensis huiusmodi causa." Quoted from Trusen, "Die Prozesse gegen Reuchlins Augenspiegel," p. 127.

6. Ludwig Geiger, *Johannes Reuchlin: Sein Leben und seine Werke* (Leipzig, 1871); Max Brod, *Reuchlin und sein Kampf: Eine historische Monographie* (Stuttgart: Kohlhammer, 1965), pp. 312–331.

7. Cf. Saverio Campanini, "Le prefazioni, le ediche, e i colophon di Gershom Soncino," in F. Tamami, ed., *L'attività editoriale di Gershom Soncino (1502–1527)* (Cremona: Edizioni dei Soncino, 1997), pp. 31–58.

8. Cf. Romans 11:25–26: "For I would not have you ignorant, brethren, of this mystery, (lest you should be wise in your own conceits), that blindness in part has happened in Israel, until the fullness of the Gentiles should come in. And so all Israel should be saved..." All biblical citations, unless otherwise noted, are taken from the Douay-Rheims edition of the Vulgate Roman Catholic Bible. This may be found online at www.catholicdoors.com/bible.

9. That is to say, the third reign after the father's first (the Old Testament), and the son's second (the New Testament).

10. Cf. Saverio Campanini, "Le prefazioni, le ediche, e i colophon di Gershom Soncino," pp. 31–58, esp. p. 49; he interprets the Hebrew epigrams of the book

as proof, esp. the last line of the third "Ishac Hispani Hebraei medici phisici, in laudem auctoris operis, carmina," which he translates as "Il tuo nome sia esaltato e il tuo santificato, come pastore del tuo gregge, cercherai le pecore smarrite."

11. Arduinus Kleinhans, OFM: De Vita et operibus Petri Galatini OFM. In Antonianum I, 1926, pp. 145–179, 327–356, esp. 168–172. François Secret, *Les Kabbalistes Chrétiens de la Renaissance* (Paris: Dunot, 1964), pp. 99–106; Paola Zambelli, *L'apprendista stregone: Astrologia, cabala e arte lulliana in Pico della Mirandola e seguaci* (Venice: Marsilio, 1995); Cesare Vasoli, "Giorgio Benigno Salviati, Pietro Galatino e l'edizione di Ortona (1518) del 'De Arcanis Catholicae veritatis,'" in Vasoli, *Filosofia e religione nella cultura del Rinascimento* (Naples: Morano, 1988), pp. 183–209.

12. Anna Morisi, *Apocalypsis nova: Ricerche sull' origine e la formazione del testo delle pseudo-Amadeo* (Rome: Istituto storico italiano per il Medio Evo, 1970), pp. 35–46; Cesare Vasoli, *Profezia e ragione* (Naples: Morano, 1974), pp. 15–128.

13. Cf. Hans Georg von Mutius, *Die christlich-jüdische Zwangsdisputation zu Barcelona. Nach dem hebräischen Protokoll des Moses Nachmanides* (Frankfurt: Lang, 1982).

14. I quote the edition of Johann Benedict Carpzov, *Raimundus Martini Ordinis Praedicatorum Pugio Fidei Adversus Mauros et Judaeos cum observationi-bus Josephi de Voisin, et introductione Jo. Benedicti Carpzovi, qui simul appendices loco Hermanni Judaei opusculum de suo conversione ex Mscto Bibiothecae Paulinae Academiae Lipsienis recensuit* (Leipzig, 1687). The text was not very well known in the early modern period; however, it was used by Nicolas of Lyra, Paulus Burgensis, and Porchetus Salvaticus in *Victoria contra Judaeos* (Genoa, 1520). Also Luther refers to the book (perhaps via Porchetus) in "Die Juden und ihre Lügen" (Cf. Carpzov, p. 89ff.). It was Scaliger who first found out that Petrus Galatinus had plagerized the *Pugio fidei*. However, Scaliger identified the author as Raymundus Sabundus and confused him with the fourteenth-century philosopher. Cf. Jacob Thomasius, *De plagio literario*, ch. 2, p. 436; Morinus, *Exerc. Biblicae*, book 1, ch. 2. Carpzov quotes a dissertation by B. Geier from 1644 named *Dissertatio inauguralis ad Jes. LIII, 8, 9, 10*.

15. This image of the rock will be of a certain importance in Paulus de Heredia's *Gale razeya*, q. 6.

16. As far as I know, the *Midrash Mechilta* that Martini quotes does not contain such a passage. Perhaps the citation was a fake, or Martini, who is usually reliable concerning his quotations, used a manuscript different from the modern editions.

17. This quote is from my (German) edition of the Talmud; Lazarus Goldschmidt, trans., vol. 12 (Frankfurt: Jüdischer Verlag 1996), p. 552, Nidda 9, 5.

18. See Saint Paul's Letter to the Romans 7:4–6: "Therefore, my brethren, you also have become dead to the law, by the body of Christ, and you may belong to another, who is risen again from the dead, that we may bring forth fruit to God. For when we were in the flesh, the passions of sins, which we were by the

law, did work in our members, to bring forth fruit unto death. But now we are loosed from the law of death, wherein we were detained, so that we should serve in newness of spirit, and not in the oldness of the letter."

19. Paulus de Heredia was born about 1405 in Aragon and died after 1486. Baptized late in life, he attacked Judaism although he had defended it and his former coreligionists. Besides the *Gale Razeya*, he published *De Mysteriis Fidei* and a *Corona Regia* on the immaculate conception (the latter dedicated to Innocent VIII), also intended to convert the Jews. De Heredia was alleged to have collaborated on the Complutensian polyglot, issued under the auspices of Cardinal Ximenez. (Hermann Kohler and Meyer Kayserling in *Jewish Encyclopedia*.)

20. The complete Latin title is extant in a manuscript in the Vatican (Cod. Vat. Lat. 4582, fol. 4r–24v), which has probably been copied from an earlier print of 1487/88. The text was also published by Julius Conrad Otto (Naphtali Margalith) (Nürnberg: Sebastian Körber, 1605) under the title "Gali Razia occultorum detectio: hoc est Monstratio dogmatum que est omnes rabbini recte sentientes, ante et post Christi nativitatem, de unitate essentiae divinae, Trinitate personarum... relinquerunt, ad fidei Christianae assertionem de Jesu Nazareno, stabiliendum." A second edition of this text appeared in Stettin in 1614.

21. The Dogma of Mary's Immaculate Conception had been officially promulgated by the Council of Basel in 1439; this decison was renewed by Pope Sixtus IV in 1476 and by Pope Pius IX in 1854. Cf. Johannes Helmrath, *Das Basler Konzil 1431–1449* (Cologne: Böhlau, 1987), pp. 383–394.

22. Cf. Arduinus Kleinhans, OFM: De Vita et operibus Petri Galatini OFM, in *Antonianum* I (1926), pp. 169–145, 179, 327–356, esp. 168–172.

23. "*Nahumiae filij Haccanae De Messiae mysterijs opusculum secretorum nuncupatorum antè salvatoris nostri adventum, anno circiter quinquagesimo ex libro galea [r]zeya Rebbeni Hàcados excerptum.*" For an English translation of this book, see Paulus de Heredia, *The Epistle of Secrets*; trans. Rodney G. Dennis, ed. J.F. Coakley (Oxford: Jericho Press, 1998).

24. Paulus de Heredia knew the history of the Jewish legal tradition from Maimonides' introduction of his *Mishneh Torah*, where Maimonides gives a detailed description of Rabbenu Hakadosh and the writing of the Mishna.

25. This is doubtless intended to be Nahumia ben Hakana.

26. De Heredia, *Epistle of Secrets*, p. 1.

27. Ibid., p. 2.

28. Mariology is the systematic study of the person of the Blessed Virgin Mary and of her place in the economy of the Incarnation. See F.L. Cross, ed., *The Oxford Dictionary of the Christian Church* (London: Oxford University Press, 1963).

29. De Heredia, *Epistle of Secrets*, p. 9.

30. The relevant passages are: (Proverbs 30:19) "and the way of a man in youth"; (Isaiah 7:14) "Behold, a virgin shall conceive..."; and (Micah 5:2-3) "and thou, Bethlehem, Ephrata art a little one..."

31. De Heredia, *Epistle of Secrets*, p. 9.

32. Ibid., p. 10ff.

33. Cf. for instance Matthew 21:42, Acts 4:11.

34. The Vulgate text which Paulus de Heredia has, reads: "Et eris vobis sanctuarium, in lapidem autem offensionis, et in petram scandali, duabus domibus Israel."

35. Perhaps the author knows and alludes here to the *topos* of the sculptor who realizes the statue inherent in the uncarved block.

36. ‏ברית=מרים וישו‎=612.

37. "Et perfice abacum quem plantavit dextera tua." More correct editions read: "Et perfice eam quam plantavit dextera tua," which translates as: "And perfect the same which thy right hand had planted."

38. De Heredia, *Epistle of Secrets*, p. 30.

39. Ibid., p. 44.

40. Cf. Anna Morisi, *Apocalypsis nova: Ricerche sull' origine e la formazione del testo delle pseudo-Amadeo* (Rome: Istituto storico italiano per il Medio Evo, 1970); Cesare Vasoli, "Notizie su Giorgio Benigno Salviati (Juraj Dagišić)," in *Profezia e ragione: Studi sulla cultura del Cinquecento e del Seicento* (Naples: Morano, 1974), pp. 17–127.

41. Ed. of 1518 fol. Iv: Georgius Benignus de Sa(l)uiatis Archiepiscopus Nazarenus ad Lectorem. "Quam ueridicum sit, candide lector, quantaeque authoritatis, Petri Galatini uiri eruditissimi, quatuorque linguarum peritissimi, opus de arcanis catholicae ueritatis, ex hebraicis libris, mirabili ingenio, & non sine diuino impulsu carptum: non solum ex hoc scire poteris. Quod Reuerendissimi quidam Domini Cardinales, diuina humanaque sapienta maxime praestantes, alijque non nulli ecclesiarum Praelati, in omni literae genere excellentissimi, opus ipsum cum eis cognoscendum missum fuisset, miris (me praesente) laudibus extulerint: quod ipse quoque cum totum uidissem, ac perlegissem, tanquam reipublicae christianae admodum profuturum, summopere laudaui. Verum ex eo etiam: quae ipsimet Hebrei sola ueritate compulsi, in laudem eiusdem operis atque authoris, pulcherrima in lingua hebraica ediderint carmina. Quod est maximum arcanorum catholicae veritatis contra eos argumentum. Cum ad probandam ueritatem, nihil sit aduersariorum testimonio efficacius."

42. The text of the "Pastor angelicus" features in Morisi, *Apocalypsis nova*, pp. 13–25.

43. Cf. note 7 above.

44. I rely on Cesare Vasoli's information. See Vasoli, "Postel, Galatino et l'Apocalypsis Nova," in *Guillaume Postel 1581–1981. Actes du colloque international d'Avranches 5–9 September 1981* (Paris, 1985), pp. 97–108. Vasoli used the following manuscripts: Firenze B.N., Cod Magliabechiano XXXIX, 1cc 289v; XXXV, 17cc 1r–215v. Conv. Soppr. J. 10.5, cc 1r–125v. Arezzo, biblioteca della Fraternita dei Laici; 436; Milano, Biblioteca del Convento dei Cappuccini, 16. Cf. Anna Morisi, "Galatino et la Kabbalae chrétienne," in *Kabbalistes*

chrétiens: Cahiers de l'Hermetisme (Paris: Albin Michel, 1979), pp. 207–231; Morisi, *Apocalypsis nova.*

45. II Corinthians 12:2.

46. This is the creation of the primordial Adam and Eve. Cf. Morisi, *Apocalypsis nova*, pp. 57ff.

47. See p. 297 above.

48. S. 271 *Arcana* (1518), "Nam ישו ומרים id est, Iesus & Maria apud Hebraeos, 612. Ratione arithmetica continent. ' ioth enim continet 10.ש sin 300. ו uau 6. Et sic ישי id est Jesus continet 316. Iterum ו uau continet 6. מ mem 40.ר res 200. ' ioth 10. 40 מ. Et sic ומרים id est & Maria 296 continet. Quare ישו ומרים id est, Jesus & Maria apud Hebraeos continet 612. Hunc eundam etiam numerum continentem apud eos ברית id est Pactum. Nam ב beth continet 2. ר res 200. ' ioth 10. ת tau 400. Ex quo patet, quòd Jesus & Maria apud Hebraeos ascendunt ad numerum Berith, id est pactum hoc est ad numerum 612. Cuius quidem numeri mentio fit non uulgaris in Cabala, quae quotiescunque huiusmodi numeros nancisci potest, eos plurimi facit, eisque non mediocrem adhibet fidem. Quam ob rem uerba ipsa Ieremiae ita interpretantur: Nisi pactum meum esset, id est nisi amore mei Iesu & Mariae, diem & noctem leges coelo & terrae non posuissem, hoc est, mundum non creassem."

49. Ibid.: "Et ideo amore Jesu & Mariae mundum creavit. Quod etiam Rabbi Ankelos confirmat, dum in glossa Chaldaica super illud Gen. 1 cap. dictum, in Principio creavit Deus coelum & terram: sic ait: ... Propter sapientiam creauit Deus coelum & terram, amore intemeratae uirginis, quae est mundi sapientia, creauit Deus coelum & terram: uel amore Messiae filij sui, cui diuinis sapientia attribuitur."

50. Ibid.: "Non solum autem totus mundus amore beatissimae uirginis conditus est, sed etiam sustentatur. Mundus enim ipse ob nostras prauas actiones, nullo pacto consistere posset, nisi ipsa gloriosa uirgo eum sua misericordia & clementia, pro nobis orando sustineret. Ex his etiam sequitur, ipsam & filium eius ab Adae peccato omnino immunes fuisse."

51. S. 272: "Nam dum Deus Adam plasmaret, fecit quasi massam, ex cuius parte nobiliori accepit intemeratae matris Messiae materiam, ex residuo uerò eius & superfluitate, Adam formauit."

52. Ibid.: "Ex materia autem immaculatae matris Messiae, facta est uirtus quae in nobiliori loco & membro corporis Adae conservata fuit, quae postea emanauit ad Seth, deinde ad Enos, deinde succedaneo ordine ad reliquos, usque ad sanctum Iehoiakim."

53. Ibid.: "Ex haec demum uirtute beatissima mater Messiae, formata fuit."

54. Cf. Romans 11:25–26.

55. Vat. Lat. 5567, Lib. V, cap. IX. Bl. CLXVv ff.: "Et soluti sunt quatuor angeli. Id est, et permissum est Turcis ipsis, adversus ecclesiam latinam tempore statuto, hoc est, in fine quinti et exordio sexti temporis exire. Qui parati erant in horam, et diem, et mensem, et annum. Hic non tam rem futuram, quam voluntatis Turcarum causam expressit. Tametsi non semper quod volunt contra

Christianos obtinent: semper tamen ad complenda contra eos sui cordis desy-
deria, parati sunt."

56. Ibid. fol. CCCLXXXIr: "*Ego Jesvs misi angelum meum, testificari vobis
haec in ecclesijs,* Misit quidem Christus *Iesvs,* angelum suum: ad testificandum
per Johannem ipsum, ac omnia, quae in libro isto scripta sunt. In ecclesijs, de
quibus in libri initio dicitur, quod vides scribe in libro, et mille septem ecclesijs:
quae sunt in Asia, Epheso, et Smyrnae, et in Pergamo, et Thyatirae, et Sardis, et
Philadelphiae, et Laodiceae. De missione vero hac dictum est, in ipso libri principio Apokalypsis *Jesv* Christi: quam dedit illi Deus palam facere servis suis, quae
oportet fieri cito: et significavit mittens per angelum suum servo Johanni. *Mittit
quoque et spiritus sanctus viros spirituales; qui haec eo spiritu quo scripta sunt,
interpretentur, atque in electorum conventibus testificentur."*

57. Cf. Guillaume Postel, *Des Admirables Secrets des Nombres Platoniciens,*
editing, translation, introduction, and notes by Jean Pierre Bach (Paris: Vrin,
2001), p. 7.

58. Jean Pierre Bach, "Introduction," in Postel, *Admirables Secrets,* p. 8.

59. For the conditions under which the books were published, cf. Carlos
Gilly, *Die Manuskripte in der Bibliothek des Johannes Oporinus* (Basel: Schwabe,
2001).

60. Guillaume Postel, *Le Thrésor des Prophéties de l'Univers,* François Secret,
ed. (The Hague: Martinus Nijhoff, 1969), p. 248: "La profecie par peincture, avec
son diction par escript, dict le mesme, qu'il sera un Pape angelike esleu des an-
ges, et afferme que de ce temps là, ou environ, il y havoit une femme au monde
qui filloit la toille de quoi faire le surplis audict Pape angelike, ce qui est pour
tout certein le laict et mystere de la Vierge Venetienne et son fils, selon que l'abbé
Joachim [de Fiore], qui ordona les peinctures et entailleures de la tres mister-
ieuses Eglise de Sainct Marc, l'ha faict entailler en la septentrionale partie partie
de ladicte Eglise, là où il ha faict en marbre la figure d'une teste de femme coiffée
à la simple contadine, du tout semblable à ladicte Vierge Venitienne, si lorsqu'elle
estoit encores en cest vie, et en fest admonester le Senat et le Prince, s'ils y eus-
sent voulu prendre garde."

61. Ibid., p. 247.

62. He quotes the Trinitarian doctrine of both in *Le Thrésor de Prophéties,*
p. 146: "Car estant chose du tout tres certeine que dieu est Maskil, Muskal, Sekel
ou Cognoissant, Cogneu et Cognoissance, et qu'il ne faut séparer en confondre
aulcunement les troys personnes, et d'avantage estant chose tres certeine que les
divines actions se font, selon la decision de la sixieme Synode ou Concile general,
par la nature divine totale et non pas par aulcun séparé ou spécial mouvement
d'alcume des troys personnes, il fault qu'il soit créateur, conservateur, redemp-
teur et mediateur du monde pour l'amour de l'homme." This idea corresponds
to Paulus de Heredia's (*Gale Razeya,* first question), and it is quoted by Petrus
Galatinus in *Arcana Catholicae Veritatis,* II, 7, p. 56ff. in the 1518 edition and p.
43ff. in the 1561 edition.

63. Postel's proof is an exegesis of Gen. 38:28, where the story of the twins
Zara (Zerach) and Pharez (Peretz) is told. *Le Thrésor de Prophéties,* p. 223: "Et

pour monstrer comment le masculin se nome feminin, cecy est testifié en Genese chap. 38 là où il est escript de Zahra ou Zerach, fère de Pharez, pere dudict Ethan etst nommé *Prima* et non point *Primus*, disant: Cestuy cy sortira la premiere, qui est pour nous donner à entendre que combien que le second estat de ce monde soit de ministere masculin comme le Papat, neanmoins il est feminin, et despend de la divinité du Fils de Dieu, qui est veritablement la divine nature passive engendrée de l'active, qui est le Pere eternel. Et affin que cecy ne demeure en obscurité qu'il y aye divinité passive ou feminine, le mesme David par un mesme relatif le monstre deux foys dedens le Ps. 115[116, 14,18] sur le nom de Seigneur *Ihovah* devant icelle, disant: Je rendray mes voeus au Seigneuer *Ihovah* devant *Icelle*, et non plus devant Iceluy, pour tout son peuple, ce qui pour faire plus grand foy de la mesme vérité est deux fois repété en un mesme mode. [i.d. Ps. 115, 16]. Et à la vérité, c'est la feminine vertu, dond procede tout le feminin distingué et sensible monde, et avant toute aultre creature la Sapience créée, *Formee* et faicte, de laquelle comme vrayement mere du monde il ne fault doubter que David au mesme pseaulme s'appelle fils."

64. For the whole affair, see François Secret, ed., *Guillaume Postel: Apologies et Rétractions. Manuscrits inédits publiés avec une introduction et des notes par François Secret* (Nieuwkoop: B. de Graaf, 1972); *Bibliotheca humanistica et Reformatoria*, vol. 3, p. 9. Here one finds the preface of his Translation of Menachem Recanati (1549), and some ideas of the combination of Mariology and female theology (pp. 15–18). Cf. also "La nouelle Eve mere du Monde" (1552), in Secret, *Guillaume Postel*, pp. 18–52.

65. Guillaume Postel, "Censure du commentaire sur l'Apocalypse... Censura auctoris," in Secret, *Guillaume Postel*, p. 13: "Quum nondum essem natus, aut Renatus potius, quando haec scripsi, sed una cum Christo corporaliter in terris sub partem agenti conversans et ab illo tantum Regnatus triennio ferme antquam restituar hos scripsi commentarios, in quibus non attigi tanta profunditate omnia Restitutionis et veritatis Rationisque aeternae mysteria quanta debebam, ideo admonendum posteritatem judicavi quum nunc instet liberatio mea ex hac carcere mortali ita ut non liceat mihi nunc ab integro repetere aut retexere. Tempus enim meae diutissimae desyderatae Resolutionis pro Patris et Matris meae veritate instat, ut propter essentiae duplicis Patris mei asservatione velim lubentissime vitam istam sensualem fundere, sicut ipse pro Gloria et essentia Patris sui asserenda mortuus est et resurrexit. Ostendet autem in me quam sit potens vita sua in suis servis, dum Judex universi in sua videbitur primogenito. Itaque et in hoc commentario et in aliis, non satis intellexeram quomodo primi hominis Mens esset in me instaurata, sed ubi aut dixi aut innuere volui (sensim enim in Restitutis emergit proficiendi veritas, sicut et in patre meo Jesu Adamo novo proficiebat experimentalis et sensu demonstrationeque acquiri solita sapienta) quod essem Restitutus aut Restituendus in Adami locum debui dicere in Caini, qui primus ex utroque parente natus est, ut statim Renato et Restituto Mater Eva nova me redarguens sugessit. De illa etiam, erubescens illam fateri ob abjectionem ejus, male scripsi quum Mariam Jochanam vocavi, ubi Jochannae et Evae novae nomine voce debeam una cum sacramenti et corporis spiritualis Christi mysterio, nam illi calicis corpus respondet sicut mascula alboque semine adventui primo corpus sub panis specie. Bis enim ea de re corpus ejusdem Christi sacrificatur Eva, itaque nova sive Christi inferio et secunda pars consummato est

Redemptionis. In partibus etiam formae humanae non satis distinxi. Nam sic habeat Mens et Spiritus ab extra, illa a Patre hic a Matre generalibus, vocat filosofus Intellectem agentem et possibilem *Intra Nos* autem sunt animus dominans ubique tanquam mas in cerebro illuminas a mente, anima dominas ubique etiam sed potissimum in corde residens, cujus lux est perfectio a spiritu sive ab intellectu possibili aut materiali sive materno. Sic volo ista a posteritae intelligi."

66. Romans 5:12–20.

67. Mark 1:2.

68. The vision of the last reconciliation is described in Postel's *Panthenosia* (Paris, 1540). Cf. W. Schmidt-Biggemann, *Philosophia Perennis* (Frankfurt: Suhrkamp, 1998), pp. 561–573.

69. The idea of a spiritual journey to Jerusalem is propagated, among others, by Quirinus Kuhlmann. Cf. W. Schmidt-Biggemann, "Salvation Through Philology: The Poetical Messianism of Quirinus Kuhlmann (1651–1689)," in P. Schaefer and M.R. Cohen, eds., *Toward the Millennium: Messianic Expectations from the Bible to Waco* (Leiden: Brill, 1998), pp. 259–298.

70. Secret, *Guillaume Postel*, pp. 217ff.

Machiavelli on Reading the Bible Judiciously

Christopher Lynch

Michelangelo's *David*, the *Door of Paradise* by Ghiberti, Donatello's *David*, the *Moses* of Michelangelo—such public masterpieces are among the more spectacular examples of a fact that strikes even the most casual tourist of Italy: the great figures and events of the Hebrew Bible lavishly adorn many of the most impressive sites of Renaissance Florence. An ordinary guidebook is all that is required to avoid perplexity as to the referents of these Renaissance icons. Given their currency during this period, what status is one to accord their appearance in writings of a thinker of the rank of Niccolò Machiavelli? Does the currency of these icons in Machiavelli's time mean that one can speak without ado about the relationship between stories of the Hebrew Bible and Machiavelli's use of them in his writings?[1] Or does it point in the opposite direction, toward the conclusion that it is difficult, perhaps even impossible, to discuss such a relationship meaningfully? For how is one to know whether Machiavelli is simply winking at the "pop culture" of his day rather than seriously engaging the political teachings of one of the great wellsprings of the Western world, the Hebrew Bible? Indeed, looking beyond Machiavelli to the relationship of the Hebrew Bible to early modern writings in general (or, still more generally, to modern writings as such), how can one ascertain whether the relationship between these two literatures is specious or genuine? In a word, how can and should one conduct the study of "political Hebraism"?

To begin with, I would suggest that considerable care be given to the question of whether any particular early modern recourse to a figure or event of the Hebrew Bible is frivolous or serious. I would consider frivolous any recourse that consists in the mere trading in readily available iconic currency that does not entail a genuine engagement with the content and foundation of the political thought contained in the Hebrew Bible. I would consider serious any recourse to such figures and events that does entail such an engagement. Lacking this distinction, one cannot speak of the relationship between the Hebrew Bible and early modern thought, since one might very well be speaking instead of the relationship of one aspect of early modern thought to another or, even worse, to a mere condition of that thought, namely, the icons of the day. Similarly, I would suggest that merely pointing to the presence of Hebraic figures and events (even their serious presence), without sufficient regard for the precise intention of the authors in whose writings they appear, would preclude any discussion of the relationship between the Hebrew Bible and such authors and periods—let alone the "influence" of the political thought of the Hebrew Bible on them.

As a step toward the meaningful study of political Hebraism, some pains will be taken in the following to distinguish among Machiavelli's references to Hebraic figures and events that clearly are not biblical, those that may or may not be biblical, and those that certainly are biblical. I will then concentrate on the last category, sketching how he both adopts a genuine teaching of the Hebrew Bible and transforms that teaching in fundamental ways. In particular, this will be done by examining what Machiavelli means when he writes of reading the Bible judiciously (*sensatamente*)[2] and outlining his purpose for engaging in this type of reading. To anticipate, reading the Bible in this manner means to read it in light of what can be known of politics and war by means of human reason, and its purpose is to resurrect political life from the tomb in which it was placed by Christianity. It will emerge that this type of reading and this purpose entail a self-consciously partial (that is, political-military) reading of a part of the Bible (namely, the "Old Testament") as a means to undermine the effectual truth of the whole Bible, namely, the weakness of the world brought about by Christianity. To make these points, I will (i) briefly survey Machiavelli's discussions of figures and events of the Old Testament in his major works with reference to relevant minor works and letters; (ii) infer from the most pertinent of these discussions what could be called his principles of biblical hermeneutics; and (iii) sketch the importance of the proper reading of the Old Testament for Machiavelli's thought as a whole.

Hebraic Figures and Events

Machiavelli made significant use of Hebraic figures and events throughout his major and minor works. In the major works, the figures of the Old Testament explicitly mentioned are Moses, Joshua, Saul, David, Goliath, Solomon, Rehoboam, and the daughters of Lot.[3] Moses is named among the four "greatest examples" of founders in chapter 6 of *The Prince*, then again with those same founders (minus Romulus) in the final chapter, which exhorts Lorenzo de' Medici to seize Italy. In the *Discourses on Livy* Moses is briefly mentioned four times: as an example of a builder of a free city taken over from previous inhabitants; then along with Lycurgus and Solon as examples of founders who had sole authority and formed laws for the common good; next as the man who named Judea; and finally, as one who slew "infinite men" (apparently in the episode of the golden calf) in order to execute his plans.[4] In *The Prince* David is mentioned once (along with the sole references to Saul and Goliath) to illustrate the necessity of possessing arms of one's own and twice in the *Discourses on Livy*, first as an example of a "strong king" who loves war but is succeeded by the weak and peaceful Solomon and the unfortunate Rehoboam (their only mentions), then along with Philip of Macedon as a monarch with absolute power.[5] Lot's daughters are mentioned by the scheming Friar Timoteo in the *Mandragola* as he seeks to persuade a virtuous young wife to cuckold her old husband so as to be able to give the husband heirs.[6] Joshua is discussed immediately on the heels of a mention of Moses[7] in the *Discourses on Livy*, but Machiavelli explicitly identifies Procopius, the sixth-century Byzantine historian, rather than the Bible as his source.[8]

Events mentioned in Machiavelli's major works that are not biblical but are nonetheless directly related to Judaism and the Jews are Vespasian's conquest of "Judea" in "Asia,"[9] his use of a "superstition" of "the Jews" to conquer them,[10] the siege of Jerusalem,[11] and the "wretched and rare" treatment of the Marranos in Spain under Ferdinand the Catholic.[12] Machiavelli also refers explicitly to one nonbiblical Jewish author: Josephus.[13]

Finally, there are numerous—Machiavelli might say "infinite"—implicit references and allusions to the Old Testament in the *Discourses on Livy*. Some are made by way of logically necessary implications. For example, any explicit discussion of "the new law," as that in *Discourses on Livy*, II 5.1, necessarily implies some thought of "the old law." When the wider context of such a discussion concerns attempts made by new religions to suppress old religions, readers' thoughts about the relationship between the old law and the new law are given a specific impetus and direction. Other references are made by way of general pronouncements regarding all events of a particular kind. For example, Machiavelli discusses floods that wipe out virtually all vestiges of human life and civilization (albeit in particular regions), whose application to biblical events is left to the reader.[14] Similarly, consideration of the question of whether the world is eternal[15] brings to mind the biblical alternative of creation. Still other references are made by way of repeated use of particular figures from pagan literature in such a manner as to emphasize parallels with Old Testament figures. One such instance is the striking similarity of Machiavelli's retelling of Manilius Torquatus' one-on-one combat with a single "Gallic" warrior to David's one-on-one combat with the Philistine Goliath.[16]

In Machiavelli's minor works, the only extended treatment of Hebraic figures or events occurs in the *Exhortation to Penitence*. In this short work David is the protagonist, both as a penitent "adulterer and murderer" and, as will become relevant below, as "David the prophet," author of the Psalms, who calls to God for mercy *de profundis*.[17] In the letters, the most significant mention of such figures is that of Moses in a letter regarding two sermons delivered by Savonarola in March 1498 when Savonarola believed himself in grave danger of injury at the hands of the new Signoria, the ruling council of Florence. In Machiavelli's retelling, Savonarola compares himself and his enemies to Moses and the Egyptian slain by him,[18] saying, "O Egyptian, I want to stab you."[19]

These, then, are the figures and episodes of the Hebrew Bible that range throughout widely divergent types of Machiavelli's writings. It is no accident that two figures in particular are predominant: Moses and David.

Moses and David of the Bible

Faced with so many instances of reference to Hebraic figures and events, one wonders how to begin to study their place in Machiavelli's writings in a nonarbitrary manner. That is, how do we keep from confounding our purposes with his, from mistaking his chief or comprehensive aims for his subordinate ones, and from confusing his ironic winks at the icons of his day with his serious strategic assault on the tradition of political philosophy? It seems highly unlikely that a study of instances in minor works would yield a complete understanding. And yet were one to launch immediately into the study of any and every apparent implicit reference to Hebrew figures and events, one's results would be as uncertain as his imagination is active. For one Gaul, as in the example mentioned above, might stand for Goliath, but another might stand for some other biblical character, and yet another might stand for no one at all, since one presumes that sometimes a Gaul is just a Gaul.

It seems, then, that one is left with instances of manifestly Hebraic figures and events as they appear in Machiavelli's major works. But even this designation is imprecise, since "major" refers to size rather than comprehensiveness. The only works in which one can reasonably hope to gain a complete understanding are those in which he conveys "everything he knows," *The Prince* and *Discourses on Livy*.[20] The most promising and safest course would therefore seem to be an examination of manifestly Hebraic characters and occurrences as they appear in these two works.

But a final hair must be split: what does it mean to be manifestly Hebraic? Are all instances of "Moses," for example, manifestly Hebraic? Consider Machiavelli's treatment, mentioned above, of Moses' successor, Joshua. If instead of naming Procopius as his authority for Joshua, Machiavelli had named no authority, the natural tendency would have been to assume that he was using or misusing the Bible. Just as we might have wrongly assumed the one explicit mention of Joshua referred to the biblical Joshua, so might we wrongly assume that each and every instance of "Moses" is Hebraic in the sense of having been deliberately derived from the Bible. In fact, at least one instance of "Moses" seems not to refer to the Moses of the Hebrew Bible or, indeed, to any Moses that is likely to have existed. For in the *Discourses on Livy*, Machiavelli implausibly asserts that Moses renamed "Judea" that part of Syria seized by him. Not

only is there no biblical support for this assertion,[21] it is doubly contradicted: Moses seized no part of Syria (Joshua did), and the use of Judea
as a place name derives from the period after the division of the kingdom
into Israel and Judah under Jeroboam and Rehoboam, generations after
the time of Moses.

Recognition of the nonbiblical character of this particular Mosaic passage leads to the further recognition that Machiavelli does not assert any
biblical support for this claim. He makes such assertions in precious few
cases. We must therefore distinguish between those instances of Hebrew
figures and events accompanied by Machiavelli's explicit assertion that
they are to be considered biblical, on the one hand, and such instances as
are not so accompanied, on the other. Only two cases fall into the former
category: one regarding David[22] and the other regarding Moses.[23] It is to
these cases that we must turn if our consideration of Machiavelli's political Hebraism is to have the most solid foundation and, in particular, if it
is to serve as a sound basis for discerning his way of reading the Hebrew
Bible. After treating these two cases, we will examine two others,[24] again
regarding David and Moses, respectively. We shall see that they too must
be considered biblical.

David

The only explicitly biblical passage regarding David appears in *The Prince*
and concerns David's encounter with Goliath. The context of the passage
speaks to its importance. The passage appears in the second of the four
main sections of *The Prince*.[25] That section concerns military matters,
and at its core is the teaching that one must possess arms of one's own.
David is a chief—arguably *the* chief—example of this teaching. Perhaps
even more significantly, when Machiavelli introduces the example of
David with the words, "I want further to recall to memory a figure[26]
from the Old Testament apt for this purpose,"[27] it is the first time in the
entire work that he explicitly names a source for an example. Hitherto,
the many examples of princes, republics, peoples, and so forth are without attribution to any authority (though one direct quotation regarding
Hiero of Syracuse is from an unknown source in *Prince*, 6.25).[28] After
this point, explicit references to ancient literature come at a fast and

furious rate. They culminate in the praise of Xenophon's Cyrus (one of the four greatest examples named in chapter 6 along with Moses) at the end of chapter 14, which in turn prepares the way for the most famous of all Machiavellian passages, his attack on imaginary republics and principalities at the beginning of chapter 15.[29] The reference to the biblical David thus represents a crucial shift: from Machiavelli's treatment of characters without respect to the authors depicting them, to his treatment of those authors themselves as expositors of the tradition of political philosophy.

As he approaches the precedent of David, Machiavelli goes out of his way to indicate that he would like to discuss only recent Italian examples. He has no difficulty finding such when it comes to how one ought *not* to behave with respect to arms. But when it comes to how one *ought* to behave, he manages to produce just one modern Italian example, that of Cesare Borgia. Then, affirming yet again that he would like to use only those examples that are both "Italian and recent," he nonetheless offers up three more examples, not one of which is both Italian and recent and one of which is neither, that of the ancient Israelite, David.

He then offers his idiosyncratic version of the David and Goliath story:

> When David offered to Saul to go and fight Goliath, the Philistine provocateur, Saul, to give him spirit, armed him with his own arms—which David, as soon as he had them on his back, refused, saying that with them he could not make good use of himself, and therefore wanted to meet the enemy with his sling and his knife. In fine, the arms of others either fall off your back or weigh you down or hold you tight.[30]

This version of the story is most often compared to biblical verses that describe the moment at which David tries but refuses Saul's arms and to those that describe the weapons used by David.[31] But Machiavelli's cue, "When David offered to Saul to go and fight Goliath, the Philistine," requires that we pick up the story many lines earlier, at the point where Saul sends for David after hearing about his interest in the rewards that will go to the slayer of Goliath. For without further setting the scene of Saul and David's meeting, the biblical text says, "Then David spoke to Saul: 'Let your majesty not lose courage. I am at your service to go and fight this Philistine.'"[32] In addition to being the verses in which David "offered to Saul to go and fight Goliath," they are the ones in which the question of losing courage or giving spirit begins to be addressed. Saul discourages David from fighting, since he is young and inexperienced in war. But Saul is apparently reassured by David's spirited tales of his killing of bear and lion while tending his flocks and by his conviction that the Lord will deliver him. Without any explicit assertion regarding Saul's reasons for arming David, the moment at which the latter tries and refuses Saul's arms is described in greater detail than—and in a manner often widely divergent from—Machiavelli's version:

> Then Saul clothed David in his own tunic, putting a bronze helmet on his head and arming him with a coat of mail. David also girded himself with Saul's sword over the tunic. He walked with difficulty, however, since he had never tried armor before. He said to Saul, "I cannot go in these, because I have never tried them before." So he took them off. Then, staff in hand, David selected five smooth stones from the wadi and put them in the pocket of this shepherd's bag. With his sling also ready to hand, he approached the Philistine.[33]

The text makes clear the weapons each combatant possessed and their significance. For when Goliath mocks David for carrying a staff, David notes that it is not by sword or spear (both of which Goliath possesses) "that the Lord saves. For the battle is the Lord's." After Goliath falls with one of the stones from David's sling embedded in his head, the text says,

> Thus David overcame the Philistine with sling and stone; he struck the Philistine mortally, and did it without a sword. Then David ran and stood over him; with the Philistine's own sword which he drew from its sheath he dispatched him and cut off his head.

It repays the effort to go through deliberately the two accounts' points of similarity and difference. The most fundamental similarity is that in both accounts David does indeed prefer his own arms to Saul's. This fact should not be discounted from a purely military-political perspective even within the Bible's own horizon. For from the biblical Saul's point of view his political downfall is directly linked to David's military victory with his own arms.[34]

On the other hand, Machiavelli has altered this story in the following six ways: (i) the Bible begins with David's expression of concern for Saul's loss of courage, which David apparently dispels by recounting his courageous deeds and professing faith in God's deliverance of him, whereas in Machiavelli's version it is Saul who seeks to give David spirit by means of giving him arms; (ii) the second alteration is a corollary of the first: whereas in the biblical version Saul gives no reason for his action, Machiavelli's Saul aims to give David spirit; (iii) Machiavelli condenses to "arms" the defensive weapons protecting head and body and the offensive weapon of a sword; (iv) in the biblical version, after walking with difficulty in Saul's arms, David refuses them with the reason that he has not tried them before; in Machiavelli's, as soon as (*come*) he has them on his back he refuses them, with the reason that with them "he could not make good use of himself" or "give a good account of himself" (*no si potere bene valere di se stesso*); (v) as the David of the Bible approaches battle he holds his staff, carries the stones in his shepherd's bag, and keeps his sling at the ready, while in *The Prince* he wants to meet the enemy with his sling and his knife; and (vi) whereas Machiavelli sends David into battle with a knife, the Bible emphasizes that it is without a sword that he fells Goliath and with Goliath's own sword that he dispatches and beheads him.[35]

The following reflections on Machiavelli's alterations are in order. They pertain to David in particular, the meaning of arms, and ways to read the Bible. First, it is not outside of Machiavelli's purposes to suppress the fact that David is endowed with the marvelous ability to sing his own praises and recount God's favoring of him so as to win over his listener. "Arms" in the full sense are both offensive and defensive, though it may behoove one to emphasize their bold and flashy offensive side and obscure their more cautious and conservative defensive side.[36] When it suits his purposes, Machiavelli will not hesitate either to use a biblical truth (as in the case of his agreement with the Hebrew Bible that having one's own arms is crucial) or to amplify and improve on it (as in point iv above, in which the emphasis on oneself crowds out any hint of divine support). Perhaps most importantly, Machiavelli is not shy about supplying reasons for unexplained biblical actions, replacing less apt reasons for actions with more apt ones, or altering actions to make them more reasonable (as in points i, ii, iv, and vi).

Machiavelli's treatment of David is digressive: it draws us away—as if by the sheer gravity of the subject matter—from the author's expressed wish to stay with examples that are modern and Italian. But near the end of the chapter, Machiavelli clearly indicates David's importance. First he includes him among "the four whom I have named above" (along with Cesare, Hiero, and Charles VIII of France) as the chief examples of those who possess arms of their own. In addition, by means of the ambiguity of this expression, Machiavelli indicates that these four are worthy of comparison to the four greatest examples of chapter 6—Moses, Cyrus, Romulus, and Theseus. In almost the final breath of chapter 13, he then completes the parallel to chapter 6 by adding a fifth example,[37] whose status vis-à-vis the others is not entirely clear. At the end of chapter 6 Hiero's name was added as "one who will have some proportion to the others"; here at the conclusion of chapter 13, a name is added that haunts David through all three of his appearances in the major works: Philip of Macedon, father of Alexander the Great. To the orders of these five, Machiavelli concludes, "I submit myself entirely."[38]

On reflection, Machiavelli's digressive treatment of David with reference to the central Machiavellian teaching of the need to rely on arms of one's own is emphatically obtrusive. His use of the biblical figure is dual: he both relies on it as an authority (in apparent contradiction to the just-mentioned teaching of relying on one's own arms) and departs from it by transforming it to suit his purposes. For as noted above, even prior to its transformation at Machiavelli's hands, the biblical passage does indeed provide support for his case for relying on arms of one's own—at least insofar as that self-reliance is opposed to reliance on the arms of any other human being. On the other hand, Machiavelli's transformation serves the purpose of placing David on more solid, that is to say, more reasonable, foundations. It is fitting that this ambiguous treatment of the authoritative text should occur at just that point in Machiavelli's own text where the question of textual authority begins to arise. For this dual use—simultaneously relying on and departing from the text—corresponds to the aforementioned shift from figures and events as products of their authors to Machiavelli's famous attack on the authority of the tradition in the work's fifteenth chapter.

Moses

Machiavelli's treatment of Moses is no less complex than that of David. The explicitly biblical passage that deals with Moses contains the sole mention of the Bible by name in the *Discourses on Livy* and the last explicit reference in that work to any human being discussed in the Hebrew Bible.[39] It occurs in the second of three main sections of book III, devoted as a whole to discussing inside things and outside things (domestic and foreign policy) as they relate to the actions of private individuals. This section considers the relationship between virtuous individuals and the multitude.[40] The chapter in which it occurs treats two subjects: eliminating envy, and how to defend a town upon seeing "the enemy." Machiavelli's examples of the first subject display a tidy symmetry: two, Moses and Camillus, eliminate envy successfully; the other two, the Dominican Friar Savonarola and Machiavelli's political patron, Piero Soderini, fail to do so and are driven from power as a result. Camillus successfully eliminated envy by displaying so many examples of virtue that those who might have envied him were more than willing to cede command to him when the very existence of the city was at stake as it came under attack. Moses was compelled to use one of the other two methods of eliminating envy: violent death to the envious.[41]

The passage in question states, "Whoever reads the Bible judiciously will see that since he wished his laws and his orders to go forward, Moses was forced to kill infinite men who, moved by nothing other than envy, were opposed to his plans." The question of why Machiavelli asserts that Moses killed "infinite" men will have to be deferred; but he kills more men than at any other time when he comes down from Sinai to find that Aaron has allowed the people to form and worship the golden calf.[42] The most striking aspect of the passage is the suggestion that at the foot of Sinai Moses wanted *his* laws, *his* orders, *his* plans to go forward. No mention of God's plans, no claim that Moses was the mere executor of God's orders.[43] Moses' own laws, orders, and plans were at issue; to see that they went forward, he was forced to kill. And just as Moses' designs are in no way God's, so the motive of Moses' enemies is in no way godly or, indeed, mixed in any way: it is envy, pure and simple.[44]

How does Machiavelli's condensed version compare with the biblical account? The passage from Exodus reads,

> When Moses realized that, to the scornful joy of their foes, Aaron had let the people run wild; he stood at the gate of the camp and cried, "Whoever is for the Lord, let him come to me!" All the Levites then rallied to him, and he told them, "Thus says the Lord, the God of Israel: Put your sword on your hip, every one of you! Now go up and down the camp, from gate to gate, and slay your own kinsmen, your friends and neighbors!" The Levites carried out the command of Moses, and that day there fell about three thousand of the people. Then Moses said, "Today you have been dedicated to the Lord, for

you were against your own sons and kinsmen, to bring a blessing
upon yourselves this day."[45]

As in his treatment of the David passages in *The Prince* and I Samuel,
there is a great deal in common between the Bible's version of the story of
the golden calf and Machiavelli's. Most importantly, it does appear to be
a moment of political truth for Moses, his enemies, and the people. For
he sees that the people have turned away in the decisive act of idolatry
and his enemies (apparently waiting in the offing to take his place) are
filled with "scornful joy."[46] He is indeed forced to act, and does so with
the killing of very many, if not infinite, men.

Concomitant to the absence of God in Machiavelli's version is that of
the Levites, who are subsumed under the phrase "Moses was forced to
kill"; for in the biblical version it is not Moses himself but the Levites who
do the killing. This brings us to the most perplexing aspect of the biblical passage: the role of the Levites.[47] When Moses says after the killings
that on that day the Levites will be dedicated to the Lord, he seems to
be inaugurating or foretelling[48] the Levites' assumption of aspects of the
priestly office. So this is a fateful moment not only for Moses but for the
politico-religious status of the Levites as well. Two questions that spring
to mind in even an ordinary reading of the passage now take on height-
ened interest: Why are the Levites the only ones ready to step forward
when Moses gives the call, and how did they manage to arm themselves
and then go from gate to gate killing 3,000 of their kinsmen (including
sons; cf. Exodus 32:29 and Deuteronomy 33:9), neighbors, and friends,
apparently without suffering any casualties themselves? We turn to the
second subject of *Discourses on Livy*, III 30, for an answer.

To be clear, I suggest that Machiavelli offers a reasonable interpretation of an otherwise mysterious passage. It is a mystery as to how the
Levites could so thoroughly dominate and kill so many others throughout the camp. I argue that just as Camillus advises to arm one's own in
advance to defend against an attacking enemy, so *must* have the equally
wise Moses. In this way, one comes to a better understanding not just of
Machiavelli but of the Bible: Machiavelli extrapolates (by means of the
symmetry of the passages as argued in this article) from the Livian text
to the biblical one, offering a reasonable interpretation of the latter.

The symmetry that obtained in Machiavelli's treatment of the subject of eliminating envy raises expectations that a similar symmetry
might emerge in the treatment of the subject of defending a city. When

Camillus, the most prudent captain of the Roman republic, again serves as the first example, such expectations are raised still further. They are apparently disappointed, however, when Camillus turns out to be the only example. Might it be, though, that Moses does in fact serve as the second example of a successful defender of a city against the enemy, just as he served as the second example of how to eliminate envy? It would be fitting if the phrase "reading the Bible judiciously" were to appear in a chapter in which such reading were demanded by such a question and taught by its answer.

Camillus' preparation for defense against the same attack discussed under the first subject provides the bridge to the second subject:

> [T]here is no more dangerous nor more useless defense than that which is done tumultuously and without order. This is shown through the third army that Camillus had enrolled so as to leave it in Rome as guard of the city. For many would have judged and would judge this part superfluous.... But Camillus, and *whosoever might be wise as he was,* judge it otherwise; for he never permitted a multitude to take up arms except with a certain order and a certain mode. So upon this example, one individual who is put in charge of the guard of a city ought to avoid like a reef having it arm the men tumultuously, but he *ought first to have those enrolled and selected whom he wishes to be armed, whomever they have to obey, where to meet, where to go*... whoever does otherwise will not imitate Camillus and will not defend *himself.*[49]

Moses, whom we just learned was "wise as [Camillus] was" when it came to eliminating envy, can also be expected to have left his "city"[50] prepared "on seeing the enemy"[51] to take up arms in an orderly manner. To be so prepared, Moses would have needed to select in advance "whom he wished to be armed" (the Levites) and tell them whom "they have to obey" (himself), then "where to meet" (with him, at the main gate), and "where to go" (the gates of the camp). Among the things learned from our consideration of the David passage was that Machiavelli seeks to supply reasoned explanations for otherwise unexplained biblical actions. In this case, he encourages us to consider a difficult-to-explain action and points us in the direction of a reasonable explanation: Moses enlisted the Levites in advance and somehow saw to it that they rather than their opponents would be armed. One can state this conclusion in literary terms as well. Since two modes were adopted in the case of eliminating envy, two examples, Camillus and Moses, were called for, whereas in the case of defending a city (or oneself), the example of Moses would have been superfluous, since Camillus and Moses adopted identical modes. None of this is to deny that Machiavelli would have preferred—had his times allowed—Camillus' bloodless mode to Moses' infinitely bloody one.

If this reading is correct, careful examination of Machiavelli's writings can then lead to better understanding of the Bible. That is, it can lead to an understanding of the Bible based on reason. The question arises as to whether the reverse is the case as well: can the careful reading of the Bible lead to a better understanding of Machiavelli? Otherwise put, how deep is the influence of the Hebrew Bible on Machiavelli's thought?

Hebraic Reading in Christian Times

Having examined the only two Machiavellian treatments of indisputably biblical figures and events, we are now in a position to sketch the purpose of such judicious readings of the Bible. To this end we should consider the implications of Machiavelli's only other reference to "reading judiciously."[52] (For there he writes not just of reading the Bible judiciously but of reading "all the histories" judiciously.) From the repetition of that phrase *chi legge sensatamente* and from the general results of the above treatments of the biblical passages, it is safe to surmise that for Machiavelli the Bible is merely one of the histories.

This suggestion should come as no shock at this stage of the argument—not to mention in this age of well-established biblical criticism. But it has far-reaching implications for the understanding of Machiavelli's political Hebraism and his thought in general. For even if the Bible is *merely* one of the histories and not of divine origin, it is, withal, one of the histories, and Machiavelli accords ancient histories a uniquely important status. For he asserts at the very outset of the *Discourses on Livy* that it is the improper reading of histories that is the cause of the characteristic modern error. That error is to fail to have recourse to the ancients in politics, war, and empire, and to believe that the imitation of the ancients in these respects is indeed impossible. It is to "turn men from this error" that he wrote *Discourses on Livy*.[53] Why the ancients can and ought to be imitated becomes clear when one looks at his formulations of the nature and cause of this modern predicament. As this predicament comes into focus, one begins to consider seriously the possibility that among the ancient histories, the Old Testament is in crucial respects the most important ancient history to read properly for Machiavelli's enterprise to be fully understood. To anticipate, it is so important because it points to both the way the West took to arrive at the degradation of human excellence in Machiavelli's day and the way out of that degradation and toward the revival of human excellence in a new form and on new foundations.

In the passage in the preface to book I of the *Discourses on Livy* referred to above, Machiavelli does not say why our failure to imitate antiquity is a problem. He does say that it

> arises, I believe, not so much from the weakness into which the present religion has led the world, or from the evil that an ambitious idleness has done to many Christian provinces and cities, as from not having true knowledge of histories, through not getting from reading them that sense [*senso*] nor tasting that flavor that they have in themselves.[54]

This credo might appear to be a frank denial of Christianity's responsibility for the problem of his times. But note that contained within the apparent denial are the positive assertions that Christianity has indeed led the world into weakness and that a certain kind of idleness that is peculiar to Christian provinces and cities has in fact done evil, as well as the unavoidable implication that the problem arises at least in part from this weakness and this evil, since "not so much" necessarily implies "some." Note too that the question arises as to why he mentions the harm done by Christianity and what that harm has to do with the cause to which he assigns the greater portion of blame, the improper reading of histories. Perhaps the first is the cause of the second; perhaps it is the condition.[55] Whatever may be the case in this regard, Machiavelli places bad reading and Christianity side by side at the moment he articulates the reason for writing his book.

Near the beginning of the second book of the *Discourses on Livy*, Machiavelli traces the weakness of the world to Christianity's valuing of contemplation over action, suffering over doing, and enduring beatings rather than avenging them. At the beginning of the third book, he points to the root of that valuation when he turns to the religious reforms of two contemplatives, St. Francis and St. Dominic. For these saints'

> [O]rders were so powerful that they are the cause that the dishonesty of the prelates and of the heads of the religion do not ruin it...

> they give [peoples] to understand that it is evil to say evil of evil,
> and that it is good to live under obedience to [the dishonest prelates
> and heads] and, if [the prelates and heads] make an error, to leave
> them for God to punish. So [the prelates and heads] do the worst
> they can because they do not fear the punishment that they do not
> see and do not believe.[56]

Machiavelli's chief motives for these accusations are not those of a twenty-first-century *Boston Globe* reporter incensed by the hypocrisy of bishops and the injustices endured by the faithful. They pertain, rather, to the utter lack of excellence with which these men are able to hold power: the Christian mode of life seems "to have rendered the world weak and given it in prey to criminal men, who can manage it securely, seeing that the collectivity of men, so as to go to paradise, think more of enduring their beatings than of avenging them."[57] Once in power, such ecclesiastical rulers maintain their rule without virtue or fortune, regardless of how they proceed, without either governing or defending their subjects, who "neither think of nor are able to alienate themselves from them."[58] For resistance is in principle impossible,[59] since there is no ground to stand on from which to resist the vicars of the all-powerful God.

As always, however, Machiavelli has left a tiny loophole through which legions of scholars have dutifully marched in their eagerness to acquit so great a thinker of the charge of impiety. For he coyly suggests that it is not Christianity itself but a false interpretation of Christianity that has weakened the world. His grounds for this suggestion are that Christianity "permits" the exaltation and defense of the fatherland. Yet to "permit" is not to require, and one is forgiven for thinking that in Machiavelli's writings, if anywhere, the effects should speak for themselves. Nonetheless, one would also like to know Machiavelli's final view of the truth about Christianity *in itself*. The only way to accomplish this task would seem to be for him to examine judiciously the text that gave rise to it: the New Testament—not to mention the tradition that composed and interpreted it. But such an examination is simply not permitted by his times.

However, to examine judiciously the text which gave rise to *that* text is indeed permitted and would perhaps provide an indirect way of laying bare the essence of Christianity by laying bare the essence of biblical religion as such. On the one hand, it is acknowledged that the "Old Testament," just by virtue of being the Old Testament, was at least incomplete, at most gravely deficient. Therefore, to interpret it in accordance with truths that came to light at a later date is altogether within the Christian tradition. On the other hand, to interpret it according to strength is altogether within Machiavelli's purposes, and we have already seen that passages in the Hebrew Bible are most amenable to being interpreted according to strength. These circumstances allow Machiavelli to praise the Old Testament insofar as it accords with his teaching, while at the same time indicating how it led, via Christianity, to the weakness of the world.

To make the point that Machiavelli put the Bible to this kind of dual use, we will briefly examine an instance of Machiavellian intertextual blasphemy. In chapter 26 of the *Discourses on Livy*, Machiavelli combines the New Testament with the Old Testament in a manner that is—or should be—as shocking as his more general combination of new and old is bewildering. The latter combination is his avowed enterprise of founding new modes and orders by returning to old modes and orders, those of the ancients. Discerning how and why he chooses to proceed in this manner is the great puzzle of his interpretation. But his particular combination in the case of chapter 26 is *sui generis*.

He prepares the way by saying at the end of the previous chapter that "he who wishes to make an absolute power, which is called tyranny by the authors, should renew everything, as will be told in the following chapter."[60] In the next chapter, the promised discussion includes David as one of two examples (the other is, of course, Philip of Macedon, Alexander's father). The examples are meant to illustrate that a new prince, especially one with a weak foundation, must make everything new in a city or province he wishes to hold. Such a prince would have to "make the rich poor, the poor rich, as did David when he was king." Then, in the same breath, Machiavelli quotes Scripture, ostensibly referring to David, "who filled the hungry with good things and sent the rich away empty." The quotation, however, is not from the Old Testament but from the New,[61] and it refers not to David but to God himself. To say in the context of a narration of God's gift of pregnancy to a faith-filled virgin that he makes "the rich poor, the poor rich," and that he "filled the hungry with good things and sent the rich away empty" is to underline God's power and will to do good to those who are faithful to him. But to remove that quotation about God from its New Testament context and to use it as though it were a quotation about a human being from the Old Testament, and to do so in the context of a discussion of how that human being was in fact a tyrant, is to underline something like the opposite. For the God who has the power to show favor and mercy to whomsoever he will[62] likewise has the power to withhold his favor and mercy. There is indeed no king but God, and that king for Machiavelli is a tyrant.

This exercise in intertextual blasphemy takes its final twist when one considers the context of the New Testament quotation, which emphasizes Christ's Davidic lineage. According to both the New Testament and Machiavelli, Christ, not Solomon, is David's true son.[63] He is the weak and peaceful king who succeeded the strong and warlike David.[64] The only New Testament quotation in Machiavelli's comprehensive works thus conflates the New Testament with the Old in a manner that reveals the character of the combination of extremes contained within both Judaism and Christianity and most clearly displayed in the opposition between the two. These extremes, well known to any reader of *The Prince*, are love and fear.[65] In a formula, Machiavelli distinguishes between the Christian testament's teaching of love, on the one hand, and the Jewish testament's teaching of fear, on the other; at the same time, he collapses that distinction. He may thereby suggest that each leads to the other within the biblical tradition. For just as Judaism clearly gave rise to Christianity, so Christianity gave rise to such acts of pious cruelty as cannot be made to gibe with human prudence—let alone human kindness. These two extremes should, in principle, be able to be combined either injudiciously or judiciously. But again, the weaker one's foundations, the more one must take the safer course, namely, to adopt modes that "are very cruel, and enemies to every way of life, not only Christian but human."[66]

Yet what does it mean to have weak foundations? Our final biblical passage implies that it does not consist in being a weak founder in the sense of lacking one's own arms, still less in the sense of lacking a legitimate title. It is rather to found oneself on that which is not and cannot be made evident to human beings as human beings. In chapter 26 of *The Prince*, Moses is again enlisted by Machiavelli. The context is the question whether in Italy the times now favor a new prince. Machiavelli notes that for Moses' virtue to be seen, "the people of Israel" (and "the Hebrews" a few lines later) had to be enslaved. He then suggests—not entirely seriously—similarities between the Italy of his day and the Egypt of Moses'. Addressing Lorenzo de' Medici, he asserts that

> where there is great readiness, there cannot be great difficulty, provided that your house keeps its aim on the orders of those whom I have put forth. Besides this, here may be seen extraordinary things without example, brought about by God: the sea has opened; a

cloud has escorted you along the way; the stone has poured forth
water; here manna has rained.[67]

At first the passage seems to be an obvious reference to the "miracles"[68]
performed as Moses and the Hebrews traveled from Egypt to the promised
land. But then one is forced to wonder whether this is instead another
instance of Machiavelli's inventiveness rather than a genuinely biblical
passage when one recognizes that the order in which the "extraordinary
things without example" are listed does not follow the chronology of
Exodus. For the sea is opened at Exodus 14:21, the cloud escorts along
the way at 13:21, the stone pours forth water at 17:6, and manna rains
at 16:4.

But doubts as to the direct biblical provenance of the passage are dis-
pelled by the discovery that the order follows exactly that given in Psalms
78:13–24.[69] On turning to this psalm,[70] one finds a story that alternates
between accounts of God's wonders and commandments,[71] the Israelites'
rebellions,[72] and God's terrifying punishments in which he "killed their
best warriors, laid low the youth of Israel. In spite of this they... did not
believe in his wonders" (31–32); "slew them" again (33–34); and "rejected
them completely[,]... gave [them] up into captivity[, and]... abandoned
his people to the sword" and to fire (59–63). The psalm culminates in
the rejection of Ephraim and the choice of Judah and of David as his
servant. This culmination points back to the beginning of the narrative
of the psalm and the disobedient retreat of the Ephraimite archers (9–11).
Although no punishment is specified in the psalm, one need only turn to
Judges 12:2–6, where Jeftah recounts their failure to fight, defeats them
in battle, and has 42,000 killed one by one as they cross the Jordan to
return home.

In sum, the psalm to which Machiavelli has drawn our attention is—
on a judicious reading—a chilling testimony to God's wrathful rule of
a people that can bring itself to believe, and then only for a time, in his
wonders only once it has "firm experience" of them. For "the nature of
peoples is variable; and it is easy to persuade them of something, but difficult to keep them in that persuasion. And thus things must be ordered
in such a mode that when they no longer believe, one can make them
believe by force."[73] Machiavelli heartily recommends such uses of force,
even—and sometimes especially—when they are not, strictly speaking,
necessary.

There is reason to think, however, that he opposes modes and orders that *make* such uses of force necessary and resistance to them impossible. For in such cases the judicious use of such extreme measures is often in practice no longer possible, since in principle there can be no limit to such force: it is infinite. Indeed, when one is the mere executor of the orders of an all-powerful and transpolitical prince, oftentimes one is compelled, as was Ferdinand the Catholic, to harm one's own people, one's own country, and oneself. Of Ferdinand, Machiavelli said, "always making use of religion, he turned to an act of pious cruelty, expelling the Marranos from his kingdom and despoiling it of them; nor could there be an example more wretched and rarer than this."[74] The overt censure contained in the word "wretched" is surpassed by the subtler criticism contained in the implication that by despoiling his kingdom of one of its finest treasures, Ferdinand behaved unreasonably.

Conclusion

This examination of Machiavelli's judicious readings of the Hebrew Bible has sought to show that careful reading of Machiavelli can lead to a better, albeit ultimately critical, understanding of the Hebrew Bible. In addition, it began to develop the possibility that careful reading of the Hebrew Bible can illuminate Machiavelli's writings and thought, in part because, by his own suggestion, the Hebrew Bible played a decisive role in his attack on the tradition of political philosophy. Indeed, it would seem that Machiavelli himself attached fundamental importance to understanding the Hebrew Bible as a means of appreciating both the perils and the necessity of properly eliciting, reading, and managing men's passions of love and fear. For although classical political philosophy was highly attuned indeed to the significance and use of these passions,[75] only in the biblical tradition, and in the Hebrew Bible in particular, does the degree to which human beings can be molded by the ultimate extremes of love and fear become clear.

Notes

I would like to thank Steven Lenzner and Nathan Tarcov for comments on early drafts of this article.

1. For a useful reprise and instance of such studies, see Alison Brown, "De-Masking Renaissance Republicanism," in James Hankins, ed., *Renaissance Civic Humanism: Reappraisals and Reflections* (Cambridge: Cambridge University Press, 2000), pp. 179–199.

2. In translating *sensatamente* as "judiciously," I follow Niccolò Machiavelli, *Discourses on Livy*, trans. Harvey C. Mansfield and Nathan Tarcov (Chicago: University of Chicago Press, 1996), pp. 28, 280; Alison Brown, "Savonarola, Machiavelli, and Moses," in Peter Denley and Caroline Elam, eds., *Florence and Italy: Renaissance Studies in Honour of Nicolai Rubinstein* (London: Westfield Publications in Medieval Studies, 1988), p. 64; and Leo Strauss, *Thoughts on Machiavelli* (Chicago: University of Chicago Press, 1958), p. 114; some alternative translations are "sensitively," "attentively," and "carefully."

3. More frequently mentioned than all of these characters is Cyrus the Great of Persia, whose *biblical* deeds and words (see Ezra 1–6) are neither cited nor alluded to by Machiavelli. His explicit source for Cyrus is Xenophon; his implicit source, Herodotus (see Christopher Nadon, *Xenophon's Prince: Republic and Empire in the Cyropaedia* [Berkeley: University of California Press, 2001], pp. 13–25). Consider also the case of Alexander the Great, for whom Machiavelli names no source while apparently drawing on many, from Plutarch and Livy to Vitruvius and Aquinas. For the possibility that Machiavelli also had in mind the Alexander of the Bible (albeit not the Hebrew Bible), compare *Discourses*, I 20, with I Maccabees 3, and Niccolò Machiavelli, *The Prince*, trans. Harvey Mansfield (Chicago: University of Chicago Press, 2nd ed., 1988), 4, with I Maccabees 5–8.

4. *Prince*, 6.22–24, 26.102; *Discourses*, I 1.4, 9.3, II 8.2, III 30.1.

5. *Prince*, 13.56; *Discourses*, I 19.2, 26.

6. Niccolò Machiavelli, *Mandragola*, 3.11.36.

7. To be discussed below.

8. More precisely, Machiavelli notes that Procopius writes of Belisarius' report of "letters written on certain columns" in Africa by the Maurusians, a people driven out of ancient Syria by "the Hebrews" (*Discourses*, II 8.2).

9. *Discourses*, I 29.2.

10. Niccolò Machiavelli, *Art of War*, trans. Christopher Lynch (Chicago: University of Chicago Press, 2003), IV 110.

11. *Discourses*, II 32.1.

12. *Prince*, 21.

13. *Art of War*, II 170. Cf. *Art of War*, II 5ff., for the apparent use of Josephus without attribution as a source for Roman heavy armaments.

14. *Discourses*, II 5.2.

15. *Discourses*, II 5.1.

16. *Discourses*, III 34, 36.1, 37.1.

17. Niccolò Machiavelli, *Tutte le opere*, ed. Mario Martelli (Florence: Sansoni, 1992), pp. 932–934. *On the Persecutions in Africa by Henry, King of the Vandals* contains several significant uses of biblical passages, one of which is attributed to David in the context of a lampoon of St. Augustine's self-imposed silence during the cruel siege of Hippo in 430 C.E. after a life of prolific writing and speaking. Machiavelli highlights the irony of the juxtaposition of such a loquacious life ("What was the need to say so many things?") against the silent retreat during such awful persecutions (Martelli, *Tutte le opere*, pp. 934–936). During this retreat, which Augustine rightly suspected would be his last due to the onset of a fatal illness, the saint is said to have posted on the walls of his room the four penitential psalms of David: Psalms 6, 32, 38, and 51 (Peter Brown, *Augustine of Hippo: A Biography* [Berkeley: University of California Press, 1967], p. 432). An exhaustive search of Machiavelli's minor works for Hebraic figures and events remains to be conducted.

18. Exodus 2:11–12.

19. Niccolò Machiavelli, *Machiavelli and His Friends: Their Personal Correspondence*, trans. and eds. James B. Atkinson and David Sices (De Kalb, Ill.: Northern Illinois University Press, 1996), p. 10. For Savonarola's appropriation of the figure of Moses and its recognition by Machiavelli, see Alison Brown, "Savonarola, Machiavelli, and Moses." Brown's interpretation of the significance of Savonarola to Machiavelli parallels this article's interpretation of the significance of Moses (see especially Brown, "Savonarola, Machiavelli, and Moses," p. 65).

20. For the claim that these works contain all that he knows, see *Prince*, dedicatory letter 3–4, and *Discourses*, dedicatory letter 3; cf. Strauss, *Thoughts*, p. 17.

21. The best support for this claim would seem to be Joshua 14:6–15 and Deuteronomy 33:7, 34:2. But the former attests only to a reminder by Caleb, descendant of Judah, that Moses had once sworn to him that "the land that you have set foot on [while reconnoitering Canaan] shall become your heritage and that of your descendants forever" (v. 9). But nowhere does Moses himself "name" a portion of Canaan "Judah" or "Judea." Even God does not so name it in Moses' time; rather, all the lands, including the land of Judah, "are shown" to him.

22. *Prince*, 13.56.

23. *Discourses*, III 30.1.

24. *Discourses*, I 26; *Prince*, 26.103.

25. The four sections are chs. 1–11 on the different types of states according especially to the means by which they are acquired, chs. 12–14 on attack and defense of such states, chs. 15–23 on modes of government with subjects and friends, and chs. 24–26 on fortune; see Strauss, *Thoughts*, pp. 55–61.

26. One should not be thrown off the scent of a genuinely literary passage by this use of "figure," for "a figure from the Old Testament" is not a mere "figure."

See Erich Auerbach, "Figura," in Auerbach, *Studi su Dante* (Milan: Feltrinelli, 1963); *The Prince by Niccolò Machiavelli with Related Documents*, trans. William J. Connell (Boston: Bedford/St. Martins, 2005), p. 83 n. 6; cf. Strauss, *Thoughts*, p. 59.

27. *Prince*, 13.56.

28. This quotation of unknown provenance bears a striking similarity to a verse from I Samuel. For of Hiero, Machiavelli says, "he lacked nothing of being a king except a kingdom" (*Discourses*, end of dedicatory letter), while of David after his defeat of Goliath, Saul, after hearing the greater praise accorded by the women to David than to him, thinks, "All that remains for him is the kingdom" (I Samuel 18:8).

29. See Strauss, *Thoughts*, pp. 58–59.

30. *Prince*, 13.56.

31. I Samuel 17:38–40, 50–51. Unless otherwise indicated, translations in this article are from Jean Hiesberger, ed., *The Catholic Study Bible: Personal Study Edition* (Oxford: Oxford University Press, 1995).

32. I Samuel 17:32.

33. I Samuel 17:38–40.

34. Cf. n. 28 above.

35. Connell, *The Prince*, p. 83 n. 7, suggests that Machiavelli's "mistake must have been prompted by his familiarity with Andrea Verrocchio's statue *David*... who holds a small sword that might easily be assumed to be David's rather than Goliath's." Two considerations work against Connell's reading. Verrocchio's David wears no belt or sheath in which to carry the sword he holds. More significantly, the following passage (as quoted in David Marsh, *The Quattrocento Dialogue* [Cambridge, Mass.: Harvard University Press, 1980], p. 57) from a widely read dialogue, *De vero falsoque bono* by Lorenzo Valla (1405–1457), suggests that the biblical presentation of David's use of Goliath's sword was well known and freighted with paramount significance: "Just as David used his enemy's own sword to kill him... so I hope in part to slay these gentiles, the philosophers, and in part to rouse them to an internecine war and their self-destruction, by the power of our faith, such as it is, and of God's word."

36. Cf. *Art of War*, III 111, where Fabrizio admits that "it is more important for one to guard against being hit than it is important to hit the enemy."

37. Making David the central example.

38. *Prince*, 13.57.

39. Cf. *Discourses*, III 33.1, 36.2.

40. Harvey C. Mansfield, *Machiavelli's New Modes and Orders: A Study of the 'Discourses on Livy'* (Chicago: University of Chicago Press, 1979), pp. 298–299.

41. *Discourses*, III 30.1. Note that the third mode is to wait for the envious to die a natural death. But in waiting for theirs, what of one's own? For Machiavelli's

answer, consider *Discourses*, II preface, III 1, together with *Discourses*, I 9.4, and *Art of War*, I 5–6.

42. Many more die in the punishments for the rebellions of Korah and of Dathan and Abiram (Numbers 16–17). However, the Bible presents not Moses or his followers as the cause of these deaths, but an earthquake and a scourge, both caused by God (notwithstanding some of Moses' enemies to the contrary [Numbers 17:6]). Despite this difficulty, these punishments could, as suggested to me by Nathan Tarcov, be the action to which Machiavelli refers, especially in light of the correspondence of Machiavelli's distinction between ordinary and violent death to Moses' distinction between ordinary death and death due to something "entirely new" done by the Lord (see *Discourses*, III 30.1, and Numbers 16:29–30); for a Mosaic Savonarola on the rebellion of Korah, see Brown, "Savonarola, Machiavelli, and Moses," p. 62.

43. *Prince*, 6.22.

44. That Machiavelli was moved to make such categorical claims due to something other than a lack of sympathy for the religious longings or experiences of others is made clear in a passage taken from a very different context, *Florentine Histories* I, 5. Machiavelli was clearly familiar with the pain that accompanies the uncertainty as to which god to turn to, if any.

45. Exodus 32:25–28.

46. Envy is both immoderate sadness at another's goods and immoderate joy at another's evils. Cf. *Catechism of the Catholic Church*, nos. 2538–2539, with the remark of the well-catechized Lonnie of Walker Percy's *The Moviegoer* (New York: Ballantine Books, 1960), p. 143: "Envy is not merely sorrow at another's good fortune; it is also joy at another's misfortune."

47. For an account of treatments of this passage by Augustine, Aquinas, and Calvin, especially as they pertain to the Levites, see Michael Walzer, "Exodus 32 and the Theory of Holy War: The History of a Citation," *Harvard Theological Review* 61:1 (1968), pp. 1–14.

48. See Deuteronomy 33:8ff.; see v. 8 for Moses' bestowal on the Levites of the Urim and Thummim, objects of "decision making" that seem to function much like a mixture of Roman auspices and Florentine *borse*, subjects about which Machiavelli has infinite things to say in the *Discourses on Livy* and *Florentine Histories*.

49. *Discourses*, III 30.2; italics added.

50. See *Art of War*, VI, where a camp is said to be like a mobile city.

51. Compare the title of *Discourses*, III 30, "...on Seeing the Enemy...," "*vedendo il nimico*," with the Vulgate version of Exodus 32:25, "*videns ergo Moses populum... hostes nudum constituerat*." In this regard also consider the ruling distinction of the structure of Machiavelli's *Art of War*, that between preparing for battle against an enemy one sees and doing so for battle against an enemy one does not see but fears (see translator's commentary in *Art of War*, p. 226).

52. *Discourses*, I 23.4.

53. *Discourses*, I preface 2.

54. Ibid.

55. Strauss, *Thoughts*, p. 177.

56. *Discourses*, III 1.4.

57. *Discourses*, II 2.2.

58. *Prince*, 11.45; translation modified.

59. Strauss, *Thoughts*, p. 185.

60. *Discourses*, I 25.

61. Luke 1:53. See Strauss, *Thoughts*, p. 49; Leo Strauss, *Studies in Platonic Political Philosophy* (Chicago: University of Chicago Press, 1983), pp. 223–225.

62. Exodus 33:19.

63. Cf. Matthew 1:1, 17, in which the numerical value of David's name (14) is used to emphasize Christ's Davidic parentage.

64. Perhaps the truly final twist is that the Magnificat from which the quotation is taken is modeled on "Hanna's Song," and the quoted line corresponds to a line from that song (see I Samuel 2:5, 7). Thus, Samuel, the origin of Christ's status *as* Christ, the anointed one, is brought to mind.

65. *Prince*, 17.

66. *Discourses*, I 26.

67. *Prince*, 26.

68. To use the traditional word. But the Hebrew Bible cannot (and Machiavelli would rather not) call such events miracles.

69. For this insight, see Hugo Jaeckel, "What Is Machiavelli Exhorting in His 'Exortatio,'" in Jean-Jacques Marchand, ed., *Niccolò Machiavelli: Politico, Storico, Letterato: Atti del Convengo di Losanna, 27–30 settemebre 1995* (Rome: Salerno Editrice, 1996), pp. 60–61. Nathan Tarcov suggested much of the following interpretation of the psalm; cf. Strauss, *Thoughts*, p. 309 n. 41.

70. It is in the third book of the Psalms, the book that produced no "orphans," that is, psalms without attribution or dedication; it is the sixth of the eleven contiguous psalms attributed or dedicated to Asaph (the Temple choir director, whose name means "collector" or "compiler"), all of which are emphatically national in character in that they make frequent allusions to the history of Israel, though this is the only one that emphasizes David; it is the eighth of thirteen *maskilim*, or psalms *eis synesin* according to the Septuagint, or *ad intellectum* according to the Vulgate. In v. 2 the psalmist opens his mouth with "story," in Hebrew, *mashal*, which "literally means 'comparison' and can signify a story with a hidden meaning" (Hiesberger, *Catholic Study Bible*, p. 699, note on Psalms 78:2). Perhaps one is thereby encouraged to compare the psalm to Exodus or—with Machiavelli's mediation—both to *The Prince*.

71. In vv. 1–8, 12–16, 21–29, 42–55.

72. In vv. 9–11, 17–20, 32, 40–42, 56–58.

73. *Prince*, 6.24.

74. *Prince*, 21.88.

75. Consider esp. Machiavelli's favorite, Xenophon's *Education of Cyrus*, I vi 20–24; cf. *Discourses*, II 13.

II. THE BIBLE AS A MODEL FOR POLITICS

Political Hebraism and the Early Modern 'Respublica Hebraeorum': On Defining the Field

Kalman Neuman

Terminology

The inauguration of a new field of study requires definition, and the rediscovery of "political Hebraism" suggests the need for clearer focus on its scope.

The term "political Hebraism" may be misleading, because it suggests a relationship with the phenomenon known as Christian Hebraism, which is often used to refer to writings of Hebraists, those versed in the Hebrew language.[1] One contemporary scholar suggests defining Hebraism as "efforts by... Christian scholars to use the Hebrew language for interpreting the Old Testament," while distinguishing between "lexical Hebraism," based on the independent ability of the Christian to read biblical and postbiblical texts, and "cultural Hebraism," in which the knowledge of Hebrew depends on conversation with a living Jew.[2]

In fact, the reach of the political reading of the *Tanach* (Hebrew Bible) exceeds the grasp of Hebraism, although it does not include all Hebraists. Hebraists (in the limited sense) did not take a special interest in political questions, and their attempt to study the text in the original focused on other areas, such as those related to theological issues or that enhanced their understanding of the New Testament. On the other hand, the investigation of the political message of the Hebrew Bible was not limited to scholars with firsthand or even secondhand knowledge of the Hebrew language, but included those who read the text in translation.[3]

Avoiding a narrow definition of "political Hebraism" raises the danger of a notion so broad as to be nebulous. The wider concept of "Hebraism" or "Hebraic writing" as a general cultural phenomenon (often contrasted with Hellenism) is an elusive concept, which has been perceived differently at different points of cultural history, most famously by Heinrich Heine and Matthew Arnold.[4]

For our purposes "Hebraic political writing" refers to texts that convey readings of the Hebrew Bible (or postbiblical Jewish texts) in a political context, whether or not the author read those texts in the original Hebrew.[5] The fact that special attention was given to the Old Testament might produce theological pitfalls. Mining the text for a relevant political message often engaged Christian writers with the question of the relevance of Old Testament law. Some of those writers could be subject to accusations of Judaizing, a claim not uncommon in the theological struggles of the sixteenth and seventeenth centuries.[6]

Now that we have focused our view on the political uses of the Hebrew Bible, we must try to identify when such use is significant for the student of intellectual history. There is a need to find criteria that will allow us to distinguish stock examples from meaningful influence on the development of ideas.

The problem at hand is exemplified by the chapter on "Hebraic politics" in Adam Sutcliffe's book *Judaism and Enlightenment*. Sutcliffe refers to the use made by Levellers, Diggers, and Quakers of "biblical rhetoric that made intensive use of the moral polarities of Abel and Cain, Jacob and Esau, and Israel and Amalek."[7] While the employment of such examples certainly reflects the common knowledge of the Old Testament among members of those groups, it is hard to see the use of such *topoi* as impacting on the content of their political thinking. Are we to see every comparison of a good king to David and an evil one to Ahab as part of "Hebraic politics"? If not, how are we to justify this exclusion? I would suggest distinguishing between rhetorical use of biblical imagery on the one hand, while on the other hand noting the more systematic use of the Bible as a source for political ideas (whether or not such use was decisive or even central in the work of a given writer).[8]

Early Modern Use of the Hebrew Bible

There is no doubt that early modern Europe saw an expansion of Hebraism in the sense of the study of the Hebrew language[9] as well as the rise of new approaches to the Old Testament.[10] Among these was reading the Old Testament as a political work. The striving to return *ad fontes*, the "struggle for stability,"[11] and the pursuit of models from the past to inform contemporary political discussions ("ancient constitutionalism") stimulated a political appreciation of the biblical text.[12]

What is new about the political Hebraism of early modern Europe? Frank Manuel notes that

> before the seventeenth century there was great reluctance to turn the narrative parts of the Old Testament into a consecutive secular story or to analyze the institutions of the patriarchal age, the period of Moses' rule or the kingships of the first and second commonwealths, as if they were states with histories similar to those of other nations.[13]

The early modern treatment of the Hebrew Republic (which begins at the end of the sixteenth century) has the Old Testament read as a consecutive narrative and not as a prefiguration of eternal truths.[14] Early modern Hebraic politics sees the polity of the Hebrews as subject to historical processes and as such may be analyzed in a way similar to political systems of other nations.

To be sure, this approach to the Bible also has its own ancient and medieval pedigree, including (to name two outstanding examples) Josephus and Thomas Aquinas. In a celebrated passage in Josephus' *Jewish Antiquities* (IV, 223), there is a depiction of the political system of the Hebrews. In that passage as well as in numerous others, Josephus is not averse to utilizing the terminology of political discourse to describe the Hebrew polity.[15] In a similar way, Thomas portrayed the regime of Moses using the classical models of political thought and introduced the concept of the mixed constitution to the study of the Israelite polity.[16]

These writings anteceded the more extensive and more systematic treatment of the ancient biblical polity in the early modern period, which was intimately concerned with the political questions of the time.

It must be emphasized that there is no common political denominator unifying the early modern political uses of the Bible. It was used to support different polarities of such questions as whether monarchy or a republic is the preferred regime. As is well known, the biblical text itself seems to present contradictory positions on the question of monarchy as opposed to other regimes. The book of Deuteronomy assumes the establishment of a king, while Samuel was opposed to the institution of monarchy. Early modern writers quoted various Old Testament and rabbinic sources (and often the same ones) both to defend monarchy as well as to attack it.[17] Typical examples of this phenomenon are two works written in 1649 and 1650, respectively, namely *Defensio regia pro Carolo I* (*Defense of the King on Behalf of Charles I*) by Salmasius (Claude de Saumaise) and the response by John Milton, *Pro populo Anglicano defensio* (*A Defense of the English People*). These works used Hebraic sources, among other arguments for and against the regicide of King Charles I, to prove their points.[18] Political Hebraism is as a whole better seen as a common mode of discourse than as a defense of a specific political position. I would suggest that it is not effective to posit an "authentic" biblical political philosophy and use that as a yardstick to distinguish between "real" political Hebraism and crass manipulation of the Bible for political purposes. Rather, it is preferable to view the Old Testament as forming one of the common bases for discourse on politics in early modern Europe. The "Mosaic moment" in political thought should take its place of honor among other languages or paradigms, which have been exposed to the light of scholarly investigation in the last forty years.[19] These works face common questions of exegesis and interpretation, promote different political and ecclesiastical images of the Israelite polity, and deal in various ways with major themes of politics and religious thought.

The Literature of the 'Respublica Hebraeorum'

What are the sources for our study of political Hebraism? In what kinds of literary works are we to find analyses of the ancient Israelite polity in terms of universal political categories? Mapping the field would include various types of religious writings (such as sermons or polemical works) as well as specifically political works of the period, a period in which historical examples were no less important than theoretical argument and in which the Bible provided examples alongside classical Greece and Rome and contemporary Venice.

There is another type of literature that describes the politics of ancient Israel. I am referring to the genre that may be called the literature of the *Respublica Hebraeorum* (Republic of the Hebrews) and that attempts to systematically study the ancient Israelite polity.

A first attempt to identify this genre is in *Bibliotheca Latino-Hebraica* (*The Latin-Hebrew Library*) by Carolo Ioseph Imbonato (Rome, 1694),[20] which lists some hundred volumes in the category of *De Republica, Synagoga, Legibus, et Ritibus Iudaeorum* (*On the Republic, the Synagogue, the Laws, and the Rituals of the Jews*). Manuel refers to this list in the context of his section in *The Broken Staff* entitled "Anatomy of the Republic of the Hebrews."[21] In this, he was judging the books by their covers (or by their titles). Many of the works in the list do not deal with the political aspects of the ancient Hebrews but with descriptions of Israelite religion.[22] Therefore, the true number of books that incorporate systematic treatments of the Israelite polity is much lower. They include works such as *De Politia Judaica tam civili quam ecclesiastica* (*On the Jewish Polity, Both Civil and Ecclesiastic*) by Cornelius Bertram,[23] *De Republica Hebraeorum* (*On the Republic of the Hebrews*) by Carlo Sigonio,[24] *Legum Mosicarum Forensium explanatio* (*Explanation of the Juridical Laws of Moses*) by Wilhelm Zepper,[25] *De Republica Emendanda* (*On How to Emend the Republic*), an early work by Hugo Grotius,[26] *De Republica Hebraeorum* (*On the Republic of the Hebrews*) by Petrus Cunaeus,[27] and *Jus Regium Hebraeorum* (*The Laws of the Hebrew Kings*) by Wilhelm Schickard,[28] as well as *De Synedriis* (*On the Assemblies*) by John Selden, probably the greatest Hebraist of his day.[29]

This genre should be seen in the context of early modern antiquarianism, a phenomenon that has been studied in the works of Arnaldo Momigliano and Anthony Grafton. Momigliano has characterized the antiquarians as describing the past in a way not based on chronological development but rather on the systematic descriptions of ancient institutions, religion, and law. The antiquarian was descriptive, attempting to reconstruct the material culture and institutions of the past, rather than explain their development. In addition, antiquarians often used nonliterary sources in order to learn about the past. This methodology found its way into biblical studies as well. Peter Miller has called the tendency of seventeenth-century biblical studies to delve into questions of biblical realia "the antiquarianization of biblical scholarship."[30] This did not only include the many works on the physical realia of the Bible. Inspired by the works of antiquarianism and by the general interest in "the ancient

constitution," the genre of the *Respublica Hebraeorum* set out to reconstruct the ancient Israelite polity.[31]

It is not always evident that the motivation for the work is other than
pure scholarship. Sigonio was first and foremost an antiquarian and historian. His attempt to describe the political system of the Hebrews after
writing descriptions of the systems of the Romans and the Athenians
seems to reflect the same academic interest.[32] Other writers had additional concerns, such as defending a view of church-state relations
(Bertram), presenting a model for the welfare of the United Provinces
(Cunaeus), or even hinting at the impossibility of reinstituting the Mosaic
state (Zepper).

The writers followed the principle of describing the Israelite polity in
terms of general political thought but did not share the same reading of
biblical history. Bertram saw the regime founded by Moses as containing
a monarchial element mixed with aristocracy (the magistrates appointed
after the reforms of Jethro) and democracy (the entire people or its representatives).[33] After the death of Moses there was no longer a king, but
military dictators were appointed in emergencies.[34] The establishment of
the king by popular demand in the days of Samuel was in effect a reinsti-
tution of the mixed constitution from the days of Moses.[35] On the other
hand, Sigonio emphasized the arbitrary power of the king, as opposed to
the rule of law that was instituted by Moses.[36] Cunaeus saw the appointment of the king as a sign of moral decay, which brought about a wish
for the opulence of a king as opposed to the ethical example of Moses.[37]
Zepper preferred a monarchy, but since he did not see the biblical example as binding, he believed that the proper regime should be determined
by rational thought and human experience.[38] Schickard seems to have had
an ambivalent attitude toward monarchy. He quotes conflicting rabbinic
opinions about kingship and also raises the question (already discussed
in the Talmud) of the king's being judged by a court of law.[39]

Methodology and Reconstruction

How did such writers go about writing the constitutional history of the
Hebrews? The reconstruction of the Israelite polity raised methodological
questions for scholars and antiquarians. Such a history has to be based
on a solitary source, the Old Testament (whether read in the original

Hebrew or in translation), and occasionally supplemented by Josephus or rabbinic texts. Obviously, the authors took for granted the historical accuracy of the biblical books (although some of these writers, such as Sigonio, might have been skeptical about the Vulgate version)[40] and the unity of the biblical text. This required them to harmonize contradictions found in the various biblical descriptions. In general, the biblical text does not easily lend itself to systematic political description. As is well known, the Tanach does not quite read like Aristotle's *Constitution of Athens*. Its depiction of political events is secondary to its status as a religious work. In addition, the events described in the Bible span hundreds of years, and it is difficult to identify the function of political institutions at any given time. On the one hand, the Bible itself describes changes in the political regime of the Hebrews, such as the institution of the magistrates by Jethro or the establishment of the kingdom in the days of Samuel. On the other hand, there are gaps in the description of the institution in each period of the biblical story. The different authors writing on the Hebrew republic had to find their own interpretative strategies to fill those lacunae.

Sigonio had previous experience in using the works of Cicero to reconstruct the mechanisms of the Roman assemblies.[41] It is not surprising that, assuming similarity between the Hebraic and Roman republics, he used the Roman model to fill in the blanks in the biblical text. For example, he assumes that when the Bible describes assemblies of the people, it is referring to a formal institution subject to precise laws. Therefore, just like in Rome, only a ruler with *imperium* (supreme political authority) could convene such an assembly. Following that assumption, he defines which offices described in the Old Testament carried with them *imperium*, trying to use the biblical terms (or their Latin equivalents—Sigonio knew no Hebrew) in a consistent way.[42] Sigonio also quotes from the appropriate passages in Josephus, using him as a major source for his recognition of the Israelite polity.[43]

Cornelius Bertram, on the other hand, seems to have used different methodological principles. He tries to base himself as much as possible on the biblical text itself (he was an accomplished scholar of Hebrew).[44] In addition, he seems to assume that institutions remained static for the extent of the biblical period, unless the text specifically describes a change. Therefore, Bertram writes that the institution of the elders that existed during the sojourn in Egypt before the Exodus continued to exist during the entire biblical period and even beyond.[45]

Wilhelm Schickard based his description of the Israelite monarchy on postbiblical texts (and, like other writers, did not question the assumption that the Jewish postbiblical texts retained authentic descriptions of the polity of biblical times). He had access to a number of rabbinic texts such as *Midrash Rabba*, *Mishneh Torah* of Maimonides (which had already been utilized by Cunaeus),[46] and various Jewish biblical exegetes.[47] Schickard's quotations from rabbinic material were used by writers such as Harrington or Milton, and even by scholars of Hebrew such as Selden.[48]

Theocracy in the 'Respublica Hebraeorum'

One of the themes that recurs in many of the works is the question of theocracy, even when the term does not appear explicitly. The notion of the "kingdom of God" appears in the Tanach as an alternative to human kingdom, but the term "theocracy" appears first as a description of the Mosaic polity in Josephus' *Against Apion*. The term is open to different interpretations (both as to the intent of Josephus and in subsequent discussions),[49] and one can distinguish between radical interpretations of theocracy that see it as direct rule of God and theocracy, which in effect is hierocracy, the rule of priests.[50]

The writers on the *Respublica Hebraeorum* often found themselves confronting the question of God as ruler. Sigonio describes the Mosaic polity as the rule of law but, utilizing a creative reading of Aristotle,[51] identifies that regime as the rule of God.[52] Despite the fact that he ignores the text in *Against Apion* and the term "theocracy," he introduces the idea through the back door. Bertram also tries to integrate the notion of God's rule in his political-historical analysis by positing God as one of the elements of a mixed constitution.[53] Cunaeus quotes the passage in Josephus on theocracy and has his own explanation about the divine nature of the Hebrew commonwealth. He does not think that the constitutional institutions of the Hebrews are worth emulating (and perhaps they are not even worth extensive discussion), but instead the United Provinces should imitate the *aequitas* (equity) and *iustitia* (justice) which are the essence of the theocracy and are reflected in the Mosaic laws (and especially in the agrarian regime).

The recurring discussion of theocracy in the descriptions of the Hebrew republic raises the question of the relation of those descriptions to the treatment of the kingdom of God by two of the major thinkers of the seventeenth century: Hobbes and Spinoza.

The descriptions of the political meaning of the kingdom of God in the third book of *Leviathan* as well as in *De Cive* (*On the Citizen*) have inspired a number of studies in recent years.[54] The details of the political history of the Bible have yet to be compared with the descriptions in the literature of the *Respublica Hebraeorum*, but they share many themes and concerns.[55]

Similarly the notion of theocracy is a central part of the description of the Israelite state in Spinoza's *Theological Political Treatise*. The affinity between Spinoza's work and the literature of the time dealing with the Israelite state has been noted by a number of scholars, but more extensive analysis of the relevant chapters and a comparison with the other writers show both the commonalities and the contrasts between the different interpretations.[56]

The study of the literature of the *Respublica Hebraeorum* and of early modern political Hebraism will certainly prove to be an important addition to the intellectual history of the period and to the role of the Bible in Western civilization.

Notes

Part of this paper is based on my Ph.D. dissertation, "The Literature of the *Respublica Judaica*: Descriptions of the Ancient Israelite Polity in the Antiquarian Writing of the Sixteenth and Seventeenth Centuries" (The Hebrew University of Jerusalem, 2002), written under the supervision of Professor Michael Heyd.

1. Moritz Steinschneider, *Christliche Hebraisten: Nachrichten über mehr als 400 Gelehrte, welche über nachbiblisches Hebräisch geschrieben haben* (Hildesheim: H.A. Gestenberg, 1973). Steinschneider's list of Christian Hebraists was originally published in the *Zeitschrift für Hebräische Bibliographie*, 1–5 (1896–1901). For an example of the use of Hebrew knowledge as the criterion for the definition of "Hebraist," see Cecil Roth, "Hebraists and Non-Hebraists of the Seventeenth Century," *Journal of Semitic Studies* 6 (1961), pp. 204–221.

2. Michael A. Signer, "Polemic and Exegesis: The Varieties of Twelfth-Century Hebraism," in Allison P. Coudert and Jeffrey S. Shoulson, eds., *Hebraica Veritas? Christian Hebraists and the Study of Judaism in Early Modern Europe* (Philadelphia: University of Pennsylvania Press, 2004), pp. 22–23.

3. The wish to avoid using the term "Hebraism" for the phenomenon we are describing is evident in one of the first academic studies in the field, the Hebrew University M.A. thesis of Shaul Robinson, submitted in 1940, entitled "The State of Israel as a Model State in the Writings of Political Thinkers of the Seventeenth and Eighteenth Centuries: Biblicism in Political Thought from Machiavelli to Adam Miller." The work, with a slight change in the title due to the establishment of the modern State of Israel in the interim, was published in a posthumous volume of Robinson's essays entitled *Education Between Continuity and Openness* (Jerusalem: Magnes Press, 1975), pp. 13–70. [Hebrew] "Biblicism," however, is also awkward for describing the field of study, especially for the Christian reader who would not understand that the reference is specifically to the Old Testament. If we accept the usual definition of Christian Hebraism, then the title of Jonathan Ziskind's article "Cornelius Bertram and Carlo Sigonio: Christian Hebraism's First Political Scientists" (*Journal of Ecumenical Studies* 37 [2000], pp. 381–400) is misleading, as Sigonio knew no Hebrew.

4. Regarding Heine and Arnold and the *topos* of Hebraism as opposed to Hellenism in general, see Yaacov Shavit, *Athens in Jerusalem: Classical Antiquity and Hellenism in the Making of the Modern Secular Jew* (London: Littman Library of Jewish Civilization, 1999). See, for example, Harold Fisch, *Jerusalem and Albion: The Hebraic Factor in Seventeenth-Century Literature* (New York: Schocken, 1964), p. 15 n. 2: "The present work is not concerned with Hebrew learning as such, but rather with the 'Hebraic factor' as a deeper and more pervasive influence…." This factor is characterized in different ways by Fisch, sometimes by referring to questions of style such as "Hebraic earnestness and sublimity" (p. 41), or "Hebrew imaginative structure" (p. 51), sometimes by alluding to the Old Testament concepts of covenant (pp. 93–114), or "the active impulse seeking… the fulfillment of a messianic hope" (p. 89). While not unaware of the dangers of "oversimplification or distortion" (p. 65), he uses different criteria for identifying "the factor of Jerusalem" (p. 114), a factor that goes far beyond references to the Old Testament. Interestingly enough, he mentions Milton's use of biblical sanction for the republican form of government as an example of "men going wrong by making false equations" (pp. 124–125).

5. The contemporary use of the term "Hebrew Bible" is an attempt to find a theologically neutral term for what for Christians is the Old Testament and for Jews is the Tanach. See Rolf Rendtorff, "Old Testament Theology, Tanach Theology, or Biblical Theology? Reflections in an Ecumenical Context," *Biblia* 73 (1992), pp. 441–451.

6. See Gerald Hobbs, "Monitio Amica: Pellican a Capiton sur le Danger des Lectures Rabbiniques," in Marijn de Kroon and Harc Kienhard, eds., *Horizons européens de la Réforme en Alsace* (Strasbourg: Istra, 1980), pp. 81–93; Jerome Friedman, "Protestants, Jews, and Jewish Sources," in Karter Lindberg, ed., *Piety, Politics, and Ethics: Reformation Studies in Honor of George Wolfgang Forell* (Kirksville, Mo.: Sixteenth-Century Journal Publishers, 1984), pp. 139–156; David S. Katz, *Sabbath and Sectarianism in Seventeenth-Century England* (Leiden: Brill, 1998).

7. Adam Sutcliffe, *Judaism and Enlightenment* (Cambridge: Cambridge University Press, 2003), p. 46.

8. Of course, the rhetorical *topoi* may also be objects of investigation. Describing the different types of such references will be an additional part of the agenda of political Hebraism. For examples, see Jacques Le Goff, "Saint Louis et Josias," in Gilbert Dahan, ed., *Le Juifs au regard de l'Histoire: Melanges en l'honneur de Bernard Blumenkranz* (Paris: Picard, 1985), pp. 157–158; Rob Meens, "The Use of the Old Testament in Early Medieval Canon Law: The Collectio vetus Gallica and the Collectio Hibernensis," in Yitzhak Hen and Matthew Innes, eds., *The Uses of the Past in the Early Middle Ages* (Cambridge: Cambridge University Press, 2000), pp. 67–77; Mary Garrison, "The Franks as the New Israel? Education for an Identity from Pippin to Charlemagne," in Hen and Innes, *Uses of the Past,* pp. 114–116; Josef Funkenstein, *Das Alte Testament im Kampf von regnum und sacerdotium zur Zeit des Investiturstreits* (Dortmund: M. Horn, 1938); Funkenstein, "Samuel und Saul in der Staatslehre des Mittelatlers," *Archiv fuer Rechtsund Sozialphilosophie* 40 (1952–1953), pp. 128–140; I.R. Robinson, "The Bible in the Investiture Contest: The South German Gregorian Circle," in Katherine Walsh and Dianna Woods, eds., *The Bible in the Medieval World: Essays in Memory of Beryl Smalley* (Oxford: Blackwell, 1985), pp. 61–83.

9. One indication of the flourishing of knowledge of Hebrew in the sixteenth and seventeenth centuries is in the list (based on Steinschneider and others) of Hebraists in *Encyclopaedia Judaica,* s.v. "Hebraists, Christian," in which those centuries represent well over 50 percent of the total number of scholars mentioned. There is not yet a synthetic work on the study of Hebrew in early modern Europe. Some important works are: Jerome Friedman, *The Most Ancient Testimony: Sixteenth-Century Christian Hebraica in the Age of Renaissance Nostalgia* (Athens, Ohio: Swallow Press, 1983); Sophie Kessler-Mesguich, "Les hebraisants chretiens," in Jean-Robert Armogathe, ed., *Le Grand Siècle et la Bible* (Paris: Beauchesne, 1989), pp. 83–95; Steven G. Burnett, *From Christian Hebraism to Jewish Studies: Johannes Buxtorf (1564–1629) and Hebrew Learning in the Seventeenth Century* (Leiden: Brill, 1996); G. Lloyd Jones, *The Discovery of Hebrew in Tudor England* (Manchester: Manchester University Press, 1983); Aaron L. Katchen, "Christian Hebraism from the Renaissance to the Enlightenment," in Charles Berlin and Katchen, eds., *Christian Hebraism: The Study of Jewish Culture by Christian Scholars in Medieval and Early Modern Times* (Cambridge, Mass.: Harvard University Library, 1988); Moshe Goshen-Gotstein, "The Revival of Hebraic Studies as Part of the Humanist Revival Around 1500," *Hebrew University Studies in Literature and the Arts* 16 (1988), pp. 185–191.

10. Ludwig Diestel, *Geschichte des alten Testamentes in der christlichen Kirche* (Jena, 1869), pp. 458–473.

11. I am alluding to the title of Theodore K. Rabb, *The Struggle for Stability in Early Modern Europe* (New York: Oxford University Press, 1975).

12. For example, see the following characterizations by G.N. Clark and Donald Kelly:
G.N. Clark, *The Seventeenth Century* (Oxford: Clarendon Press, 1931), p. 215: "A tendency of the political thought of the period... was the comparative study of political phenomena. Studies of the actual constitutions of different countries, of which there are few earlier examples, now became common. Particular attention was paid to states like Venice, which were supposed to be models of good government, but no state was neglected...."

Donald R. Kelly, "Elizabethan Political Thought," in J.G.A. Pocock, ed., *The Varieties of British Political Thought* (Cambridge: Cambridge University Press, 1993), p. 72: "[P]olyhistorical learning and legal, biblical, and classical tradition, tended to prevail in political debate, and demonstrations of antiquity or particular precedents were the basis of disputation, a mode of argumentation reinforced by the increased availability of printed records and sources...."

13. Frank Manuel, *The Broken Staff: Judaism Through Christian Eyes* (Cambridge, Mass.: Harvard University Press, 1992), p. 118.

14. Auerbach notes that in the Middle Ages "the figural interpretation changed the Old Testament from a book of laws and a history of the people of Israel into a series of figures of Christ and the Redemption." Eric Auerbach, "Figura," in his *Scenes from the Drama of European Literature* (Minneapolis: University of Minnesota Press, 1984), pp. 52–53; see Annette Weber-Möckl, *Das Recht des Königs, der über euch herrschen soll: Studien zu 1 Samuel 8:11ff. in der Literatur der frühen Neuzeit* (Berlin: Duncker and Humblot, 1986).

15. See Daniel R. Schwartz, "Josephus on the Jewish Constitutions and Community," *Scripta Classica Israelica* 7 (1983–1984), pp. 30–33. Schwartz claims that Josephus is consistent in his use of political terminology. Cf. Yehoshua Amir, "Josephus on the Mosaic Constitution," in Henning G. Reventlow et al., eds., *Politics and Theopolitics in the Bible and Postbiblical Literature*, Journal for the Study of the Old Testament Supplement Series 171 (Sheffield: Sheffield Academic Press, 1994), p. 16; Masateru Hayashi, *Moses in the Jewish Antiquities: Josephus' Political Philosophy* (Ann Arbor, Mich.: University Microfilms, 1992).

16. Thomas Aquinas, *Summa Theologica*, I–II, q. 105; Douglas Kries, "Friar Thomas and the Politics of Sinai: An Inquiry Concerning the Status of the Mosaic Law in the Christian Theology of Thomas Aquinas" (Ph.D. diss., Boston College, 1988); Kries, "Thomas Aquinas and the Politics of Moses," *Review of Politics* 52 (1990), pp. 84–104; Weber-Möckl, *Das Recht des Königs*, pp. 98–99.

17. It would be difficult to accept Salo Baron's sweeping statement that "the adherents of a republican constitution always referred to the Jewish Bible while the advocates of monarchy looked for support to the New Testament." See Salo Baron, "Azariah De Rossi's Attitude Towards Life," in Arthur Herzberg and Leon A. Feldman, eds., *History and Jewish Historians: Essays and Addresses by Salo Baron* (Philadelphia: Jewish Publication Society, 1964), p. 188.

18. Falconer F. Madan, "A Revised Bibliography of Salmasius' *Defensio regia* and Milton's *Pro populo Anglicano defensio*," *The Library*, 5th ser., 9 (1954), pp. 101–103; Katheryn A. McEuen, "Salmasius: Opponent of Milton," in *Complete Prose Works of John Milton*, vol. 4, pt. 2 (New Haven: Yale University Press, 1966), pp. 962–982. I hope in the future to publish a detailed study of the use of biblical and postbiblical Judaic sources by the two writers.

19. I am, of course, speaking of the study of languages of political thought exemplified in the works of Pocock and Skinner. See, for example, J.G.A. Pocock, *The Ancient Constitution and the Feudal Law: A Reissue with a Retrospect* (Cambridge: Cambridge University Press, 1987); Pocock, *The Machiavellian Moment: Florentine Political Thought and the Atlantic Republican Tradition*

(Princeton: Princeton University Press, 1975); Pocock, "The Concept of a Language and the *Métier d'Historien*: Some Considerations on Practice," in Anthony Pagden, ed., *The Languages of Political Theory in Early-Modern Europe* (Cambridge: Cambridge University Press, 1987), pp. 19–40; James Tully, ed., *Meaning and Context: Quentin Skinner and His Critics* (Cambridge: Polity Press, 1988); E.O.G. Haitsma Mulier, *The Myth of Venice and Dutch Republican Thought in the Seventeenth Century* (Assen: Van Gorcum, 1980).

20. Regarding the work, see Shimeon Brisman, *A History and Guide to Judaic Bibliography* (Cincinnati: Hebrew Union College Press, 1977), p. 8.

21. Manuel, *Broken Staff*, p. 120.

22. A typical example is the famous work of John Spencer, *De Legibus Hebraeorum Ritualibus et earum Rationibus*. The book (despite the fact that it is mentioned by Manuel on p. 123) does not contain a description of the political system (but rather, one isolated chapter is devoted to an explication of the concept of theocracy, in which the political is subsumed under the religious).

23. Geneva, 1574. Bertram (1531–1594) taught Hebrew in the Academy of Geneva and was close to Theodore de Béze, the successor of Calvin.

24. Bologna, 1582. Sigonio (1522–1584) was one of the most important historians in sixteenth-century Italy. His most significant works were on the history and institutions of the Roman republic.

25. Herborn, 1604. Zepper (1550–1607) was a major figure in the development of Calvinism in Germany, as part of the process known as the "Second Reformation," which centered on the *Hochschule* of Herborn. He wrote extensively on church government.

26. Even though the work was written before 1609, it was published first in 1984. See Arthur Eyffinger et al., "De Republica Emendanda: A Juvenile Tract by Hugo Grotius on the Emendation of the Dutch Polity," *Grotiana*, n.s. vol. 5 (1984), pp. 3–121.

27. Leiden, 1617. Cunaeus (1586–1638) was a professor of law at Leiden. His work on the Hebrew republic achieved great popularity and was translated into English in the course of the English Revolution. See Petrus Cunaeus, *The Commonwealth of the Hebrews*, trans. Clement Barksdale (London, 1653). This English translation is available in an edition prepared in 1996 in Italy with an introduction in Italian by Lea Campos Boralevi: *De Republica Hebraeorum (The Commonwealth of the Hebrews)* (Florence: Centro Editoriale Toscano, 1996).

28. Strasbourg, 1625. Schickard (1592–1635) taught Hebrew and astronomy at the University of Tübingen. *Jus Regium Hebraeorum* is a study of the Hebrew monarchy based on an extensive range of rabbinic sources. See Friedrich Seck, ed., *Wilhelm Schickard: 1592–1635* (Tübingen: Mohr, 1978).

29. London, 1650–1655. Selden (1584–1654) was a jurist, antiquarian, and scholar who wrote many works on the history of English law as well as works that showed his erudition in rabbinics. His Hebraic scholarship has not yet been studied systematically. See Jonathan Rosner Ziskind, *John Selden on Jewish Marriage Law: The Uxor Hebraica* (Leiden: Brill, 1991).

30. Arnaldo Momigliano, "Ancient History and the Antiquarian," in Momigliano, *Studies in Historiography* (London: Weidenfeld and Nicolson, 1966), pp. 1–40, first published in *Journal of the Warburg and Courtnauld Institutes* 13 (1950), pp. 285–315; Arnaldo Momigliano, "The Rise of Antiquarian Research," in Momigliano, *The Classical Foundations of Modern Historiography* (Berkeley: University of California Press, 1990), pp. 54–79; Anthony Grafton, *Defenders of the Text: The Traditions of Scholarship in an Age of Science: 1450–1800* (Cambridge, Mass.: Harvard University Press, 1994); Peter N. Miller, *Peiresc's Europe: Learning and Virtue in the Seventeenth Century* (New Haven: Yale University Press, 2000); Miller, "The 'Antiquarianization' of Biblical Scholarship and the London Polyglot Bible (1653–1657)," *Journal of the History of Ideas* 62 (2001), pp. 463–482. See also Brevard Childs, "Biblical Scholarship in the Seventeenth Century: A Study in Ecumenics," in Samuel E. Balentine and John Barton, eds., *Language, Theology, and the Bible: Essays in Honor of James Barr* (Oxford: Oxford University Press, 1994), pp. 325–333.

31. Miller, *Peiresc's Europe*, pp. 80–81.

32. William McCuaig, *Carlo Sigonio: The Changing World of the Late Renaissance* (Princeton: Princeton University Press, 1989). McCuaig does not discuss the work of Sigonio on the Israelite polity, but his description of Sigonio as a scholar leaves no doubt as to the nature of his antiquarian interests. A comparison of the table of contents of Sigonio's work on the Hebraic state with that of his book on the Athenian state highlights the common denominator between them.

33. Bertram, *De Politia Judaica*, p. 39.

34. Ibid., pp. 50–51.

35. Ibid., p. 53.

36. Carlo Sigonio, *De Republica Hebraeorum*, annotated by Johann Nicolai (Leiden, 1701), p. 86.

37. Petrus Cunaeus, *De Republica Hebraeorum*, annotated by Johann Nicolai (Leiden, 1703), p. 11.

38. Wilhelm Zepper, *Legum Mosicarum Forensium*, p. 218.

39. Wilhelm Schickard, *Jus Regium Hebraeorum*, p. 55ff.

40. See William McCuaig, "The Tridentine Ruling on the Vulgate and Ecclesiastical Censorship in the 1580s," *Renaissance and Reformation* 18 (1994), pp. 43–55.

41. William McCuaig, "Sigonio and Grouchy: Roman Studies in the Sixteenth Century," *Atheneum* 74 (1986), pp. 147–183.

42. Sigonio, *De Republica Hebraeorum*, pp. 590–595.

43. Ibid., pp. 174, 177, 231, 274, 353, 402, 433, 599, 605, 613, 617, 622.

44. Bettye Thomas Chambers, *Bibliography of French Bibles* (Geneva: Librairie Droz S.A., 1983), pp. 479–480; S.L. Greensdale, *Cambridge History of the Bible*, vol. 3 (Cambridge: Cambridge University Press, 1969), p. 119; Robert D. Linder,

"The Bible and the French Protestant Reformation of the Sixteenth Century," *Andrews University Seminary Studies* 25 (1987), pp. 145–161.

45. Bertram, *De Politia Judaica*, pp. 30–31, 53.

46. See Aaron Katchen, *Christian Hebraists and Dutch Rabbis* (Cambridge, Mass.: Harvard University Press, 1984).

47. In his introduction he mentions Kimhi, Ibn Ezra, Rashi, Gersonides, Nahmanides, Bahai, and Abraham Seba.

48. Harrington's list of rabbinic opinions on monarchy is identical to the sources listed by Schickard on the same subject. See J.G.A. Pocock, ed., *The Political Works of James Harrington* (Cambridge: Cambridge University Press, 1977), p. 575. Schickard was not mentioned in S.B. Liljegeren, *Harrington and the Jews* (Lund: C.W.K. Gleerup, 1932), the only work devoted to this topic. Salmasius' *Defensio regia* and Milton's *Pro populo Anglicano defensio* show use of Schickard's *Jus Regium Hebraeorum*, which also appears frequently in Selden's marginal notes.

49. See Martin Selman, "The Kingdom of God in the Old Testament," *Tyndale Bulletin* 40 (1989), pp. 161–184; Wolfgang Hübener, "Die verlorene Unschuld der Theokratie," in Jacob Taubes, ed., *Religionstheorie und Politische Theologie, Theokratie*, vol. 3 (Munich: W. Fink, 1978), pp. 30–37; Jürgen Gebhardt, "Alle Macht den Heiligen–zur frühneuzeitlichen Idee der Theokratie," in Taubes, *Theokratie*, pp. 206–232; Schwartz, "Josephus on the Jewish Constitutions"; Amir, "Josephus on the Mosaic Constitution."

50. *Encyclopedia of Religion* (Eliade), s.v. "Theocracy."

51. Aristotle, *Politics* 1287a.

52. Sigonio, *De Republica Hebraeorum*, p. 86.

53. Bertram, *De Politia Judaica*, p. 39.

54. J.G.A. Pocock, "Time, History and Eschatology in the Thought of Thomas Hobbes," in Pocock, *Politics, Language and Time* (New York: Macmillan, 1971), pp. 148–201; Patricia Springborg, "*Leviathan* and the Problem of Ecclesiastical Authority," *Political Theory* 3 (1975), pp. 289–303; Pocock, "Hobbes on Religion," in *The Cambridge Companion to Hobbes*, Tom Sorell, ed. (Cambridge: Cambridge University Press, 1996), pp. 346–380; Quentin Skinner, "Hobbes' 'Leviathan,'" *The Historical Journal* 7 (1964), pp. 321–331.

55. See in the meantime Johann P. Sommerville, "Hobbes, Selden, Erastianism, and the History of the Jews," in G.A.J. Rogers and Tom Sorell, eds., *Hobbes and History* (London: Routledge, 2000), pp. 160–188.

56. Richard Popkin, "The Marranos of Amsterdam," in Popkin, *The Third Force in Seventeenth-Century Philosophy* (Leiden: Brill, 1992), p. 165; Amos Funkenstein, "Comment on R. Popkin's Paper," in James E. Force and Richard Popkin, eds., *The Books of Nature and Scripture: Recent Essays on Natural Philosophy, Theology and Biblical Criticism in the Netherlands of Spinoza's Time and the British Isles of Newton's Time*, Archives internationales d'histoire des idées (Dordrecht: Klüwer, 1994), p. 22 n. 139.

Some Thoughts on the Covenantal Politics
Of Johannes Althusius

Alan Mittleman

The *Politica* of Johannes Althusius (Althaus) is a classic of Reformed Protestant political theory. While Zwingli, Bullinger, Calvin, Bucer, and others contributed to political theory or, more properly, political theology, Althusius produced the first truly comprehensive and systematic Protestant political science. Unlike the earlier Reformed figures, who wrote, as biblical theologians, on political topics only when necessary, Althusius writes as a political scientist.[1] Although trained as a lawyer and employed as a professor of law at a fledgling Reformed university in Westphalia, Althusius has clearly differentiated the concepts of politics and society from that of law. He writes in what today would be called the fields of political science and sociology. Like Machiavelli, with whose *Discourses* he was familiar, he is concerned about the formation, preservation, and destruction of states. He distinguishes private from public morality and is not above believing that the end can justify the means in the business of statecraft. He combines the naturalism, humanism, and political realism of the Renaissance with the austere moral requirements of the Reformed faith. To what extent his work is essentially secular and to what extent it is permeated by religion remains controversial.[2] At any rate, the controversy that ensued in the seventeenth century surrounding his work had less to do with its secular tone than with its sturdy opposition to monarchical absolutism, its "Monarchomach" endorsement of disobedience and resistance to tyranny and its advocacy of popular sovereignty.[3]

Althusius' erudition ranged from the Bible, Roman law, and classical philosophy to the humanistic learning of the Renaissance and the legal and political traditions of the German city-state. In the style of the day, he relies on thousands of textual citations from these sources as illustrations of his theoretical points. Of these, the largest number—several thousand—are biblical, primarily from the Hebrew Scriptures but also from the New Testament.[4] The Hebrew Scriptures provide realistic examples of political behavior, virtues, and institutions. The New Testament sources give rather more idealistic examples of Christian love and charity; of the high normative vision of a Christian communism. Whether these impulses pull in different directions is an open question. The next-largest number of citations in Althusius is from Jean Bodin, the most important political theorist of the previous generation, with whom he often differs on crucial political matters. This paper will provide an overview of several important topics in the *Politica*, including Althusius' concept of covenant and its implications for a federal arrangement of political life, his use of the Hebrew Scriptures, and his potential for contemporary political thought, both Jewish and general.

Covenantal and Federal Motifs in Althusian Thought

The *Politica* is a work of description and analysis, as well as a grand design for a good commonwealth in which people can lead holy lives together. It is firmly rooted in empirical observation and conditioned throughout by a realistic understanding of human limits and possibilities. Although it proposes a model of an ideal, Christian society, it does not impress the reader as utopian, at least not naïvely or fervently so. As noted above, the work has a predominantly rational, logical, and secular-scientific tone. Althusius' background in the law, coupled with his lengthy experience as the lawyer and diplomat (namely, syndic) for the Reformed Protestant city of Emden, constrained whatever tendencies toward the visionary his faith might have inspired in him. Like Calvin—but unlike Luther—Althusius pays great attention to the form of the polity, to its constitution and internal relations. Unlike Calvin, his writing reveals a disciplined insight into and a profound respect for political institutions and their ability to facilitate the achievement of the good life that is reminiscent of Aristotle. The role of the polity goes far beyond the restraint of sin. The version of the Reformed faith that came to Emden—as well as to Herborn, where Althusius was a professor—was influenced as much by Zwingli and Zurich as by Calvin and Geneva.[5] Zwingli, a Swiss, was more humanistic and republican than Calvin. These emphases are evident in Althusius.

The *Politica*, like Aristotle's *Politics*, proposes to take account of man as he is and to order political life according to a moderate, religious, yet this-worldly appraisal of man's possibilities and limits as a political animal. The *Politica* begins with the natural, with our divinely created nature as social beings, and takes care at every step not to offend against it. True to his Protestant roots, Althusius understands that man has a fallen nature, that his nature has been corrupted by sin. But although the belief in human depravity is present in Althusius, it is not pervasively so. It appears in his low opinion of the masses, who are "inconstant, violent, lacking in judgment, credulous, envious, wild, turbulent, seditious, frivolous, ungrateful, changeable, and aping those who govern."[6] Despite this, Althusius has a sober, relatively optimistic confidence that people have the reason and the will to choose arrangements that will allow them to flourish in common.[7] This de-emphasis on the Calvinist theme of depravity is partly an artifact of his naturalistic and empirical approach, of his aspiration to create a scientific study of politics. Its consequences are significant. Due to his belief in depravity, he rejects democracy as such. On the other hand, in line with his naturalistic and empirical approach, he derives political authority from popular sovereignty. For Calvin or Luther, authority derives from God alone. For Althusius, political authority derives from human delegation, albeit under the terms of a covenant sanctioned by God. Hence, Althusius validates resistance to unjust government to a far greater extent than either Luther or Calvin.

Althusius' thought stresses concepts such as *communicatio, communio*, and *koinonia* (he sometimes favors Greek terms over Latin ones): sharing, communing, and communal association. All human social and political arrangements are built upon the "communication" or sharing of things (*communicatio rerum*), of services (*communicatio operarum*), and of rights and duties (*communicatio juris*) between and among individuals and groups. Society and polity are associations (*consociatio symbiotica*) where individuals and groups (*symbiotici*) choose to live a life in common, out of both natural necessity and divine grace, and who scale their desires, actions, and expectations to the requirements (*jus symbioticum*; *lex consociationis*) of the arrangement that they have chosen. Althusius constantly emphasizes choice and consent—pact making or covenanting—as the basis of a good politics. Hence, the opening sentences of the *Politica*:

> Politics is the art of associating men for the purpose of establishing, cultivating, and conserving social life among them. Whence it is called "symbiotics." The subject matter of politics is therefore association (*consociatio*), in which the symbiotes *pledge themselves each to the other, by explicit or tacit agreement* (*qua pacto expresso vel tacito*), to mutual communication of whatever is useful and necessary for the harmonious exercise of social life. The end of political, "symbiotic" man is holy, just, comfortable, and happy symbiosis, a life lacking in nothing either necessary or useful.[8]

God has made humans as social beings; their task is to help and to love one another. Althusius emphatically rejects the philosophic and monastic preference for the antipolitical, contemplative life. Indeed, his first extensive use of Hebrew Scripture (Genesis 4:14, Deuteronomy 28:64, Psalms 107 and 144) is to argue against the presumptive Catholic misuse of the New Testament to validate monasticism. Althusius displays the "inner-worldly asceticism," to use Weber's apt phrase, of Reformed Protestantism. "Examples of pious men embracing an active political life are to be found throughout sacred scripture."[9]

God and nature endow humans with sociality. How humans realize this disposition, however, is a matter of choice, enacted ultimately through covenants. "The efficient cause of political association is consent and agreement among the communicating citizens (*consensum et pactum civium communicantium*)."[10] Humans choose to live in families for mutual assistance. The symbiosis of the family is initiated through a special covenant (*pactum*) among the founding members to share in a way of life and cultivate a common interest. This is no mere contract. Pledges of mutual aid must be met with trust and fidelity, reminiscent of the biblical concept of *hesed*—the dimension of mutual, loving solidarity which makes a covenant deeper and more enduring than a contract. In Althusius' terms, good will (*benevolentia*) and amity (*concordia*) are prime civic virtues without which association is not possible.[11] The family is the fundamental form of association. It is technically a "simple" and "private" association in Althusius' typology, but it is the basis of all subsequent "mixed" and "public" ones. Without it, the other associations are "able neither to arise nor to endure."[12] Families choose to link with other families and create kinship networks (another form of private association) and eventually hamlets and villages. Villages covenant together to form towns. Such associations are chosen and consensual but reflect a high degree of natural necessity. More voluntaristic are the civic associations, the *collegia*, which for Althusius are principally guilds. Collegia covenant together with towns to form cities. Cities join with others into provinces, the federation of which ultimately constitutes a commonwealth (*respublica*), or a realm (*regnum*). At every step, the lower or prior orders delegate power to representatives, who enter into covenants (*pacta*) to faithfully fulfill their administrative duties.[13] Should they fail to do so or abuse their delegated authority, the representative authorities of the lesser order can remove them. Everything rises from the bottom up. The private is the seedbed of the public. Authority is diffused among many levels and types of association. Human beings live in different types of authoritative community simultaneously.

The commonwealth or realm is a federal union of numerous groups, which covenant together to create a sovereign magistrate. At no point, however, does the creation of the universal sovereign absorb or suspend the fundamental rights of the covenanting bodies, nor does it eliminate their independent identities.[14] The sovereign is transient; the people, articulated through the network of associations, are enduring. The communities that compose the polity are never *aufgehoben* in the state, nor do they relinquish the authority that their members have consented to vest in them. Althusius is thus a principal philosopher of federalism—a powerful if largely unheeded voice in a seventeenth-century world of centralizing states and absolutizing monarchies. He derives his federal views both from the actual political experience of the German cities under the Holy Roman Empire and from the covenantal theology of Reformed Protestantism, which held that the various governments of the biblical Hebrews were the only examples of political rule directly approved by God. In the biblical examples, the covenantal consent of the people to the rule of prophets, judges, or kings was necessary. Explaining how a supreme magistrate, whether king or republican ruler, is properly elected through the representatives of the various private and public associations that comprise the commonwealth, Althusius describes the covenantal procedures of ancient Israel:

> God marvelously governed this people [Israel] for about four hundred years, just as if he himself were king. He led the people first through Moses out of Egypt, then through Joshua, and afterwards through a long series of vigorous judges. Then, when the people requested a king, he was indignant and gave it Saul, who was designated and chosen immediately by himself through the service of a prophet. When he afterwards rejected Saul... he substituted David in the same manner, and by his word established the descendants of David in the control of the realm. These actions, however, were so performed by him that *the consent and approval of the people were not excluded from the process of designating these kings and putting them in control of the realm. Rather the matter was so handled that the kings were considered to be chosen by the people as well,* and to receive therefrom the right of kingship (*jus regis*).... Indeed, it is evident that the supremely good and great God has assigned to the political community this necessity and power of electing and constituting. "You shall establish judges and moderators in all your gates that the Lord your God gave you through your tribes, who shall judge the people with a righteous judgment" (Deut. 16:18, see also Deut. 17:14, 15; II Samuel 5:3, I Kings 1:34 inter alia).[15]

Althusius generalizes from this that God has formed "in all peoples by the natural law itself the free power of constituting princes, kings, and magistrates for themselves."[16]

Althusius' views are in sharp contrast to Bodin, who also bases his approach to sovereignty on the Hebrew Scriptures. In Bodin's reading, since all power comes from God, the right to command is independent of the consent of the commanded.[17] The differences between them emerge in their treatments of the family, with which they both begin their works. Bodin, like Althusius, sees the family as the seedbed for the state. Unlike Althusius, the family, for Bodin, is characterized by the husband's (and father's) absolute right to rule over his wife (and children). Where Althusius saw marriage as a covenant between the parties, Bodin sees marriage as the divinely sanctioned rule of one man over others, that is, over wife and children. Bodin goes so far as to recommend that the state restore to fathers the power of life and death over their children![18] It would be wrong, however, to see Althusius as an early advocate of women's rights. He believes, no less than Bodin, that men are superior

to women, that hierarchy is, to a large extent, natural (although, interestingly, Bodin rejects slavery). Althusius believes that the different roles
of men and women are divinely sanctioned vocations. Like all vocations,
they confer different levels of merit upon us. (In society and the polity at
large, those whose services are most essential for the good of the public
have the greatest dignity. A well-governed community accords its most
useful citizens the greater merit.) For Althusius, the family comes into
being through the free choice of husband and wife, concretized by covenant. For Bodin, the family comes into being when the woman obeys
the commandment to subordinate herself to her husband. Although the
latter entails a choice, the only correct choice is to subjugate flesh to spirit—which is how Bodin symbolizes the male-female relationship—and
accept the authority of man over woman. The father's authority in the
home is indivisible and permanent. On Althusius' account, his authority
is real and consequential but contingent on his fulfillment of his promises to advance the welfare of his family. The same is true of sovereignty
in the state. For Bodin, in order for persons to follow the first command
of the natural law they must subordinate animal appetite (their natural
liberty) to reason and submit to a sovereign. After this, they have alienated their rights. The sovereign rules absolutely and is answerable only to
God. For Althusius, authority remains with the people as a whole, who
delegate it to administrators at various levels of the social order. Their
remaining in authority is contingent on their fidelity to their covenant
with the people.

The Althusian alternative of a covenantal or federal (from *foedus*, "covenant") polity to the Bodinian tradition of unitary, indivisible sovereignty,
which became dominant in modernity, has once again become attractive
in late modern times. European nations are in a protracted (and con-
tested) process of relinquishing aspects of their national sovereignty. The
future of Iraq may lie in a federal union of three ethnic-religious cantons.
In the United States, since the Reagan administration's New Federalism,
the national government has returned power and discretion in some areas, such as welfare policy, to the states. Public policy increasingly looks
to local communities, faith-based groups, and civil society per se for
solutions that eluded the "Great Society." Furthermore, a keen sense of
the limits and excesses of a purely secular, individualistic, rights-driven
liberalism has fueled philosophical interest in traditions that emphasize
community without entirely compromising liberty. The emphasis on consent and the depiction of the political community as a community of

communities continues to ring true to the reality or at least to the ideals of a democratic, pluralistic society. Does Althusius remain a useful theorist in this respect? We will consider the extent to which Althusius' approach to politics has enduring salience in the final section of this paper. For the present, let us proceed to an analysis of Althusius' use of the Hebrew Scriptures. While Althusius refers to biblical examples throughout his text, his most sustained treatment is in his several essays on the Decalogue.

A Biblical Foundation for the Good Polity

"No polity," Althusius writes, "from the beginning of the world has been more wisely and perfectly constructed than the polity of the Jews (*Judaeorum politia*). We err, I believe, whenever in similar circumstances we depart from it."[19] Although his praise of the biblical polity is fulsome, Althusius limits the applicability of a biblical model of politics to similarity of circumstances. There is no Puritan attempt here to recreate the Mosaic polity or the primitive church. The biblical teaching contains both the enduring and the ephemeral. Unlike Spinoza, Althusius believes that there are permanently valid elements of biblical politics, as well as time-bound, provisional ones.[20] In keeping with Protestant theology, the Decalogue is the lead example of eternally valid and politically salient commands, whereas the subsequent legislation no longer suits our "circumstances." Moses, who is not only a prophet bringing a divine law (*ius divinum*) but a prudent legislator and administrator, prescribed many laws to explain and adapt the Decalogue (the *lex moralis*) "to the varying circumstances of place, time, persons, and the thing present within the commonwealth.... Such laws can therefore differ in certain respects from the moral law, either by adding something to it or by taking something away from it."[21] Laws change on the surface because a prudent legislator understands how to achieve justice under changing historical conditions. Nonetheless, the deep nature of law is immutable conformity with the higher principles of the Decalogue: in its correspondence with the *lex moralis*, valid law does not change.[22]

In Protestant thought, our comprehension of the law of nature has been compromised by the Fall. The divine law is necessary to correct our perversion of the law of nature. Althusius' preferred term for the law of nature corrected by the divine law is "common law" (*lex communis*). *Lex communis* is also synonymous with *lex moralis*. As with the law of nature in the Reformers, although this law is common to all, all do not apprehend it equally well, nor are all identically inclined to follow it. The magistrate and legislator have, therefore, to produce new laws, appropriate to the historical circumstances. These supplementary laws are called *lex propria*, "proper law."[23]

The first table of the Decalogue sets forth the *lex communis* of our relationship with the divine, the second of our relationship with one another. The second table, in addition to its detailed prescriptions, provides for civic virtue, which may be summarized as: "whatever you wish to be done to you, do also to others," and conversely, "whatever you do not wish to be done to you do not do to others."[24] The second table is "more civil and political," but both sets of precepts are necessary for the well-ordered commonwealth. The first four precepts of the Decalogue "are always, absolutely, and without distinction binding upon all, to such a degree that the second table... ought to yield precedence to the first table as to a superior law." Althusius continues: "If a precept of God and a mandate of the magistrate should come together in the same affair and be contrary to each other, then God is to be obeyed rather than the magistrate.... These precepts of the first table can never be set aside or relaxed, and not even God himself is able to reject them."[25] The length to which Althusius goes in insisting on the absolute authority of the Decalogue is striking. Even God is bound by his law. Bodin too makes the sovereign responsible to the Decalogue but only in his conscience. If he violates God's law, that is between him and God. The people still owe him absolute obedience. Luther too would not sanction resistance to an impious sovereign. It is in the Reformed tradition, well represented by Althusius, where a sovereign's violation of divine law makes him a tyrant, whom the people are required first to disobey and then, if necessary, to resist.[26]

"The right of realm (*jus regni*) is twofold. It pertains to both the welfare of the soul and the care of the body. Religion, by recognizing and worshipping God, seeks the welfare of the soul."[27] Thus, the state is equally concerned with piety (defined by the first table of the Decalogue) and with justice (defined by the second table). The first table of the Decalogue contains the precepts whereby the "true and correct worship of God," both public and private, is to be regulated. Althusius, like other Protestants, envisions a state-church in which there is both ecclesiastical independence from and dependence on the organs of state. The church has its own extensive internal organization and procedures. It must have liberty in preaching, teaching, ordaining, and governing the life of citizens with respect to sacred duties. These duties are outlined by the first table of the Decalogue:

> Private and internal worship consists of the expression of confidence, adoration, and thankfulness, the first precept of the Decalogue. Private and external worship consists of rites and actions that revere God, the second precept, or of words that do the same, the third precept. Public worship of God consists of holy observance of the Sabbath by corporate public celebration, the fourth precept.[28]

The role of the civil authority is to support the church by using its sword, if necessary, to maintain the good moral and spiritual order of society. Although Althusius recognizes the occasional need for religious toleration, any thought of religious liberty for dissenters is foreign to his system. This is a problem to which we will return.

The second table of the Decalogue, precepts five through ten, comprises the civic or political duties as such. Although the precepts belong to the common law, the form that some of them have is contingent, that is, "proper" or positive, as we would say. Althusius offers an imaginative, politically salient reading. The fifth commandment is an endorsement of the legitimacy of social hierarchy. Inferior persons owe superior persons—defined as persons who bring gifts, talents, or services to the public or private offices of the commonwealth—"respect, obedience, compliance, subjection, and necessary aid." Every positive precept also has negative implications; in this case, we are to refrain from "despising, scorning, or depreciating our neighbor by word or deed." Althusius derives from "honor your father and mother" the general principle of "not destroying order among the various stations of human society and not introducing confusion into them."[29]

The sixth commandment ("you shall not kill") "requires the defense, protection, and conservation of one's own life and that of the neighbor." Althusius derives an expansive set of works and virtues from this precept. "Conservation of the neighbor's life is his protection through friendship and other duties of charity, such as provision for food, clothes, and anything else he needs for sustenance. Negatively, this precept prohibits enmity, injury to the human body, assault, mutilation, blows, murder, terror, privation of natural liberty, and any other inhuman treatment."[30]

The seventh commandment ("you shall not commit adultery") "concerns the conservation of the chastity of one's own mind and body, and that of one's neighbor, through sobriety, good manners, modesty, discretion, and any other appropriate means. Negatively, it pertains to the avoidance in word or deed of fornication, debauchery, lewdness, and wantonness."

The eighth commandment ("you shall not steal") "concerns the defense and conservation of one's own goods and those of one's neighbor, and their proper employment in commerce, contracts, and one's vocation." One notes here the Protestant validation of emerging capitalism in the emphasis on commerce and vocation. Negatively, the commandment "condemns deceit in commerce and trade... any injustice that can be perpetrated by omitting or including something in contracts, and an idle and disordered life." Althusius draws a rather extensive Protestant halacha and *musar* from the precept.

The ninth commandment ("you shall not bear false witness") requires the conservation of one's own and one's neighbor's reputation. It implies an ethic of honesty and truthfulness, and the rejection of defamation, insult, and hostility.

Finally, the tenth commandment concerns concupiscence. Curiously, Althusius' gloss on the commandment is a direct quote from Cicero: "We are taught by the authority and bidding of laws to control our passions, to bridle our every lust, to defend what is ours, and to keep our minds, eyes, and hands from whatever belongs to another." The quotation from Cicero underscores the fundamental identity of natural and divine law. It also illustrates Althusius' de-emphasis of depravity. The pagan philosopher knows through (an ostensibly uncorrupted) reason what Jew and Christian have been vouchsafed through revelation.[31]

It is within God's power to occasionally suspend his commandments, as when he ordered Abraham to kill Isaac or when he permitted polygamy or levirate marriage to the Jews. But this dispensation has not been given to humans. The Decalogue is a universal common law, prescribed for all peoples. The proper law, which peoples such as the Jews built up upon the common law to achieve justice under their peculiar circumstances, varies, but not infinitely. Common law requires that evildoers be punished; proper law defines and prescribes what punishment means under given historical circumstances. While the latter is variable, it is nonetheless tied in starting point, purpose, and subject matter to the *lex communis.* Insofar as humans are by nature social beings, the fundamental problems of social and political life will always be the same. The Bible, in its exposition of the common law, will always be relevant to the human situation. The Bible will always be as much political as it is spiritual:

> At this point we encounter the controversy over what we maintain to be the political doctrine of the Decalogue. In the judgment of others the Decalogue should instead be considered theological. Some persons consider that we thus sin against the law of homogeneity. Whence there is this deep silence among them about the role of the Decalogue in politics. But this is wrong in my judgment. For the subject matter of the Decalogue is indeed political insofar as it directs symbiotic life and prescribes what ought to be done therein.[32]

Unlike the New England Puritans, Althusius would not try to resurrect and implement the public law of the Protestant Old Testament. He holds to both the enduring validity of biblical political teachings and legal norms and the need to view these through the lens of what counts as justice for us now. Common law regulates proper law, but it is also lame without it. The law of nature, divine law, depends on the insight and skill of the prudent legislator. That prudence is developed by the political experience of citizens' learning to live together in multiple, overlapping, consensual communities.

Althusius and Jewish, Democratic Thought

Given the foregoing analysis, to what extent can Althusius be a philosopher for us? By "us," I mean both citizens of late modern democracies and Jews, who seek to discern and rehabilitate elements of the Jewish political tradition. The answer to this depends in part on how strongly one wants to hold on to core features of liberalism. Is it possible to sustain the high degree of symbiosis—consensual life in common—that Althusius requires without unacceptably compromising individual rights and liberties? Carl Joachim Friedrich, writing during the rise of Nazism, did not think so. Daniel J. Elazar, writing at the end of the twentieth century, disagreed. Elazar sees Althusius as a corrective to the philosophical and practical "consequences of unrestrained liberalism." "Political

scientists [have] begun to explore problems of liberty in relation to primordial groups—families, particularly, and ethnic communities. Here it
was discovered that Althusius has much to offer contemporary society."[33]
I am inclined to agree with Friedrich. An Althusian state would be far
more intrusive than a liberal democrat could accept. Although Althusius
distinguishes between the public and the private, he is aggressively republican enough to obliterate his distinction. At the end of the day, all social
life must serve the polity. There is no right to be left alone. There is only
the freedom to belong, to contribute, to "communicate." It goes perhaps
too far to see Althusius, as Friedrich does, as the father of the collectivist
state. After all, he does not advocate *Gleichschaltung* ("homogenization").
The power of the sovereign remains contingent, almost provisional, and
the concern for tyranny is pervasive. Nonetheless, the core liberal idea
of individual rights is alien to Althusius, an insuperable defect from a
liberal point of view.

Another defect of Althusius, from a liberal point of view, is his insistence on the ineluctability of group membership. It is true, as Elazar
notes, that we are today coping with the consequences of unrestrained individualism. But the alternative to that excess, I would think, is prudent,
"restrained" individualism rather than the obliteration of individualism
that is a concomitant of Althusian thought. Althusius is correct to give
a foundational place in his account of society and politics to primordial
groups. It is philosophically unsatisfying, however, to envision the human good as entirely comprised by republican citizenship on the one
hand, and membership in the church on the other. Contemporary political thought has sought a good for the liberal soul, a deeper account
of individuality than classical liberalism provided.[34] Althusian thought
forecloses on this possibility.

This is a sensitive point for contemporary Jews. Committed modern
Jews want both the depth of belonging to a historic primordial group, the
Jewish people, and, for some at least, their historic covenantal faith, *and*
the liberty to participate in modernity in ways that do not easily harmonize with their Jewish commitment. They want the liberty to seek their
own path that is constitutive of the modern project. Althusian thought
does not conceive of the relationship between persons and groups as
dialectical, that is, as entailing both belonging and estrangement simultaneously. The Althusian individual is nested within the federal structure
of associations like the infant at the center of a Russian *matrushke* doll.

Whether this manner of thinking can become *aufgeklärt*, in Kant's sense, that is, able to shed a self-imposed immaturity and to realize the complexity of choice, is an open question.

Althusius is a federalist, but he is not—despite the immense role that groups play in his thought—a pluralist. His system requires, ideally, a religiously uniform citizenry. As Elazar writes, "The Althusian version of the Calvinist model of the religiously homogenous polity is not likely to be revived in the postmodern epoch. On the other hand, we are beginning to revive an old understanding that no civil society can exist without some basis in transcendent norms that obligate and bind the citizens and establish the necessary basis for trust and communication."[35] Elazar has limned an essential moment of conflict in the modern polity. Struggles in the United States over the public display of the Decalogue, and other indicia of biblical faith, controversy in Europe over the preamble of the (now rejected) EU constitution, or abiding controversy in Israel over the relationship between "Jewish" and "democratic" dimensions of the Israeli state all point toward the desire of modern people for conflicting goods: an affirmation of a transcendent ground for law and social order, on the one hand, and an affirmation of radical immanence, of a self-sufficient secular cosmology, on the other. These struggles are not likely to abate. Althusius is not yet at the point where toleration and then religious liberty were achieved to restrain, subordinate, and diffuse these struggles within the modern sovereign state. When state sovereignty and national sentiment weaken, does primordiality assert itself more fiercely? Would a modern Althusian state—something more like Canada, say, than France—reduce the need for an overarching civil religion, or would it increase it? Althusius, the secular dimension of his political science notwithstanding, cannot envision a good polity without a holy purpose, nor can Elazar, it would seem. Jewish thought is, to say the least, divided on this matter.

Althusius' enduring contribution is his emphasis on choice as the basis of covenant and covenant as the basis of society. This emphasis, of course, does not do justice to the accidental and alien nature of social reality, or to our experience of *Geworfenheit* ("thrownness"), as Heidegger put it, the strange and unchosen quality of the world in which we find ourselves. Perhaps it attributes more control to humans and more design to social reality than is the case. It also captures an essential truth and recognizes a pillar of human dignity. The truth is that we have made some crucial features of our world, however objectified, accidental, or alien they come to appear to us. The dignity of man, as a co-creator with God, is an essential feature of Jewish thought. From this point of view, covenanting as a way of facilitating moral and purposive human association, is of Jewish value. From a democratic point of view, as many as possible should participate in creating, sustaining, and directing "symbiotic" life. Althusius would agree. Despite his endorsement of the patterns of hierarchy and social status of his time, his vision of a universe of diverse, interacting associations includes everyone, even as active participants. Althusius does offer resources for democratic thought and, by holding out a fairly temperate vision of a politics informed by biblical faith, for Jewish thought as well.

Notes

1. Althusius refers to politics as an *ars*, that is, an art or science in the sense of the *Geisteswissenschaften,* or humanities. Johannes Althusius, *Politica Methodice Digesta*, ed. Carl Joachim Friedrich (Cambridge, Mass.: Harvard University Press, 1932), p. 15.

2. The great nineteenth-century student of medieval law and politics, Otto von Gierke, characterizes the *Politica* as "a purely secular book in content and purpose," which, despite "its stern Calvinistic spirit… shakes off the whole theocratic conception of the State." Cf. Otto von Gierke, *The Development of Political Theory*, trans. Bernard Freyd (London: George Allen & Unwin, Ltd., 1939), p. 71. By contrast, a contemporary commentator, Daniel J. Elazar, sees Althusius as an exponent of Reformed Protestant "Federal Theology." Elazar, *Covenant and Commonwealth: From Christian Separation Through the Protestant Reformation* (New Brunswick, N.J.: Transaction, 1996), ch. 8. Carl Joachim Friedrich, writing in the 1930s, defends Althusius against a German theologian who claimed that his biblical references are only window dressing on an essentially secular project. Friedrich, following Max Weber, by whom he is much impressed, sees a secular ethic deeply implicated in Calvinism from the beginning. Althusius is working out the implications of Calvinist worldliness and disenchantment. "This so-called naturalism is implicit in the Calvinist cosmology," writes Friedrich. Althusius, *Politica*, p. xviii.

3. Gierke, *Development of Political Theory*, pp. 16–18.

4. Althusius, *Politica*, p. xliii.

5. Elazar, *Covenant and Commonwealth*, p. 194. Neither Gierke nor Friedrich draw this conclusion. Both see Althusius as firmly in the Calvinist camp.

6. Althusius, *Politica*, p. lxxi.

7. Friedrich, in his analytic introduction to Althusius, is insistent that Althusius is a determinist (i.e., that he believes that humans are so social by nature that they have no control over the sorts of groups that they form and join). He rejects the notion, so crucial to Elazar, that choice and consent—voluntarism—have anything to do with politics. In Althusius' anthropology, according to Friedrich, the Calvinist "rigid determinism" of predestination has been transformed into a mechanical necessitarianism, with God demoted to an "impersonal, normative force." "Althusius does not know, and cannot know a *free will*" for both Calvinistic and naturalistic reasons. Cf. Althusius, *Politica*, pp. lxviii–lxix. I don't think that this position can be coherently maintained both in light of Althusius' references to choice and consent, and in light of Friedrich's own attribution of voluntaristic elements to Althusius. See, for example, Althusius, *Politica*, p. lxxxviii: "It [i.e., the social contract] is the fundamental organizing decision of a living group whose common life transcends this organizing act.... How these decisions were actually made is something which Althusius by no means pretends to know. But that every type of living group comes into existence through a series of such decisions Althusius does, I believe, maintain."

8. Johannes Althusius, *Politica*, trans. and ed. Frederick S. Carney (Indianapolis: Liberty Fund, 1995), p. 17; emphasis added. All English translations in this paper are taken from Carney's edition. Occasional words or phrases of the Latin original are taken from Friedrich's edition.

9. Althusius, *Politica*, ed. Carney, p. 24.

10. Ibid.

11. See especially ibid., ch. 31, pp. 180–182.

12. Ibid., p. 27. The discussion of the family provides Althusius with an opportunity to make a strong distinction between politics and economics. The main activities of the family are political rather than economic, such that writers who leave the family out of political analysis are mistaken. Although family members do engage in purely economic activities (i.e., matters of household sustenance), these are directed in a political manner: "by politics alone arises the wisdom for governing and administering the family" (p. 32).

13. The first eight chapters of the *Politica* treat the private and public associations out of which the commonwealth arises (i.e., the family, the *collegium*, the city, and the province).

14. Friedrich argues that Althusius is ultimately a statist and not, as Gierke and Elazar characterize him, a federalist: "What Althusius is setting forth is the theory of a corporative state. This state is characterized by the fact that in the last analysis it devours the entire community, becomes one with it." *Politica*, Friedrich, ed., p. lxxxvi. I believe that Friedrich is mistaken. In his zeal to defend individual rights, which are indeed lacking in Althusius, against the fascist and

communist totalitarians of his day (1930s), Friedrich associates Althusius' corporativism with theirs (see p. lxxxviii). This seems to me to be a lapse of judgment in this otherwise exceedingly careful scholar.

15. Althusius, *Politica*, ed. Carney, pp. 95–96; emphasis added.

16. Ibid.

17. Jean Bodin, *Six Books of the Commonwealth*, ed. and trans. M.J. Tooley, (Oxford: Basil Blackwell, 1955), p. xxiv.

18. Ibid., p. 12.

19. Althusius, *Politica*, ed. Carney, p. 13. See p. 131: "Such is the example of the Jewish polity, which is the best of all."

20. *Briefwisseling Hugo Grotius* 9 (1638), republished in The Hague in 1973 as *RGP*. With respect to biblical law, Althusius calls the enduring precepts *lex communis*, "common law," and the contingent, presently invalid statutes *lex propria*, "proper law." See below for discussion.

21. Althusius, *Politica*, ed. Carney, p. 81.

22. Ibid., p. 145.

23. Althusius has a comment about Jewish "proper" law. It is "twofold. It is in part ceremonial, and in part forensic or judicial. The ceremonial law… was directed to the observance and support of the first table of the Decalogue through certain political and ecclesiastical actions and things; it was devoted to piety and divine worship…. The forensic law was the means by which the Jews were informed and instructed to observe and obey both tables, or the common law, for the cultivation of human society among them in their polity, according to the circumstances of things, persons, place, and time…. What is moral in such a law is perpetual; what is judicial can be changed by the change of circumstances; and what is ceremonial is considered to have passed away." Ibid., p. 146.

24. Ibid., p. 22. Althusius uses Hillel's negative formulation of the golden rule without attributing it to the talmudic source (*Babylonian Talmud*, Shabbat 31a).

25. Ibid., pp. 141–143.

26. Althusius devotes chapter 38 of the *Politica* to an analysis of tyranny, prescribing a proportional approach to opposing it relative to its severity. He constitutionalizes opposition to tyranny by making opposition the duty of the elected representatives of the people, who constituted the sovereign in the first place and from whom he derives his authority.

27. Ibid, p. 74.

28. Ibid., p. 52.

29. Ibid., p. 142.

30. Ibid.

31. All of the above is taken from ibid., pp. 142–143.

32. Ibid., p. 147.

33. Ibid., p. xxxix.

34. See, for example, David Walsh, *The Growth of the Liberal Soul* (Columbia, Mo.: University of Missouri Press, 1997); William Galston, *Liberal Purposes* (New York: Cambridge University Press, 1991); Stephen Macedo, *Liberal Virtues* (New York: Oxford University Press, 1991).

35. Althusius, *Politica*, ed. Carney, p. xliii.

Why Draw a Politics from Scripture?
Bossuet and the Divine Right of Kings

———✦———

Emile Perreau-Saussine

Jacques-Bénigne Bossuet (1627–1704) started writing *Politics Drawn from the Very Words of Holy Scripture* in the 1670s, while educating the son of Louis XIV. As the work of a Catholic, it is an odd book. First, it seems too Protestant. Fairly literal in its interpretation of Scripture, it pays little attention to philosophy or natural law; it savors of "Scripture alone." Second, it seems too Jewish: it hardly mentions the New Testament, drawing mainly on the book of Kings, and seems to prefer King David to Christ the King. Bossuet's book prompts a simple question, but most commentators mention it only in passing: why a politics drawn from holy Scripture? More specifically, why from the book of Kings? Many political philosophers have found their inspiration in the history of Greece or Rome; few have done so in the history of the Jewish people. And even among those who *have* offered a political interpretation of Israel's history, not many since the Renaissance have recommended it for imitation by their readers.[1] Why is Bossuet an exception? And why does his *Politics* take David as its main model? These are some of the questions I intend to examine, less through an analysis of Bossuet's thought than through placing it in a broad context that I hope will shed light on its significance.[2] This article will explore whether the oddities of Bossuet's book result from his attempt to offer a political theology for the modern state.

1. Louis XIV: Absolute Monarch and Most Christian King

One commonplace of medieval political thought, reinforced by the second scholastics, is that with the exception of the chosen people, the most immediate origin of the authority of the state lies in the consent of the people: *omnis potestas a Deo sed per populum* (all power comes from God but through the people). At times, Bossuet writes in a medieval vein, explaining, for example, that "after establishing temporal power, God left the choice of form of government to the will of the people."[3] Overall, however, he tries to defend and justify Louis XIV's absolute political regime, which means parting with medieval tradition.[4] One way of making this break—as Luther did—is through a return to Scripture itself. To establish monarchy as directly rooted in God's will, Bossuet transforms the Jewish people's God-given exceptional status into the norm. He discovers in Scripture a "people whose legislator is God himself."[5] In the Bible, God names kings in a fairly direct manner. And in the kingdoms of David and Solomon, Bossuet finds the precedent he seeks: kings owe their legitimacy to God, without the mediation of the people. "Princes act as God's ministers, and as his lieutenants on earth."[6]

Bossuet reads the Bible in a notoriously one-sided fashion. He considers the glorious period of the monarchy as the most significant one, in effect the *only* significant one, without exploring the theological meaning of its short duration.[7] He suggests that David and Solomon were absolute monarchs, ignoring the tribal structure of Israel.[8] And he is so attached to French mores that he justifies primogeniture without paying much attention to God's preference not for the firstborn but for younger brothers—Abel, Jacob, Joseph, and David, for instance.[9]

The absolutist thesis of the divine right of kings was already at least a hundred years old when Bossuet turned his attention to it; in drawing his politics from the Bible, however, he transformed a traditionally rather dubious thesis into a position fairly "natural" or "obvious" for Christians. The divine right claimed by James I and Louis XIV was supposed to justify a doctrine of passive obedience and put the king above the law. It also had to promote some degree of independence from the pope: relative independence in the case of Louis XIV, absolute in the case of James I. According to the theory of the divine right of kings, the king receives and holds his legitimacy directly from God, just as does the pope, his equal. The theoreticians of divine right were trying to diminish or abolish the pope's influence: subjects were to obey the monarch without taking much notice of injunctions and excommunications from Rome. To the divine right of the pope, they juxtaposed another divine right, no less important in their eyes: the divine right of kings.[10]

In this context, Bossuet's constant reference to the books of Kings has two advantages. I have already mentioned the first, the generalization of the cases of David and Solomon. The second is subtler. The political life of Israel's kings does not take place amid a dual legitimacy of civil and religious authorities; only with the exile in Babylon is politics detached from religion. There is tension in the book of Kings between Samuel and Saul, of course, but Bossuet downplays it. While Spinoza focuses on the separation of administrative and religious functions after Moses, as well as on the distinctive character of the Levites, Bossuet tends to remain silent on these matters.[11]

Instead, Bossuet transforms the political imagination of his readers by relating biblical monarchy to seventeenth-century France's absolute monarchy. He replaces the duality of *sacerdotium* and *imperium*, of church and state, of natural and sacred, with a landscape void of separation. Louis XIV can thus be an absolute monarch *as well as* a most Christian king. The medieval tradition avoids absolutism by maintaining a certain tension between church and state: Bossuet tries to relativize this tension in order to justify absolutism.

In other words, as a work by a Catholic scholar, *Politics Drawn from the Very Words of Holy Scripture* seems too Protestant, because the best way to part with a non-absolutist Christian tradition is to go back to Scripture alone, and it seems too Jewish, because the Old Testament depicts kings directly appointed by God without much human mediation.

Bossuet breaks with his own tradition so radically that Joseph de Maistre could say that he "leaves far behind him all the other worshippers of Louis XIV."[12] At times, it seems that the title of his book should be "Holy Scripture Drawn from Bossuet's Politics." Why did Bossuet defend such a political theology?

2. The Sacralization of the State as a Means of Assertion

In the Middle Ages and the Renaissance, philosophers had no qualms about invoking Aristotelian arguments. But in the context of church-state relations, this reference was essentially ambiguous. It is a commonplace in the history of political thought that the translation of Aristotle's texts in the thirteenth century led to an intellectual revolution. Some writers, like Marsilius of Padua and Dante, drew on Aristotelian arguments to limit the church's place in the political sphere. A focus on "nature" (rather than on more theological arguments in terms of "grace") freed intellectuals to understand the polis at least partially independently of faith. Marsilius pulled Aristotle in a democratic direction, and Dante in an imperialistic one, but both used him to confine the church to what they defined as its proper sphere. They contended that, besides the *corpus mysticum* of the church, there was a *corpus politicum et morale* best understood through concepts already known to the pagans. From this perspective, building on Aristotle's thought allowed separation of the sacred from the profane and fostered a form of "secularism": politics could recover its "naturalness," that is, its proper natural ends.

There is truth in this commonplace but also in its inversion. Aquinas' baptism of Aristotle subordinated nature to grace. Thomists like Francisco Suarez turned the Marsilian approach on its head, using Aristotle to subordinate civil authorities to religious authorities. To defend papal authority, Suarez developed a striking response, using a theory of the natural character of the polis to *subordinate* kings to the church. The institution of the body politic had to be understood as *purely natural*: the state pursues its own ends. Since these ends are inferior to the supernatural ones pursued by the church, kings must obey the pope. The separation of nature and grace could thus be an efficient way of subordinating civil authorities to religious authorities. Supernatural ends' being higher than natural ones, the exaltation of nature offered a splendid opportunity for an even greater exaltation of grace. The teleological arguments made by Aristotelians keen to limit the power of the church were readily trumped by Aristotelians keen to reaffirm the authority of the church.

There remained a way to avoid politically ambivalent arguments based on the relationship between nature and grace. Instead of naturalizing the state, one could sacralize it, making it imitate the church. This process as it took place in the Middle Ages has been well documented by Ernst Kantorowicz, who describes how secular power took on the attributes of the church in order to dominate it, analyzing the mimetic rivalry with which monarchs adopted the model of Christ's two natures to attribute to themselves a mystical body. Since the mystical body of the king "never dies," the continuity of the state could be asserted.[13] In an essay on the

"Mysteries of the State," Kantorowicz describes this transition from the *arcana ecclesiae* to the *arcana imperii,* allowing princes to put their feet into pontifical mules. And in his *"Pro Patria Mori,"* he underlines how, while Christians were not supposed to sacrifice themselves for a republican ideal (their true city being the city of God and not the earthly city), from the twelfth century onward, their "true" city returned to earth. The idea of a holy war was replaced by that of a quasi-holy war: the defense of the kingdom, of the nation, of the crown, allowing Joan of Arc to proclaim, "those who wage war against the holy realm of France wage war against King Jesus." "The quasi-religious aspects of death for the fatherland," Kantorowicz concludes, "clearly derived from the Christian faith, the force[s] of which were now activated in the service of the secular *corpus mysticum* of the State."[14]

This process, described by Kantorowicz, culminated in the Reformation. In the Middle Ages, Paul's claim of *non est potestas nisi a Deo* (there is no authority that does not come from God) in the Epistle to the Romans had been understood to require obedience to civil authorities, albeit subordinated to religious authorities. The pope could excommunicate kings and authorize forms of resistance. But Luther challenged the mediating function of the clergy, criticized the pope, and rejected what he called the "visible Church." In delegitimizing this "visible" church, Luther sanctified the civil power and justified passive obedience. The defense of religious truth and practice, until then entrusted mainly to the church, was now turned over to the state: although Luther initially defended freedom, he quickly turned against it. In weakening the clergy, in depriving the pope of any authority over reformed countries, Luther undermined the medieval balance in favor of kings. Contrary to the duality of the civil and religious order, he proposed a unified order. In abolishing canon law and the coercive strength of the church, Luther entrusted former church responsibilities to the state. The church dissolved in the state, which assumed the new body of Christ.[15] Luther reassigned the church's aura of holiness to the state, with the state becoming newly visible as the church became invisible. The principle *cuius regio, eius religio* recognizes the superiority of the civil power and its position as the interpreter and expositor of religious truth. In this way, monarchs overcome religious wars by becoming emperors within their kingdoms and, more often than not, heads of national churches. Absolutism is the result of this transformation: the power of the king is no longer counterbalanced by the people or the (visible) church.

In Catholic France, a similar outcome emerged through a different process. Wars of religion and divisions among the people undermined the medieval tradition of power emanating from God through the people. Since legitimacy no longer derived from popular consensus, it had to come from above, from the will of the prince. If legitimacy no longer came from the people, it had to come without them—hence the divine right of kings. Again, the weakening of the church accompanied a sacralization of the king. In France, absolutism prevailed in the wake of the wars of religion; the king claimed to rise above the warring parties, with the Edict of Nantes separating politics from religion and conferring a new prestige on the monarchy. The king was raised from the body of the kingdom to new summits.[16] That is why the Edict of Nantes led dialectically to its own revocation: it granted the king such dominion that he could abolish the policy of tolerance if he so wished.

The medieval period was not without its own absolutist stream.[17] Following Kantorowicz, historians have shown how, in asserting their increasing power, kings emphasized their "sacred ministry." Many of the themes "typical" of the seventeenth century in fact developed in the fourteenth or the fifteenth century. The comparison between David and the king of France was used in the time of Philip the Fair to assert his sovereignty.[18] The designation of the French monarch as the "most Christian king," common in the fifteenth century, could already be seen as a way of avoiding the very notion of contract and pact.[19] But only in the wake of the Reformation was the church weakened to the extent that absolutism became not just a stream but a political reality.

For the purpose of the present discussion, I have emphasized how deeply the Reformation undermined the medieval hierarchical vision of society. On the one hand, on a theoretical level, the Reformation questioned the need for mediation between God and his people and therefore for mediation in general. On the other hand, on a practical level, it divided the people into competing sects and confessions, undermining the very unity required for the king's legitimacy to come through "the" people. Thus, in one way, the Reformation weakened the king, neutralizing his dominance of the social hierarchy. In another way, it strengthened the king, who was no longer confined within the limits of a hierarchical view of the world.

Insofar as the Reformation deprived political authorities of guarantees in a nature understood hierarchically, two possibilities remained: conventionalism (the Hobbesian solution) or supernaturalism (Bossuet's solution). For Hobbes, order rests on the will of the Leviathan, the "mortal God." For Bossuet, order rests on God's direct appointment of the monarch, whose authority is thus rooted "in conscience, in presence, and in the eyes of God himself."[20] Both thinkers fear that men without a strong state will lapse into disunity and violence. Both share a sense of the fragility of the civil and political order: the extreme character of their absolutism testifies to the depth of this shared fear.[21]

Thus, the divine right of kings appeared to solve the problems accompanying state recognition of religious pluralism. In the conflicts between Catholics and Protestants throughout the sixteenth and seventeenth centuries, the monarchical state became a *tertius gaudens*. It reinforced its power not by invoking Aristotelian naturalism but by appropriating the symbolism and power of a weakened church. Lawyers defended the modern state by refusing to relegate it to the realm of nature or to allow the church a monopoly on grace: imitation became a means of differentiation. Temporal and spiritual power, they asserted, had one and the same origin, which meant that the latter could not claim primacy; the sanctity of royal power put it on equal footing with ecclesiastical power.

Bossuet did justify the revocation of the Edict of Nantes. His *Politics Drawn from the Very Words of Holy Scripture* is one of the most accomplished manifestoes for Louis XIV's state. Its subject is a self-conscious political theology: "*L'Etat, c'est moi.*" The constant references to the book of Kings are a good illustration of the defense of a conflation of church and state against Christian tradition in a manner typical of absolutism. Bossuet's strange, systematically anachronistic comparisons between Louis XIV and David represent, if not the canonical version, at least one of the most acute expressions of a theology of the state.

3. An Anti-Machiavellian 'Mirror of the Prince'

Non est potestas nisi a Deo, says St. Paul: there is no authority that does not come from God. Perhaps one of the most famous statements of Christian political theology, as suggested above these words were not traditionally understood to justify anything like a divine right of kings. In the Middle Ages,

> St. Paul's formula, "authority comes from God," is repeated less to invite subjects to obey power than to invite power to obey God.

By calling the princes "representatives" or "ministers" of God, the church does not want to transfer to them God's all-powerful nature; on the contrary, the church hopes to remind them that they hold their authority as a mandate and must use it according to the intention and the will of the Master from whom they received it. The purpose is not to allow the prince legislative omni-competence, but to make sure that power will give way to the divine law which dominates and binds him.[22]

Kings did not wait for absolutism to assert the sacred character of their authority. Consider, for example, the notion of the royal touch.[23] As Walter Ullmann writes:

It was, on the one hand, the nature of the theocratic office which supplied the strength of the king, but it was also, on the other hand, the same office which placed severe limitations on the king. [...] The dramatic assertion of Henri IV that God himself had conceded him power, that Gregory VII should recognize this divine origin of Henry's power and that he was a Lord's anointed, could do nothing to avert his deposition by the pope. In fact, one might go as far as to say that it was the theocratic king himself who had opened up the gates; for the emphasis on God as the source of his power made it less difficult for the pope to pronounce upon this very issue.[24]

By regarding the royal office as an ecclesiastical office in a broad sense, medieval lawyers and theologians raised the prince above the people and the nobles but subordinated him within the hierarchy of the church.

The sacralization of the medieval monarch remained confined within a hierarchical vision of the world, with which absolutism breaks. The divine right associated with the aftermath of the Reformation belongs to a different conceptual universe, in which the king is no longer to be thought of as a *primus inter pares*, or as the top of the pyramid or the feudal organization. Unlike most medieval authors, Bossuet interprets St. Paul's statement as a sanctification of royal authority: "the royal throne is not the throne of a man, but the throne of God himself."[25] Bossuet's divine right of kings differs from the medieval versions (as described by Marc Bloch, for example).[26] This change can be explained in a sentence: the divine rights of thirteenth- or fourteenth-century monarchs fall within a hierarchical worldview, while "modern" divine rights express the crisis of this hierarchical vision. The question is no longer where to place the king in a pyramid, but how to anchor a political world without support for its order. The riddle of the foundation of power, of little interest to medieval thinkers, becomes closer to an obsession. Both symbolically and philosophically, the king constitutes no longer the highest order, but the very principle of the order itself. Law and order no longer rest on a hierarchy of nobles or clergy, but depend on the absolute authority of the prince.

Why should a Catholic theologian like Bossuet justify an absolutism that seems to serve one purpose, that of humiliating the pope and the Catholic church? One can understand why a Protestant theologian, an Erastian philosopher like Hobbes, or a legist like Domat might defend absolutism. But why should Bossuet offer such praise of a prince, breaking with Catholic tradition and possibly diminishing the authority of the church? I believe that there are two answers to these questions.

First, Bossuet's Gallican ecclesiology fits comfortably with absolutism. Bossuet is above all a defender of episcopal dignity against the "ultramontanes." Gallicans dispute Rome's likening of the pope and the church to *caput* and *corpus*, respectively. The body is not purely a product of the head; it has its own reality and life. For Gallicans, bishops do not derive their authority through participation in papal authority; episcopal power is not simply a reflection of that of the pope. Rather, episcopal endorsement of papal decisions actually makes them binding. "Bossuet's Gallicanism is primarily a defense of the original power of bishops," asserts Yves Congar.[27] Bossuet mentions in the same breath the "temporal independence of kings, the episcopal jurisdiction immediately from Jesus Christ, and the authority of councils."[28] By supporting Louis XIV in his quarrels with the pope, Bossuet did not so much exalt the power of the king over the church as defend episcopal authority against the ultramontanes. He tries not so much to give all power to kings as to remind the pope of the limits of his own authority.

Second, rather lacking in political imagination, Bossuet regards absolutism as inevitable; he wonders not whether it is necessary to be for or against it, but whether the absolute monarch will behave in a Christian manner. He tries to baptize (or confirm the baptism of) a power that he believes bound to remain absolute. In the Gallican dispute, Bossuet acted as a moderator; he sought to constrain absolutism in a way that would render it compatible with the unity of the church.[29] Favoring the freedoms of the Gallican church, Bossuet explains them "in the manner that the bishops understood them, and not in the manner that the magistrates understood them."[30] His absolutism implies neither an Erastianism nor a French Anglicanism.

The *Politics Drawn from the Very Words of Holy Scripture* belongs to the genre of the "mirror of the princes," which it renews in an anti-Machiavellian spirit.[31] In this respect, Bossuet's absolutism differs deeply from Hobbes' or that of the "magistrates." He offers no equivalent of the principle *salus populi suprema lex esto*; inverting Machiavelli, he substitutes providence for chance or fortune. More specifically, by showing that it is possible to draw a politics from Scripture, the Old Testament being most useful for that purpose, Bossuet seeks to establish both that Christianity is not as oblivious to the demands of politics as the author of *The Prince* argued, *and* that good politics will be Christian politics.

The end of Bossuet's foreword announces, "those who believe that piety weakens politics will be refuted." In this respect, book 5 is particularly important. Bossuet traces a description of the prudence, skill, intelligence, capacity for attention, and knowledge of the human soul that one will find in a good prince: "Under a skillful and well-informed prince, nobody dares do anything wrong. One always believes that he is present, and even that he guesses everyone's thoughts.... Nothing escapes his knowledge."[32] Bossuet insists on the higher intelligence of the wise man, that is, on the cognition accompanying Christian virtues. He suggests, against Machiavelli, that the prince need not "enter evil." Bossuet's King David is a holier leader than most other Davids.[33]

The modern state has built itself in confrontation with the church. In this confrontation, one of its favorite weapons has been the political theology that asserts at least equality with if not superiority over the church. In response, Christians can either denounce this political theology or restore it to Christianity. Suarez chose the first option, Bossuet, the second. Taking advantage of the theological element at the heart of the state, Bossuet reinstates Scripture and, with it, the church. But few Christians today lament the failure of his bold attempt. The thesis of the superiority of the state over religion takes two forms: an anti-liberal one (Bossuet) and a liberal one (Locke). In the long run, the liberal solution has been widely preferred.

4. From Divine Right to the Nation-State

Absolutism was to prove fragile and to characterize only a transitional period. In *The Ancien Régime and the Revolution*, Tocqueville traces how by depriving the nobility of its functions, absolutism paved the way for equality: the French Revolution completed a process initiated by Richelieu and Louis XIV, the culmination of the nobility's loss of function. The critique of hierarchical principles had already partially delegitimized the nobles, and the centralization of power rendered them increasingly parasitical. The nobility retained privileges but without any of the responsibilities or duties that could justify them. It thus became unbearable. Absolutism ruined the aristocratic order it crowned; it cut the trunk that bore it. In a similar way, the notion of the divine right of kings benefits from the very theological framework it questions. What one calls "secularization" is not only or not even mainly the result of an occlusion of religion. Oddly enough, secularization is perhaps, above all, the consequence of the sacralization of what was once regarded as secular. In his *Protestant Ethics and the Spirit of Capitalism*, Max Weber posits that the sacralization of work, the Protestant glorification of everyday life, paved the way for a secular vision of the world. This thesis fits the phenomenon sketched here rather well: a sacralization of the state led to a desacralization of the religious sphere. Such is the paradox around the notion of the divine right of kings. Its theorists secularize politics by "theologizing" it. They increase the freedom of the state with regard to the church thanks to the divine right, but once the church is marginalized, divine right loses its significance, and the king is left naked. Tocqueville argued that absolutism saws off the aristocratic branch that carries it; it should be added that it also saws off the religious trunk that bears it.[34]

There is something contradictory at the heart of Gallicanism. The movement was radicalized by the French revolutionaries and later Napoleon: the former via the civil constitution of the clergy, the latter via his own form of absolutism. Although he signed a concordat, Napoleon humiliated the church. By treating bishops as glorified civil servants, he isolated them from their flock, in effect disestablishing the Church of France. In treating the bishops as his religious "*préfets*," Napoleon's policy intended to isolate further the French church from Rome. But it had the opposite consequence. No longer recognizing themselves in their bishops, French Catholics became ultra-montane.[35] The radicalization of Gallicanism and of the logic of the divine right of kings by Napoleon revived claims of the pope's own divine right.

In the 1820s, the Bourbons attempted to resurrect the divine right of kings, but it no longer made sense. The secularization of political life precluded reliance on the absolutism of kings who were no longer, by any stretch of the imagination, "most Christian." In their periodical *L'Avenir* (*The Future*) in the early 1830s, the founders of liberal Catholicism attacked the political theology that I have sketched in these pages. The periodical's manifesto condemned Louis XIV's despotism and his legacy to both state and church. Catholics who wanted the government to protect religion were mistaken, the authors argued; even if this vision had once made sense, it no longer did, not least since it required that "papal infallibility be replaced with ministerial infallibility, the Sinai with the golden calf."[36] In their assault on absolutism, these liberal Catholics rediscovered their own history, realizing that "the church's close alliance with absolute power, an alliance Bossuet and his followers had made a kind of article of faith among us, was a novelty originating in the seventeenth century, and one that has against it one thousand years of tradition and contrary precedents."[37]

The state is tempted to sacralize itself in order to avoid succumbing to an ecclesiastical trumping that places the ends of the city below those pursued by the church. But the solution fails, because ultimately the political theology of divine right subverts Christianity as well as the state it is supposed to legitimate. Modern political philosophy has preferred the Hobbesian solution, built not on Bossuet's fear of God but on fear of death; it has preferred to elude evil rather than seek good.[38] Both Bossuet and Hobbes tried to reunify the two heads of the eagle; both endeavored to avoid, at least partially, the medieval dualism of civil and religious authority. And even Hobbes could not help employing a vocabulary that echoes notions of the divine right of kings: as already remarked, his state is a 'mortal God.' In this sense, Bossuet's political theology has endured. It reveals a face of the state, a face still to be seen.[39] After all, Bossuet's political theology remains alive.

In an essay to which I referred earlier, "*Pro Patria Mori*," Kantorowicz mentions the abnegation of soldiers during the First World War, then under Italian Fascism: "*Chi muore per Italia non muore*."[40] For Kantorowicz, the sacralization of the state is related to nationalist passion. One can wonder whether Bossuet's much earlier identification of the French with the chosen people contributed to the consolidation of the nation-state. In likening Louis XIV's monarchy to David's, and the French to the Jewish nation, the nation par excellence, Bossuet ennobles the modern nation-state.[41] Nationalism, whose birth is often located at Valmy in 1792 with the French Revolution's termination of absolutism, adapted the same political theology of that late absolutism: the sacralization of the state and therefore of the body politic. The extraordinary sacrifices made during the First World War can be understood only, if at all, by reference to this sacralization. Modern nationalism draws its energy from that which it inherits: the confusion within the doctrine of the divine right of kings of the sacred and the profane, nature and grace. "*Je ne sais quoi de divin s'attache au prince*," wrote Bossuet.[42] "*Je ne sais quoi de divin s'attache à la nation*,"[43] claim nationalists. King David has two bodies: one buried in Jerusalem, and another mystically kept alive by any nation worth its salt.

Notes

1. See in particular Benedict de Spinoza, *Theological-Political Treatise*, ch. 18.

2. On absolutism in France generally, see Nannerl O. Keohane, *Philosophy and the State in France* (Princeton: Princeton University Press, 1980); Fanny Cosandey and Robert Descimon, *L'absolutisme en France* (Paris: Seuil, 2002).

3. Jacques-Bénigne Bossuet, *Défense de la Déclaration* (Paris, 1709), I, 2, *in fine*.

4. Cf., for instance, Walter Ullmann, "Towards Populism," in Ullmann, *Principles of Government and Politics in the Middle Ages* (London: Methuen, 1961), pp. 231–279.

5. Jacques-Bénigne Bossuet, *Politique tirée de l'Ecriture sainte* (Paris, 1709), dedication.

6. Bossuet, *Politique*, III, 1, ii.

7. Compare with Sir Robert Filmer's *Patriarcha*, on the one hand, and with Thomas Paine's later biblical critique of monarchy (*Common Sense* II), on the other.

8. In this respect, as in others, Bossuet's interpretation of the Bible opposes Spinoza's; see Spinoza, *Theological-Political Treatise*, ch. 17.

9. Bossuet, *Politique*, II, 1, ix. Cf. John Locke, *First Treatise on Government*, ch. 11; Martin Buber, "Biblical Leadership," in Buber, *Israel and the World: Essays in a Time of Crisis* (New York: Schocken, 1948), p. 124.

10. John Neville Figgis, *The Divine Right of Kings* (Cambridge, 1896).

11. Spinoza, *Theological-Political Treatise*, ch. 17.

12. Joseph de Maistre, *De l'Eglise gallicane* (Paris, 1821), II, 12.

13. Ernst H. Kantorowicz, *The King's Two Bodies: A Study in Medieval Political Theology* (Princeton: Princeton University Press, 1957).

14. Ernst H. Kantorowicz, "*Pro Patria Mori* in Medieval Political Thought," in Kantorowicz, *Selected Studies* (Locust Valley, N.Y.: J.J. Augustin, 1965), pp. 318, 320–321. Cf. Kantorowicz, "Mysteries of the State: An Absolutist Concept and Its Late Medieval Origins," in Kantorowicz, *Selected Studies*. Cf. also Joseph R. Strayer, "France: The Holy Land, the Chosen People and the Most Christian King," in Theodore Rabb and Jerrold Seigel, eds., *Action and Conviction in Early Modern Europe* (Princeton: Princeton University Press, 1969), pp. 3–16.

15. Cf., for instance, John Neville Figgis, *Studies of Political Thought: From Gerson to Grotius* (Cambridge: Cambridge University Press, 1916), pp. 55–72.

16. G. Lacour-Gayet, *L'éducation politique de Louis XIV* (Paris, 1898), pp. 330–338.

17. Jacques Krynen, *L'empire du roi: Idées et croyances politiques en France XIIIe–XVe siècle* (Paris: Gallimard, 1993), pp. 339–414.

18. Aryeh Graboïs, "Un mythe fondamental de l'histoire de France au Moyen Âge: le 'roi David', précurseur du 'roi très chrétien,'" *Revue Historique* 287 (1992), pp. 29–30.

19. As Krynen writes, "*Le thème du roi très chrétien, thème obligé pour la pensée politique française au XVe siècle, a pour effet d'évacuer du royaume toute idée de contrat, de pacte constituant conclu entre le monarque et son peuple, idée tellement caractéristique du Moyen Age occidental.*" Krynen, *L'empire du roi*, p. 360.

20. Jacques-Bénigne Bossuet, "Panégyrique de saint Thomas de Cantorbéry" (1668), in Bossuet, *Œuvres Complètes*, 43 vols. (Paris, 1864), vol. 12, pp. 42–43.

21. Gustave Lanson, *Bossuet* (Lecène & Oudin, 1890), pp. 184–281.

22. Bertrand de Jouvenel, *Du pouvoir: Histoire naturelle de sa croissance* (Geneva: Constant Bourquin, 1947), p. 43.

23. Marc Bloch, *The Royal Touch: Sacred Monarchy and Scrofula in England and France*, trans. J.E. Anderson (London: Routledge, 1973 [1924]).

24. Ullmann, *Principles of Government*, pp. 139, 140–141.

25. Bossuet, *Politique*, III, 2.

26. See n. 23, above.

27. Yves Congar, *L'Eglise: De saint Augustin à l'époque moderne* (Paris: Cerf, 1970), p. 398. Cf. Aimé-Georges Martimort, *Le gallicanisme de Bossuet* (Paris: Cerf, 1953), pp. 549–563.

28. Jacques-Bénigne Bossuet, "Lettre au cardinal d'Estrées" (1681), in Bossuet, *Œuvres Complètes*, vol. 26, p. 292.

29. Martimort, *Le gallicanisme de Bossuet*, pp. 361–523.

30. Bossuet, "Lettre au cardinal d'Estrées," p. 291.

31. Bossuet owned Machiavelli's *Complete Works* and two copies of *The Prince*.

32. Bossuet, *Politique*, V, 1, xiv.

33. Compare with Pierre Bayle's or Voltaire's Davids, for instance (in *Dictionnaire historique et critique*, 1697, and in *Dictionnaire philosophique*, 1764, respectively).

34. Marcel Gauchet, *Le désenchantement du monde: Une histoire politique de la religion* (Paris: Gallimard, 1985), pp. 221–231.

35. Hyppolite Taine, *Les origines de la France contemporaine* (1876–1891), III, book 5, ch. 2.

36. Quoted in Lucien Jaume, *L'individu effacé ou le paradoxe du libéralisme français* (Paris: Fayard, 1997), pp. 197–198.

37. C. de Montalembert, *Des intérêts catholiques au dix-neuvième siècle* (1852), in Montalembert, *Œuvres* (Paris, 1860), vol. 5, pp. 63–64.

38. Pierre Manent, *An Intellectual History of Liberalism*, trans. Rebecca Balinski (Princeton: Princeton University Press, 1995), pp. 3–38.

39. Hegel even suggests that the visible church was only a poor imitation of the state, just as speculative theology parodied philosophy. Cf. Jacques Maritain, "L'homme et l'Etat" (1953), in Maritain, *Œuvres Complètes*, vol. 9 (Paris: Fribourg, 1982), pp. 513–539.

40. "He who dies for Italy does not die."

41. Cf. Adrian Hastings, *The Construction of Nationhood* (Cambridge: Cambridge University Press, 1997); Steven Grosby, *Biblical Ideas of Nationality* (Winona Lake, Ind.: Eisenbrauns, 2002).

42. "There is something mysteriously divine about the prince." Bossuet, *Politique*, V, 4, i. Bossuet alludes to Psalm 138.

43. "There is something mysteriously divine about the nation."

III. THE DUTCH REPUBLIC

'How Wondrously Moses Goes Along with The House of Orange!' Hugo Grotius' 'De Republica Emendanda' in the Context of the Dutch Revolt

Arthur Eyffinger

Dutch Political Hebraism

Within the wider context of the fascinating early modern European phenomenon we have now come to identify as political Hebraism, the Dutch chapter constitutes a truly intriguing phase. Far from being a mere academic exercise, political Hebraism in the Dutch Republic was prompted by urgent social debate. Indeed, it was part of a very deliberate reflection on a prolonged political crisis, in an attempt, however futile, to help avert catastrophe. The gist and drift of the Dutch Revolt can be summed up in its leading mottos *Haec Libertatis Ergo* (*This Is for the Sake of Freedom*) and *Haec Religionis Ergo* (*This Is for the Sake of Religion*)—and so can the constitutional crisis of the young Republic. As would soon dawn on the Dutch, political tolerance and Calvinist orthodoxy made for poor bedfellows.[1] The crisis came to a head in 1618, with the *coup d'état* by Prince Maurice of Orange, which sealed the fate of the early aristocratic republic and yet did not resolve the riddle that had brought that political experiment to its knees.[2] The small corpus of tracts that can be identified with political Hebraism eminently addressed the two signal defects of the early Republic throughout: the absence of a sense of unity and of religious tolerance.

Dutch political Hebraism, aside from being acutely linked to political circumstances, also coincided, and not incidentally so, with two other phenomena, one being of an intellectual nature, the other of a social nature. The first was the rise of Hebrew studies and biblical research at Leiden University, the other the growing influx of Jews, mostly merchants, into the United Provinces as a result of political circumstance elsewhere in Europe.[3] The close interrelation of all these elements has, in the present author's opinion, not been appreciated to the full by modern research.

Symptomatic of this circumstance is the relative disinterest of scholars regarding the most representative tract of the period in this field, Petrus Cunaeus' *De Republica Hebraeorum* (*On the Republic of the Hebrews*), due mostly to ignorance of its acute social commitment. Far from being a work of speculation and mere historical research, Cunaeus' treatise was urged, if nothing else, by the complexities of the Remonstrant troubles. Indeed, as is amply attested to by its beseeching letter of dedication to the States of Holland, the treatise was precisely meant as a piece of advice to help steer the States' policy. It was, in fact, a fairly courageous attempt on the part of the gifted Leiden professor of political science to voice what he saw as his personal responsibility to the benefit of the public domain, and to put all his learning and authority as a foremost Hebrew scholar at the service of his nation's future.[4]

But modern scholarship has also neglected to investigate the links between Cunaeus' treatise and another intriguing tract of the period, that here under consideration, Hugo Grotius' *De Republica Emendanda* (*On How to Emend the Dutch Polity*). These links too can be easily established. In all likelihood, it was Hugo Grotius who inspired Cunaeus' work in the first place. Both the genesis and later reorientation of Cunaeus' treatise attest to his having been intellectually and politically backed by this dear friend of his, who was the foremost political thinker and publicist of the period. In addition to this, Grotius' many works on the relationship between state and church in the years leading up to the crisis of 1618 were, without exception, reviewed prior to their publication by Cunaeus. Indeed, in some cases these works were actually withheld from publication at the instigation of the small circle of tried and trusted friends, Cunaeus among them, on whom Grotius relied unreservedly.[5]

If Grotius' *De Republica Emendanda* of around 1600 was a counsel's plea aimed at the revision of the Dutch constituency by reference to the ancient Hebrew constitution, Cunaeus' *De Republica Hebraeorum* of 1617 served precisely as a reminder to the States of Holland of the innate shortcomings which had brought down that ancient model confederacy, the republic of the Hebrews, these defects being, in the author's appraisal, the inevitable outcome of religious friction and fanaticism. The Hebrews had been affected by an ailment common to so many nations: civil strife. There is no other recipe, Cunaeus holds, to bring nations down so effectively. In fact, the Romans employed it in their foreign policy—and conquered the world. The Achaean League once, just like the Dutch League today, seemed invincible, based as it was on inner strength, unity, and inviolable laws. This until the Romans, "the plague of the world" as they were once called, interfered. The technique Cunaeus cites as having been used by Jeroboam to divide the twelve tribes was to corrupt true religion and replace it with empty superstition: "What had been a battle about freedom and power came to be one about sacred rituals and places of worship."

No phrase could have better summarized the acute problem of the Dutch Republic. From here, not surprisingly, the perspective of Cunaeus' dedication shifts from Hebrew history to Dutch topicality:

> You, State Members are aware, better than anyone, that harmony creates success as sure as disharmony causes ruin. Right now, after a long uphill battle, and thanks to your unity, you have reached the peaks of power. I feel confident that this unity will be preserved, and success will be durable. And yet... there is reason to draw lessons from the experience of others. Recently, factions and sections tend to multiply in our Republic. And the bones of contention seem to be rather obscure and fairly pointless issues of religious doctrine, which, most of the time, the rivaling factions don't even understand themselves. The mobs, as usual are left to follow their whims and passions.[6]

From here, Cunaeus' tenor becomes positively imploring:

> It is in your interest to apply a timely remedy. Therefore, study, over and again, the fate of this holiest and best of all Republics.[7]

Grotius' and Cunaeus' tracts were flip sides of a coin. For all their differences of perspective, both essentially belong to that fascinating genre of state parallels, which were such a favorite tool for humanists to make

their point. Actually, as can be established from Cunaeus' correspondence, his tract was intended to be merely the first part of a far more
ambitious program, namely the comprehensive comparison of a wide
range of constitutions. In the end, the realization of this program was
forestalled only by the author's untimely death.

Dutch political Hebraism, in short, was spurred on by sociopolitical
crisis if nothing else. Two of the foremost political minds of the period,
Petrus Cunaeus and Hugo Grotius, may pose as its godfathers. In my
introductory note on the new English edition of Cunaeus' tract from
Shalem Press, I have elaborated on the complexities of Dutch society of
the period and the immediate context of Cunaeus' life and works. The
present contribution focuses rather on Grotius and on the juvenile tract
De Republica Emendanda as a first step toward the overall interpretation
of Grotius' personal views, academic research, and political tenets vis-
à-vis contemporary Jewry, biblical and Hebrew studies, and the Dutch
constituency, respectively. My two texts, that presented here and the
introduction to Cunaeus' book, may be read as complementary and as
preliminary to an overall interpretation of Dutch political Hebraism.

For, to be sure, as the widely acclaimed intellectual product of Scaliger's
school of biblical and Hebrew studies at Leiden and the self-imposed
heir to the irenic legacy of Erasmus and Franciscus Junius, the intensely
socially engaged Grotius—who was no less formidable as a theologian
than as a lawyer and politician—could not fail to recurrently address
the topical issues of his day and age, either at his own initiative or at
the insistence of authorities and in an official capacity. In Grotius' life
and works all the vicissitudes of early-seventeenth-century Dutch society are eminently reflected. In 1614, Grotius was invited by the States of
Holland to formulate an answer to the highly controversial immigration
of Jews and define a formal state policy. Later on, in his great apology of Christianity, *De Veritate* (*On Truth*), he volunteered an influential
analysis of ancient and contemporary Jewry. Finally, in his *Annotationes*
(*Notes*) to the Testaments, he compiled a wealth of philological and historical research to the same purport. His contacts with Hebrew scholars,
other than with the Jewish community, were impressive. This paper will
insist on the urgency of the debate in the context of which Grotius wrote
his *De Republica Emendanda* and will retrace the way in which he was
first put on this lifelong quest.

Hugo Grotius: A First Appraisal

To our day and age, Hugo Grotius is almost exclusively renowned for his pioneering role in the domain of international law.[8] Lost to the world at large, along with his many philological and poetical endeavors, are his impressive historical and exegetical pursuits, which never failed to charm the European world of humanism. With time, and due mainly to the sharp turn Western society took in subsequent decades, the lasting fame of "*le miracle de la Hollande*" came to rest on his *Laws of War and Peace.*[9] Meanwhile, most of Grotius' versatile intellectual pursuits date from his long years in exile following the sudden foundering of his dazzling political career, an event which, at home at least, would forever taint his reputation. Whatever Grotius' merits may be in the eyes of the world at large, to the Dutch these can never be abstracted from his steering role in that first moment of crisis of the young Republic, the so-called Remonstrant troubles,[10] troubles which, with hindsight, can be viewed as part of Europe's deep intellectual crisis and the Dutch variation of that social tragedy which on the French stage prompted St. Bartholomew's Day and in Britain the beheading of Charles I.

By that moment of crisis in 1618, Hugo Grotius—thirty-five at the time—was the widely acclaimed, up-and-coming man in the Dutch Republic, generally expected to become its first servant and *Landsadvocaat* in good time. Only three years later he found himself in Paris, in exile for the remainder of his days. He was, however, lucky enough to have escaped the scaffold by the narrowest of margins, and to have fled state prison and a life sentence by that romantic escape in a book chest which possibly inevitably registered his name in the realm of folklore. Grotius' life, in short, epitomizes the drama of the early Dutch Republic. Documented to have been without peer, from his earliest teens he had been recruited to serve the public interest, first by the curators of Leiden University, then by leading Hague political circles, and shortly afterward by the administrators of that bulwark of Dutch pride, the VOC (*Verenigde Oostindische Compagnie*—East India Company). Still, Grotius first applied his astounding genius toward the effort of putting a haphazard band of rebelling provinces on the map of Europe as a legitimate sovereign state. He was a leading actor in the making and a major victim in the disappointment of that experimental undertaking to attain a precarious political balance. Nor was his downfall incidental. In all frankness, the political riddle Grotius got entangled in was not to be solved throughout the full span of two centuries, until the Republic was finally rolled up as an anachronism in the Napoleonic onslaught. Prior to that, protagonists might change, and so might the labels of factions, their pretensions and pretenses, but, far from healing, the ulcer was only inflamed. Various moments of crisis, maimings of justice, and outbursts of violence would mark the road. Of the three most gifted politicians the Republic brought about, the first, Oldenbarnevelt, was beheaded, the second, Jan de Witt, lynched by the mobs; Grotius alone got away with his life.[11]

The drama of Grotius' life might be said to equal the Achilles' heel of his beloved country. Indeed, his never-ending struggle was aimed precisely at achieving the entwining of those two proud mottos raised on the banners of the Dutch Revolt that we signaled above, by helping to improve the country's constitution and legislation and by settling the vexing issue of the relationship of church and state.[12] Still, if on the European stage Grotius readily succeeded in becoming "the New Justinian" Justus Lipsius had been urging,[13] within the domestic sphere his efforts to secure harmony (apart from the sphere of civil procedure)[14] were mostly frustrated—as were the efforts of succeeding generations for that matter. The short tract that we will now discuss stands out as Grotius' first attempt ever, indeed the opening move in this long game of chess, to tackle the intrinsic shortcomings of the Dutch experiment. From that perspective, the relevance of De Republica Emendanda, however immature its presentation both intellectually and stylistically, and for all its flaws by comparison with Grotius' majestic works written at a more advanced age, can never be seriously questioned.

'De Republica Emendanda': Identification of Authorship

In many respects, the tract here under consideration is a Fremdkörper in the Grotian canon.[15] So much so indeed that its authenticity has long been questioned on solid grounds. It reached us in a single manuscript copy, hidden in an omnibus codex in Vienna[16] stemming from a Venetian diplomat and collector,[17] and was identified as a result of a chance discovery by a prominent Dutch law professor back in 1964.[18] The manuscript is unmistakably a copy, its handwriting very unlike Grotius' scribblings or the known hands of any of his private secretaries. The author's name in the heading is added by yet another hand that likewise baffles verification. Apart from this, the tract abounds with misspellings of biblical proper names and syntactical irregularities that put into question the expertise of the transcriber. Moreover, its contents are sometimes at variance with the tenets maintained by Grotius on other occasions, such as in *De antiquitate* (*On the Ancients*, 1610), *Apologeticus* (*Defense*, 1622), and *De jure belli ac pacis* (*On the Laws of War and Peace*, 1625).[19]

Whereas, consequently, circumspection and caution were imperative, a clean dismissal of Grotius' authorship was forborne by the sheer topicality of the issue throughout his life. Also, in the tract, its author clearly presents himself as a Dutchman and alludes to social and political circumstances which fit in wondrously with Grotius' early Dutch years. In 1983 identification was much enhanced by the establishment of a cursory reference in a letter from one of Grotius' sons to his father and dated 1638, to the purport of his having perchance stumbled across a manuscript: "*inveni ibi librum tuum De emendanda Republica tua manu descriptum*" ("I found there your book *On How to Emend the Dutch Polity*, written in your own hand").[20] In the provisional 1984 edition of the tract, the watermark evidence of the Viennese copy was elaborated upon to help sustain identification of the manuscript with Grotius' immediate surroundings.[21] Also, on that occasion, the eventualities which led to the manuscript ending up in the hands of the Venetian collector were amply discussed.[22] By all appearances, a former pupil and private secretary of Grotius, Dirck Graswinckel, himself the author of *Libertas Veneta* (*Venetian Freedom*), a tract on the Venetian commonwealth and constitution, was instrumental in the process through his many contacts with Venetian diplomats.[23] The manuscript's recipient, incidentally, Count Marco Foscarini, himself authored *Ragionamento politico sulla perfezione della Repubblica* (*Political Reasoning on the Perfection of the Republic*).[24]

The Dating of the Tract

While the above strongly suggested Grotius' authorship, it left the pinpointing of the date and the tract's insertion into Grotius' intellectual development and political thought still very much an open question. Suffice it to say here that the sum of positive and negative internal

evidence—more specifically, the absence of references to either acute religious troubles, the political watershed of 1618, or even the Twelve-Year
Truce with Spain, which was concluded in 1609—helped trace the draft-
ing of the document to the opening years of the seventeenth century at
the latest.[25] This in itself much enhanced the probability of Grotius' authorship, as the work's intellectual status would rule out any later dating
within his career. In fact, if the manuscript is indeed to be attributed
to Grotius, the very tenor of the tract would strongly suggest its dating prior to Prince Maurice's epochal victory over the Spanish *tercios*
at Nieuwpoort in Flanders (1600), as its atmosphere seems curiously at
odds with the jubilation breathing from whatever Grotius produced in
the years immediately following this major feat of arms.

This in itself is an intriguing observation inasmuch as the years 1598–
1600 coincide wondrously with Grotius' first established pursuits in the
field of constitutional comparative law and the growing topicality of the
issues to Dutch political circumstance. By virtue of Maurice's successful
campaigns and the first exploits overseas, the Dutch, after some twenty-five years of bitter, uphill fighting, had finally managed to somewhat
shift the balance toward the offensive. They were now confidently looking forward to triumphantly crowning three cumbersome decades by
establishing a sovereign nation of their own, albeit one based on a trun-
cated body of seven provinces out of the seventeen that had revolted back
in 1568. Ever since the recapture of Brussels and Antwerp by Parma in
1585, the Southern Provinces, by all appearances, had been lost for good.
Before analyzing the tract here under consideration, we will now briefly sketch the sociopolitical circumstance by which it was prompted and
young Grotius' position at the time.

The Rise of the Dutch Republic

The political experiment of the Confederacy that constituted the Dutch
Republic stands out as a *rara avis* amidst the absolutism on the rise
throughout Europe at the time. The centralizing of power seemed the
virtually inevitable answer to the chaos of the previous century; to that
extent at least most commentators throughout Europe, whatever their
origin and perspective, readily agreed.[26] Prominent humanists such as

Melanchthon, Budé, and the then-Leiden scholar Justus Lipsius, in his influential *Politica* of 1589, essentially coincided with these views.

However, in 1585, when the urgency of the debate dawned on the Dutch, political observers in the Netherlands concluded on a different course. This was not primarily the outcome of in-depth theoretical speculation, for which, initially at least, the intellectual cadre was far too meager, but rather on the urge of circumstance. If the Dutch revolted against their Hapsburg overlord, it was precisely because, in their opinion, Philip II had alienated himself from his legitimate role, overstepped his invested rights, and usurped what made up the inalienable tenure of the *Staten*, the sovereignty of the provinces. It was Hugo Grotius himself who, in his celebrated *De antiquitate* of 1610, probably best transmitted this message to the outside world, indeed in unequivocal, be they highly controversial terms.[27] The flip side of this medal was of course that to many Dutch observers a constitutional monarchy was never a preferred option. Indeed, the full history of the Dutch Republic (1588–1795) can be encapsulated as an intellectual dilemma and political struggle to safeguard unity and secure an effective administration without relapsing into monarchic rule.

In the complex political debate of the first half century of the Dutch Revolt a few crucial periods can be identified: The first immediately following the disastrous Leicestrian interlude (1585–1587), the second during the years leading up to the Twelve-Year Truce (1609–1621), and the third spanning the years from the 1618 crisis up to the end of the truce in 1621. Both the core thought and all durable problems intrinsic to the Republic over the next two centuries surfaced during these periods.

The tracts of the first period, consisting mostly of anonymous pamphlets, appeared in the aftermath of Leicester's rule and with ensuing resistance to any longer investing a foreign overlord with sovereignty. Understandably, the authors of these pamphlets readily shared an uncompromising stance on provincial sovereignty. The pamphlets led up to the *Korte verthooninghe* of 1587, a first substantial treatise by a Gouda pensionary, François Vranck, which advocated a form of aristocracy mixed with democracy that respected the privileges and obliged the interests of both the landed gentry and the city regents, this last category being recruited from the bourgeois and merchant classes.[28]

All this is not to say that the pro-monarchist argument was entirely absent from the debate.[29] In fact, shortly before 1584, there were numerous calls to invest the popular William of Orange with sovereignty. After the latter's assassination, his son, Prince Maurice, was another ready candidate. However, with the years, and spurred on by the dominant province of Holland and its influential Landsadvocaat, Johan van Oldenbarnevelt, the preference for an aristocratic form of government within a true republic, a so-called aristocratic republicanism, prevailed.

By the same token, in their day-to-day lives, the Dutch were, from very early on, faced with the somewhat embarrassing flip sides of provincial sovereignty—overall particularism, regional friction, and the pettiness and *eigensouckelijkheid* of city magistrates. The seven provinces, thrown together in their outcry over the alleged abuse of power by the Hapsburg king, soon found out that, apart from sharing a common enemy, there was nothing much to bind them. In fact, in political terms, conflicts were lurking around every corner. Traditions and insights varied enormously, whether social stratification, religious denomination, or commercial interests were considered. In short, numerous were the stumbling blocks precluding the provinces from growing into a veritable union and confederacy.

It is this circumstance that, quite naturally, prompted commentaries such as the one here under consideration for the improvement, or rather implementation, of a true republic.[30] By and large, these commentaries can be divided into three classes: theoretical expositions on the best form of government, such as Paulus Buys' *De Republica* (1613) and Paulus Merula's *Commentariolus de statu Confederatorum Belgii* (1618); reprints or translations of foreign authors, such as Johannes Meursius' critical edition of Constantinus Porphyrogenetes' *De Administrando Ingenio* of 1611 or editions of Althusius' pivotal *Politica* in 1602, 1610, and 1614; and finally, descriptions of foreign constitutions, which we will discuss later.

Meanwhile, for all their efforts, the influence of these authors was never decisive enough to heal the wound. It was only on the strength of this circumstance that an essentially theological conflict such as the one which kept two professors at Leiden University, the bulwark of Calvinist orthodoxy, divided could surface as social strife and from there flare up to political crisis. Indeed, nothing much was required to unbalance the Republic's fragile equilibrium. In a way, the crisis of 1618 was the virtually inevitable outcome of a long process of fermentation, fostered as much by the innate zealousness of ministers or the inveterate rivalry of city councils as it was spurred by the conflicting ambitions of the strong-headed

Landsadvocaat Oldenbarnevelt and proud Prince Maurice of Orange.[31] Inasmuch as the first contestant represented the enlightened regents and merchant class of the dominant province of Holland, with time the other quite naturally came to pose as the self-imposed champion of the States General and the common man.

At a fairly early phase, young Grotius, who had migrated from Leiden to The Hague by 1600, there to become an attorney at the bar and a private counselor to Oldenbarnevelt himself, was keenly aware of his nation's precarious position. This can be documented with reference to public memorials from around the second period of 1607, the opening months of the protracted negotiations which would result in the Twelve-Year Truce of 1609.[32] There is every reason to suggest their endorsement by Grotius, if not to actually ascribe their authorship to him, inasmuch as their tenets are in line with his private correspondence.[33]

The United Netherlands, it is argued here, is not really a republic but actually seven separate provinces, which among themselves have nothing in common but a military defensive alliance, a contract that is otherwise respected only too lukewarmly. During long decades of war, it is asserted, nothing anywhere aspiring to a common administration or a steady republic had ever materialized, apart from a kind of provisional arrangement as if *sede vacante* or *durante interregno*. And even this in itself precarious, if not downright dangerous, arrangement was only upheld precisely on account of the imminent peril of foreign invasion. Any overtures to peace that abated the urgency of this threat would render the fabric torn. Peace would rend asunder, from sheer jealousy and slackness, whatever unity had prevailed so far; indeed, it would prompt the very anarchy and confusion that had induced the Spanish to make their peace proposals in the first place. In short, as the ready conclusion read, a central administration had to be installed, to be recruited from the regent class and profiting from its civic virtues. It was to be vested with full authority to govern the lands without prior consultation of the unifying elements, and rally provinces and city magistrates, perforce if need be— or else the so-called republic would be lost.

It was Grotius' intimate Johannes Meursius, tutor to the sons of Oldenbarnevelt himself, who, with hindsight, would formulate this ideal in his *Areopagus* of 1624. Still, as early as 1595, the visionary Justus Lipsius, in a private *sendtbrief*, had ruefully advised the Spanish king to conclude a truce with the Dutch, arguing that their republic was internally divided to the bone and unity about to collapse.[34] Himself victimized by the jealousy and intolerance at Leiden, Lipsius had by then once more found refuge in Louvain and the Catholic faith.

If the above-mentioned memorials would lead us to conclude that by 1607 Hugo Grotius, for his part, had become a steadfast opponent to the peace Oldenbarnevelt championed, it must be said that ever since 1604 the Landsadvocaat had been in a tight spot. His once staunch allies, France and Britain, had both reached peace with Spain in 1598 and 1604, respectively. In the military sphere, the clash between Prince Maurice and Count Spinola had ended in a perfect deadlock. Facing an empty war chest, an imminent failure of the VOC, and a French king only too keen to expand his protectorate, Oldenbarnevelt must have felt caught between a rock and a hard place.

In the overtures to peace, Dutch aspirations of unrestricted sovereignty were crushed by the Spanish demand that the Dutch forthwith abandon their profitable overseas trade. A diplomatic stalemate presented itself, which was then wound off in a truce that would soon make Grotius' worst fears come true. In September 1609, he intimated to the French diplomat Jeannin, a friend of his, that a recent visit to the province of Zealand had perfectly disillusioned him. If the consensus among the other provinces was mediocre at best, quarrels with Zealand were endless. Also, the incessant internal strife among Zealand's various cities and factions—which he deemed as imprudent as they were impudent—undermined, indeed ridiculed, the authority of the States General and any concept of common justice, with the predictable outcome: *quae quo tendant facilis est coniectura* (it is easy to guess where they are headed).[35] It is interesting to see the considerable extent to which these views coincide with the apprehensions first expressed in *De Republica Emendanda*.

The crisis, in short, came as no surprise, and the conclusions to be drawn from the experience with Oldenbarnevelt's aristocratic republic were neatly summarized in 1621 by the Zealand pensionary Johannes de Brune in his *Grond-steenen van een vaste regieringe* (*Foundations of a Firm Government*), a steadfast plea for a mixed form of government with the *duplex ordo* of piety and justice as cornerstones of the Republic, and an appeal for the abolition of the previous tolerance, which had merely prompted license.[36] Sovereignty without popular support, it was argued here, only invited the craving for self-interest and power of the *raison d'état*, while religious issues were discussed in the marketplace only at the risk of civil strife. After a long quest which had ended in crisis, the republicanism that represented the optimism of the early decades of the Dutch Revolt was to be supplanted by a mixed constitution. We will now turn to the role of state parallels in the process sketched above.

Political Parallels

Within the Dutch debate, among the political models that were hailed as exemplary or worthy of imitation, one must distinguish between contemporary and historical parallels.[37] Prominent within the first category was the model of the Swiss Confederacy, a genre represented by Simler's *De Republycke van Switserlandt* (*Republic of Switzerland*) of 1613 and François le Petit's *Nederlandsche Republycke... vergeleken met die van de Swytsersche cantoenen* (*Dutch Republic Compared with the Swiss Cantons*) of 1615. Tracts on the Venetian constitution are in a distinct class of their own. These too have a long pedigree in the Dutch Republic, which amounts to what has been coined as "The Venetian Myth."[38] Admittedly, most of these tracts date from a slightly later period, opening with a 1628 Leiden edition of Contarini's *De Republica Venetorum* (*On the Republic of the Venetians*). This is followed in 1631 by the edition of Giannotti's *Dialogi*, which was rendered into Dutch in 1667; followed by Graswinckel's *Libertas Veneta* of 1634; Thysius' panegyric on Venice of 1645; translations of Nanni's historiography in 1685–1700; and finally, Van Hoogstraten's monograph on Venice of 1715.

If this sequence attests to the lasting topicality of the issues to the Dutch intellectual debate, still, the keen interest of the Dutch, indeed of Hugo Grotius himself, in the Venetian model is documented well before 1628. Among Grotius' earliest works is his 1599 translation of a tract on piloting, by a lifelong friend of his, Simon Stevin of Bruges, Maurice's tried and trusted engineer, who incidentally authored *Vita Politica* (*Political Life*) in 1590.[39] Grotius' dedication of this *Limenheuretike* (*Finding a Harbor*), or *Havenvinding*, of 1599 is addressed to the Venetian doge.[40] Again, the following year, when publishing his astronomical treatise *Syntagma Arateorum* (*Collection of Aratus' Works*), otherwise an astounding philological achievement, Grotius once more addressed his dedication to the doge in a vast eulogy of Venice and a lengthy comparison of the mercantile aspirations and aristocratic constitutions of both republics.[41]

If the above attests somewhat to Grotius' acute interest in state parallels already by 1600, he would soon provide further testimony. This leads us to consider the second category of state models, being the historical parallels. During 1600–1602 Grotius had completed ample research for a comprehensive comparison of Dutch society with the ancient Greek and Roman commonwealths in three books entitled *Parallelon rerumpublicarum*, of which only a single book has come down to us.[42] We will elaborate on this later; for now this suffices to establish Grotius' keen interest in not only contemporary but also ancient constitutions. The relevance of this observation becomes manifest once we turn to discuss another great tradition in Holland, the mirroring of the Dutch with the ancient Hebrew confederation.

In the period under consideration, both political observers and religious leaders in Holland were positively inspired by what they saw as a wondrous resemblance of the vicissitudes of the tribes of Israel and the Dutch Republic. Both nations, the Hebrew and the Dutch, had rewon their independence and regained the true faith by trial. The idea is suitably epitomized by the prince of Dutch poets, Joost van den Vondel, in the line cited in the title of this paper.[43] Clearly, this parallel was gratefully acknowledged by politicians to underscore the righteousness of their cause and the privileged status of the Dutch as God's chosen people, as much as it was by clergymen with a view to imposing the most stringent orthodoxy, indeed to the point of aspiring to turn the Republic into a theocracy. Biblical references, imagery, and similitudes became ubiquitous in Dutch society, as attested to by the works that emerged from the worlds of scholarship, literature, and the visual arts alike.

Among the earliest political tracts in the field is *De observatione politiae Moysis* (*On the Preservation of the State of Moses*) of 1593 by no less a figure than Franciscus Junius, author of *Grammatica linguae Hebreae* (*Grammar of the Hebrew Language*) of 1590 and, more important for our purposes, prominent among Grotius' early teachers. Junius was the man with whom the young genius found lodgings during his student years and who, in Grotius' own words, was decisive in instilling an essentially irenic imprint on him for the remainder of his life.[44] Again, in 1608, Sigonius' *De Republica Hebraeorum* was reprinted in the Netherlands, followed in 1617 by the epitome of the tradition there, Petrus Cunaeus' authoritative treatise, which bore the same title as Sigonius' and incorporated all the lore accumulated by him, Pagninus, and Bertram or, for that matter, by Fricius Modrevius of Poland.[45]

Now to return briefly to Junius. According to both Cunaeus and Scaliger, Franciscus Junius, for all his renown, was not much of an authority on Hebrew studies. For expertise in that field they much preferred another scholar, far less widely known, Johan Boreel, a politician and pensionary from Zealand who wrote a learned commentary on the book of Daniel, was an expert in Oriental languages, had traveled extensively in the Middle East, and, along the way, had amassed an extremely valuable collection of manuscripts and Orientalia, which mostly ended up in Cambridge University Library. Boreel was also an intimate of Hugo Grotius.[46] Actually, it was Boreel who first interviewed the Alexandrian patriarch Meletius Pegas, who lent his name to Grotius' well-known "open letter" to Boreel of 1611, entitled *Meletius*, in which Grotius first developed his essentially irenic thesis. This is the same Boreel who was given credit by Cunaeus for having introduced him to the works of Maimonides, Sigonius, and all the others and who probably inspired him to conceive his *De Republica Hebraeorum* in the first place.

Meanwhile, throughout the period here under consideration, Hebrew and Oriental studies flourished at Leiden, and young Grotius was on intimate terms with all of the most prominent figures: Scaliger himself, first and foremost; but likewise the longstanding professor of Hebrew Franciscus Raphelengius, who taught him some elementary Arabic in 1605; or for that matter Thomas Erpenius, who was of particular assistance during Grotius' years of imprisonment and in a way was instrumental in his spectacular escape.[47] Again, in the north of the country, at Franeker, another former Leiden professor of international standing, Joannes Drusius, spearheaded a booming center of Oriental studies. Drusius' courses were attended by Cunaeus.

And this brings us to Cunaeus. He and Grotius were on fairly intimate terms throughout. Grotius was involved with the genesis of Cunaeus' *De Republica Hebraeorum*, which was ready by 1614, as much as Cunaeus was involved with Grotius' many tracts in the years 1610–1618, which dealt with all the vexed and intertwined issues of the day, ranging from predestination and the Lord's grace to appointments at Leiden University, matters of church and state, and irenicism. Prior to their publication, drafts of all these tracts were sent to Cunaeus for review.[48] A professor of Latin at Leiden from 1612 onward, added to by a tenure in politics soon afterward, Cunaeus with time felt ever more attracted to the study of law. A restless and brilliant mind, he seems to have been a courageous enough character as well. Amid the growing tension at Leiden in 1613, he ventured to publish a satire, *Sardi Venales* (*Fools for Sale*), in which he ridiculed pedant university dons and dismissed the Remonstrant troubles as the plaything of arrogant theologians and perfectly ignorant clergymen. The pamphlet caused student riots and the canceling of courses for weeks on end—apparently without at all damaging Cunaeus' reputation in official circles. Having completed his legal thesis in 1615 and following a brief interval at the Hague court, Cunaeus soon returned to his alma mater to be entrusted with the teaching of courses on Justinian's *Digests* and later on the *Pandects* and *Codex*.

In his varying capacities as a first-rate linguist and Hebraist, a prominent literator, and a student of both law and politics, Cunaeus may justly be called the Dutch counterpart of John Selden in Britain. The interesting thing is that the two foremost Dutch and British protagonists of the Hebrew confederacy were to cross swords over quite a different issue, and this leads us back to Grotius. At some stage, Selden was commissioned by his government to formally counter Hugo Grotius' *Mare Liberum*, the Dutchman's pivotal tract from 1609 on the freedom of the seas. In 1635, Selden, to that end, published his *Mare Clausum* (*A Closed Sea*). The following year, with Grotius himself in exile in Paris, it was Petrus Cunaeus who was commissioned by the States of Holland, in his capacity as counsel on matters of commerce and trade, to pass judgment on Selden's thesis.

The Context of 'De Republica Emendanda'

The above has served to establish Grotius' keen and lasting interest in all three elements which together must have brought about the tract here under consideration: an acute political awareness, an inclination to state parallels, and some familiarity with the ongoing debate on the relevance of the Hebrew confederacy to contemporary commonwealths. We will now see what expertise Grotius could have mustered by about 1600, the most likely date of origin of the tract.

By 1598, at the age of fifteen, the precocious youngster's mostly philological pursuits over the preceding four years at Leiden University were cut short by his attendance of Oldenbarnevelt's diplomatic mission to Fontainebleau in a futile attempt on the part of the Dutch administration to preclude the Peace of Vervins between France and Spain. Grotius eminently availed himself of the trip abroad to earn a doctorate of law at Orléans. Upon his return he published two astrological tracts, produced a wealth of liminary poetry that glorified the feats of arms of Prince Maurice,[49] and intriguingly commented in verse on the political barometer of Europe.[50] By December 1599, Grotius had definitely turned to The Hague and to practicing law.

In 1601 the first of Grotius' three biblical tragedies along Senecan lines, *Adamus exul* (*Adam in Exile*), saw light.[51] In an epilogue to this publication, *Lectori* (*To the Reader*), which incidentally contained a wealth of poetical paraphrases of texts from both Testaments, the young genius proudly refers to his "work in progress."[52] Of all the titles advertised here, nothing ever materialized in printed form, due precisely to the subsequent spectacular rise of his professional career—already by 1604 he had been officially appointed state historiographer. The following year saw him at work on behalf of the VOC in defense of the capture of a Portuguese *caraque*. From this emanated *De jure praedae* (*On the Laws of Booty*) and eventually the celebrated *Mare Liberum*.[53]

Meanwhile, the drafts referred to in the epilogue to *Adamus exul* are not without interest in our context. Reference is made to a dialogue entitled *Philarchaeus* (*The Lover of Antiquities*), which was lost altogether, but in which, according to its author, Moses' sacred history was confirmed by numerous pagan testimonies—"that is, if one may say so of something which is inherently certain and is not in want of external support to lend credibility to it."[54] In this dialogue, numerous data on Egyptian, Phoenician, Orphic, and Pythagorean theology were amassed. In other words, in the period here under consideration, Grotius was well steeped in Mosaic law. This is also testified to by the proficiency in Mosaic law he displayed in *Adamus exul*, his tragedy on "paradise lost," which served as a model for Milton's epic.

Are these projects and his network of Orientalists to suggest a solid command of Oriental languages, particularly of Hebrew, on Grotius' part? Commentators have widely disagreed on this.[55] At the end of the day it would seem that his knowledge of rabbinical literature was rudimentary and his command of postbiblical Hebrew slight at best. So much for certain, the *sine qua non* at the time for the intimate reading of the Talmud, namely a Jewish teacher, is not documented in Grotius' case, unlike in the cases of Scaliger, Drusius, and Erpenius. It would seem that whatever knowledge of Hebrew young Grotius had mastered was based on the teachings of Junius, himself a pupil of Tremellius, along with snatches gained from his intimacy with Scaliger. One should recall and appreciate that it was quite probably Scaliger himself who steered Grotius' early projects. If Grotius' courses in Arabic with Raphelengius as late as 1605 suggest a sincere scholarly interest, by the same token, the singular increase of references to and quotes from Judaic sources in Grotius' works from the last decade of his life coincides with the increasing availability of Latin translations. To conclude, it would seem that Grotius' eagerness, throughout his life, to have a network of specialized contacts ready at hand was precisely meant to succor his own rudimentary knowledge whenever this seemed opportune.

Now, to return to *Adamus exul*, in its above-mentioned epilogue another intriguing reference is found to his ongoing work on "*nostratis reipublicae cum aliis olim nobilibus, successuumque inter se comparatio*" ("comparison of our own state with the great states of the past, and of their respective successes"),[56] in short, historical state parallels. This reference has always been interpreted as referring to the above-mentioned *Parallelon rerumpublicarum*; the draft of the preserved part of this project was clearly finished by the summer of 1602, and from there the manuscript circulated among Grotius' friends until the project was abandoned altogether by 1606.[57]

Now there can be no doubt that *De Republica Emendanda* and *Parallelon rerumpublicarum* are works of essentially different natures. The most conspicuous aspect of the latter tract is its endless eulogy of the unity of the seven provinces, to the point where the author begs the question. If anything, whether or not against his better judgment, this approach was brought on by Grotius' wishful thinking. Be that as it may, the tract definitely attests to his keen eye for the acuteness of the situation and the relevance of this genre of writing. Primarily meant for the general public, *Parallelon*, one may conclude, was intended as an admonition to his compatriots not to fall into the same traps that had brought down the Greek and Roman commonwealths. Now, this jubilant tone is singularly absent from Grotius' comparison between the Dutch and Hebrew constitutions, which, if anything, shows the author's sincere concern with the *mesalliance* of the seven provinces. This in itself may suggest that *De Republica Emendanda* was meant for private circulation and internal debate. Meanwhile, Grotius' reference in the 1601 epilogue to *Adamus exul*, if deemed to definitely allude to his *Parallelon*, should not as a consequence be precluded from referring also to his *De Republica Emendanda*.

The Contents of the Tract

The text of *De Republica Emendanda* consists of sixty-four paragraphs that fall into three well-distinguished segments:

First, a comparison of the Hebrew and Dutch constitutions in most general terms (pars. 1–27), including:

(i)   A comparison of legislation in the fields of sacred and civil law (pars. 6–13)

(ii)   A discussion of the best possible constitution according to political theorists and divine revelation (pars. 14–19)

(iii) An inquiry into the nature of the Hebrew kingship (pars. 20–27).

Second, a full analysis of the Hebrew constitutions (pars. 28–42), covering:

(i)   A proposition of method and a working definition of the true republic (pars. 28–29)

(ii)   A structural examination of the Hebrew commonwealth at the levels of township, tribe, and nation (pars. 30–32)

(iii) A structural examination of the major bodies operative at each level: the principal, council, and assembly (pars. 33–34)

(iv)   The council as supreme authoritative body at each level, and the conclusion as to the role of this council as the sovereign body within the unity of twelve tribes (pars. 35–42).

Last, a discussion of the form of government operative in the republic (pars. 43–64), consisting of:

(i)   A historical synopsis of the genesis of the republic (pars. 43–49)

(ii)   Its shortcomings at each level (pars. 50–58)

(iii) Recommendations for emendation: the centralization of power and the sovereignty of the council (pars. 59–64).

The tract abounds with references to suggest that, whether based on original research or not, Grotius' command of biblical and historical sources was impressive. There is nothing surprising here. Grotius pursued biblical studies throughout his life. His bulky *Annotationes*, the harvest of a lifetime of painstaking research, are an acknowledged source of exegesis in the Netherlands and exemplary in their philological approach.[58]

Having said this, and in all fairness to the author, *De Republica Emendanda*, in spite of all the humanist lore, philosophical niceties, and historical parallels, is, first and foremost, a very practical proposal for the emendation of the Dutch Republic, and we should never be fooled about its ultimate purport. If, rather than drawing parallels with contemporary polities, Grotius harks back to the Hebrew commonwealth, he had very good reasons to do so. First, he paid lip service to the widely felt affinity in Calvinist Holland toward the ancient Hebrew nation and to the popular belief, so readily kindled by the zealot clergy, of a far-reaching similarity between the natures, constitutions, and statuses of the two commonwealths. To this end, Grotius emphasizes the parallels between the salutary history of the Jewish nation up to the Roman domination and the history of the Dutch Revolt.[59] This parallel was suggestive of a special kind of divine patronage the Dutch Republic was supposed to enjoy and which only confirmed the truth of Calvinist orthodoxy. In the dedication of Cunaeus' tract of 1617, a much similar approach can be observed in the reference to the "*coniunctio animorumque conspiratio*" with the Hebrew nation "*qua nulla umquam in terris sanctior, nec bonis exemplis ditior fuit*" ("the holiest ever to have existed in the world, and the richest in examples for us to emulate").[60]

Still, a more powerful argument is advanced. The current shortcomings of the Dutch polity and its defective political practice only served to emphasize the imperfections of the *ratio humana*, for all its good intentions. Human political insights must by their very nature be inferior to that superior source of knowledge, *divina revelatio*, as contained in the laws of Moses. Since the Hebrew nation was the only one to have drawn from this source, its constitution must, by its very nature, be the superior one.[61] Clearly, there was nothing new about this line of reasoning. The argument was advanced and elaborated in full detail by prominent sixteenth-century authors in the field such as Bertram and Sigonius, to whom we have referred above—and Grotius was well aware of the tradition, which he invokes consistently, without otherwise bothering too much over credentials. In his turn, Cunaeus draws from the same source: "*quoniam illa hercle non hominem quemquam mortali concretioni satum, sed ipsum Deum immortalem, autorem fundatoremque habet*" ("because its creator and founder was not some man sprung from mortal matter, but immortal God himself").[62]

All this seems nice and innocent enough. From here on, however, Grotius brings down his main argument with full force. In paragraphs 14–17 he presents a survey of human reasoning throughout the ages with

respect to the three main constitutional concepts: Monarchy, aristocracy, and democracy. His conclusions are as one would expect: Grotius'
outspoken preference for the *optimates*, that is, the aristocratic form of
government, is well known from many sources, as, for that matter, is
his abomination of tyranny and his abhorrence of the *vulgus*. In this
context it is opportune to point out the importance of Grotius' biblical
dramas as a vehicle for his political tenets. Sixteenth- and seventeenth-
century drama all over Europe was eminently politicized. These were
pièces à clé, pièces à thèse mostly. Grotius' three plays—on *Adamus exul*
(*Adam in Exile*, 1601), *Christus patiens* (*The Passion of Christ*, 1608),
and *Sophompaneas* (*Joseph in Egypt*, 1635)—for all intents and purposes,
comment on acute topical issues, echoing the author's personal tenets under the veil of biblical circumstance. We will have occasion to illustrate
this below. To return to the tract here under consideration, in spite of a
wealth of treatises to the contrary and contemporary practice all around,
Grotius readily argues:

> Some support the idea of monarchy as being the reflection of this
> supreme power which so intelligently rules the universe. Some in-
> sist on investing the people with autonomy and assert that nature
> itself strongly suggests that all men are equal. But then there are
> men to whom neither the rule of a single man nor that of all men
> together is pleasing, and they maintain that it is inherent in hu-
> man destiny that the best way always turns out to lie in the middle.
> Most sensible indeed are they who insist on a certain combination
> of these, in the sense that a single state embraces the majesty of a
> prince, the authority of a senate, and the freedom of a people.[63]

He then concludes:

> Also, it should be stipulated that the same things do not equally
> befit all people. However, an aristocratic government seems to suit
> the nation best which loves its freedom as much as it shows re-
> spect to virtue; and experience teaches us that whenever a nation
> shakes off the yoke of tyranny, this is the most likely alternative to
> replace it.[64]

The Hebrew King

Grotius then turns to the core of his argument, the form of constitution which "God himself selected for his chosen people." Drawing from Josephus,[65] he argues that both Samuel and Moses readily agreed on aristocracy. He cites Moses as having said:

> [T]he best thing is aristocracy and the way of life that is associated with it. May the longing for another civil regime never creep upon you, but rather cherish this kind of constitution, respect the authority of my laws, and live up to them. For God is the only supreme emperor you need.[66]

In similar tenor God, through Moses, explicitly disapproved of democracy[67] and of monarchy, as Grotius argues with reference to Samuel[68] and Gideon.[69] However, one way or the other, Grotius could not possibly dismiss forthwith the unequivocal references in Deuteronomy in which God actually recommended a king to the Israelites once they had taken possession of the promised land,[70] or the references in Judges to the license of the mob due precisely to the absence of a king.[71] This spurred him into a commentary on the nature of this kingship.[72] Having discussed the absolute nature of Oriental kingdoms[73] and observed in passing that both Moses and David, in their respective capacities of lawgiver and military commander, were addressed as "king,"[74] he concludes that there were two categories of monarchy, dependent on the king's position before the law. With reference to Aristotle and Homer,[75] he comments on the nature of the so-called kings who ruled among the Spartans, and who, in all respects but their military command alone, acted effectively as *primus inter pares*. Quoting from Josephus, he has Moses himself comment: "Consider God as your supreme commander with plenary powers; but elect as his lieutenant a man of outstanding virtue."[76] This "Laconian" kingship, in Grotius' perception clearly the one recommended by the Lord, he finds documented in the figures of Samuel[77] and Joshua.[78] Acting to the contrary was the damnable figure of Abimelech, who seized power, abolished the aristocracy, and proclaimed himself above the law and the judiciary.[79]

The latter phenomenon was not incidental. In biblical practice, numerous indeed were the kings who freely committed adultery and robbery without ever being called to account in the way the Spartan kings were, for the very reason that their absolute power made them untouchable. The story of Absalom was enlightening in this respect.[80] However, this ran counter to Jahweh's intentions, inasmuch as there was no point in concluding a covenant with him in the first place when a king who felt like violating the treaty could not be stopped anyway. As Aristotle, "the first of philosophers," had wisely observed: "he who confers power upon the law joins forces with God, whereas he who entrusts power to man joins the Beast."[81] References to a "king" in the Mosaic tradition, Grotius concludes, may well have implied a kind of collective authority, combining political and judicial elements, rather than a single head of state.[82]

Historicity

The above is highlighted as exemplary of Grotius' kind of reasoning, a method which is upheld throughout the tract and notably in its second major excursus, an extensive description of the Sanhedrin. The role of the Sanhedrin is emphasized by Grotius as much as by any of his predecessors, and again for very pragmatic reasons. The method applied throughout is typical of the eclectic humanist approach, and Grotius would avail himself of the concept time and again, in his *Parallelon rerumpublicarum* and, most conspicuously, in his celebrated *De antiquitate*, in which the time-honored supremacy of the States General is reconstructed from Roman and medieval sources and "proved" beyond dispute.[83]

Clearly, there is no need for further scrutiny of the historicity of these biblical references. They are selected and arranged to serve a well-defined, preset purport, to mirror the ideal Grotius has set himself for the Dutch Republic. In paragraph 42 he draws his major conclusion, to wit, that "the true Hebrew republic" was not the township or tribe but rather the society made up of the twelve tribes together and in which the senate held supreme power. Twenty-seven paragraphs later, having dealt with the Dutch constitution in much similar terms, he draws the conclusion that the similarities between the Hebrew and Dutch republics are indeed "so many and so striking that you might rightly wonder why we should not reasonably hope that, given such a similar model, we can simply adapt the few remaining points of difference."[84] These "few remaining points," however, concern the two major features of the Hebrew constitution, to wit, the primacy of the union and the central role of the Sanhedrin! To be sure, changes should not be implemented overnight, the invariably conservative Grotius argues: "Every nation has its own morals and a nature of its own, and particular institutions corresponding to them." To copy these "just like that" would lead to a "complete dissimilar duplicate." Also, and here the Grotius of *De antiquitate* comes to the fore: "if there is no obvious advantage in change, then as a rule the change itself causes great inconvenience."[85]

Shortcomings of the Dutch Constitution

The last fifteen paragraphs of *De Republica Emendanda* are reserved for a survey of shortcomings of the Dutch Republic and specific recommendations for its amendment. The Republic's major defects, it is argued here, concern both the interrelation of the various bodies within its respective communities (townships and provinces) and the attitude of the communities toward each other. In this respect, precious lessons could be drawn from the Hebrew model. In that ancient commonwealth, obviously, the council constituted the highest authority within each community, and the greatest community equaled the true republic. Given this model the current Dutch equivalent fell short in both respects. Within the townships, a proper hierarchy was lacking, in that the citizenry increasingly exerted its influence upon the magistrates, while the latter, in turn, tended to affect the supreme power of the senate and, by party strife and turmoil, jeopardize overall stability.

Likewise, at the provincial level, Grotius considered the states too powerful and the role of the councilors too restricted. Delegates, more often than not, acted primarily in the interest of the township that delegated them and to which they were bound by oath, rather than keeping in mind the overall interest. This circumstance prompted endless disagreement, again at the cost of the public interest. The same could be observed at the highest level, the union of the provinces. Here, councilors who were held under obligation by their provinces actually eroded the authority of the Council of State, the body which should have represented and preserved the highest common interest.

As Grotius concludes in paragraph 55, unlike the Hebrew model, the so-called United Provinces did not constitute a true republic, but merely a confederacy and a kind of alliance in case of war. The best proof thereof was that the leaders of the confederate body lacked the authority to reform provincial laws, and in case of a dispute between provinces there was no constitutional court of justice to which to appeal. In short, every province possessed the full rights of a true republic. This situation, Grotius argues, mirrored that of the Hebrew state between the days of Joshua and Samuel, as recorded in Judges,[86] when each tribe adopted a policy of its own and waged wars of its own, which resulted in the neglect of the true faith, worship of idols, internal strife, tyranny, and, the greatest of all evils, civil war. Grotius then cites the well-known saying of Tacitus about the Greek city-states of old and the Germans and Britons of his own time: "inasmuch as they fought individually, they were collectively conquered."[87] By comparison he praises the Achaean League, which united the whole of the Peloponnese and to that extent could serve as a great model for the Dutch Republic.[88]

Recommendations

Grotius then concludes upon a set of very specific recommendations. The central organ of the true Dutch Republic should be the Council ("Senatus"), which should be authorized to enact laws of general purport and decide autonomously on all matters of war, peace, and alliances. This Council should comprise the wisest men from all provinces, though not in their capacity as representatives of these provinces. They should be elected for a life term and the body be replenished through co-optation. In much the same way as with the Hebrew priests, this Council should include pious men with expertise in church administration. Meanwhile, it should be presided over by the highest prefect, who is to act as commander in chief. In a similar vein, Grotius concludes, taxes should be centralized, a single Treasury established, and a united military and a single currency imposed. Grotius then invites others to elaborate on these outlines.

Grotius' Position circa 1600 and Subsequent Views

From the above it can be established that, as early as 1600, young Grotius entertained sincere apprehensions about the consistent discord within and among the townships, provinces, and various classes of the Dutch population and genuine concern with their widely dissenting views on many fundamental issues of general purport. What Grotius claims, in as many words, is that the widely acclaimed "republic" had actually never materialized and should indeed be implemented forthwith. It is a fairly bleak picture he sketches of a society running wild. As stipulated above, the sketch is singularly at odds with the picture drawn some three years later in the *Parallelon rerumpublicarum*. Is this to say that in between things had dramatically changed for the better? Certainly not. Admittedly, the military victory in Flanders had come as a great relief, but the hazardous expedition, pushed through by Oldenbarnevelt against the better judgment of the much more cautious Prince Maurice, had brought to the surface the widely differing views and personal antagonism between the Republic's two leading politicians. None of the core issues had changed, and Grotius must have been well aware of this. Clearly, the *Parallelon* was meant for a different audience, the critical angle for once having been supplanted by an adhortative approach.

Still, one recalls the *Memorien* mentioned above and dating from approximately 1607. Here a tenor is felt to prevail that is much similar to *De Republica Emendanda*, with a desperate tinge at that. For this, there was ample reason. By that juncture, the military deadlock resulting from Count Spinola's counteroffensive against Maurice, along with the financial dire straits of the leading province of Holland, had definitely cornered Oldenbarnevelt. With James I alienated and the French king lying in wait to take over sovereignty, the Dutch by 1608 were left with little choice but to accept the ingeniously alluring terms presented by Madrid and Brussels. At that critical moment, Grotius once more voiced protest, advancing that the worst enemy was actually lurking inside the body politic and that foreign war, whatever its cost, would at all times be preferable to civil strife. In his second biblical drama, *Christus patiens* of 1608,[89] which at heart is a warm plea for conciliation, he vividly portrays the blind frenzy of the mobs and the unsettling zealousness of the pharisaeans in terms which echo his own experience with the Dutch clergy.[90]

Within a year from the day the truce was concluded, in 1610, the bomb exploded at Leiden University. Three years later, discord on Calvinist orthodoxy had divided the nation to the bone.[91] Grotius' next reference to the problem is to be distilled, again in an almost oblique way, in his very deliberately irenic tract *Meletius* of 1611, an open letter to his friend Boreel, which lends a penetrating insight into Dutch society.[92] In the opening paragraphs, Grotius muses philosophically on this curious phenomenon that Europeans, when roaming the Middle East, tend to greet any fellow Europeans they meet as dear friends and almost as relatives, whereas they would perfectly ignore the same men when coming across them within the European compass.

> Likewise we ourselves who live in these parts not only consider the other Europeans as foreigners, but even we as Germans are differentiated as High and Low Germans. Firstly, the Low Germans are kept divided by the recollection of a war which is hardly over; next, some are Guelders and others Frisians; and would that the peoples of Holland and Zealand, who always used to be closely connected, differed only in name and not also in sympathy! Not to mention at this point the cities—rival centers rather—the quarrels between city districts, or the enmity between the great families. When we take all this into consideration, there is no doubt that neighbors and relatives seem more alien to one another than Italians or even Spaniards seemed to you when you stayed in Syria.[93]

The year 1613 was to become the crucial one. Misinterpreting the outcome of a lengthy personal interview with James I when visiting London as the head of the Dutch delegation to the Colonial Conference,[94] and erroneously satisfied with the king's support for Oldenbarnevelt's essentially Erastian policy, Grotius, provoked by a vehement pamphlet questioning the States' policy,[95] and for once throwing all warnings from friends to the winds, penned a vehement treatise on the authority of the States in church matters.[96] The repercussions were disastrous. In fact, the total of irenic tracts written by Grotius throughout his lifetime would not add up to counterbalance the damage done by this single invective and its sequels. In the year when, at Oldenbarnevelt's instigation, he was being appointed pensionary of Rotterdam and thereby offered the stepping-stone to the eventual position of Landsadvocaat, Grotius, through the *Ordinum Pietas* (*On the Discretion of the States*), lost all credibility with the strict orthodox clergy in Holland. As his spouse would correctly analyze in retrospect, from that moment on his career was doomed.

Ever-more cornered, Oldenbarnevelt, also at Grotius' prompting, decided on ever-more stringent resolutions to enforce peace in the land. In 1616, Grotius himself rendered a gem of a speech in the Amsterdam City Council in a desperate but futile attempt to win the city over to Oldenbarnevelt. By then, Maurice had made up his mind and thrown in his lot with the other faction. And Grotius? The man who in 1601, when proudly presenting a copy of his *Adamus exul* to no less a figure than Justus Lipsius, had argued in a complementary letter that whatever he would write in his life would be devoid of all partisanship and be aimed exclusively at the *katholikon kai oikoumenikon*,[97] had nonetheless been lured by party politics into irreparable bias.

At that juncture of 1616, Grotius was consulted by a dear friend of his, the prominent literator P.C. Hooft, on the epilogue of his forthcoming political play *Baeto*, which focuses on the life of the legendary ancestor of all Batavians.[98] The play was meant to grace the ceremonial opening of the new playhouse in Amsterdam.[99] Hooft's dilemma was whether or not *Baeto* should be raised on the shield, according to German custom (the *elevatio*). In other words, should one present the prince of Orange with the *principatus* so as to unite the people under his banner? Grotius, who in 1610, in his *De antiquitate*, before all Europe had steadfastly advocated the time-honored and unrestricted sovereignty of the States General, after ample consideration seems to have reluctantly concluded to the affirmative. One is inclined to read in this counsel Grotius' implicit admission of the failure of Oldenbarnevelt's policy, which had also been his own.

Fate, however, would ordain differently. The tumor would linger on for another two years, then finally come to a head in Prince Maurice's *coup d'état* of August 1618, which brought Oldenbarnevelt to the scaffold and Grotius to Loevestein, as a mere prelude to twenty-five years of exile and a complete reorientation of his life and thought. Maurice's *coup* would never solve the riddle. The innate particularism, political bipartition, and, to a lesser extent, religious strife would keep the Republic divided until the Napoleonic era, and numerous were the victims that would fall on the anvil.

The Intrinsic Value of 'De Republica Emendanda'

As we stipulated above, the tract here under consideration abounds with shortcomings. Still, these seem to evaporate instantly before the incontestable fact that *De Republica Emendanda* stands out as a first-ever synopsis on the part of the most outstanding and consummate intellectual of the first quarter of the seventeenth century in the Netherlands with regard to the most crucial dilemmas that clung to, indeed paralyzed, the political experiment that was meant to shoulder the triumphant Dutch Republic. From his early teens, Grotius' life was determined by precisely the issues that were first tackled, ever so hesitantly, in this tract. Its feeble voice from the first decade of the Republic prefigures the virtual inevitability of the crisis twenty years later.

This on the matter of political substance. To what extent should the comparison with the Hebrew commonwealth be called incidental or fundamental? Clearly, as with the *Parallelon* of 1602 and *De antiquitate* of 1610, we have little difficulty in unmasking its lack of historicity and in identifying the innate shortcomings of this typical humanist approach, which aimed at summoning so-called evidence by reference to citations that were, often enough, distorted out of all context, to serve a preset objective. Clearly, the biblical research underlying *De Republica Emendanda* is worlds apart from Grotius' painstaking, indeed epochal research of later decades, which has reserved a well-deserved and lasting place in the prestigious history of biblical exegesis in the Netherlands. Although steeped in Mosaic law, there is very little originality or creativity in either its references or its line of thought. In about 1600, the youngster availed himself readily, indeed shamelessly, of authors such as Bertram and Sigonius.[100] Still, there was no better way for Grotius to try and persuade dissenters of his advocacy of a temperate aristocracy within a centralized and united confederacy than by reference to God's chosen people, with whom Dutch Calvinists so readily identified themselves. There is much to be said against the historicity of Grotius' presentation of the ancient Hebrew commonwealth, but this leaves the topicality of the comparative element to contemporary political reality unscathed.

Epilogue

Even in exile, Grotius never lost sight of the fatherland or interest in its vagaries.[101] In 1632, after ten years of exile—with Maurice long succeeded by Prince Frederic-Henry, with most Remonstrant clergymen long recalled from exile, and the sharp edges of the Synod of Dordrecht blunted—Grotius, ill-advised by friends, ventured his return. Within a matter of weeks he had to beat a hasty retreat to Hamburg. It meant a painful disillusionment and psychic upheaval. Then, out of the blue, Axel Oxenstiern's invitation to represent the Swedish Crown in Paris was dropped in his lap like manna.

The next year, his third biblical drama was published, *Sophompaneas*, which depicts the life of Joseph as deputy king of Egypt.[102] The play reveals Grotius' consummate literary skills, as he had given earlier proof of his versatility in so many other disciplines. But more than this, unlike any playwright before him on this extremely popular theme in the seventeenth century,[103] Grotius presents the patriarch, in reference to Mosaic law, as the perfect administrator, the epitome of political wisdom, and a great conciliator.[104] Well positioned to make his brothers repay the pit at Dothan, instead he reaches out to them in a truly brotherly manner. But apart from this, the deputy king is presented reorganizing Egyptian society and redrafting a new constitution for his people. Dozens of lines are devoted to this model constitution,[105] and there is little coincidence here. Grotius was not the only one to be struck by the parallel of his life with that of Joseph. Given the clear parallel drawn throughout, Joseph's new constitution mirrors the one that this humanist in Paris wished to convey to his compatriots as the ideal polity for the Dutch Republic. Needless to say, in many respects, this constitution reveals particulars which we find first drafted in *De Republica Emendanda*. A full thirty-five years later, and with an accumulated wealth of political experience, Grotius' views had not changed fundamentally, and neither had the inspiration he, like so many of his compatriots in Holland, drew from the Mosaic law and the Hebrew constitution.

A final issue which perhaps imposes itself here concerns the extent to which the above affected Grotius' position with respect to contemporary Judaism, also given the growing influx of Sephardic Jews and Marranos into the northern Netherlands—following their expulsion in previous centuries—since the fall of Antwerp in 1585. We can only touch on this ever so briefly. The first two decades of Jewish immigration are discussed in more detail in my introductory note on Cunaeus' treatise. Meanwhile, commentators have traditionally disagreed widely as to Grotius' position.[106] Diehard Calvinists have accused him of philo-Semitism, calling him *judaizans* as much as others have accused him of being *papizans*, "catchall epithets" of the period, as they have wisely been called by one modern commentator.[107] According to one colorful tradition, Grotius would at some stage even have considered converting to Judaism. More recent appraisals reveal him as having been far less benign to Judaism. As Rabbie observes correctly, Grotius' references to Judaism should never be taken at face value but carefully weighed within their context. Still, there are a few benchmarks to guide us in properly evaluating his attitude toward Jews and Judaism.

In 1614–1615, Grotius, in an official capacity, drew up a memorandum "concerning the order which should be imposed upon the Jews" in Holland.[108] It is a reflection upon the immigration process to which Grotius first refers in his *Meletius* of 1611 in otherwise commonplace terms, which betrays neither special interest nor sympathy with the Jewish community in Holland.[109] The same holds true for the 1615 *Remonstrantie*. The dilemma that vexed the authorities at the time was that, while these Jews were political refugees from Spanish tyranny as much as the Dutch themselves, to officially grant them freedom of religion would imply a curious "positive discrimination" vis-à-vis the Roman Catholics and certain Protestant denominations who were formally denied the possibility of freely exercising their beliefs. To solve this riddle, two champions of orthodoxy—Hugo Grotius, the Rotterdam city pensionary, on behalf of the (more lenient) followers of Arminius, or Remonstrants; and Adriaan Pauw, the Amsterdam city pensionary, on behalf of the (more stringent) adepts of Gomarus, or Contra-Remonstrants—were invited to submit propositions. The outcome, predictably, was inconclusive. As before, Jewish policy was left to city magistrates, a decision that was formalized by resolution of the States of Holland in December 1619.[110]

Meanwhile, the debate on the substance of this matter is of some interest. Grotius advocated a policy that, from our point of view at least, appears as rather ambivalent. In viewing this, however, one must take into consideration all the prejudices of the period. The pogrom that took place that very year in Frankfurt is symptomatic of the ways ministers mobilized the rudimentary resentments of the mobs against all dissentients. Reactions to recent incidents in Holland had been very similar.[111] The core of Grotius' views was the following: the Jewish religion is not even remotely akin to the Christian religion. Still, it is extremely useful to learn Hebrew, if only for biblical research, and to that extent contacts with Jews are helpful. Also, a Christian is bound to try and convert Jews. By the same token, Jews must be forbidden by law to try and convert Christians. To that extent, freedom of the press for the Jews should be restricted. Again, public ceremonies in synagogues are out of the question. Intermarriage or intercourse with Christians, even with prostitutes, must be prohibited, nor should a Christian be submitted to the ignominy of serving a Jewish household. Jews are not to be admitted to public office, however, they are at liberty to study at university centers, notably Leiden. Again, inasmuch as Jews serve commercial interests, no restrictions whatsoever should be imposed on them in this domain, as long as Jewish shopkeepers observe Sundays and Christian holidays. Finally, ghettos or restricted areas are not to be imposed.

It is not difficult to see that the *Remonstrantie* is the product of very peculiar circumstances and conflicting interests. Well aware of the sensitivities on both sides, Grotius advocated a pragmatic, considerate approach in which, clearly, mutual commercial interests and intellectual exchange played a substantial role. Stock elements of similar edicts abroad—as well as in other provinces of the Republic—such as the wearing of special attire, the interdiction of circumcision, or restrictions in terms of numbers of immigrants, are not to be found here. As for the interdiction of *connubium*, against the backdrop of similar prohibitions of Sephardic and Ashkenazic Jews amongst one another, one can hardly call this notion far-fetched or reactionary. The same held for most other suggestions by Grotius, as subsequent practice would demonstrate. In Amsterdam, by decree in November 1616, the exercise of religious practice by Jews, if in silence and unobtrusive, was granted. But the restrictions on synagogues, sexual intercourse, and the conversion of Christians were stringently upheld. With respect to ghettos, the States Resolution of December 1619 gave city councils license to open restricted areas for Jews.

Five years later, Grotius tackled the issue from a completely different angle. During his imprisonment he drew up an apologetic poem, *Bewijs van den waren Godsdienst* (*Proofs of the Proper Worship of God*), later to be elaborated in his scholarly *De Veritate religionis Christianae* (*On the Truth of the Christian Faith*) of 1627.[112] Within this apologetic context of traditionally staunch refutation of Judaism, Grotius' verdict on the Jews stands out as surprisingly mild by comparison. Inevitably, post-Christian Judaism is refuted as a superseded, intermediate stage between paganism and Christianity but in no harsh terms. Book 5 of *De Veritate* deals exclusively with Judaism, notably the refutation of traditional Jewish arguments against Christianity, such as Jesus' status as the Messiah, his miracles, and his position toward Mosaic law. The book reveals far more sympathy than shown in Book 6 toward Islam and enters into much more detail. However, in these references it is never quite clear to what phase of Jewish tradition Grotius is referring. Clearly, the Old Testament is the major reference for his entire text. As Heering argues,[113] Duplessis-Mornay's *L'Advertissement aux Juifs* (1607) must have been one of Grotius' principal sources and may even have inspired its mildly philo-Semitic tone. Grotius readily acknowledges the debt of Christianity toward Mosaic law and the Jewish tradition, extensively praises the Jewish religion on the grounds of its antiquity,[114] meanwhile making short shrift of later talmudic tradition, and ending with a prayer to God to enlighten the Jews and forgive them. Later in life, in his *Annotationes* on the Testaments, Grotius once more discussed many issues relating to Jewish history and customs in full detail. His undogmatic approach would invoke incriminations of Judaizing by stern Calvinists.[115] Even so, Grotius concludes with infamy and ridicule of the Talmud. It would seem that, in drawing up his final verdict, he was preoccupied with the Old Testament rather than contemporary Judaism. In this context, commentators have rightly pointed to Grotius' scarce contacts with the Jewish community in the Netherlands and the absence of any affection toward its figurehead, the Amsterdam rabbi Menasseh ben Israel. In this, one should appreciate that, from 1621 onward, the role of the Jewish community in the Netherlands can have hardly been a priority for the lifelong exile. Meanwhile, as is well known, in his otherwise poor estimate of later Jewish literature, Grotius makes explicit exception for Maimonides, for whose merits as a scholar he reserves a place of honor throughout his works.[116]

A last benchmark is Grotius' massive *Annotationes* on the Bible, the work of a lifetime, most of which was published posthumously. Inevitably, these impressive commentaries on the Old and New Testaments abound with references to Jewish history, literature, society, and religion, and it is here that we can observe the above-mentioned increase of factual knowledge of customs and rituals—and accordingly of sympathy—which seem the harvest of intimate reading of texts in Latin translations. Even so, also later in life, Grotius' interest in Judaism, historical and contemporary, seems to have been spurred primarily by the demands of his philological research, indeed as much as the historic parallel in *De Republica Emendanda* was urged on by Dutch sociopolitical conditions.

Notes

1. For a recent evaluation, see R. Po-Chia Hsia and Henk van Nierop, eds., *Calvinism and Religious Toleration in the United Provinces* (Cambridge: Cambridge University Press, 2002). See also Douglas Nobbs, *Theocracy and Toleration: A Study of the Disputes in Dutch Calvinism from 1600 to 1650* (Cambridge: Cambridge University Press, 1938); and, generally, Jonathan Israel's classic *The Dutch Republic: Its Rise, Greatness, and Fall, 1477–1806* (Oxford: Clarendon Press, 1995).

2. For a consummate overview of the history of political thought and social processes in the Netherlands of the period, see, for example, E.H. Kossmann, *Political Thought in the Dutch Republic* (Amsterdam: Edita—The Publishing House of the Dutch Republic, 2000); Israel, *The Dutch Republic*; Hans Blom, *Morality and Causality in Politics: The Rise of Naturalism in Dutch Seventeenth-Century Political Thought* (Ph.D. diss., University of Utrecht, 1995); Martin van Gelderen, *The Political Thought of the Dutch Revolt (1555–1590)* (Cambridge: Cambridge University Press, 1992); Leonard Leeb, *The Ideological Origins of the Batavian Revolution* (The Hague: Martinus Nijhoff, 1973).

3. On these aspects see J. van den Berg and Ernestine G.E. Van der Wall, eds., *Jewish-Christian Relations in the Seventeenth Century: Studies and Documents* (Dordrecht: Kluwer, 1988); Hans Bots and Jan Roegiers, eds., *The Contribution of the Jews to the Culture in the Netherlands* (Amsterdam: Holland University Press, 1989); J.C.H. Blom, R.G. Fuks-Mansfield, and I. Schöffer, eds., *The History of the Jews in the Netherlands* (Oxford: Littman Library of Jewish Civilization, 2002); Jonathan Israel and Reinier Salverda, eds., *Dutch Jewry: Its History and Secular Culture* (1500–2000), Brill's Series in Jewish Studies, vol. 29 (Leiden: Brill, 2002). Earlier surveys: Da Silva Rosa, *Geschiedenis der Portugese Joden in Amsterdam, 1593–1925* (Amsterdam: Hertzberger, 1925); H. Brugmans and A. Frank, eds., *Geschiedenis der Joden in Nederland* (Amsterdam: Van Holkema and Warendorf, 1940). A comprehensive survey of European Jewry can be found in Jonathan Israel, *European Jewry in the Age of Mercantilism, 1550–1750* (Oxford: Littman Library of Jewish Civilization, 1998), which appeared in Dutch in 2003 under the title *De Joden in Europa, 1550–1750* (Franeker: Uitgeverij Van Wijnen, 2003).

4. For an extensive review of the genesis and purport of Cunaeus' tract, see my introductory note on Petrus Cunaeus, *On the Hebrew Republic* (Jerusalem:

Shalem Press, 2006). Literature on Petrus Cunaeus' life is scant outside biographical dictionaries. See notably *NNBW* I, pp. 658–660 (v. Kuyk). A summary of his
life is to be found in the funeral address pronounced by Adolphus Vorstius in
1638. A bibliography of Cunaeus' works appears in M. Ahsmann and R. Feenstra,
Bibliografie van hoogleraren in de rechten aan de Leidse Universiteit tot 1811
(Amsterdam: KNAW, 1984), pp. 85–102. On Cunaeus' political studies in Leiden,
see H. Wansink, *Politieke wetenschappen aan de Leidse Universiteit 1575–1650*
(Utrecht: HES, 1981).

5. Grotius notably sent copies of his *Meletius, Ordinum Pietas*, and *De
Satisfactione Christi* to Cunaeus for review purposes. See the introductory notes
in Edwin Rabbie's critical editions of *Ordinum Pietas* (Leiden: Brill, 1995) and
De Satisfactione (Leiden: Brill, 1990).

6. Petrus Cunaeus, *De Republica Hebraeorum* (Leiden, 1617). While a translation of the entire work has been published by Shalem Press in 2006, the first of
the three books that compose this work can be found in an English translation
by Clement Barksdale, *The Commonwealth of the Hebrews* (London, 1653), which
is currently available with an introduction in Italian by Lea Campos Boralevi:
Petrus Cunaeus, *De Republica Hebraeorum (The Commonwealth of the Hebrews)*
(Florence: Centro Editoriale Toscano, 1996). Quotes here are my own translation and can be found in a slightly different form in the Boralevi edition on
pp. 21–22.

7. Cunaeus, *The Commonwealth of the Hebrews*, p. 22.

8. See, for example, Hedley Bull, Benedict Kingsbury, and Adam Roberts,
eds., *Hugo Grotius and International Relations* (Oxford: Oxford University Press,
1990).

9. Hugo Grotius, *De jure belli ac pacis* (Paris, 1625).

10. On these matters see *The World of Hugo Grotius, 1583–1645: Proceedings
of the International Colloquium* (Amsterdam: Holland University Press, 1984);
Henk J.M. Nellen and J. Trapman, eds., *De Hollandse Jaren van Hugo de Groot,
1583–1621* (Hilversum: Verloren, 1996).

11. A comprehensive survey can be found in E.H. Kossmann, "Politieke the-
orie in het zeventiende-eeuwse Nederland," *Verh. Kon. Ned. Akad, Wet.*, Afd.
Letterkunde, N.R. LXVII (1960).

12. On these matters see Harm J. van Dam's critical edition of Hugo Grotius,
De imperio summarum potestatum circa sacra, to be found as *Studies in the
History of Christian Thought*, vol. 102/1 (Leiden: Brill, 2001).

13. In the final paragraphs of his *Politica*.

14. The reference is to Grotius' *Inleiding tot de Hollandsche Rechts-geleertheyd*
(*Introduction to the Dutch Jurisprudence*) (The Hague, 1631).

15. On *De Republica Emendanda*, see Fiorella De Michelis, *Le origini storiche
e culturali del pensiero di Ugo Grozio* (Florence: La Nuova Ilania, 1967); Arthur
C. Eyffinger, "*De Republica Emendanda*: A Juvenile Tract by Hugo Grotius on
the Emendation of the Dutch Polity," in *Grotiana*, n.s. vol. 5 (1984), pp. 3–135;

Leonard Besselink, "The Place of *De Republica Emendanda* in Grotius' Works," in *Grotiana*, n.s. vol. 7 (1986), pp. 93–98.

16. See *Tabulae codicum manu scriptorum praeter graecos et orientales in BibliothecaPalatina Vindobonensi*, Band 4 (1870), cod. 6256, pp. 288–289.

17. Marco Foscarini (1695–1763), a Venetian doge, diplomat, and historiographer.

18. See J.Th. de Smidt in *Hugo de Groot 1583–1645* (Zwolle: Tjeenk Willink, 1983), pp. 18–31, esp. p. 27.

19. On these issues, see Eyffinger, "Grotius on the Dutch Polity," pp. 8–10; Besselink, "The Place of *De Republica Emendanda*." .

20. *Briefwisseling Hugo Grotius* 9 (1638), republished in The Hague in 1973 as *RGP Great Series* 142, pp. 338–339, no. 3605: "Letter from Pieter de Groot dated May 31, 1638."

21. Eyffinger, "Grotius on the Dutch Polity," pp. 12–13.

22. Ibid., pp. 13–16.

23. Dirck Graswinckel (1600–1666), a lawyer from Delft who served at the bar in The Hague and Malines, was a prolific author on issues of constitutional law and notably relating to the Venetian republic. His *Libertas Veneta sive Venetorum in se ac suos imperandi ius* was first published in Leiden in 1634.

24. Eyffinger, "Grotius on the Dutch Polity," p. 8.

25. Ibid., pp. 52–56.

26. From Machiavelli, Guicciardini, Paruta, and Botero in Italy; along with Ferrault, Gousté, De Grassaille, Le Roy, Hurrault, and Bodin in France; to Elyot, Gardiner, Merbury, Barclay, and Hobbes in Britain.

27. Grotius' *De antiquitate* constitutes one of the pivotal tracts in the debate on Dutch sovereignty. Critical edition by Jan Waszink, Bibliotheca Latinitatis Novae 1 (Assen: Van Gorcum, 2000).

28. Eyffinger, "Grotius on the Dutch Polity," p. 41.

29. Hence, Thomas Wilkes' remonstrance in his debate with Vranck. On this see P.A.M. Geurts, *De Nederlandse Opstand in pamfletten, 1566–1584* (Utrecht: HES Uitgevers, 1983).

30. Eyffinger, "Grotius on the Dutch Polity," p. 44ff.

31. See Jan den Tex, *Oldenbarnevelt*, 2 vols. (Cambridge: Cambridge University Press, 1973).

32. Eyffinger, "Grotius on the Dutch Polity," pp. 41–43.

33. See, for example, P.C. Molhuysen, ed., *Briefwisseling van Hugo Grotius* 1 (The Hague: Martinus Nijhoff, 1928), p. 85, no. 100, letter dated April 21, 1607, that is, from the months of peace negotiations, in which Grotius argues: "*Nam hactenus, ut verum fateamur, interregnum est, et dilapsuris sponte sua partibus*

ferruminis usum praebuit metus communis, quo remittente fit locus privatis studiis, quae in tam populari imperio facile ad discordias et factiones abeunt." ("For to be honest, thus far we have had an interregnum, and only the general state of tension has served to cement together elements that are on the verge of flying apart of their own accord; once this tension has relaxed, individuals will have the opportunity to pursue their own agendas, which—in a government so under the control of the people—will quickly lead to strife and political faction.")

34. In an appendix to Erycius Puteanus, *Burgerlijk Discours over de Nederlandsche Treves* (1617). See Hans Blom, "Politieke theorieën in het eerste kwart van de 17e eeuw: Vaderland van aristocratische republiek naar gemengde staat," in Henk J.M. Nellen and C. Ridderikhof, eds., *Hollandse Jaren van Hugo de Groot* (The Hague: Constantijn Huygens Instituut, 1996), p. 149.

35. Molhuysen, *Briefwisseling* 1, p. 149, no. 170, letter dated September 18, 1609.

36. See Blom, "Politieke theorieën," pp. 146–149.

37. For an overview of these issues in the wider European context, see Martin van Gelderen and Quentin Skinner, eds., *Republicanism: A Shared European Heritage* (Cambridge: Cambridge University Press, 2002).

38. See E.O.G. Haitsma Mulier, *The Myth of Venice and Dutch Republican Thought in the Seventeenth Century* (Assen: Van Gorcum, 1980).

39. Eyffinger, "Grotius on the Dutch Polity," pp. 46–47.

40. Ibid., pp. 46–47, 132–133.

41. Ibid., pp. 47–48, 133–135.

42. On these matters, see Arthur Eyffinger, ed., *The Poetry of Hugo Grotius*, vol. 2, 1.3 (Assen: Van Gorcum, 1988), pp. 45–50; the same can also be found in *Grotiana*, n.s. vol. 2 (1981), p. 116ff. This and further citations of *The Poetry of Hugo Grotius* in this essay are from the multiple-volume *De Dichtwerken van Hugo Grotius* (*The Poetry of Hugo Grotius*) (Assen: Van Gorcum, 1970-).

43. "O Wonderbaerlyck schict sich Moyses met Orangien!" in Joost van den Vondel, *De Werken van Vondel*, eds. J.F.M. Sterck et al. (Amsterdam: Wereldbibliotheek, 1927–1937), 1.46, p. 263. See H. Smitskamp, *Calvinistisch nationaal besef in Nederland voor het midden der 17e eeuw* (The Hague: Ôs-Gravenhage, 1947); A.C. Duke and C.A. Tamse, eds., *Britain and the Netherlands VI: War and Society* (The Hague: Martinus Nijhoff, 1977).

44. Among the works of François Dujon (F. Junius; 1545–1602) dating from Grotius' student days are *Le paisible Chrétien* and *Eirenicum,* both published in Leiden in 1593. See Eyffinger, "Grotius on the Dutch Polity," p. 29.

45. Ibid., p. 51.

46. As witnessed by Grotius' correspondence and poetry over his early years. Grotius composed an epithalamium for Boreel's wedding in 1608.

47. A sister of Erpenius was married to a merchant in Gorcum, near Loevestein Castle. The latter volunteered a book chest to facilitate the regular

transport of books from Erpenius in Leiden to Loevestein, so as to support the prisoner's biblical research. It was with the help of this book chest that, two years later, Grotius made his escape.

48. This holds true for *Meletius*, which was written in 1611 but suppressed; *Ordinum Pietas* (1613), which can be found in a critical edition with English translation and commentary by Edwin Rabbie, to be found in *Hugo Grotius, Ordinum Hollandiae ac Westfrisiae Pietas, 1613* (Leiden: Brill, 1995); *De Satisfactione Christi* (1617), which can be found in Edwin Rabbie, ed., *Defensio fidei catholicae De satisfactione Christi adversus Faustum Socinum Senensem* (*A Defense of the Catholic Faith Concerning the Satisfaction of Christ, Against Faustus Socinus*) (Assen: Van Gorcum, 1995); *De imperio summarum potestatum circa sacra* (conceived 1614–1617, published 1647), to be found in van Dam, *De imperio summarum.*

49. Notably *Scutum Auriacum* and *Mirabilia* concerning the Battle at Nieuwpoort, 1600. See B.L. Meulenbroek, ed., *Poetry of Hugo Grotius*, vol. 1.2.1 (Assen: Van Gorcum, 1972), pp. 59ff., 131ff.

50. The reference is to *Pontifex Romanus*, from the days of the Triple Alliance, in Meulenbroek, *Poetry of Hugo Grotius*, vol. 2.1, p. 73ff.

51. *Adamus exul*, reprinted in Meulenbroek, *Poetry of Hugo Grotius*, vol. 1.1 (Assen: Van Gorcum, 1970).

52. Ibid., p. 294ff.

53. See L.E. van Holk and G.C. Roelofsen, eds., *Grotius Reader: A Reader for Students of International Law and Legal History* (The Hague: T.M.C. Asser Instituut, 1983).

54. *Adamus exul*, p. 295.

55. For a survey of the *quaestio*, see Edwin Rabbie, "Grotius and Judaism," in Rabbie and Henk J.M. Nellen, eds., *Hugo Grotius Theologian: Essays in Honor of G.H.M. Posthumus Meyjes* (Leiden: Brill, 1994), pp. 99–120. So much for certain, from the 1630s onward, also thanks to the publications and personal advice of such scholars as Cocceius, Schickard, De Voisin, and L'Empereur, Grotius' intimate knowledge of rabbinical literature, ranging from early medieval sources, along with Maimonides, to his contemporary Menasseh ben Israel, grew considerably. Cf. also Manfred Lachs, "Hugo Grotius' Use of Jewish Sources in *On the Laws of War and Peace*," *Renaissance Quarterly* 30 (1977), pp. 181–200; A.W. Rosenberg, "Hugo Grotius as Hebraist," *Studia Rosenthaliana* 12 (1978), pp. 62–90. All in all, it is remarkable that no intimate links and personal relationships between Grotius and representatives of the Jewish community, either in Holland or abroad, can be attested to.

56. *Adamus exul*, p. 297.

57. See Eyffinger's contribution to Nellen and Trapman, *De Hollandse Jaren*, pp. 92–93.

58. See H.J. De Jonge, "Hugo Grotius, exégète du Nouveau Testament," in Robert Feenstra, ed., *The World of Hugo Grotius* (Amsterdam: Holland University Press, 1984), pp. 97–115.

59. Grotius, *De Republica Emendanda*, pars. 6, 13.

60. Cunaeus, in the preface to his *De Republica Hebraeorum* (1617).

61. Grotius, *De Republica Emendanda*, pars. 1–3.

62. Cunaeus, *De Republica Hebraeorum*, preface.

63. Grotius, *De Republica Emendanda*, par. 14.

64. Ibid., par. 16.

65. Flavius Josephus, *Jewish Antiquities*, IV, 223; XI, 111; XIV, 91; XX, 251; Josephus, *Wars of the Jews*, I, 170.

66. Grotius, *De Republica Emendanda*, par. 17.

67. Deuteronomy 12:8ff.; Exodus 15:24, 16:2, 17:2; Numbers 11:1, 14:1, 16:1; Josephus, *Jewish Antiquities*, III, 7; IV, 14ff.

68. I Samuel 8:7, 10:17–19; Josephus, *Jewish Antiquities*, VI, 35ff.

69. Judges 8:22–23.

70. Deuteronomy 17:14–20; cf. Josephus, *Jewish Antiquities*, IV, 223–225.

71. Judges 17:6, 21:24.

72. Grotius, *De Republica Emendanda*, pars. 19–20.

73. See Jeremiah 50–52 for Babylonian and Chaldaean kings; Daniel 1:21, 13:65, for Medean and Persian kings; Ezekiel 29–30 for Egyptian pharaoh.

74. Deuteronomy 33:5; I Samuel 21:12; cf. Josephus, *Jewish Antiquities*, VI, 245.

75. Aristotle, *Politics* 1285–1286; Homer, *Iliad*, 2.447–483, 3.166–1709.13, 14.64ff.

76. Josephus, *Jewish Antiquities*, IV, 297.

77. Deuteronomy 17:14–20; I Samuel 8:11–18.

78. Exodus 17:9; Josephus, *Jewish Antiquities*, III, 49; Joshua 13–19.

79. Judges 9; Josephus, *Jewish Antiquities*, V, 233ff.

80. II Samuel 13–19; Josephus, *Jewish Antiquities*, VII, 181ff.

81. Aristotle, *Politics* 1287a28ff.

82. Genesis 36:31ff.

83. Jan Waszink, introduction to Waszink, ed. and trans., *Hugo Grotius: The Antiquity of the Batavian Republic*, with notes by Petrus Scriverius (Assen: Van Gorcum, 2000), p. 13ff.

84. Grotius, *De Republica Emendanda*, par. 49.

85. Ibid.

86. Judges 17:6, 21:25.

87. Tacitus, *Agricola* 12.2.

88. Polybius, *Universal History* 2.37–40.

89. Meulenbroek, *Poetry of Hugo Grotius*, vol. 1.2.5.

90. *Christus patiens*, II. 379ff., 421ff., 539ff. (on the pharisaeans), and 359ff. (on the commoners).

91. See Nobbs, *Theocracy and Toleration*; and the introduction to van Dam, *De imperio summarum*.

92. Critical edition by G.H.M. Posthumus Meyjes, *Meletius sive de iis quae inter christianos conveniunt epistola* (Leiden: Brill, 1988).

93. See *Meletius*, par. 1. Many similar observations, also regarding the strait-jacket of dogmas, are made throughout pars. 2–5 and 89–91.

94. See G.N. Clark and W.J.M. van Eysinga, "The Colonial Conferences Between England and the Netherlands in 1613 and 1615," *Bibliotheca Visseriana* 15 (1940).

95. The reference is to the attacks by Sibrandus Lubbertus, a Franeker theologian, on the States' policy in appointing Conrad Vorstius at Leiden.

96. The reference is to *Ordinum Pietas*.

97. Molhuysen, *Briefwisseling* 1, p. 20, no. 25, letter dated November 1, 1601.

98. Ibid., pp. 530, 531, 560, nos. 476, 479, 500, letters written between October and December 1616.

99. In the end publication was postponed, mainly out of political considerations, until after Maurice's demise in 1625; the play was first staged in 1626.

100. Incidentally, apart from his evaluation of the Hebrew commonwealth, Sigonius, like Grotius, also produced a tract *De Republica Atheniensium* (*On the Athenian Republic*).

101. Grotius would include further critical surveys of the Dutch constitution in *De antiquitate* (1610), chs. 1 and 6–7, and in *Annales et Historiae* (1657), p. 107ff. See Eyffinger, "Grotius on the Dutch Polity," pp. 122–132.

102. See Eyffinger's critical edition of *Sophompaneas* in Eyffinger, *Poetry of Hugo Grotius*, vol. 1.4. On the biographical context see pp. 67–76.

103. See Jean Lebeau, *Salvator Mundi. L'exemple de Joseph dans le théatre Allemand au XVIe siècle*, 2 vols. (Nieuwkoop: De Graaf, 1977); *Sophompaneas*, pp. 46–53.

104. *Sophompaneas*, pp. 126–133. On these matters see Arthur Eyffinger, "The Fourth Man," in H.W. Blom and L.C. Winkel, eds., *Grotius and the Stoa* (Assen: Van Gorcum, 2004), pp. 117–156. This was also published in *Grotiana*, n.s. 22/23 (2001/2002), pp. 117–156.

105. *Sophompaneas*, pp. 112–138, 773–828.

106. In his "Grotius and Judaism," Rabbie presents an interesting overview of these traditions.

107. Jerome Friedman, *The Most Ancient Testimony* (Athens, Ohio: Swallow Press, 1983), quoted in Rabbie, "Grotius and Judaism," n. 3.

108. Hugo de Groot, *Remonstrantie nopende de ordre dije in de landen van Hollandt ende Westvrieslandt dijent te worden gestelt op de Joden*, ed. J. Meijer (Amsterdam: Coster, 1949).

109. Rabbie, "Grotius and Judaism," pp. 106–107.

110. See on this in my introductory note on Cunaeus' *De Republica Hebraeorum*.

111. Such as in Hoorn, where Mennonites had converted to Judaism, or in Amsterdam, where a Jew was caught having intercourse with a Christian girl, let alone the incident of the married Jewish pharmacist who was caught committing adultery with a Christian maidservant in 1616.

112. *De Veritate religionis Christianae* of 1627 is a great apology of Christianity in the tradition of Vives and Duplessis-Mornay (the two sources explicitly acknowledged by Grotius). On the tradition, see Avery Dulles, *A History of Apologetics* (London: Hutchinson, 1971). In *De Veritate*, Grotius argued not so much against the increasing atheism and skepticism of his day and age as rather against the devastating discord among the endless Christian denominations. In this, he focused on ethics above all: piety, rather than dogma, should inspire Christians, he felt, and practical toleration rather than learned doctrine. He then elaborated his theory of necessary and unnecessary doctrines as first developed by Erasmus and later by Junius in his *Eirenicon* of 1593. On the latter treatise, see Christiaan De Jonge, *De irenische ecclesiologie van Franciscus Junius (1542–1602)* (Nieuwkoop: De Graaf, 1980). Already in 1616, Grotius had ardently advocated the same in his eloquent and impressive but futile address to the Amsterdam City Council of May 1616. Again, in his *De Imperio*, Grotius argued that theologians would do wise in following the example of lawyers who had long since realized the dangers implicated in all-too-strict definitions.

113. Jan-Paul Heering, *Hugo Grotius as Apologist for the Christian Religion: A Study of His Work 'De Veritate Religionis Christianae' (1640)* (Leiden: Brill, 2004), p. 146.

114. Ibid., p. 106ff.

115. Cf. Rabbie, "Grotius and Judaism," pp. 99–101.

116. Ibid., pp. 112–113. Cf. Cunaeus' appraisal of Maimonides, which is expounded upon in my introduction to Cunaeus' *De Republica Hebraeorum*.

The Biblical 'Jewish Republic' and the Dutch 'New Israel' in Seventeenth-Century Dutch Thought

Miriam Bodian

There is now a considerable scholarly literature on early modern Dutch identification with the biblical Israelites. Scholars have located the earliest popular expressions of this "Neerlands Israel" discourse in the pamphlets and songs of the so-called Sea Beggars, the rebels who led the uprising against Spain in the 1560s. They have examined its expression in sermons, paintings, coins, literary works, and political speeches.[1] And they agree that translations of Luther's German Bible and, eventually, the *Statenvertaling* of the Bible—the Dutch translation of the Bible from the original Hebrew and Greek (1625–1637), financed by the States General—played an important role in familiarizing a growing reading public with the historical and prophetic texts that nourished this sort of identification.

There is also agreement that fashioning the story of Dutch national birth around the Old Testament theme of redemption from slavery provided ballast for a political narrative that lacked the weight of history, not to mention antiquity. When the Reformed minister Jacob Lydius wrote in 1668, "Above all I thank him / Who made Holland Jerusalem," he was elevating this former backwater province of the Holy Roman Empire to the center of the universe.[2] To be sure, there was an alternative effort to create historical roots for the evolving republic, namely, the elaboration of Tacitus' history of the Batavian revolt against Rome. Without denying the importance of this effort to root the Dutch polity in classical antiquity, however, there seems little doubt that the Old Testament was a more powerful instrument in shaping Dutch collective consciousness.

It may seem obvious why the Old Testament, not the New, was the key source in the development of a national discourse. Simon Schama argued succinctly that

> The gospels of the New Testament were self-evidently universal in their import, and ultimately personal in their theme (at least to a Protestant). But the Old Testament was patriotic scripture, the chronicle of a people chosen by God to reveal his light to the world through their history.[3]

This is certainly so. Yet the simple fact that the Old Testament provided particularly suitable material was not the only reason for its appropriation. It is no accident that medieval Spaniards, for example, did not seize on the Old Testament for inspiration when they drove the Muslims from their soil. That the Old Testament *could* be mobilized this way by the Dutch was partly the result of shifts in how the Bible was being read in sixteenth-century Protestant Europe.

This reading reflected a sharp break with centuries-old patterns. Since late antiquity, Christian exegesis had drawn a sharp distinction between the Old Testament figures who preceded Christ (who were righteous) and the Israelites and Jews of Jesus' time (who embodied every imaginable vice). The early Dutch crypto-Protestants, in contrast, reading the Bible as the many Lutheran tracts circulating among them encouraged them to do, were swept up by the story of oppression and liberation that lay at the heart of the Pentateuch. They identified not only with the righteous patriarchs and prophets (as Catholics also might, insofar as the actions of these figures were associated with Christ) but with the entire Israelite nation. To illustrate this novel identification with the Israelites—all of them—let me quote some verses by the Reformed preacher and poet Jacob Revius (1586–1658), interpreting the Twelve Years' Truce with Spain (1609–1621):

> The Jews marched through the desert forty years
> In trouble, danger and want of everything;
> But in the end and after that sad time
> Joshua led them into the promised land.
> The war forced us to march through the desert for forty years;
> Now the Truce opens to us the promised land.[4]

It was not so much that the Old Testament was "patriotic scripture" as that it was being *read* that way.

This kind of rhetoric was by no means distinctively Dutch. The fashioning of a collective self-image in terms of the "New Israel" could be found among Calvinist populations everywhere—in France, Switzerland, Germany, England, and New England, among other places. The Dutch discourse, then, was part of a broader development. But it became absorbed into a debate that was peculiarly Dutch.

II.

Initially, the rhetoric of the Beggars played a primarily unifying role, mobilizing widespread support for the rebels across confessional and provincial boundaries. Perhaps for this reason, some scholars have viewed the Dutch discourse of "Neerlands Israel" entirely in light of its unifying function. Schama is a case in point:

> In the Dutch Republic, the Hebraic self-image functioned much more successfully as a unifying bond than as a divisive dogma. It flowed out of the pulpit and the psalter into the theater and the print shop, diluting Calvinist fundamentalism as it did so, but strengthening its force as a national culture for the very same reason. Indeed it was just because the roots of Netherlandish Hebraism were not exclusively Calvinist, but reached back to an earlier and deeper humanist reformation, that it could exert such broad appeal. ...[I]t was a sign of the versatility and inclusiveness of the idiom that opposing political factions could both resort to it to argue their respective positions. This interpenetration with profane history lent Dutch scripturalism its tremendous strength. It was used not in order to swallow up the secular world within the sacred, but rather to attribute to the vagaries of history... the flickering light of providential direction.[5]

The eminent Dutch scholar Willem Frijhoff writes in a similar vein:

> Dutch society, in constant danger of splitting up, needed symbols of unity to stay together. It was the Reformed church that, better than any other, stood out as a centralizing and unifying element.... Among the religious models of unity, the notion of the new Israel, or "Dutch Israel," was particularly important.... The central notion

was well and truly that of being chosen; Israel being the chosen people of God, the new Israel was the instrument that God had recently chosen to realize his kingdom on earth and spread his message. ... Since the Revolt, which was seen as a war of independence just like the struggles of the Jewish people, the Protestants had got into the habit of comparing themselves with biblical heroes, particularly those of the Old Testament. The Prince of Orange had become the new Moses, Gideon, or David, the enemy being the Spanish Sennacherib (Philip II) or the French Nebuchadnezzar (Louis XIV), both descendants of Cain. The very existence of the Dutch Republic was literally a miracle for many.[6]

Both Schama and Frijhoff imply that behind the richly varied contents of this rhetoric, Netherlanders of all backgrounds—Schama mentions as examples (along with the Reformed *predikanten*) a humanist, an Arminian, and a Catholic—shared a single basic vision of "Neerlands Israel."[7] This was true, but only up to a certain point: once the Spanish forces had been turned back decisively, two competing camps emerged in a fundamental debate about the character of the Dutch polity. Spokesmen for each camp mobilized the common founding myth to serve their different political goals. A bystander in the Netherlands of the mid-seventeenth century would have been acutely attuned to the different agendas that were promoted using the common framework of the New Israel. It is striking that modern scholars have seemed rather oblivious to this bifurcation.[8] In what follows, I will try to show how a fundamental fissure in Dutch society impacted on the development of the "Neerlands Israel" theme and how, in an essay written in the 1680s, an author within the Portuguese-Jewish community of Amsterdam produced a Jewish formulation of this theme that both appropriated and subverted the gentile discourse.

III.

The conflicting camps in Dutch society confusingly assumed different names at different junctures in Dutch history but are perhaps best known as Remonstrants and Counter-Remonstrants, associated with the States-party (confederate) and Orangist (monarchist) factions, respectively. Broadly speaking, the two sides of the protracted conflict over church-state relations in the Netherlands can be said to have crystallized with the installation of the Reformed church as the "public church" of the Seven Provinces in 1575. The Calvinists, having spearheaded the Dutch Revolt, possessed a clear popular advantage over the Catholics. Moreover, as elsewhere in Europe, the Calvinists were quick to establish an effective, three-tiered organization of synods, classes, and consistories. But most Netherlanders were not devotees of *any* church. As Jonathan Israel writes:

> In the late sixteenth century, the majority of the Dutch popula-
> tion... cannot unequivocally be described as Protestant or Catholic.
> For the majority constituted a non-confessionalized, or barely con-
> fessionalized, bloc, undecided and unformed.[9]

Despite their privileged position, the dogmatically orthodox Calvinist preachers did not speak even for their own congregants in the late sixteenth century, and undertook the daunting task of what has come to be known as "confessionalization."

By the early seventeenth century, the ranks of the Calvinist ministers had split decisively along theological lines that would eventually coincide with a political-ideological divide. The Counter-Remonstrants insisted on an uncompromisingly confessionalizing agenda, which they expected the state to support. For them, victory over the Spanish had been a victory for the "true faith." They regarded it as their duty to enforce that faith through the close supervision of religious life in the new republic—that is, by exercising police powers in the spiritual realm.

The Remonstrants, on the other hand, shared the humanist spirit of most of the regent ruling class. For them, victory over the Spanish had been a victory over tyranny and oppression. An authoritarian enforcement of religious norms, then, was contrary to the principles for which they had fought. They favored freedom of conscience. Yet they supported the establishment of the Reformed church as the public church, lest a lack of formal consensus on religion invite bloodshed and theological chaos. They viewed the public church as an instrument for maintaining civil peace, not as an instrument for imposing orthodoxy and uniformity.

Tensions between the two sides reached a crisis point in 1617-1618, with the battle lines drawn between the orthodox Reformed preachers and Prince of Orange Maurits of Nassau (stadholder of five of the seven provinces), on the one hand, and the Remonstrants and the so-called *Landsadvocaat* (leader of the States of Holland), Johan van Oldenbarnevelt, on the other. What transpired is a complex story. To simplify greatly,

Prince Maurits engineered a successful coup d'état. As a result, a National Reformed Synod (with foreign participants) was convened at Dordrecht in late 1618 and the spring of 1619, and Remonstrant theology was declared heretical. Oldenbarnevelt was executed that May, and unrepentant Remonstrant preachers were banished. In a republic widely viewed as a bastion of tolerance in early modern Europe, the winning party now sought to initiate a sweeping program of religious purification (the so-called "Further Reformation" [*nadere reformatie*]), including additional suppression of Remonstrants, Catholics, Lutherans, and Jews.

The Counter-Remonstrant "revolution" petered out by the mid-1620s, but the resounding success of the orthodox ministers fueled Counter-Remonstrant/Orangist ambitions for generations. The alliance of the House of Orange and the orthodox Reformed ministers proved enduring. It was not without political logic. The powerful states of Holland resisted the stadholders' domination for the same reason they sided with the Remonstrants: Their primary interests (aside from securing their position of power) were to maintain peace and prosperity, which precluded religious conflict or adventurism in foreign policy. In time the identification of the strict Reformed clergy with the quasi-monarchist Orangists, and of the Remonstrants with the States of Holland, became a fixture of the ongoing Kulturkampf.[10]

IV.

It was only natural that the rhetoric of "Neerlands Israel" would assume a different thrust in each of the two camps. For the Counter-Remonstrants, the New Israel was not a national entity based on *patria*, but a religious community consisting of Reformed believers.[11] The Counter-Remonstrant preacher Florentius Costerus (1656–1703) explicitly stated that while the Old Testament term "Zion" applied to the *nation* of Israel, in the New Testament the church—the community of believers—had replaced the ethnic, national entity.[12] (Counter-Remonstrant insistence on this point has convinced some scholars that the rhetoric of "Neerlands Israel" rejected the Old Testament notion of chosenness, but that generalization is misleading and apologetic.)[13] God's Law was intended for all men and women; it was the task of the Reformed ministers and secular rulers to establish it on earth.[14]

Though the Reformed were the "Second Israel," they were no more inherently righteous than the "First Israel," the biblical Israelites. In fact, the latter's ingratitude and backsliding—and their consequent punishment—were frequently held up as an example and warning. Article 36 of the Synod of Dordt's revision of the *Confessio Belgica (Nederlandse Geloofbelijdenis)* justifies and underscores the need for political supervision of moral life. It states "that our good God, because of the corruption of the human race, has ordained kings, princes, and authorities, intending that the world should be governed by laws and policing, in order that the dissoluteness of men should be suppressed and everything should proceed according to good ordinances."[15] While "nationalist" biblicist rhetoric externalized the "villain" (the Spanish, the pope, the French), the rhetoric of Reformed orthodoxy reflected more strongly the fear of the "Babel" within. God had planted his church in the Netherlands, but he could uproot it, as Reformed ministers emphasized by quoting Jeremiah 45:4: "The Lord says thus: Behold, that which I have built I break down, and that which I have planted I pluck up, namely this whole land."[16] The fate of the *patria*, a blessing from God, was in the hands of the Reformed church.

Good order required clear hierarchy, whereas seventeenth-century Dutch society suffered from an unresolved relationship between stadholders and states (both the provincial states and the States General) and a public church lacking the powers of a state church. What the Counter-Remonstrants sought was a society in which God was recognized as the sole sovereign, with the church granted spiritual preeminence, and stadholders, political preeminence. The biblical functions that best symbolized this dual form of authority were, for many ministers, those of prophet and king. As vessels for God's message, the ministers were "ambassadors of God" (*Godsgezanten, ambassadeurs*) or "watchmen on the walls" (from Isaiah 62:6), who, like the Old Testament prophets, brought the word of God to the people and rulers of Israel.[17] But the Counter-Remonstrants were also profoundly aware of the need for real, institutionalized authority. Thus, at times they chose to depict the church's ministers and preachers as functionaries akin to the priests of the Temple in Jerusalem. (The tripartite organization of the Reformed church under ministers, elders, and deacons was compared to the Old Testament hierarchy of priests, Levites, and elders.)[18] The contrasting images of prophet and priest may reflect the ambivalence of a once insurgent movement seeking its place in a new regime.

A similar ambivalence can be perceived in the Counter-Remonstrant model of the king. The archetype was William the Silent, not in fact a king but a stadholder, whose legitimacy stemmed from his role in the Netherlanders' liberation from the Spanish. The biblical image for William the Silent, Joshua leading the New Israelites into the promised land, remained forever integral to the Orangist legacy, with the ideal stadholder continually associated with Joshua. But the liberation phase had passed, and the task of the stadholder in the new regime—as Counter-Remonstrants envisioned it—was to provide godly rule and maintain public morality. In this mode, the ideal stadholder was likely to be represented as Hezekiah, uprooting idolatry from within, cleansing the Temple (in cooperation with the Levites), defending against the idolatrous enemy from without, and relying on the word of the prophet.[19] Josiah served as an alternative image, teaching the "words of the book of the covenant," commanding obedience to the law, and taking action (in cooperation with the high priest) to eliminate idolatry.[20] Such was the glorious, if imaginary, "tradition" of the House of Orange-Nassau.[21]

V.

In contrast, the Remonstrants clung to an irenic and patriotic idea of the New Israel. In this respect, they revealed a sense of destiny that was rather free of confessional anxieties. Thus, for example, the Remonstrant preacher Johannes d'Outrein (1662–1722):

> God chose the Jewish people to be his people. We may say that God has done the same for the *Netherlands people* (although not to the disparagement of other peoples).[22]

Remonstrant thinkers had their own anxieties, but they were more likely to be about the dangers of ecclesiastical power. In a properly ordered sovereign state, both ecclesiastical and secular institutions were to be subordinate to the sovereign. The influential Remonstrant Johannes Uytenbogaert (1557–1644) pointed to the biblical king Jehoshaphat as a model of such a sovereign. When magistrates and ministers are summoned by the sovereign "to come to court and render a reckoning of their proceedings to him," Uytenbogaert wrote, "they must not any of them [that is, any of the ministers] give for an answer that such matters are ecclesiastical [and thus not under the king's jurisdiction]."²³ This idea of Jehoshaphat's authority over ecclesiastical matters may have been drawn from the fact that he appointed (and thus authorized) the priests and Levites to adjudicate disputes "in matters of the Lord."²⁴ Such an arrangement made sense to the Remonstrants, because they saw the purpose of government as serving the needs and providing for the welfare of the people rather than bending them to the will of God.

Remonstrant theology was thus relatively compatible with contemporary republican notions that drew on a classical philosophical tradition. The great jurist Hugo Grotius (1583–1645), among others in this camp, cited both biblical and classical examples to support his arguments about ideal government. Liberty, stability, and prosperity were best nurtured, he maintained, by an aristocracy, a government by the social elite. Such was the government of ancient Judea under the Judges. Such was the government of democratic Athens and republican Rome. And such was the government of the Dutch regents. In the 1650s, Jacob Cats (1577–1660) formulated very similar arguments.²⁵ Likewise, Johan de Wit (1618–1676) maintained in his *Public Gebedt* (1663–1664) that the "aristocratic republic" of the regents of Holland was the best form of government, chosen by God himself "for his people, the children of Israel."²⁶

It need hardly be pointed out that the rule of the Judges over Israel after Joshua's death bears little resemblance to the Aristotelian conception of aristocratic government. But the Remonstrants, like their opponents, sought scriptural backing. And what these thinkers regarded as important about the biblical precedent was not the structure of the regime of the Judges, which bore little resemblance to that of the regents, but the fact that God disapproved of anointing a king over Israel. God himself was an anti-Orangist.

VI.

On some level, such rhetoric was undoubtedly flattering to the Jews of Amsterdam. It would be a mistake, however, to assume that the positive association of the Dutch with the ancient Israelites in the rhetoric of "Neerlands Israel" necessarily indicated a more positive view of contemporary Jews. Neither the Remonstrants nor the Counter-Remonstrants particularly befriended the Jewish community, though members of both engaged in cordial relations with Menasseh ben Israel and other Jews. Yet in principle there was never any doubt that Jewish interests were better served by the Remonstrants than by the more intolerant Counter-Remonstrants.

Indeed, insofar as political biblicism was expressed in the language of national consensus, drawing from humanist sources that predated Calvinism and emphasizing the liberation of the Dutch from the tyrannical Spanish, it could be cautiously enjoyed even by Jews. The model of the biblical Jews as a people bound together by a covenant with God coincided with the contemporary Jewish self-image. The patriotic self-depiction of the Dutch vis-à-vis the Spanish (or, in 1672, the French) as David before Goliath, as Moses before Pharaoh, as Gideon before the Midianites, as Hezekiah before Sennacherib, or as the Maccabees before Antiochus created, in a way, symbolic and emotional common ground between Jews and Christians. So did the Dutch adoption of Moses the lawgiver as the emblem of good government. There was surely something reassuring to Jews about the scenario sketched by the Catholic poet Joost van Vondel (1587–1679) in 1659, in his poem "On Moses Receiving the Law":

> Hebrew Moses received the Law from God
> With which he returns from above to the people
> So they become respectful and welcome them with longing.
> As the people honor the laws, so shall a free state stand.[27]

This sort of political biblicism could particularly be appreciated by descendants of baptized Jews who had fled the Iberian Peninsula, among whom the image of the Spanish monarch as an enslaving Pharaoh was cultivated long before the Beggars fomented rebellion in the Low Countries. These Jews, of course, did not accept that the Dutch had superseded them as the "true Israel." (In fact, this proposition was absurd from their point of view. They were much more likely to express competitive attitudes toward Spain than toward the Netherlands.)[28] Still, they could well believe God sided with the Dutch, and they could identify with the Dutch in their victory against Spain.[29]

In contrast, the more confessional political biblicism of the orthodox Reformed preachers was threatening to the Jews (and other non-Reformed groups). It is true that, in general, within the dynamics of Reformed Old Testament moral theology, the Jews were a side issue, essentially absent from the religio-moral equation. Reformed preachers regarded their church—*the* church of the new covenant—as the moral and religious backbone of Dutch society. The nation's fate depended on *their* behavior. God's own people were punished for their own sins, not those of their neighbors who lived in error. As the Reformed minister Herman Witsius (1636–1708) wrote in 1669 about his flock, "You are God's own people to whom the Lord has come so close and whom he has elected as his own in a special way from among so many other peoples, and of whom he therefore reasonably expects more than of the rest."[30] God could be called "the Netherlands' God," one minister wrote, "though we have in our midst idolaters and the remnant of the Canaanites [the Jews], [because these people] are reckoned merely as inhabitants."[31] But at the same time, the Counter-Remonstrants believed the Dutch "Israelite" ruler should eliminate false religious doctrines and support true religion. "Oh, if only the pious zealots—the Hezekiahs, Jehoshaphats, and Josiahs—would entirely extirpate the detestable idolatry in 'Nederlandts Israël,'" one Reformed minister urged, "putting it on ever more flimsy foundations!"[32] This sentiment was probably more a pious wish than an expectation, but such intolerance was at odds with the well-being of the Jewish community.

We might ask at this point whether either camp's political Hebraism had any practical impact on political life. The biblical analogues never served as actual models for the structure and operation of Dutch political institutions. That is, the oligarchic regime of the regents might be imaginatively regarded as a replication of the regime of the biblical Judges, but it had not been created to reproduce the biblical form of rule, which no good burgher could possibly have wanted. Nonetheless, the rhetoric was not empty. It was intertwined with Dutch society's contemplation of the proper exercise of power in a republic—a discourse that rested on classical philosophical and ancient Christian, including Old Testament, foundations.

From the point of view of the Jews, who stood at the sidelines of the debate, there was no pressing need to respond directly to the Dutch appropriation of Old Testament imagery and political models, or to the struggle between the Counter-Remonstrants and the Remonstrants. The Portuguese Jews of Amsterdam naturally followed events closely but prudently withheld comment, preferring to work behind the scenes to cultivate the support of the regents, who were in any case inclined to curb the zealotry of the orthodox preachers. A fascinating exception is an essay by the ex-*converso* litterateur Daniel Levi de Barrios, published in 1683 or 1684 as an introduction to his *Triumpho del govierno popular*, a lengthy institutional portrait of the Spanish and Portuguese Jewish community of Amsterdam written for a Jewish audience.[33] Let us briefly examine this unique Jewish response to the Dutch notion of "Neerlands Israel."

VII.

De Barrios' analysis makes an important polemical point at the very outset. There was, he insisted, no single model of Israelite government. Under Moses, Saul, David, and Solomon, Israelite government was monarchic. Under Joshua, the Judges, and the Maccabees, it was aristocratic. In exile—in Egypt, Babylonia, and the post-antique diaspora (including his own time)—it was democratic.[34] The assertion that God did not ordain a certain form of Israelite government as the proper one for all time was significant because it allowed De Barrios to argue that the destruction of the Temple and the exile of the Jews were not indications that the Covenant had been nullified or replaced. Rather, the Jews were entering a new phase of their history which required a different form of governance.

Still, in principle, De Barrios preferred democracy, eagerly noting its prevalence among the Jews of Amsterdam in his own day. (His wish to identify Jewish government with "democracy" is revealed in his claim that even in antiquity, Moses had desired a democratic regime.)[35] Politically, De Barrios seems to have sympathized with more radical currents that were beginning to emerge in Dutch society, articulated by such figures as Pieter de la Court (1618–1685) and Benedict de Spinoza (1632–1677). Democracy was best, he asserted, because it eliminated the misuse of power for personal gain, which was the chief danger of government by the few. Monarchy almost inevitably degenerated into tyranny, "for rare is the monarch who puts the good of his subjects before his own, and rare are the subjects who serve God more than the king."[36]

De Barrios further asserted that throughout their exile (or, more correctly, exiles), even in pre-Mosaic Egypt, the Jews had been "democratic." Democracy was thus the most ancient and long-lived mode of government.[37] The second "democratic" regime of Jewish congregations or settlements discussed by De Barrios was that of the Jews during the Babylonian exile,[38] and in this discussion he first hinted at what he understood to be the salient feature of Jewish communal "democracy." He referred to Strabo's contention (cited in Josephus) that the Jews of

Alexandria lived on their own streets under their own laws and rulers, "with absolute power as if they were a republic unto themselves."[39] De Barrios struck a similar note in discussing the Jews' third "democratic" period, extending from the destruction of the Second Temple to his own time—the period of the "*Sustentadores o Parnasim*."[40] He referred to "all the Israelites who were dispersed among the nations" as "governing themselves with the Mosaic Law."[41] These two statements strongly suggest that De Barrios associated democracy first with liberty in its ancient sense, i.e., collective freedom from foreign interference or tyranny, and second with rule by one's own laws and customs.

These two themes—political independence (that is, communal autonomy) and self-government founded on the Law of Moses—recur throughout De Barrios' *Triumpho del govierno popular*. He also expatiated on the antiquity, immutability, and eternity of Mosaic Law, comparing a united Jewish people with an unstable, fragmented gentile world. While the Chaldaeans, Phoenicians, Egyptians, Persians, Medeans, Greeks, and Romans had all perished along with their monarchies and laws, "the Law of Moses persists among the people who observe it."[42] And while the Christian sects proliferated, each with its different rites—"Papists," Socinians, Lutherans, Quakers, Calvinists, "and many other sects"—only Mosaic Law retained its original, uncorrupted form.[43] The antiquity, continuity, and stability of government so sought after by the gentile nations were in fact, De Barrios implied, achieved only by the Jews.

De Barrios' use of the term "democratic" government, or *govierno popular*, in reference to the Jewish community is highly misleading. He seems to have meant government brought into being by the people and based on their sovereignty. But political thinkers could enlist such a notion to support various types of government, including absolute monarchy, and they had done so in the past. Indeed it might be said that De Barrios himself used it to justify any Jewish regime based on the Law of Moses—a regime that could assume a variety of structures, according to circumstances.

Insofar as his essay was a rebuttal of Dutch political Hebraism, De Barrios underscored the problem of dissent. The Reformed ministers sought to impose a godly regime on an unwilling (or partially unwilling) people. In contrast, he implied (with considerable distortion of both the biblical narrative and the contemporary reality), the Jews had always freely chosen to live under the Law of Moses, whether by "electing"

Moses to be their leader or by "electing" the *parnasim* of the Amsterdam community.[44]

In escaping the tyranny of Spain and opting to live by the Law of Moses, then, the Portuguese Jews of Amsterdam were echoing the Israelites at the Red Sea and at Mount Sinai. The ancient liberty of the Jews to govern themselves by the Law of Moses had been denied them many times in history, but they had always restored self-government by common agreement after their liberation from captivity. There was, in other words, no New Israel, only the original Israel, with whom God had made a covenant through Abraham.

Yet De Barrios was not without sympathy for the Dutch and their rhetoric of Neerlands Israel. He shows this clearly at the end of his introductory essay. It may be appropriate here to point out that the full title of his work is *Triumpho del govierno popular y de la Antiguedad Holandesa* (*The Triumph of Popular Government, and of Dutch Antiquity*). His biblical plays on words suggest that the Jews and the Dutch actually shared ancient ancestral ties: They both descended from Shem (the Dutch through Shem's great-great-grandson Yoqtan). More significantly, they had parallel histories. According to the *Antiquitates* of Pseudo-Philo, Yoqtan had intervened heroically to rescue Abram and other dissenters who refused to cooperate in the plan of the evil Nimrod to build the tower of Babel. Yoqtan ultimately failed to prevent Abram from being thrown into the brick kiln, but Abram was saved by a miracle, while Nimrod and his followers suffered death by fire.[45]

De Barrios' version of history associated Nimrod with tyranny, tyranny with imperial Spain, the Spanish with Catholic idolatry and the Inquisition, and the Inquisition with fire. The Dutch, in contrast, were linked spiritually with the Jews. The non-idolatrous, Noahide beliefs of the sons of Eber (father of Yoqtan), it was suggested, could be found in the Calvinist doctrines of their seventeenth-century counterparts. These convictions had stirred Yoqtan's descendants in the Spanish Netherlands to rise up and overthrow an idolatrous, tyrannical monarch, and afterwards it was they who offered the sons of Abraham a refuge from the flames of the autos-da-fé.

In proposing an ancient bond between Portuguese Jewry and the Dutch people, De Barrios was experimenting with the discourse of his Dutch contemporaries, politely rejecting their version of divine history while offering them a minor role in the epic of the "true Israel." Yet consciously, and perhaps unconsciously as well, he drew his entire conception from the rhetoric of Dutch political Hebraism in both its variants:

The Counter-Remonstrants depicted the New Israel as a community of believers without borders, a diaspora people that could nevertheless claim hegemony over a sovereign nation. Not surprisingly, De Barrios emphasized that even in exile the Jews resembled a sovereign nation, with a structure of leadership and governance.

The Remonstrants, on the other hand, accentuated the national traits and history of the New Israel. In doing so, they frequently referred to the Exodus story, in a way that paralleled crypto-Jewish and ex-converso identification with the same narrative. It may have been refreshing for ex-conversos to live amid a people with whom they could share the experience of Spanish oppression and the Inquisition. The "Neerlands Israel" rhetoric of magistrates and preachers may also have been irritating, however, in its displacement and marginalization of the Jews.

On one level, De Barrios' essay can be read simply as a flattering representation of Jewish political life in biblical and post-biblical times, aimed to please a Jewish audience. But it was also a response and a challenge to the Dutch appropriation of Israelite history. In this regard, it was an effort at reclamation accomplished by adopting the very idiom the Dutch had used in their appropriation.

Notes

1. For a summary of this material see Lea Campos Boralevi, "Classical Foundational Myths of European Republicanism: The Jewish Commonwealth," in Martin van Gelderen and Quentin Skinner, eds., *Republicanism: A Shared European Heritage*, 2 vols. (Cambridge: Cambridge University Press, 2002), vol. 1, pp. 248–250.

2. "Maar boven als bedank ik hem / Die *Holland* maakt *Jeruzalem*." Jacob Lydius, *'t Verheerlikte, ofte 't Verhoogde Nederland* (Dordrecht, 1668), fo. 1v.; G. Groenhuis, *De Predikanten: De sociale positie van de gereformeerde predikanten in de Republiek der Verenigde Nederlanden voor 1700* (Groningen: Wolters-Noordhoff, 1977), p. 81.

3. Simon Schama, *The Embarrassment of Riches: An Interpretation of Dutch Culture in the Golden Age* (New York: Knopf, 1987), p. 68.

4. "De Joden veertich jaer de wildernis doorgingen / In moeyte, in gevaer, in schaers-heyt aller dingen; Opt eynde van dien tijt en na dien droeven stant / Brocht haer Jehosua in het beloofde lant. / Den oorloch veertich jaer int wild en ons dee lopen; Nu doet den treves ons 't lant van beloften open." Jacob Revius, "Die tyrannie verdrijven. Godsdiensten onafhankelijkheidsstrijd in de 16e en 17e eeuw," in *Spectrum van de Nederlandse Letterkunde*, ed. M.C.A. van der Heijden, 25 vols. (Utrecht and Antwerp, 1967–1972), vol. 7, p. 148. See also Groenhuis, *De Predikanten*, pp. 79–80. Translation from G. Groenhuis, "Calvinism and National Consciousness: The Dutch Republic as the New Israel," in *Britain and the Netherlands: Papers Delivered to the Conference*, vol. 7, *Church and State Since the Reformation* (The Hague, 1981), p. 120.

5. Schama, *Embarrassment of Riches*, p. 97.

6. Willem Frijhoff, "Religious Toleration in the United Provinces: From 'Case' to 'Model,'" in R. Po-Chia Hsia and Henk van Nierop, eds., *Calvinism and Religious Toleration in the Dutch Golden Age* (Cambridge: Cambridge University Press, 2002), pp. 50–51.

7. The same basic position is adopted by Campos Boralevi, "Classical Foundational Myths."

8. Recently, Lea Campos Boralevi has pointed to this tension, without elaborating on it. See her "Classical Foundational Myths," p. 252.

9. Jonathan Israel, *The Dutch Republic: Its Rise, Greatness, and Fall, 1477–1806* (Oxford: Clarendon Press, 1995), p. 366. For a detailed analysis of the large population of "unchurched" Christian Netherlanders, see Benjamin Kaplan, "'Remnants of the Papal Yoke': Apathy and Opposition in the Dutch Reformation," *The Sixteenth Century Journal* 25 (1994), pp. 653–669.

10. Jonathan Israel recently argued for a modification of the traditional, rigid conception of these two camps as dominating the Dutch sociopolitical landscape. He describes the emergence in the later Golden Age of an "Orangist democratic republicanism" that was anti-clerical, on the one hand, and critical of the regent class, on the other. This important modification does not, however, significantly affect the developments we will be describing in the two camps, which emerged earlier and continued to do battle later. See Jonathan Israel, *Monarchy, Orangism, and Republicanism in the Later Dutch Golden Age: Second Golden Age Lecture, Delivered on Thursday 11 March 2004* (Amsterdam: Amsterdam Centrum voor de Studie van de Gouden Eeuw, 2004).

11. See Roelof Bisschop, *Sions vorst en volk: Het tweede-Israëlidee als theocratisch concept in de Gereformeerde kerk van de Republiek tussen ca. 1650 en ca. 1750* (Veenendaal: Kool, 1993), p. 71.

12. Bisschop, *Sions vorst en volk*, p. 91.

13. See E.H. Kossmann, *In Praise of the Dutch Republic: Some Seventeenth-Century Attitudes* (London: H.K. Lewis, 1963), p. 12; H. Smitskamp, *Calvinistisch national besef in Nederland voor het midden der zeventiende eeuw* (The Hague: Daamen, 1947), pp. 14–18. The denial that "chosenness" was part of the Neerlands Israel discourse may reflect an effort to distance Dutch nationalism from the

white supremacist convictions of the Dutch settlers in South Africa, whose conception was explicitly one of racial "chosenness." On the South African development, see G.J. Schutte, *Het Calvinistisch Nederland: Mythe en werkelijkheid* (Hilversum: Verloren, 2000), pp. 27–75.

14. See Bisschop, *Sions vorst en volk*, pp. 111–112.

15. "Dat onze goede God, uit oorzaak der verdorvenheid des menselijken geslachts, koningen, prinsen en overheden verordend heeft; willende, dat de wereld geregeerd worde door wetten en politiën, opdat de ongebondenheid der mensen bedwongen worde en het alles met goede ordinatie onder de mensen toega."

16. See Bisschop, *Sions vorst en volk*, p. 73.

17. See Groenhuis, *De Predikanten*, pp. 122–123; Bisschop, *Sions vorst en volk*, p. 103.

18. See Groenhuis, "Calvinism and National Consciousness," p. 125.

19. II Kings 18:1–20:21; II Chronicles 29:1–32:33.

20. II Kings 22:1–23:25; II Chronicles 34:1–35:27.

21. See Douglas Nobbs, *Theocracy and Toleration: A Study of the Disputes in Dutch Calvinism from 1600 to 1650* (Cambridge: Cambridge University Press, 1938), pp. 1–24.

22. My emphasis. "God had het Joodsche Volk tot sijn Volk verkozen. Dit mogen we seggen, dat God ook gedaan heeft ontrent Neerlands volk. Hoewel niet met uitsluiting van andere volkeren." Johannes d'Outrein, *De opening van de veld-tocht, des jaars 1706 en 1708: Door twee boet-predikatien over Joël 2:12-18* (Amsterdam, 1708), second sermon, p. 30. See also Bisschop, *Sions vorst en volk*, p. 175.

23. "Ende niet seggen als sy van Josaphat dat is de Hooghe Overheydt te Hove ontboden worden om reeckenkenschap te gheven dattet kerkelijck is." Jan Uytenbogaert, *Tractaet van t'Amt ende Authoriteyt eener hoogher Christelicker Overheydt in Kerckelicke Saecken...* (The Hague: Hillebrant Jacobz, 1610), p. 39. Nobbs, *Theocracy and Toleration*, pp. 30–31.

24. See II Chronicles 19:8–11.

25. See Campos Boralevi, "Classical Foundational Myths," p. 251.

26. Johan de Wit, *Public gebedt, ofte Consideratien tegens het nominatim bidden in de publique Kerken*, 3 vols. (Amsterdam: Cyprianus vander Gracht, 1663–1664), vol. 2, p. 2; and see Israel, *The Dutch Republic*, pp. 421–422, 598, 763.

27. "Hebreeusche Moses heeft de wet van Godt ontfangen, / Waermede hy naer 't volk van boven wederkeert, / Dat hem eerbiedigh groet, en welkomt met verlangen. / De vrye Staet luikt op, als 't volk de wetten eert." Joost van den Vondel, *Poëzy, of, Verscheide gedichten*, 2 vols. (Franeker: Leonard Strick, 1682), vol. 2, p. 327. Schama, *Embarrassment of Riches*, p. 120. I have used Schama's translation.

28. On competitive attitudes toward Spain, see Miriam Bodian, "Some Ideological Implications of Marrano Involvement in the International Arena," in Abraham Haim, ed., *Society and Community: Proceedings of the Second International Congress for Research of the Sephardi and Oriental Jewish Heritage* (Jerusalem: Misgav Yerushalayim, 1991), pp. 207–210.

29. Simon Schama has emphasized this broad-based, patriotic use of biblical rhetoric in his chapter, rich in example, on "Patriotic Scripture." See *Embarrassment of Riches*, pp. 51–125.

30. "En zijt Gods volk daar de Heere soo na by gekomen is die hy uit soo veel andere volken op een bysondere wijse hem tot een eigendom verkooren heeft, en daar hy dan bilijck wat meerder van verwacht als van de rest." Herman Witsius, *De Twist des Heeren met syn wyngaert* (Utrecht, 1719), p. 388.

31. "Niettegenstaande we midden onder de Afgoden-dienaars en overgeblevene Canaäniten woonen, die slechts by ons als bywoonders moeten gerekent worden." J. van Boskoop, *Het in beginselen verhoogde Nederlandt verder opgeluistert, inzonderheit door het Erffelyk verklaaren der Hooge Waardigheid des Stadhouderschaps* (Rotterdam, 1748). See also C. Huisman, *Neerlands Israël: Het natiesbesef der traditioneel-gereformeerden in de achttiende eeuw* (Dordrecht: J.P. van den Tol, 1983), p. 57. This passage shows very clearly, incidentally, that orthodox Reformed ministers used the language of chosenness in their conception of Neerlands Israel.

32. "Och, of 'er godvrugtige yveraars, Hiskiassen, Josaphats en Josiassen opstonden die den verfoeilyken beeldendienst in Nederlandts Israël geheel uitroeiden, immers die binnen enger palen zetteden!" C. van Velzen, *Kerkelyke Redevoeringen*, 2 vols. (Groningen, 1758), 1:212. See also Huisman, *Neerlands Israël*, p. 57.

33. Daniel Levi de Barrios, *Triumpho del govierno popular y de la Antiguedad Holandesa* (Amsterdam, 1683–1684) (hereinafter *TGP*), pp. 1–58. Extant copies of this work vary somewhat; I have used Exemplar B (*Etz Haim*, Ms. 9 E 43). For a more detailed description of this work, see Miriam Bodian, "Biblical Hebrews and the Rhetoric of Republicanism: Seventeenth-Century Portuguese Jews on the Jewish Community," *AJS Review* 22:2 (Fall/Winter 1997), pp. 209–221.

34. *TGP*, p. 2.

35. On the basis of Numbers 11:25–29, De Barrios noted that Moses "humbly desired that all should be prophets, so that all should be equal; and that all being equal, there would be no occasion to envy the government either of an individual or of the elect few" (*TGP*, pp. 5–7).

36. *TGP*, p. 4.

37. Ibid., pp. 23–24.

38. Ibid., pp. 28–33.

39. Ibid., p. 31. For the passage from Strabo, see Menachem Stern, *Greek and Latin Authors on Jews and Judaism*, 3 vols. (Jerusalem: Israel Academy of Sciences and Humanities, 1974), vol. 1, p. 278.

40. *TGP*, p. 28.

41. Ibid., p. 35.

42. Ibid., p. 623.

43. Ibid., pp. 646–647.

44. In fact, the Mahamad, or board of *parnasim*, was a self-perpetuating body dominated by a close-knit group of wealthy merchants. See Miriam Bodian, *Hebrews of the Portuguese Nation* (Bloomington: Indiana University Press, 1997), p. 111.

45. See *Pseudo-Philo's Liber Antiquitatum Biblicarum*, ed. G. Kisch (Notre Dame, 1949), pp. 123–130. For an English summary of this legend, see Louis Ginzberg, *The Legends of the Jews*, 7 vols. (Baltimore: Johns Hopkins University Press, 1998), vol. 1, pp. 174–176.

Spinoza's Theological-Political Problem

Menachem Lorberbaum

1. Introduction: The Theological-Political Problem

Spinoza's *Tractatus Theologico-Politicus* (*TTP*), known in English as his *Theological-Political Treatise*,[1] is an uneven book. Its tone shifts easily from rigorous analysis and argumentation to a dismissive—or at times heated—rhetoric of pamphleteering. Spinoza masters the philosophical exposition of clear and distinct ideas and of axioms of reason but is also well versed in the religious "history and language,"[2] that is to say, in theological discourse. The stylistic unevenness of the text has much to do with the fact that the book was composed over more than a decade. The *TTP* was published anonymously in 1670, but its earliest components may date back to the 1650s, and Spinoza included in it material written for philosophical but also polemical purposes.[3]

The very title of the book is misleading as to its genre. It is not, strictly speaking, a work of theology. Classic themes of theological works, such as the existence of God and the validity of religious language, are absent from the treatise. Neither is it a political treatise in the sense that Machiavelli's *Prince*, Hobbes' *Leviathan*, or Locke's *Treatise of Government* are political treatises. Political themes—the social contract, a conception of the best regime, and the theory of rights—are stated and defended in the *TTP*, but they lack the comprehensive theoretical development typical of the other treatises mentioned.[4] While the book discusses these themes, they are not its focal point. The *TTP* is neither a proper work of theology nor of political philosophy. It is a unique blend of the two; but perhaps the price it pays for achieving this mixture is that neither is complete.

The problems encountered when reading the *TTP* run even deeper: stylistic incongruity alludes to seemingly substantive contradictions of position and of doctrine. Spinoza is committed to a liberalism that celebrates freedom of opinion and expression. "After thus making clear the freedom [*libertatem*] granted to every man by the revelation of the Divine Law," he seeks to establish the declared aim of the treatise: "that this freedom can be granted without detriment to public peace or to the right of civil authorities... and cannot be withheld without great danger to peace and grave harm to the entire commonwealth [*Reipublicae*]."[5] The introduction to the book, however, espouses a grim account of the multitude of human beings. "The mass of mankind [*vulgus*, the vulgar]," he declares, "remains always at about the same pitch of misery."[6] As victims of their affectations, they are "prone to every form of credulity." Doesn't this view of the multitude undermine the very liberalism Spinoza seeks to promote? How democratically committed—if at all—is his liberalism?

In the first five chapters of the book, Spinoza criticizes, and hopes to undermine, the fundamental principles of Judaism as they are constructed by the political theologies of medieval Jewish philosophy. He delivers a bitter critique of all the central themes of medieval Jewish political theology, rejecting the major tenets of its various paradigms. Election, he argues, is no more than a promise of material good fortune, the law is no longer binding after the destruction of the Judean state, and biblical prophecy has little to do with philosophical excellence.

Maimonides is Spinoza's favored foil for an attack on what he calls dogmatic conceptions of the Bible. The dogmatists maintain that "the meaning of Scripture should be made to agree with reason."[7] Spinoza promotes a different relationship between reason and Scripture, where it is not the meaning of Scripture that should conform with reason, but rather the method used to interpret Scripture. The method he provides for interpreting Scripture is thereby modeled on the interpretive method of nature deployed by science:

> For as the [method of] interpretation of nature consists in the examination of the history of nature, and therefrom deducing definitions of natural [things] on certain [data], so Scriptural interpretation proceeds by [forming a history] of Scripture, and inferring the intention of its authors as a legitimate conclusion from [certain data and] principles.[8]

Spinoza has great confidence in the possibility of conjuring a method for stable readings of texts. This is in contrast to the interpretive method employed by Maimonides in *The Guide of the Perplexed*, which presupposes that the God of nature and the God of the Law are one but also assumes that nature is stable while texts are not. According to Maimonides, texts are objects of interpretation while nature is the object of knowledge, of physics and metaphysics, the sciences of being. Texts should therefore naturally be subject to an interpretation congruent with science.[9] In other words, Maimonides' theology of nature guides his theology of law.[10] It is precisely this presupposition that Spinoza finds intolerably prejudicial in its approach to Scripture.[11]

But Spinoza's textual analyses in the political and theological chapters of the *TTP* are not always scrupulous in their fidelity to his own interpretive guidelines. His portrayal of Jesus as a philosopher is as little convincing as the model whose nemesis he hopes it to be: Maimonides' portrayal of Moses as a Platonic prophetic leader.[12] And Spinoza's adaptation of Maimonides' thirteen principles or dogmas of belief indicates a greater affinity for the dogmatic enterprise than he might wish to acknowledge.

Although these tensions do not constitute outright contradictions, Spinoza does confront us with sufficient unevenness in style and substance to warrant the search for an overall organizing principle for the book. The present study examines Spinoza's concepts of religion and politics and how these two endeavors provide conflicting solutions to the same fundamental problems of human existence.

I argue that the tensions we note in the book are rooted in the conflict inherent in Spinoza's theological-political agenda. The very title of the book, *Theological-Political Treatise*, assumes a theological-political question or problem that must be attended to.[13] This problem can be formulated as follows. On one hand, following Hobbes, Spinoza believed that no sovereign can afford to be indifferent to religion, and that therefore no sovereign can do without a political theology to buttress his reign. On the other hand, he viewed (at least) popular religion to be no more than superstition, and the church's institutionalization of religion to be the greatest threat to the legitimacy of any sovereign. The agenda of the *TTP* is hence twofold: it seeks to destroy, to the extent possible, the theological foundations of institutionalized religion, and concomitantly to salvage a significant kernel that would enable the channeling of the elements of existing historical religions for the purposes of the sovereign.

The project of political theology as Spinoza conceives of it is therefore conflictual, seeking to retrieve as much as possible from the historical religions for the very purpose of undoing the institutions their beliefs traditionally supported.[14]

2. Phenomenology of Religion and Politics: Religion

Spinoza's assessment of the human condition is vividly set out in the opening lines of the book:

> Men would never be superstitious, if they could govern all their circumstances by set rules,[15] or if they were always favored by fortune [*fortuna*]: but being frequently driven into straits where rules are useless, and being often kept fluctuating pitiably between hope and fear by the uncertainty of fortune's greedily coveted favors, they are consequently, for the most part, very prone to credulity.[16]

Spinoza begins his treatment of political theology from a realistically inclined assessment of the inability of human beings to "govern all their circumstances" and the resulting susceptibility to superstition. In his *Political Treatise* (*PT*),[17] he defines this realistic treatment of politics in contradistinction to the philosophers who "conceive of men, not as they are, but as they themselves would like them to be."[18] Indeed, his analysis takes its cue from both Machiavelli and Hobbes, whose discussions he echoes.

Machiavelli's realism is famed for its unflinching attitude toward dirty hands in his development of the prince's virtue.[19] No less important is the awareness of the constraints of fortune in defining the horizons of meaningful and effective political agency.

> It is not unknown to me that many have held and hold the opinion that worldly things are so governed by fortune [*fortuna*] and by God, that men cannot correct them with their prudence, indeed that they have no remedy at all; and on account of this they might judge that one need not sweat much over things but let oneself be governed by chance [*sorte*].[20]

Machiavelli begins his discussion on "How much Fortune can do in human affairs, and in what mode it may be opposed" by distinguishing between fortune and chance: chance implies a fatalistic view of affairs stemming from indolence, whereas fortune assumes the possibility of agency, such that fortune presents opportunity. "It might be true that fortune is arbiter of half of our actions, but also that she leaves the other half, or close to it, for us to govern."[21] Machiavelli seeks to articulate guidelines for the prince's contention with fortune.

But aside from practical guidelines, Machiavelli's theoretical contribution lies in the very conceptualization of fortune by means of which he can sketch the general constraints imposed on viable political activity. His realism not only recognizes the role of power in politics; it also stresses the awareness of constraints as part of the adequate assessment of meaningful political agency.

Spinoza begins his treatise with a bleaker appraisal of the general ability to resist fortune. "Being frequently driven into straits where rules [*consilium*] are useless, and being often kept fluctuating pitiably between hope and fear by the uncertainty of fortune's greedily coveted favors," the human response does not exude the self-confidence, let alone the impetuosity or audacity, Machiavelli urges. The typical human response is that of credulity:

> The most frivolous causes will raise them to hope, or plunge them into despair—if anything happens during their fright which reminds them of some past good or ill, they think it portends a happy or unhappy issue and therefore... style it a lucky or unlucky omen.[22]

Superstitions are unfounded beliefs in the portentousness of natural events.[23] And not only the plebes are prone to this response. In dire straits, even great princes of the rank of Alexander the Macedonian will behave with credulity.[24]

Human beings are particularly inclined toward superstition because of a psychological instability, an oscillation between fear and hope, due to the unmanageable circumstances of their existence. Ritual is an organized form of this response to the human situation: "If they are struck with wonder at some unusual phenomenon, they believe this to be a portent signifying the anger of the gods or of a supreme deity, and they therefore regard it as a pious duty to avert the evil by sacrifice and vows, susceptible as they are to superstition and opposed to religion."[25]

Hobbes provides a parallel analysis of this mindset:

> And they that make little, or no enquiry into the naturall causes of things, yet from the feare that proceeds from ignorance it selfe, of what it is that hath the power to do them much good or harm, are

> enclined to suppose, and feign unto themselves, severall kinds of
> Powers Invisible; and to stand in awe of their own imaginations...
> making the creatures of their own fancy, their Gods.... And this
> Feare of things invisible, is the naturall Seed of that, which every
> one in himself calleth Religion.[26]

Hobbes stresses a one-dimensional "Feare of things invisible"; Spinoza's analysis of the fundamental human response to its existential situation is, psychologically speaking, subtler. Though he acknowledges "that only while fear persists do men fall prey to superstition,"[27] Spinoza takes an additional step, stressing the sway between the poles of hope and fear, the rise and plunge of oscillating affectations in response to the inscrutability of fortune.[28]

Furthermore, and in contradistinction to Hobbes, who speaks of the natural seed of all religious phenomena, Spinoza cautiously differentiates between superstition and religion. It is not merely a rhetorical difference, but one of substance. Spinoza indeed viewed much of institutionalized religious phenomena to be rooted in the human propensity to superstition. "All men are by nature liable to superstition."[29] And to the degree that men are prone to superstition, they are prone to its manipulation. Yet despite the tight weave between the affectations of fear and hope, the cognitive response of superstition and the institutional cultivation of cult, Spinoza is also committed to a notion of love of God that Hobbes does not seem to share or cultivate in *Leviathan*. This might be the background for Spinoza's choice of verse from the First Epistle of John as the motto for the book: "Hereby know that we dwell in him, and he in us, because he hath given us of his Spirit" (4:13). The verse preceding this states that "if we love one another, God dwelleth in us, and his love is perfected in us" (4:12).[30]

Maimonides, Spinoza's intimate medieval interlocutor, begins his great legal work, the *Mishneh Torah*, stressing the sublimity of the love of God:

> And what is the way that will lead you to the love of Him and the
> fear of Him? When a person contemplates His great and wondrous
> works and creatures and from them obtains a glimpse of His wis-
> dom which is incomparable and infinite, he will straightway love
> Him, praise Him, glorify Him, and long with an exceeding longing
> to know His great Name... and when he ponders these matters, he
> will recoil frightened, and realize that he is a small creature, lowly

and obscure, endowed with slight intelligence, standing in the presence of Him who is perfect in knowledge.[31]

Spinoza gives expression to the sublimity of love of God in all his works. "The love of God is man's highest happiness and blessedness, and the ultimate end and aim of all human actions [*amor Dei summa hominis foelicitatis sit, & beatitudo, & finis ultimus, & scopus omnium humanarum actionum*]."[32] Therefore, he argues, "he alone lives by the Divine Law who loves God not from fear of punishment, or from love of any other object, [thing]... but solely because he has knowledge of God, or is convinced that [it] is the highest good."[33] Spinoza's formulation clearly echoes that of Maimonides' Laws of Repentance:

> Whoever serves God out of love, occupies himself with the study of the Law and the fulfillment of commandments and walks in the paths of wisdom, impelled by no external motive whatsoever, moved neither by fear nor calamity nor by the desire to obtain material benefits—such a man does what is truly right [*ha-emet*, true] because it is truly right [lit., true], and ultimately, happiness [*ha-tova*, the good] comes to him as a result of his conduct....
>
> It is known and certain that the love of God does not become closely knit in a man's heart till he is continuously and thoroughly possessed by it and gives up everything else in the world for it.... One only loves God with the knowledge with which one knows Him.[34]

Spinoza purges the Maimonidean formulation of all fidelity to halacha as law and focuses exclusively on the philosophical love of God. Furthermore, contrary to Maimonides, Spinoza does not begin his phenomenology of religion from an experience of the sublime that is open to all human beings. For Spinoza's differences with Machiavelli and Hobbes notwithstanding, his treatment of religion and politics shares their fundamental realism with regard to the all too human, fickle motivations of politics and religion. He also shares the latter's conservative anxiety to mitigate potential sources of instability. The political responsibility of his liberal individualism is to create a polity congenial to individuals seeking their own good, not a polity charged with realizing human perfection (although the polity has a crucial role to play in its enhancement).[35]

3. Phenomenology of Religion and Politics: Politics

The firm connection between fortune and fear is the key to Spinoza's understanding not only of religion but also of politics. Politics is another human answer to fortune, to the impermeability of contingency. Chapter 4 of the *TTP*, "The Divine Law," begins by defining "law" as "that by which an individual, or all things or as many things as belong to a particular species, act in one and the same fixed and definite manner, which manner depends either on natural necessity or on human decree."[36] The word "law" denotes two radically different forms of regularity. One kind, natural regularity, is necessary and analytic to the essence of any given thing. Spinoza provides two examples of such regularity:

> The law that all bodies impinging on lesser bodies, lose as much of their own motion as they communicate to the latter is a universal law of all bodies.... So, too, the law, that a man in remembering one thing, straightway remembers another either like it, or which he had perceived simultaneously with it, is a law which necessarily follows from the nature of man.[37]

According to Spinoza, then, natural determination governs, by law, both inanimate bodies and psychological phenomena. Both physics and psychology may exemplify the necessary laws of nature.[38]

The other type of regularity, humanly decreed moral or legal behavioral regularity, is contingent upon human choice and the human assessment of particular life circumstances:

> But the law that men must yield, or be compelled to yield, somewhat of their natural right, and that they bind themselves to live in a certain way, depends on human decree.[39]

Political life, the very yielding of natural right for the sake of creating a law-governed polity, is posed as the realm of contingency in contradistinction to the natural-law-governed physics and psychology.

Spinoza's twofold definition of law begs the question of the mutual relation of both types of law: what is the metaphysical status of man-made law? How can Spinoza declare that he freely admits that "all things are determined by the universal laws of Nature" and at the same time "still say that these... laws depend on human will"?[40] On the other hand, how does humanly decreed law view the metaphysically based analysis of nature in general and of human law in particular?

Spinoza provides two answers to the metaphysical question of the possibility of humanly decreed law. First he argues that "man, insofar as he is a part of nature, constitutes a part of the power [*potentiae*] of nature."[41] Hence, all human capacities are particular instances of natural power. "Whatever, therefore, follows necessarily from the necessity of human nature... follows... from human power"—including lawmaking as a product of the human mind. Spinoza does not elaborate on this point, and it should be treated as a sketch of the general direction to be taken.

Related to Spinoza's determinism is his metaphysical monism. This theme finds its political expression in his theory of power and right: "the rights of an individual extend to [his determinate] power."[42] Whether Spinoza's identification of right with power is interpreted as a reduction of right to power[43] or only as a statement regarding the coextensiveness of the two,[44] it typifies the monistic tendency of his thought, which is reluctant to accept the bifurcation of right and power as metaphysically warranted. The epistemic status of this very identification of right and power, however, remains unclear. It is not a law of nature, but a semantic point rooted in his metaphysical monism. In any case, Spinoza's position on right and power is congruent with his political realism and remains a constant component of his political theory.

For the present discussion it is Spinoza's second argument that is crucial. Although his metaphysics is deterministic in principle, it does not follow that he could provide a full and detailed account of natural contingency in practice. To state the matter in Spinoza's own words, "I [absolutely] grant that, ...all things are determined by universal laws of Nature to exist and to act in a definite and determinate way."[45] At the same time, "as to the actual co-ordination and concatenation of things, that is how things are [ordered and concatenated], we are obviously ignorant [*plane ignoremus*]; therefore, it is more profitable for right living, nay it is necessary for us to consider things as contingent [*possibiles*]."[46] Because we do not have a full account of nature, the adequate practical management of human affairs necessitates a notion of contingency—a point reiterated in Spinoza's major works although overlooked by most of his readers.[47] It is because science, the tool that advances our knowledge of nature and its law, does not cover the range of our experiences in this world that law in the sense of human decrees is a necessary feature of life.

> I have stated that these laws depend on human decree because it is well to define and explain things by their proximate causes. The general consideration of fate [*fato*] and the concatenation of causes would aid us very little in forming and arranging our [thoughts] concerning particular [things].[48]

Legislation, or put differently, politics, is thus espoused not only by the ignorant but by the knowledgeable too.

Spinoza is unclear as to the precise causes of the epistemic status of politics. The fact that we lack a full account of nature may be due to the present state of human scientific achievements that could in principle be overcome with due progress over time. It is possible, however, that the inability to offer a comprehensive account of natural law that would cover the range of detail we experience is due to a theoretical impasse. On this reading, it is principally impossible to deduce detailed phenomena from the clear and certain knowledge we do possess of the general essence of things. I am inclined toward the latter interpretation, which views the inability to provide a complete science as a theoretical problem.[49] Either way, even according to the nontheoretical interpretation, there is (at least to date) no political "science" in the strict sense of the word. Politics is the field of human legislation precisely because our daily affairs cannot be subsumed under recognizable laws of nature. Our daily affairs are to be treated as contingent.[50]

Spinoza further expounds his basic orientation to politics in his last work, the incomplete *Political Treatise*. He introduces this work with a critique of philosophers for their inadequate accounts of politics:

> Philosophers conceive of the passions which harass us as vices into which men fall by their own fault, and, therefore, generally deride, bewail, or blame them, or execrate them, if they wish to seem unusually pious.[51] ...For they conceive of men, not as they are, but as they themselves would like them to be. Whence it has come to pass that, instead of ethics [*Ethica*], they have generally written satire, and that they have never conceived of a theory of politics [*Politicam*], which could be turned to use, but such as might... have been formed in Utopia, or in that golden age of poets when, to be sure, there was least need of it.[52]

The traditional philosophic treatment of politics has been based on an unreal conception of human psychology. As philosophical ethics are grounded not in reality but in the dreams of authors, the resultant politics are equally utopian and useless as guides for the practical challenges of policy making.

> Accordingly, as in all sciences, which have a useful application, so especially in that of politics [*Politices Theoria*], theory is supposed to be at variance with practice [*Praxi*]; and no men are esteemed less fit to direct public affairs [*regendae Reipublicae*] than theorists or philosophers.[53]

Spinoza here does not rule out the possibility of a science of politics (the precise meaning of which will soon be elaborated). He decries the failures of philosophers that have led people to generally assume a sharp divide between theory and practice in a matter in which theory might be of the utmost importance: the ruling of the republic.

Spinoza contrasts the worldly experience of statesmen and politicians[54] with the practical futility of philosophers. "[Experience] has taught" politicians "that vices will exist, while men do."[55] On the one hand, this has brought upon them the ire of theologians, for

> While they study to anticipate human wickedness, and that by arts, which experience and long practice have taught, and which men generally use under the guidance more of fear than of reason, they are thought to be enemies of religion, especially by the divines [*Theologis*], who believe that supreme authorities [*summas potestates*] should handle public affairs in accordance with the same rules of piety, as bind a private individual.[56]

Spinoza implies here, presumably following Machiavelli, that princes have a different set of virtues than that of private individuals.[57] And as regards the quality of their written works on politics, "there can be no doubt, that statesmen [*Politicos*] have written about politics more happily than philosophers." The reason for this success is their respect for experience: "For, as they had experience for their [master], they taught nothing that was inconsistent with practice."[58]

Spinoza charts his own project against the background of these two poles: the theoretical failure of philosophers and the writings of statesmen rich with experience. We may formulate Spinoza's question as follows: is there a middle ground that is not a science on the one hand, yet is not superstition on the other, on which we might base politics? Political theory is for him an empirical science that draws its foundational data from experience, not concepts:

> I am fully persuaded that experience has revealed all conceivable sorts of commonwealth [*Civitatum*], which are consistent with men's living in unity, and likewise the means by which the multitude may be guided or kept within fixed bounds. So that I do not believe that we can by meditation discover in this matter anything not yet tried and ascertained, which shall be consistent with experience or practice. For men are so situated, that they cannot live without some general law. ... Therefore, on applying my mind [*animum*] to politics, I have resolved to demonstrate by a certain and undoubted course of argument, or to deduce from the very condition of human nature, not what is new and unheard of, but only such things as agree best with practice.... We must not, therefore, look to proofs of reason for the causes and natural bases of dominion [*imperii*], but derive them from the [common] nature or position of mankind.[59]

The science of politics begins with human political experience as recorded for the most part in the works of statesmen. Indeed, both the *TTP* and the *PT* are replete with citations of classic works of political history. The theoretician then seeks to ground the practical lessons of experience and generalize these lessons by deductions from the theoretical data regarding human psychology and the human condition.[60]

As an illustration of the human condition leading to political life, we can recall the description of the human oscillation between hope and fear in encountering fortune and its reversals. As an example of the lessons of human psychology, Spinoza goes on to say that "men are of necessity liable to passions, and so constituted as to pity those who are ill, and envy those who are well off; and to be prone to vengeance more than to mercy: and moreover, that every individual wishes the rest to live after his own mind."[61] Spinoza states that these are psychological truths regarding human nature that he has already deduced in his *Ethics*. Summarized here in the *PT*, they form the psychological constraints of the political that might be paralleled to Hobbes' sociological analysis of power necessitating the creation of an agreed-upon sovereign. "And so it comes to pass," Spinoza argues, "that as all are equally eager to be first, they fall to strife, and do their utmost mutually to oppress one another; and he who comes out conqueror is more proud of the harm he has done to the other, than of the [profit] he has done to himself."[62] Politics begins from the mixture of contentiousness inherent in human relations and human credulity in contending with the circumstances of fortune.

Political science contends with the human condition by structuring stable political institutions independent of the quirks of human character so as to promise both order and security in human life.

> A dominion [*Imperium*] then, whose well-being depends on any man's good faith, and whose affairs cannot be properly administered, unless those who are engaged in them will act honestly, will be very unstable. On the contrary, to insure its permanence, its public affairs should be so ordered, that those who administer them, whether guided by reason or by passion, cannot be led to act treacherously or basely. Nor does it matter for the security of a dominion, in what spirit men are led to rightly administer its affairs. For liberality of spirit, or courage, is a private virtue; but the virtue of a state is its security [*imperii virtus securitas*].[63]

Constitutionalism, in the sense of the stable structuring of the basic institutions of society, resolves the tensions between reason and passion as sources of human motivation. Contra Hobbes, constitution—the regime structure, not the sovereign—is the soul of the polity.[64]

4. Political Theory

The proposed analysis of the scientific status of political theory has important implications for understanding the goals of Spinoza's major works and their interrelations.

First, it follows from this analysis that there is no direct systemic, architectonic link to be sought between the *Ethics* and the *TTP*. I am not denying the compatibility of the works, but rather critiquing the assumption that the political messages of the *TTP* are derivative of the *Ethics*. Given the epistemological constraints barring the possibility of constructing a complete science of being in practice, a student of the *Ethics* would still need the practical guidance of the *TTP*.[65] Put otherwise: although the *Ethics* provides directives for the philosopher's political life (for example, *Ethics* IV:35–37, 70, 73), the *TTP* provides the political guidance for a polity of the masses.[66]

I have already noted that the principle identifying right and power continues to function as a constant factor in Spinoza's political theory. But unlike the psychological truths he mentions, this is not a substantive natural law. The principle functions more as a regulating rule to ensure that the political theory stemming from experience will not develop into a moral science independent of the tight constraints of Spinoza's monism.[67] However, the bulk of his political theory treats politics as an empirical science.

Second, the *TTP* is often treated as an enlarged and sophisticated political pamphlet. According to such a reading, Spinoza the philosopher is enlisted there for the purpose of a particularly acute and pressing political conflict of religion and state. Hence, the book is particularly situated, and it would conceivably be unnecessary if the historical circumstances were different. But my analysis of religion and politics as two fundamental responses to the fortunes of the human condition, along with the analysis of the empirical nature of political science, suggests otherwise. When writing the *TTP*, Spinoza may have believed it the only way to engage in political theory. Politics in the Platonic sense is indeed impossible, but an account can be given—drawing from experience and elucidating it—of the various political-theological regimes existing in history. In his *PT*, Spinoza continues this basic undertaking but focuses on regime structure. Constitutionalism rather than political theology is the central concern of that work.

The analysis of political theology necessitates not only a different institutional focus. Both Judaism and Christianity are text-centered religions, and in that respect theology is a hermeneutical project. The political theory of the *TTP* engages in both conceptual analysis and hermeneutics, the latter presented as a method following natural history. In fact, the *TTP* develops two readings of the Bible. One legitimates an interpretation of the Bible in the spirit of Spinoza's preferred political theology while criticizing the traditional medieval version (chapters 1–5). The other utilizes the hermeneutical principles developed in the middle chapters of the *TTP* to religiously sanction an interpretation of the Bible as a work of political history (chapters 17–18).[68] The former views Moses primarily as a theologian; the latter, primarily as a statesman and founder of a polity.

5. Conclusion

Religion and politics are the two most basic human responses to the instability of human existence and fortune. Both attempt to connect particular events and draw operative conclusions for organizing the human response to fortune. Religion makes these connections by omens that it then interprets and stabilizes by means of ritual, whereas politics seeks causal connections culled from experience in order to create political structures that would provide peace and security. Politics is more rational than religion in its mode of connecting events, but it is still not a science in the sense that metaphysics is. The latter deduces causal connections from the essence of things, but due to the incompleteness of human knowledge there is no escaping the need for politics as an empirical resource for conducting our lives in a relative veil of ignorance regarding the interconnectedness of phenomena. It is this incompleteness that also explains why politics cannot be deduced from metaphysics. Most readers of Spinoza approach the *TTP* from the geometrical structure of the *Ethics* and therefore miss the independent character of the *TTP* as a work conceived within the strictures of Spinoza's concept of politics. Political theory is not a fiction, but it is not a science either. It is a scientifically informed and empirically based study and therefore more rational than religion, but it is also ultimately imaginative, as are other fields of knowledge that are not metaphysical.

This duality of the human response to the contingencies of fortune explains the ongoing need for a political theology. Politics must find a way to deal with religion as a permanent form of human response to fortune.

Notes

I thank Yuval Jobani for our many intensive hours of joint study of Spinoza's works, the fruits of which have nuanced my entire presentation.

1. Citations follow Benedict de Spinoza, *A Theological-Political Treatise and A Political Treatise*, trans. R.H.M. Elwes (New York: Dover, 1951), hereinafter *TTP, E*; and Spinoza, *Tractatus Theologico-Politicus*, trans. Samuel Shirley (Leiden: Brill, 1991), hereinafter *TTP, S*. As neither of these translations is satisfactory, I use that which best fits my understanding of the text, inserting occasional emendations marked by square brackets. Latin originals follow *Spinoza Opera*, vol. 3, ed. Carl Gebhardt (Heidelberg: Carl Winters Universitaets Buchhandlung, 1925), hereinafter *TTP, G*.

2. *TTP, E*, p. 189.

3. See Steven Nadler, *Spinoza: A Life* (Cambridge: Cambridge University Press, 1999), pp. 135, 175; W.N.A. Klever, "Spinoza's Life and Works," in Don Garret, ed., *The Cambridge Companion to Spinoza* (Cambridge: Cambridge University Press, 1996), pp. 36–46.

4. At the beginning of chapter 18, Spinoza states that it is not his intention "*de Republicae ex professo agere*" (*TTP, G*, p. 221), to provide an exposition of the republic.

5. *TTP, S*, p. 55. The formulation of the title page, however, suggests a restricted freedom to philosophize: "that freedom to philosophize [*Libertatem Philosophandi*] can not only be granted without injury to Piety and the Peace of the Commonwealth [*Reipublicae Pace*], but that the Peace of the Commonwealth and Piety are endangered by the suppression of this freedom" (*TTP, S*). Translating "republic" as "commonwealth" is at least as old as Hobbes' *Leviathan*. But whereas Hobbes' politics demanded distancing himself from republicanism, Spinoza's text demands a highlighting of his republicanism.

6. *TTP, E*, p. 5. In the course of his discussion, Spinoza uses the terms "multitude," "vulgar," and "people" as technical terms for different purposes. See Robert J. McShea, *The Political Philosophy of Spinoza* (New York: Columbia University Press, 1968), pp. 92–95; Warren Montag, *Bodies, Masses, Power: Spinoza and His Contemporaries* (London: Verso, 1999), pp. 74–80; and Menachem Lorberbaum, "Republic in Hebrew: On the Hebrew Translations of Spinoza's Political Terminology," *Iyyun* 53 (2004), pp. 194–196. [Hebrew]

7. *TTP, E*, p. 190. Cf. Leo Strauss, *Spinoza's Critique of Religion*, trans. E.M. Sinclair (Chicago: University of Chicago Press, 1997), pp. 108–109.

8. *TTP, E*, p. 99.

9. See Moses Maimonides, *The Guide of the Perplexed*, trans. Shlomo Pines, with an introductory essay by Leo Strauss (Chicago: University of Chicago Press, 1963), 2:25, pp. 327–328.

10. See Maimonides, *Guide of the Perplexed*, 3:32, pp. 525–531. See also David Hartman, *Maimonides: Torah and the Philosophic Quest* (Philadelphia: Jewish Publication Society, 1976), pp. 122–124, 160–164; Joseph Stern, *Problems*

and Parables of Law (Albany: SUNY, 1998), pp. 15–33. On Spinoza's critique of Maimonides, see Strauss, *Spinoza's Critique of Religion*, p. 147ff.

11. As is often the case, Spinoza may be steering a midway course between Maimonides and Hobbes. Hobbes' stated hermeneutic principle with regard to supernatural Scripture is that "wee are bidden to captivate our understanding to the Words"; see Thomas Hobbes, *Leviathan*, ed. Richard Tuck (Cambridge: Cambridge University Press, 2001), p. 256. This principle notwithstanding, Hobbes' interpretive practices are often close to those of Maimonides.

12. See Shlomo Pines, "Spinoza's *Tractatus Theologico-Politicus*, Maimonides and Kant," in *The Collected Works of Shlomo Pines*, in Warren Zev Harvey and Moshe Idel, eds., *Studies in the History of Jewish Thought*, vol. 5 (Jerusalem: Magnes Press, 1997), pp. 668–670, 676–682. See also Etienne Balibar, "*Jus-Pactum-Lex*: On the Constitution of the Subject in the *Theologico-Political Treatise*," in Warren Montag and Ted Stolze, eds., *The New Spinoza* (Minneapolis: University of Minnesota Press, 1997), pp. 187–192. Balibar analyzes Moses and Jesus as two opposing yet complementary moments of the dialectic of obedience.

13. For an analysis of the title, see Lorberbaum, "Republic in Hebrew," pp. 204–205.

14. For a detailed discussion of and comparison to Hobbes, see Menachem Lorberbaum, "Making Space for Leviathan: On Hobbes' Political Theology," in Cristoph Schmitt, ed., *Leviathan: Jewish Modernity as Political Theology* (Berlin: Vorwerk, forthcoming).

15. *Certo consilio*, which might also be rendered "firm counsel." The difference would relate to the specific role rules or laws might serve in political circumstances. See below.

16. *TTP, E*, p. 5.

17. All citations of *PT* are in traditional notation with page numbers that follow Spinoza, *A Theological-Political Treatise and A Political Treatise*. Latin originals follow *Spinoza Opera*, vol. 3, and are in traditional notation only.

18. *PT* I:1, p. 287. McShea describes Spinoza's position as "moderately pessimistic." See McShea, *Political Philosophy of Spinoza*, pp. 55–56 and, regarding the permanency of social conflict, pp. 78–80.

19. See Michael Walzer, "Political Action: The Problem of Dirty Hands," *Philosophy and Public Affairs* 2 (1973), p. 170ff. Spinoza's definition of virtue in the *Ethics* clearly echoes Machiavelli: "By virtue [*virtutem*] and power [*potentiam*], I understand the same thing, namely (*Ethics* III, prop. 7), virtue insofar as it is related to man, is the very essence, *or* nature, of man, insofar as he has the power [*potestatem*] of bringing about certain things...." Benedict de Spinoza, *The Collected Works of Spinoza*, vol. 1, trans. and ed. Edwin Curley (Princeton: Princeton University Press, 1988), p. 499. See also Benedict de Spinoza, *The Ethics and Selected Letters*, trans. Samuel Shirley, ed. Seymour Feldman (Indianapolis: Hackett, 1982), IV, def. 8. Spinoza here defines *potestatem* as the power of bringing about. Sovereignty, *summum potestatem*, then, is the supreme possibility of

bringing about desired effects. *Potentiam* relates to the range of possibility at one's hand. Cf. Spinoza, *Ethics* I, props. 34–35.

20. Niccolò Machiavelli, *The Prince*, trans. Harvey C. Mansfield (Chicago: University of Chicago Press, 1985), 25, p. 98. Italian original in Niccolò Machiavelli, *Il Principe e altre Opere Politiche* (Milan: Garzanti, 1981), p. 91.

21. Machiavelli, *Prince*, 25, p. 98.

22. *TTP, E*, p. 3.

23. According to Spinoza, "the fickle disposition of the multitude" (*TTP, E*, p. 216) is a permanent feature of the psychological foundations of a polity. As we will show, his construction of the basic power equation between sovereign and multitude at the basis of the polity continues to be informed by this infirmity.

24. "Superstition, then, is engendered, preserved, and fostered by fear. If anyone desire an example, let him take Alexander, who only began superstitiously to seek guidance from seers, when he first learnt to fear fortune in the passes of Sysis... whereas after he had conquered Darius he consulted prophets no more, till a second time frightened by reverses" (*TTP, E*, p. 4).

25. *TTP, S*, p. 49.

26. Hobbes, *Leviathan*, p. 75.

27. *TTP, S*, p. 50.

28. Hobbes describes a similar oscillation in his discussion of the passions (*Leviathan*, p. 44) but stresses the cognitive response of deliberation rather than emotional instability. This example underscores Hobbes' positive assessment of ordinary human deliberative and rational capacities. He therefore claims that "he who hath by Experience, or Reason, the greatest and surest prospect of Consequences, Deliberates best himselfe; and is able... to give the best counsel unto others" (*Leviathan*, p. 46). We have already noted Spinoza's skepticism as to good counsel in managing human affairs.

29. *TTP, S*, p. 50. Throughout the *TTP* Spinoza stresses that all people are prone to their affectations. Even philosophers are not immune, besides the fact that it takes many years of ethical training to achieve a state of freedom: "...the right and ordinance of nature, under which all men are born, and under which they mostly live, only prohibits such things as no one desires, and no one can attain" (*TTP, E*, p. 202); "However, it is far from being the case that all men can always be easily led by reason alone; everyone is drawn away by his pleasure, while avarice, ambition, envy, hatred, and the like so engross the mind [*mens*] that reason has no place therein" (*TTP, E*, p. 204).

30. See Spinoza's interpretation of these verses in *TTP, E*, pp. 184–186. The distinction between superstition and religion, as we shall see, should be understood in terms of the parallel and further distinction between the religion of subjugation and what he terms "universal religion" (*Catholica Religio*), on one hand, and his commitment to cultivate a piety that is consonant with the civic virtues, on the other.

31. Maimonides, "Laws of the Foundations of the Torah" 2:2, in Isadore Twersky, ed., *A Maimonides Reader* (New York: Berman House; Philadelphia: Jewish Publication Society, 1972), p. 45. For a "mystical" interpretation of Spinoza's conception of love of God see J. Ben-Shlomo, "Reply to Professor Hampshire," in Nathan Rotenschtreich and Norma Schneider, eds., *Spinoza: His Thought and Work* (Jerusalem: The Israel Academy of Sciences and Humanities, 1983), pp. 142–146; cf. David Blumenthal, "Maimonides: Prayer, Worship, and Mysticism," in Blumenthal, *Approaches to Judaism in Medieval Times*, vol. 3 (Providence: Brown University, 1988), pp. 1–16.

32. *TTP, E*, p. 60; *TTP, G*, p. 46.

33. Ibid.

34. Maimonides, "Laws of Repentance" 10:2, 6, in Twersky, *Maimonides Reader*, pp. 83–85.

35. The laws of human reason aim at "man's true [utility] and preservation" (*TTP, E*, p. 202): "The object of government [*finis Reipublicae*—the end of a republic] is not to change men from rational beings into beasts or puppets [*automata*], but to enable them to develop their minds and bodies in security, and to employ their reason unshackled; neither showing hatred, anger, or deceit, nor watched with the eyes of jealousy and injustice. In fact, the true aim of government [*Reipublicae*—of a republic] is liberty" (*TTP, E*, p. 259).

36. *TTP, E*, p. 57.

37. Ibid.

38. Not all physical and psychological science is of the epistemological stature of metaphysics. Spinoza includes these particular laws in the extended discussion of *Ethics* II between propositions 13 and 18. He does not provide arguments justifying the *a priori* nature of the laws mentioned but simply states that they are so in a series of lemmas and axioms. Spinoza seems to distinguish between physical and psychological laws that are analytic to his notions of body and mind and those that are reconstructed by an empirical physics and psychology known by the imagination. These two sources are ultimately rooted in the difference between rational conceptions of adequate ideas and sense perceptions (cf. props. 14, 19, 22–24).

39. The Latin word used is *placito*—decision, resolve; cf. *TTP, S*, p. 101, where *placito* is rendered "will." My suggestion that *placito* be rendered "human decree" follows the Hebrew translation by Chaim Wirszubski, *Tractatus Theologico-Politicus* (Jerusalem: Magnes Press, 1961), p. 44. [Hebrew] Spinoza stresses the volitional character, the *decision* involved in human law. On this see the formulation in chapter 16 regarding the social contract formed "by the power and will [*voluntate*] of the whole body," that "they must, therefore, most firmly decree [*statuere*] and establish that they will be guided in everything by reason" (*TTP, E*, p. 203). See also the distinction between the *decreto* of human sovereigns and the *decreta* of God in chapter 19 (*TTP, G*, p. 231; *TTP, E*, p. 248).

40. *TTP, S*, p. 101.

41. *TTP, E*, p. 57.

42. Ibid., p. 200.

43. See McShea, *Political Philosophy of Spinoza*, pp. 56–59.

44. *TTP, S*, p. 237, renders *extindere* as "coextensive." Edwin Curley points out that this interpretation is not a trivial point; see Curley, "Kissinger, Spinoza, and Genghis Khan," in Garret, *Cambridge Companion to Spinoza*, pp. 318–322. For Spinoza, as for any form of moral political realism, the moral point is that all political rights ultimately depend on adequate power to ensure their applicability. See Spinoza's letter 50, available in Latin in *Spinoza Opera*, vol. 4, pp. 238–241.

45. *TTP, S*, p. 101.

46. *TTP, E*, p. 58.

47. "Nature is not bounded by the laws of human reason, which aims only at man's true benefit [*utile*] and preservation; her limits are infinitely wider, and have reference to the eternal order of nature, wherein man is but a speck; it is by the necessity of this alone that all individuals are [determined as existing and operating] and acting in a particular way.... Nevertheless, no one can doubt that it is much better for us to live according to the laws and assured dictates of reason [*rationis dictamina*, rational dictates], for [their intention is] men's true [utility]" (*TTP, E*, p. 202). Spinoza elaborates on this position in Spinoza, *Ethics*, letter 32, p. 244. He defines the term "contingency" in the spirit of the limits of human knowledge in *Ethics* I, prop. 33, s. 1.

48. *TTP, E*, p. 58.

49. See the discussion of experience as a source of knowledge in Spinoza, *Collected Works*, letter 10, p. 196. Curley explores the constitutive role of experience in Spinoza's epistemology and discusses the distinction between knowledge through essence and knowledge through proximate cause in "Experience in Spinoza's Theory of Knowledge," in Marjorie Grene, ed., *Spinoza* (New York: Anchor, 1973), pp. 24–59.

50. The difficulty of retaining philosophical repose in the face of such contingency is expressed in Spinoza's correspondence. In letter 30 he expressly connects his musings on this issue with the *TTP*; cf. Nadler, *Spinoza*, p. 220.

51. Cf. Hobbes, *Leviathan*, p. 89: "The Desires, and other Passions of man, are in themselves no Sin. No more are the Actions, that proceed from those Passions, till they know a Law that forbids them: which till Lawes be made they cannot know: nor can any Law be made, till they have agreed upon the Person that shall make it," which is to say until they form a body politic.

52. *PT* I:1, p. 287.

53. Ibid.

54. Spinoza's *Politici* is translated as "statesmen" by Elwes.

55. *PT* I:2, p. 288.

56. Ibid.

57. Machiavelli states that his "intent is to write something useful" in contrast to "many [that] have imagined republics and principalities that have never been seen or known to exist in truth; for it is so far from how one lives to how one should live that he who lets go of what is done for what should be done learns his ruin rather than his preservation. For a man who wants to make a profession of good in all regards must come to ruin among so many who are not good. Hence it is necessary to a prince, if he wants to maintain himself, to learn to be able not to be good, and to use this and not use it according to necessity." Machiavelli, *Prince*, 15, p. 61.

58. *PT* I:2, p. 288.

59. *PT* I:3–4, 7, pp. 288, 290.

60. In order to overcome what he perceives to be "a possible confusion of aims here" between deductive reasoning and practice, McShea suggests recasting the paragraph from the *PT* (I:4) as an enthymeme "taking Spinoza to mean that he will not deliberately seek novelty and that he will as far as possible adapt to each other the requirements of human nature and historically known political patterns or, that in some unexpressed way, common political patterns already contain important adaptations to the necessities of human nature." McShea, *Political Philosophy of Spinoza*, p. 106. My own reading proposes that Spinoza is describing an agenda for politics as an empirical science. As I continue to argue above, this "confusion of aims" is reflective of the in-depth tension permeating his project of political theory within a system that otherwise has a thoroughly *a priori* and deductive conception of science. Cf. McShea, *Political Philosophy of Spinoza*, p. 125 n. 93.

61. *PT* I:5, p. 289.

62. *PT* I:5, p. 289. See the laws cited in *TTP*, chapter 16, as guidelines for formulating the foundations of the republic (*TTP, E*, pp. 200, 203). Such psychological truths condition the political, but political policy cannot be described as a derivative of these truths; contra Hampshire's assertion that "there can be a rational political science founded on psychological truths." Stuart Hampshire, "The Political and Social Philosophy of Spinoza," in Rotenschtreich and Schneider, *Spinoza: His Thought and Work*, p. 138.

63. *PT* I:6, pp. 289–290.

64. *Anima enim imperii jura sunt*, translated by Elwes, "For the constitution is the soul of a dominion" (*PT* X:9, p. 383). McShea, presumably hesitant to render *jura* as constitution rather than law, omits the first part of the statement and writes, "The constitution, then, 'is the soul of the state'" (*Political Philosophy of Spinoza*, p. 109). *Imperii* can also be rendered "sovereignty," and this would underscore Spinoza's affinity to Locke rather than Hobbes; cf. John Locke, *Two Treatises of Government*, 2:149–150, 212, with Hobbes, *Leviathan*, pp. 9, 153, 228–229.

65. Yirmiyahu Yovel argues that Spinoza envisages "a gradual growth of rationality from within the domain of *imaginatio*, and he thinks it is the philosopher's task to provide tools for dealing with the various forms of this transition—as he himself does [in the *TTP*]." Yovel, *Spinoza and Other Heretics: The Marrano*

of Reason (Princeton: Princeton University Press, 1989), p. 145. Steven Smith too, in *Spinoza, Liberalism and the Question of Jewish Identity* (New Haven: Yale University Press, 1997), argues that "The task of the *Treatise* as a whole is... to liberate its readers from the terrors of superstition and prepare the way for the transition from a life dominated by the passions to one directed by reason" (p. 30). These readings of Spinoza would be more appropriate as readings of Maimonides, who clearly has a history of religious progression in *Guide* 3:32. Amos Funkenstein highlighted the proto-Hegelian character of *Guide* 3:32 in his analysis of Maimonides' messianism; see Funkenstein, *Perceptions of Jewish History* (Berkeley and Los Angeles: University of California Press, 1993), pp. 131–155. My formulation above, however, need not contradict Edwin Curley's more restrictive claim that "The *TTP* is a prolegomenon to the *Ethics*." See Curley, "Notes on a Neglected Masterpiece [II]: *The Theological-Political Treatise* as a Prolegomenon to the *Ethics*," in J.A. Cover and Mark Kulstad, eds., *Central Themes in Early Modern Philosophy* (Indianapolis: Hackett, 1990), p. 113.

66. Cf. Antonio Negri, *The Savage Anomaly*, trans. Michael Hardt (Minneapolis: University of Minnesota Press, 1991), pp. xviii–xix, for a neo-Marxist interpretation of the politics of the masses. The nature of Spinoza's interest in politics ultimately depends upon his conception of freedom. Thus, Hampshire ("Political and Social Philosophy of Spinoza") provides an individualistic interpretation of freedom and derives from it a liberal interpretation, while Ben-Shlomo ("Reply to Professor Hampshire"), highlighting the mystical interpretation of unity with God, the only substance, stresses Spinoza's ultimate philosophical indifference to history and, by implication, to politics.

67. In terms of substance, the principle ensures a conception of political life true to Spinoza's realism regarding human political motivations based, inter alia, on his *a priori* psychology. Hence, Spinoza's political history (that is, his reading of the Bible) expresses this political empiricism and provides some of the realistic content of the identification of right with power. On the other hand, and on the theoretical level, politics is dissociated from metaphysics. This is the unique Spinozist combination of realism and liberalism. In terms of his actual political positions, it reverberates in Spinoza's formulation of the dogmas of belief, as has been argued by Pines, "Spinoza's *Tractatus Theologico-Politicus*, Maimonides and Kant," pp. 688–692.

68. "I will touch on the teaching of Divine revelation to Moses in this respect, and we will consider the history and the success of the Jews, gathering therefrom what should be the chief concessions made by sovereigns to their subjects, with a view to the security and increase of their dominion" (*TTP, E*, p. 216). See too Shlomo Pines, *Studies in the History of Jewish Philosophy, the Transmission of Texts and Ideas* (Jerusalem: Bialik Institute, 1977), pp. 300–305 [Hebrew]; Yosef Hayim Yerushalmi, "Spinoza on the Existence of the Jewish People," in *Proceedings of the Israel Academy of Sciences and Humanities*, vol. 6 (Jerusalem, 1984), pp. 175–181. [Hebrew]

IV. SEVENTEENTH-CENTURY ENGLAND

Rabbinic Ideas in the Political Thought of John Selden

Jason P. Rosenblatt

Acting on the belief that the stories we tell about others reveal even more about ourselves, recent and justly well-regarded studies of England and the Jews have argued that a culture's representation of "otherness" has important consequences for its own self-imagining.[1] In his *Shakespeare and the Jews*, James Shapiro unearths many of the vile racist stereotypes common in the English Renaissance in order to suggest that our fantasies about others reveal our deepest fears about ourselves. For Shapiro, the fear and loathing of Jews as child abductors, murderers, and cannibals can help to explain the confused struggles among the English in the early modern era to develop a religious and national identity in a turbulent time. Judaism as a race, nation, and religion is defined as different in every way from the English Protestantism that it threatens to contaminate.

Inevitably, Shapiro's exhaustive and valuable attempt to reconstruct a Renaissance audience's experience of *The Merchant of Venice* in the light of its preconceptions about Jews involves recourse to the most destructive myths. He acknowledges but understandably does not concentrate on an exception such as John Selden (1584–1654), the most learned person in seventeenth-century England, whose rabbinic researches, unlike those of his other great contemporary English talmudic scholar, John Lightfoot, are free of Judeophobia.[2] One might argue that Selden is precious precisely because he is uncommon, like the courageous few who throughout history have refused to be swallowed up by the mob. Generally skeptical toward harmful myths, Selden has a humanist's respect for historical investigation and an antiquarian's interest in the documents of the past simply because they exist.[3] A polymath, he wrote a half-dozen rabbinic works, some of them immense, which respect, to an extent remarkable for the times, the self-understanding of Judaic exegesis. *De Diis Syris* (1617), an analysis of the pagan gods of the Hebrew Bible, is a pioneering study of cultural anthropology and comparative religion. *De Successionibus ad Leges Ebraeorum in Bona Defunctorum* (1631) addresses the question of intestate succession according to Jewish law. *De Successione in Pontificatum Ebraeorum* (1638) explores the laws relating to the ancient Jewish priesthood. *Uxor Ebraica* (1646) analyzes the theory and practice of the Jewish laws of marriage and divorce, which Selden admired. On the very last page he suggests parenthetically (because it was a point of honor for him to bury the lead) that the canon law of divorce still in force in England be reformed and brought more closely into conformity with Jewish law. Selden's motto was "περί παντός τὴν ἐλευθερίαν" ("liberty above all things"), and *De Synedriis et Praefecturis Juridicis Veterum Ebraeorum* (1650–1655), a study of the Sanhedrin written shortly after the execution of Charles I, contains a remarkable Maimonidean discussion of whether that court could try kings not only for crimes like murder, which anyone could commit, but also for those which only kings could commit. Occupying 1,132 huge folio columns in the *Opera*, *De Synedriis* deals primarily with the constitution of Jewish courts, including the Sanhedrin, which, as Selden notes pointedly, was not priestly in composition. Its understated argument is thoroughly Erastian, demonstrating that matters at present under the jurisdiction of ecclesiastical courts in England were in ancient times decided by Jewish courts that could well be called secular.[4] The implicit argument is that the Sanhedrin might serve as a positive model for Parliament. Taken together, these rabbinic works constitute a notable exception to those products of the English Renaissance that emphasize otherness and difference.

Selden's important contribution to political theory and international law, *De Jure Naturali et Gentium juxta Disciplinam Ebraeorum* (1640), 847 folio pages, is surely one of the most genuinely philo-Semitic works produced by a Christian Hebraist in early modern Europe. Selden accepts the universal validity of the non-biblical, rabbinic *praecepta Noahidarum*, the seven Noahide laws, which serve for him as the law of nature. Selden bases his theory on the Talmud, which he believes records a set of doctrines far older than classical antiquity.[5] Natural law consists not of innate rational principles that are intuitively obvious but rather of specific divine pronouncements uttered by God at a point in historical time. Selden discusses the rabbinic identification of natural law with the divinely pronounced Adamic and Noahide laws, considered by rabbinic tradition as the minimal moral duties enjoined upon all of humankind. He quotes from the *locus classicus* in tractate Sanhedrin (56a–b), which includes the traditional enumeration of the laws: the prohibitions of idolatry and blasphemy; the injunction to establish a legal system; commandments against bloodshed, sexual sins, and theft; and a seventh law, not applicable to vegetarian Adam but added after the flood and based on Genesis 9:4, forbidding anyone to eat flesh cut from a living animal. Selden devotes an entire book of *De Jure* to each of the seven commandments, and he follows the order set by Maimonides, which emphasizes their decalogic nature. The first two, like the first tablet of the law, deal with the relations between human beings and God, while the rest govern relations among human beings.[6] While Selden accepts the authority of this postbiblical, rabbinic, universal law, he rejects the absolute authority of the biblical Ten Commandments on the grounds that they were given only to the Jews.

In *De Jure* Selden sets down ideas regarding the nature of Judaism and its attitude toward gentiles that are far more charitable than those circulating in other contemporary works addressed to Christian audiences. Selden did not live to see Cromwell's Whitehall Conference, and one can never be certain that his reverence for ancient Jewish learning and toleration of contemporary Jews would have extended so far as activity on behalf of readmission. It is clear, however, that his writings had a positive influence on both the readmission question and, in the next century, the Jewish Naturalization Act, or the Jew Bill of 1753. Regarding the former, on the occasion of Jews' making application to Cromwell and "at the request of a person of quality," Thomas Barlow (1607–1691), bishop of Lincoln, wrote a tract on the "Toleration of the Jews in a Christian State." Published posthumously, it was probably written not long after 1650, since Barlow refers to Selden's *De Synedriis* as having been written "of late." The person of quality and addressee of the opening epistle is "the Honorable Robert Boyle, Esq." The argument in favor of admission—arranged according to numbers and lists, perhaps to please the great scientist who occasioned it—derives entirely from Selden's rabbinic writings. The proviso that eighteen regulations and limitations on freedom be imposed originates with Barlow himself. In the following century, the learned English printer William Bowyer offered a humane argument in favor of the Jew Bill, citing such sources as *Seder Olam*, an obscure, midrashic, chronological work of the second century. Bowyer, who wrote an epitome of Selden's immense, three-book study of the Sanhedrin, superintended the printing of Selden's *Opera Omnia* and took his rabbinic scholarship from those six vast volumes.

In light of Selden's scholarly range and depth of thought, it is difficult to limit oneself to one or two ideas. In the brief space that remains, I would like to discuss two ideas from *De Jure Naturali et Gentium*, selected because of their very difference, one asserting the absolute power of the law, the other authorizing the abrogation of the law under certain circumstances: first, Selden's folding of English common law into the Noahide law of *dinim*, and second, his Talmud-based discussion of the "*Ius Zelotarum*" ("the right of zealots").

Unlike most of his contemporary natural law theorists, who look for innate laws as universal moral imperatives, Selden in *De Jure* postulates a hypothetical state of total natural freedom, upon which the laws of nature supervened. Those laws were not innate but had to be learned, so that the only condition truly natural to human beings was freedom. Selden identified natural or universal law with the rabbinic Noahide laws, uttered by God at a specific moment in historical time when he made plain to mankind what he would punish them for.[7] There is no other universal law apart from this divine revelation, which is a positive, or voluntary, law of perpetual obligation. It is important to remember that when Selden speaks of the negative laws against stealing and adultery, he is thinking not of the biblical prohibitions in the Ten Commandments, which are binding only on the Jews, but rather of the *praecepta Noahidarum*, which originate in the Talmud:

> I cannot fancy to myself what the law of nature means, but the law of God. How should I know I ought not to steal, I ought not to commit adultery, unless somebody had told me so. 'Tis not because I think I ought not to do them, nor because you think I ought not; if so, our minds might change: whence then comes the restraint? From a higher power; nothing else can bind. I cannot bind myself, for I may untie myself again; nor an equal cannot bind me,

for we may untie one another. It must be a superior, even God Almighty.[8]

Selden, who distinguishes between the universal and the natural, rejects the view of other theorists that the consensus of all nations ought to be considered evidence of a law of nature, in part because for him Noahide law is divine and positive rather than natural and innate. Perhaps equally important, and overlooked, is Selden's radical idea of the common law of England as a limited law of nature. What may have been for Selden the most attractive of the Noahide laws is *dinim* (adjudication), the injunction that every nation establish its own civil laws. Where the other six laws are examples of what the Talmud calls *"shev v'al taaseh"* ("sit and do nothing"), the law of adjudication is an example of its opposite, *"kum aseh"* ("get up and do"), a positive commandment whose fulfillment requires a specific action. In *De Jure*, Selden quotes the Talmud, Maimonides, and other rabbinic sources to make the point: "Surely it has been taught: Just as the Israelites were ordered to set up law courts in every district and town [Deuteronomy 16:18], so were the sons of Noah likewise enjoined to set up law courts in every district and town":[9]

> How are they [the Noahides, i.e., non-Jews] commanded concerning the *dinim* [adjudication]? They are obligated to install judges and legal authorities in every district and to judge according to these six commandments and to warn the people.[10]

As Selden himself is well aware, he introduces this law belatedly and appears to devote less space to it than to the other precepts, to each of which a whole book in *De Jure* is dedicated.[11] But in fact it is treated at greater length than the others. The many laws of the written and oral Torah discussed throughout *De Jure* constitute for Selden the civil law of the Jews. For him, as for the rabbis, Noahide law has a double jurisdiction. It is the system of law for which non-Jews are universally obligated, and it was the system of law followed by the Jews before the revelation of the 613 commandments of the Torah at Sinai. As David Novak has pointed out, "the correlation between these two jurisdictions is that Jews began as Noahides."[12] According to Selden, the other six Noahide laws, repeated in the Torah, are universal, while the law of adjudication ("*de Judiciis*") comprises all the other Torah laws and obligates only the people of Israel. Hence his view that Christians are not bound even by the Decalogue.

The view that Noahide law was original and universal, and that it was supplemented by civil laws that have the same force within a specific nation as natural laws, dovetails in Selden's mind with the view that the original natural law evolves for his own countrymen into the English common law, the highest legal authority, from which there is no appeal. As early as the *Notes on Fortescue* (1616), he called the common law of England a limited law of nature:

> Although the law of nature be truly said immutable yet it is as true, that it is limitable, and limited law of nature is the law now used in every state. All the same may be affirmed of our *British* laws, or *English*, or other whatsoever. But the divers opinions of interpreters proceeding from the weakness of man's reason, and the several conveniences of divers states, have made those limitations, which the law hath suffered, very different.[13]

Years later, Selden would assimilate this view of the common law into the Noahide precept of *dinim* (*de Judiciis*), a religious injunction to "install judges and legal authorities in every district." For Selden, whose "Torah" is law, the English common law has an added status as a natural law ordained by God. There could then be no appeal to a higher law or to general principles outside of the law. Alan Cromartie is entirely persuasive when he notes that Selden's passionate commitment to the common law gave him an advantage "in coping with the tactics of the crown"— particularly with the king's attempt to appeal "outside the common law to an inalienable prerogative." Bate's case (1606) involved the king's right to levy customs without Parliament's consent; the Five Knights case (1626), in which Selden defended Hampden, involved imprisonment of the king's opponents without revealing cause; and *R. v. Hampden*, the Ship Money case (1638), involved the power of emergency taxation.[14]

In both the *Notes on Fortescue* and *De Jure*, there are universal laws as well as a law of particular places, issuing from divine commandments for the children of Israel and with roots in arbitrary arrangements entered into by common consent for England and other countries. The insularity implicit in "the several conveniences of divers states," which make the shape of the common law "very different" for each of those states, does not bother Selden, who asserts with equanimity the view that "the opinions, customs, constitutions, and measures of all, or at least many, other nations carry no weight with the Hebrews in their decisions about the nature of natural or universal law." But this statement infuriates the generally humane Cambridge Platonist Nathanael Culverwel (1618–1651), in *An Elegant and Learned Discourse of the Light of Nature*, published post-humously, who sees it, understandably, as a sign of Jewish triumphalism and quotes it as an example of "how that learned and much honoured Author of our own, does represent their minde unto you."[15] Since all of his knowledge about such matters derives from Selden, implicit in his complaint is either the question of why Selden isn't complaining or the assumption that he is:

> Why then do the Jews look upon the *goyim* [nations, gentiles, idola-ters] with such a disdaining and scornful eye, as if all the Nations in comparison with them, were no more than what the Prophet saies they are in respect of God, *as the drop of a bucket, as the dust of the Ballance* [Isaiah 40:15], that cannot incline them one way or other.[16]

This is an ambivalent quotation from the Hebrew Bible, since Isaiah, of-fering comforting words to Zion, speaks in the voice of God, disparaging foreign nations.

Culverwel's *Discourse* is an attempt at bridge-building, and the passag-es in Selden asserting Jewish superiority distract him from his message. (Christian superiority he both assumes and asserts.) Selden's sympathy with the earliest rabbis, who saw themselves as heirs to the Pharisees, is harder to understand. After all, as a Christian he knows that the Pharisees had acquired a terrible reputation, in large part because of the intense hostility toward them expressed in some chapters of the New Testament. Part of the answer must remain a mystery, though connected with Selden's magnificent Hebrew scholarship and a love of learning for its own sake. It is also true that the Pharisees attempted to extend holiness from the limits of the Jerusalem Temple to a wider range of everyday life. Concern for ritual detail exposed them to attack by early Christians, but it also turned quotidian existence into a vast array of opportunities to fulfill divine law and thus to sanctify life.[17] According to Cromartie, Selden's priorities "satisfied a puritan need by heightening the significance of or-dinary life. The law of the Jews was established by God, but the laws that were made by the English played precisely the same role: they were in fact a duty, religious in authority and content, that a people could estab-lish for itself."[18]

Although they are essentially opposites, it is sometimes hard to tell the difference between an Erastian position and a theocratic one. It is impossible to read Selden's heart and to tell whether he really believes in the Noahide law or sees it merely as set of minimum legal requirements, supported by ancient tradition, that might justify a civil religion. In Selden's rabbinic writings, the sacred and the secular become inextricably intertwined. Does he, like the Pharisees, want to extend holiness beyond the church to everyday life, or does he want to turn law into religion? According to Robert Baillie, a hostile fellow member of the Westminster Assembly, "this man is the head of the Erastians; his glory is in the Jewish learning; he avows every where that the Jewish state and church was all one, and that so in England it must be, that the Parliament is the church."[19]

The second and concluding rabbinic argument of this talk, taken from Selden's *De Jure*, caused something of a stir among his contemporaries, including a positive response from Anthony Ascham and a negative one from Thomas Hobbes. In a series of comprehensive and ultimately Maimonidean chapters on the right of zealots, the *Ius Zelotarum*, Selden interprets the New Testament account of Jesus' scourging of the money-changers as an act in accordance with the laws of normative Judaism.

Selden fills his chapters with diverse biblical examples of zeal, including Numbers 25:6–15 (Phinehas' slaying of Zimri and Cozbi, which earns him a covenant of perpetual priesthood), I Maccabees 2:23–26 (Mattathias' slaying of a Jew who was about to offer a sacrifice in public on a pagan altar), Matthew 21:12–17 (Jesus' scourging of the moneychangers and driving them from the Temple), John 18:22 (one of Caiaphas' officers striking Jesus on the face), Acts 7:57 (the stoning of Stephen), and Acts 23:13 (the oath to kill Paul).[20] Despite these examples, Selden's argument is decidedly rabbinic rather than biblical. He begins with a central text to explicate, a *mishna* from tractate Sanhedrin that he cites in both the Babylonian and Jerusalem texts of the Talmud, even noting a textual variant in the latter. The mishna promulgates a law whereby zealots are to punish one who commits an act of sacrilege by stealing the service vessels of the Temple, or curses by enchantment, or cohabits with an Aramean woman [i.e., a Gentile]. If a priest performs the Temple service while ritually unclean, his fellow priests do not charge him with this offense in a court (a *bet din*). Rather, the young priests take him out of the Temple court and crush his skull with cudgels.[21]

In this instance, the different moral valences of the acts of zeal recorded in Scripture are of less interest to lawyer Selden than the binding precept of the mishna, an example of *halacha*, that is, a rabbinic "legal decision regarding a matter or case for which there is no direct enactment in the Mosaic law, deduced by analogy from this law or from the Scriptures" (*O.E.D.*). What should be emphasized is the fact that where other exegetes in seventeenth-century England blame the rabbis for distorting the meaning of the Hebrew Bible with the severity of their laws, Selden, throughout *De Jure*, recognizes that halacha imposes restrictions in order to prevent the enforcement of laws that authorize violence. In this case, the Talmud requires that the zealot act only at the moment the offense is being committed and that ten Israelites witness it.[22] And Maimonides, the great codifier cited more often by Selden than any other authority, Christian or Jewish, goes much farther, moderating even the strictures of the rabbis. In a commentary on the *mishna* in question to which Selden refers, Maimonides limits the various punishments. To be punished by a zealot, one must be an apostate who has denied the fundamental tenets of the religion ("הכופר בעקר, *eo qui renuntiasset Fundamento*"). Moreover, one who cohabits with a heathen woman must do so in the presence of ten Israelites or more. After the intimate act, or if there is no assembly of Israelites present, or if she is not an idolatress, the zealot is forbidden to kill the offender. And if the transgressor killed an attacking zealot in order to save his own life, he is not liable to be executed, because the zealot was pursuing him to kill him, and the Torah does not decree the death penalty except in the manners prescribed. However, the offender is liable to "*karet*" ("extirpation") by Heaven for [cohabiting with] an idolatress. Even though such extirpation is not mentioned in the Torah and is not enumerated among the list of those liable to extirpation, nevertheless, it is a tradition, and its explanation is based on a scriptural phrase: "and hath been intimate with the daughter of a strange god; the Lord will extirpate the man that doeth this" (Malachi 2:12).[23]

In both *De Jure* and *De Synedriis*, Selden cites striking pronouncements—both pagan and Jewish—on the *Ius Zelotarum* unchecked by the merciful limitations of rabbinic Judaism. He quotes extensively from Philo, whose comments on subversives who entice their fellow Israelites into the worship of other gods (Deuteronomy 13:1–18) ignore that chapter's insistence (in verse 14) that inquiry and thorough investigation precede the bringing of charges and punishment: "And his seductions ought to be made known to all lovers of piety, who [may be expected to] attack the wicked one without delay, having deemed it their holy duty [lit.

"the duty of sanctity"] to kill such a man."[24] Selden takes note of the medieval law of England's ordaining that an outlawed person be given over to the power of everyone that would kill him. Some thought that those persons who incurred a praemunire were liable to the same fate, but this was expressly guarded against by parliamentary statute, not an insignificant fact for an advocate of parliamentary rights.[25]

In a *tour de force* in *De Jure* 4.5, a commentary, informed by rabbinic scholarship, on the cleansing of the Temple (Matthew 21:12–13, Mark 11:15–19, Luke 19:45–48, John 2:13–22), Selden sees Jesus as a Jew acting according to the *Ius Zelotarum*. Relying on numerous talmudic texts and the commentaries of Maimonides and Obadiah of Bertinoro, among others, Selden describes in meticulous detail each of the thirteen chests, called *shofarot* (trumpets), with narrow mouths and wide bellies, that collected monies in the Temple in Jerusalem: in the first, the money of the present year; in the second, that of the year past; in the third, the money that was offered to buy pigeons, etc.[26] Each person, no matter how poor, was required to pay exactly half a shekel. Therefore, when he sought to change a shekel for two half shekalim, he was obliged to allow the moneychanger some gain, which was called *kalbon* (related to the Greek *kolluboj*). And even when two paid one shekel between them, each person was obliged to allow the same gain or fee to the exchanger.[27]

Selden knows the *kalbon* is a minute amount—one twenty-fourth of a half shekel, which Jesus paid for himself and Peter, presumably without objection (Matthew 17:24–27)—but it still symbolizes trafficking for unholy gain. Jesus' action can then be seen as a protest against the commercialization of the Temple. His driving out of the sheep and oxen disrupts the sacrificial offerings, reminding the Christian reader of their replacement by the one unrepeatable sacrifice soon to come. What really captures Selden's imagination is John 2:16: "and said unto them that sold doves, Take these things hence; make not my Father's house a house of merchandise." This immediately puts the disciples in mind of Psalms 69:9: "The zeal of thine house hath eaten me up." And it dovetails in Selden's mind with a long-familiar talmudic passage that helps to explain Christ's vehemence: a *mishna* in tractate Sanhedrin (24b) declares ineligible as legal witnesses or judges gamblers with dice, "pigeon-flyers," usurers, and traders in the produce of the Sabbatical year. Selden discusses the various interpretations of the meaning of pigeon-flyers, including those who bet that their pigeon can outrace another's, and the view in Rashi's commentary (the "*Glossa*") that it refers to those who train pigeons (*columbas*, pigeons or doves) to fight with each other—a form of cockfighting.[28] As early as *De Diis Syris* (1617), before he could have been aware of the talmudic source, Selden notes that the Jews regarded those who handled doves as too low to give testimony and placed them on the same level as thieves, pimps, and dice-players ("*fures nempe, lenones, aleatores*"). This information Selden found in Philippus Ferdinandus' translation of a commentary on the 613 precepts by the obscure Abraham ben Hassan (incorrectly transcribed by Philippus as "Kattan"), *Praecepta in Monte Sinai* (Cambridge, 1597).[29]

A favorite theme, repeated in Selden's mature scholarship, and occasioned by the references to pigeons and doves in the Gospels and in tractate Sanhedrin, is the importance of contributing to the public good. In both *De Jure* and *De Synedriis*, Selden quotes the *mishna* in Sanhedrin 24b, the *gemara* that develops the *mishna*, and the commentaries on the Talmud, to emphasize the importance of productivity and the moral imperative to contribute to the welfare of civilization. The four types of people enumerated in the *mishna* have not habituated themselves to "performing acts of charity and humane conduct." Maimonides, in his commentary on the *mishna*, explains further: "[such a person] is occupying himself with something that has no value for the general welfare of human society. It is a fundamental principle of Judaism that a person should occupy himself in this world with one of two things: either with Torah, to perfect his soul with its wisdom, or with an occupation which contributes to the general welfare of society, such as a trade or a business. It is proper to lessen the latter and increase the former, as the Sages said: 'Lessen your involvement in business activities, and occupy yourself with the Torah'" (Avot 4:10).[30] This injunction must have resonated with Selden, whose "Torah" was law and legal history and who turned down offers of high office and additional income (he was wealthy enough already) in order to concentrate on his studies. His endorsement of the view that productivity should be a prerequisite for full citizenship is reflected in his various positive formulations of the ancient passages requiring the promotion of public good.[31] Indeed, the Talmud itself objects to the profiteering from the sale of doves in the Temple.[32]

In conclusion, I have chosen two very different discussions from *De Jure Naturali* in order to suggest the range of Selden's thought. For each of the diverse individuals influenced by him—Ben Jonson, John Milton, James Harrington, Thomas Hobbes, John Locke, and Giambattista Vico, among many others—Selden represented something different. One might call him the English Osiris, remembering the famous passage in Milton's *Areopagitica* that compares the body of truth to the body of Osiris, "torn into a thousand peeces, and scatter'd to the four winds. From that time ever since, the sad friends of Truth, such as durst appear, imitating the careful search that Isis made for the mangl'd body of Osiris, went up and down gathering up limb by limb still as they could find them." The figure is evocative for various reasons: the cross-cultural implications of the story of an Egyptian god, found in Plutarch's *Moralia* and adapted by Milton, an English Puritan; the extraordinary mastery of Eastern learning by the young Selden, who writes brilliantly of Osiris in his great work of cultural anthropology and comparative religion, *De Diis Syris*; and even the images of scattering and gathering, diaspora and ingathering, that suggest the Jews' dispersion and the controversy over their readmission in the 1650s. Osiris, for Milton, is the body of truth. For most English intellectuals in the mid-seventeenth century, Selden, a Christian, embodied rabbinic thought; and even today no one has been able to see him whole. Like his contemporaries, the few who study him today are slowly gathering him up, limb by limb, as we can find them. More than seventy-five years ago, David Ogg described him accurately as one who stands out alone in a century of greatness, "seeking not fame but truth in an erudition more vast than was ever garnered by any other human mind." And even Ogg, concentrating on Selden as a historian of the laws and constitutional institutions of England, has not a word to say about the half-dozen rabbinical works that constitute his most mature scholarship.

Notes

Heartfelt thanks to Meirav Jones and Gordon Schochet, two guiding spirits of the conference on Hebraic political thought at the Shalem Center in August 2004; and to Oxford University Press for permission to reprint material from my new book *Renaissance England's Chief Rabbi*.

1. See especially Michael Ragussis, *Figures of Conversion: 'The Jewish Question' and English National Identity* (Durham and London: Duke University Press, 1995); James Shapiro, *Shakespeare and the Jews* (New York: Columbia University Press, 1996).

2. Shapiro makes the important point that in his scholarship Selden draws upon examples from the Bible, the Talmud, and medieval Anglo-Jewish history, thus "collapsing any simple distinction between the ancient Israelite and the modern Jewish nation" (*Shakespeare and the Jews*, p. 174).

3. A serious and unfortunate example of antiquarian devotion to documents overcoming skepticism would seem to be the records of Jewish ritual murder in Selden's brief *Treatise on the Jews in England* (1617). Gerald J. Toomer, who generously read a draft of this lecture, argues that Selden's position on the matter cannot be so easily determined. His history of the Jews appears in the third edition of Samuel Purchas' *Pilgrimage* (1617), and parts of it—such as a reference to "one cruell and (to speake the properest phrase) Jewish crime... usuall amongst them"—sound like Purchas rather than Selden. More important, in a transcript provided by Professor Toomer of the relevant sections of William Prynne's *Short Demurrer to the Jewes Long Discontinued Remitter into England* (1656), Prynne asserts that Purchas did not print unaltered what Selden submitted to him, and Selden was angry with Purchas "for abusing him in such a manner, and his Readers likewise" (p. 1). Selden took the stories of ritual murder from Matthew Paris, who had a virulent hatred of the Jews. A number of questions complicate the matter, including the relation of Selden's original *Treatise* to what Prynne calls "such a poor maimed account given of [the Jews]... so different from that delivered [to Purchas]" (p. 1). Professor Toomer believes that Selden, reproducing his sources in a mostly straightforward narrative, "was already too much of a skeptic to endorse the stories of Matthew Paris as is done in Purchas' rendering." The one example in the *Treatise* that seems to derive directly from an archival source and is accompanied by one of Selden's characteristic learned notes is an accusation not of ritual murder but rather of forced circumcision in Norwich. But "the Jewes after procured the boy to be seene, and his member was found covered." Selden then refers to an ancient Hellenistic technique of "Chirurgery, [whereby] the skinne may be drawne forth to an uncircumcision" (Purchas, *Pilgrimage*, p. 173; John Selden, *Opera Omnia*, ed. David Wilkins [1726], 3:1461). Does Selden believe that the Jews of medieval Norwich practiced this surgical technique? There are more questions than answers. What can be asserted is that no Christian can be found in early modern England who unequivocally rejected the blood libel.

4. See, on this point, Jonathan R. Ziskind's introduction to his edition, *John Selden on Jewish Marriage Law: The Uxor Hebraica* (Leiden, New York: Brill, 1991), p. 18.

5. See Richard Tuck, *Philosophy and Government 1572–1651* (Cambridge: Cambridge University Press, 1993), p. 214. I am greatly indebted to all of Professor Tuck's writings on Selden, especially *Natural Rights Theories: Their Origin and Development* (Cambridge: Cambridge University Press, 1979).

6. John Selden, *De Jure Naturali et Gentium juxta Disciplinam Ebraeorum* (London, 1640), pp. 118–119. He lists the ordinances as "*de Cultu extraneo*," "*de Maledictione Nominis sanctissimi seu Numinis*," "*de Effusione Sanguinis* seu *Homicidio*," "*de Revelatione Turpitudinum* seu *Turpitudine ex concubitu*," "*de Furto ac Rapina*," "*de Judiciis* seu *Regimine forensi ac Obedientia Civili*," and "*de*

Membro animalis viventis non comedendo." His list is based on Maimonides' distinction between those commandments that are *"inter Hominem & Numen sanctissimum"* and those that are *"inter Hominem & proximum suum."*

7. See the lucid and concise discussion of Selden's theory of natural law in Richard Tuck, "The Ancient Law of Freedom: John Selden and the Civil War," in John Morrill, ed., *Reactions to the English Civil War 1642–1649* (London: Macmillan, 1982), esp. pp. 139–145.

8. John Selden, *Table Talk* (Freeport, N.Y.: Books for Libraries Press, 1972), p. 101.

9. Selden, *De Jure*, 7.5, p. 805, citing *"Gem. Bab. ad. tit. Sanhed. cap.7. fol. 56b"*: *"Traditio est, quemadmodum in praeceptis accepere Ebraei, constituere tribunalia per omnes pagos & urbes (quo referunt illud [Deuter. 16.18], Judices & Magistros constitues in omnibus portis tuis) ita praeceptum est Noachidis constituere Tribunalia per omnes pagos & urbes."*

10. Ibid., citing Maimonides, *Hal. Melakim cap. 9: "Quomodo intelligendum est praeceptum Noachidarum de Judiciis?* [806] *Ex eo debent constituere Iudices & Praefectos pagatim, qui tum judicent de Sex illis praeceptis ceteris, tum populum (de eorum observatione) commoneant."* On this point he also cites *"Moses Mikotzi praecept aff. 122; & videsis* Aiin Israel *part 2. fol. 111. col. 2."*

11. Selden, preface, *De Jure*, sig. b3: "Et demùm accedit ibi *Caput de Judiciis seu Regimine Forensi atque Obedientia Civili."*

12. David Novak, *The Image of the Non-Jew in Judaism: An Historical and Constructive Study of the Noahide Laws* (New York and Toronto: Edwin Mellen, 1983), p. 53.

13. Selden, *Opera*, 3:1891.

14. Alan Cromartie, *Sir Matthew Hale (1609–1676)* (Cambridge: Cambridge University Press, 1995), p. 31.

15. Nathanael Culverwel, *An Elegant and Learned Discourse of the Light of Nature* (1652), p. 82, quoting the chapter heading of *De Jure*, 1.6, p. 75: "Gentium (saies he) *sive omnium, sive complurium opiniones, mores constitutiones, mensurae apud Hebraeos, in eo decernendo quod jus esse velint Naturale, seu universale, lucum habent nullum."*

16. Culverwel, *Discourse*, p. 82. The complaint is based entirely on Selden, including *De Jure*, 1.6, p. 119, on "אומות העולם *gentes* seu *populos munde* atque גוים *id est Gentes seu Barbaros."*

17. This paragraph is indebted to Robert Goldenberg, "Talmud," in Barry W. Holtz, ed., *Back to the Sources: Reading the Classic Jewish Texts* (New York: Summit, 1984), pp. 129–175, esp. p. 130.

18. Cromartie, *Hale*, p. 161.

19. Robert Baillie, *Letters and Journals of Robert Baillie*, ed. D. Laing (Edinburgh, 1861), 2:265–266.

20. Selden, *De Jure*, 4.4, p. 490; 4.5, p. 498.

21. Selden, *De Jure*, 4.4, p. 487, citing *Tit. Sanhedrin* cap. 9, [sect.] *ult. Gemar. Babylon. ibid. fol.* 81 b. &c. *Hierosolymit. eod. tit. fol.* 27. col. 2. [sect.] 11: "*Qui Sacrilegium commiserat (et sacra nempe supellectili quid furatus erat;) qui per Idolum maledixerat (Numini) qui coitu se miscuerat cum foemina Aramaea, id est extera seu plane Gentili, Zelotis fas fuit incurrere in eum* [marginal note: "בהן *in eos codice Hierosolymitano*"]. *Sacerdotem in immunditie sua sacra obeuntem, non erat necesse ut sacerdotes caeteri in forum deducerent: sed sacerdotes qui per aetatem nondum ministerio sacro pares erant, eum extra atrium protrahebant, & cerebrum ejus fustibus elidebant.*"

22. Selden, *De Jure*, p. 487, where the opening words of the chapter emphasize that the zealot must act while the crime is being committed: "*in ipso dum committebatur facinus duntaxat momento.*" For required witnesses, see ibid., p. 488, "in Publico."

23. Selden, *De Jure*, p. 488: "*vide Maimonid. Halach. Rotzach.* cap. 4. & *halach. Sanhedrin* cap. 18. & *halach. Aboda Zara* cap. 10." See the next marginal note on the same page, which includes references to Moses of Coucy's commentary on the positive and negative laws of the Torah, which draws heavily on Maimonides' *Mishneh Torah*, and to Joseph Caro's *Code*, which relies for its decisions on Maimonides, Isaac Alfasi, and Asher b. Jehiel: "*Videsis, etiam Maimonid. halach. Memarim* cap. 3. *Mos. Mikotzi praec. Negativ.* 163. *Shulcan Aruch tit. Iore dea cap.* 158."

24. John Selden, *De Synedriis*, 2.3, in Selden, *Opera*, 1:1529: "*Et illecebrae ejus emittendae sunt ad omnes pietatis amatores, qui absque mora in scelestum irruant, rati sanctitatis officium talem hominem occidere*"; Philo, *De Specialibus Legibus*, I, 315–316, in *Philo*, ed. F.H. Colson, Loeb Classical Library (London and Cambridge, Mass.: Heinemann and Harvard University Press, 1937), 7:283. See also *De Specialibus Legibu*, I, 55, Loeb edition, 7:131. For the editor's attempt to temper Philo's brutal comments, see appendices, *Philo*, 7:617: "That [Philo] should be seriously encouraging his fellow Jews in Alexandria, where we know that the Jews had independent jurisdiction, to put apostates to death without any legal trial seems to me almost impossible. But was it perhaps otherwise in other cities of the Dispersion, where the Jews had no such privilege and knew that the ordinary courts would not take cognizance of apostasy or heresy?"

25. Selden, *De Synedriis*, 2.3, in Selden, *Opera*, 1:1531: "*Sed sub Elizabetha regina sancito parliamentario* [marginal note: "*Stat. 5. Eliz. cap.* 1"] *opinio abolita est.*"

26. Selden, *De Jure*, 4.5, pp. 492–493.

27. Ibid., pp. 492–494.

28. Selden, *De Jure*, pp. 494–495: "*columbas volare docentes,*" "*excitant eas ad certamen mutuum.*" For a reminder that real doves may differ from our "dream of a dove that saves, / Picasso's or the pope's," see Anthony Hecht's poem "Birdwatchers of America," in Hecht, *The Hard Hours: Poems* (New York: Atheneum, 1981), p. 57.

29. John Selden, *De Diis Syris* (1617), p. 185. Regarding the source of additional information on the *venditores*, the sellers of doves, Selden notes: "*quod*

appendix Ferdinandi Poloni ad Abrahamum Ben-Kattun me primum docuit."
G.J. Toomer points out that Selden underlines *"Qui alunt columbas"* among
those barred from giving testimony in his copy of *Praecepta in Monte Sinai* at
the Bodleian. For information on the author and his book, see Siegfried Stein,
"Philippus Ferdinandus Polonus," in I. Epstein, E. Levine, and C. Roth, eds.,
Essays in Honor of the Very Rev. Dr. J.H. Hertz (London: Edward Goldston, 1942),
pp. 397–412. Stein notes that Philippus' book lists the seven Noahide laws, perhaps the first occasion on which Selden came across them. Abraham ben Hassan's
list of the Torah's precepts was published in the Bomberg Rabbinical Bible of
1516–1517, which Selden also owned. In his later scholarship Selden understandably preferred the fuller commentary on the precepts by Moses of Coucy.
Philippus Ferdinandus was a converted Jew of Polish origin (hence "Polonus"),
who spent time with the Karaites in Constantinople and taught Hebrew and
Arabic at Cambridge, then went to Leiden, where he taught Scaliger Hebrew.
Another underscored passage in Selden's copy of Philippus' book, noted by Stein,
is a reference to the patriotic sincerity of the Jews, not found in other early
modern Christian sources. Regarding what he identifies as the Torah's sixty-fifth
negative commandment, "Thou shalt not revile judges or curse the ruler in thy
people" (Exodus 22:27), Philippus comments: "This the Jews observe, and they
pray for the king under whom they live and honor him as if he had come from
their own people" (Stein, "Philippus Ferdinandus Polonus," p. 402).

30. For Selden on what can loosely be called *tikkun olam* ("repairing the
world"), see *De Jure*, 4.5, pp. 494–495, where he cites Obadiah of Bertinoro
on the *mishna*; and *De Synedriis*, in *Opera*, 1:1425–1426. In the latter, Selden's
long list of sources may constitute a tactful way of emphasizing, in the face of
Christian detraction, the consonance of biblical and talmudic disapproval of usu-
ry. He makes it clear that the prohibition applies to the borrower as well as to the
lender: "*Foeneratorum nomine non solum continetur hic* המלוה *seu qui mutuo dat
foenore, verum etiam* הלוה *qui mutuo accipit. Nam ad utrumque interdicta sacra
de foenore attinere scribunt. Ad hunc in Deuteronomio* [note: "Cap. xxiii.19"]; *ad
illum Levitico* [note: "*Levit. xxv.37. Videsis ibid. Sal. Jarchium* [Rashi], *Mosem
Kotzens.* [Moses of Coucy] *in Praecept. Negat. 193. praeter commentarios ad su-
pra e Talmude locos indicatos*"]." Among the many examples in English literature
of thieving, dicing, whoring, swearing, and borrowing—and thus of failing to
advance public welfare—the figure of Falstaff looms large. See, e.g., *1 Henry IV*
3.3.14–18: "I was as virtuously given as a gentleman need to be, virtuous enough:
swore little, dic'd not above seven times—a week, went to a bawdy-house not
above once in a quarter—of an hour, paid money that I borrowed—three or four
times...."

31. Selden, *De Jure*, pp. 494–495: "*incumbit rebus quae ad firmitudinem seculi,
id est ad bonum publicum seu vitae humanae commodum spectant*"; "*quibus in-
est firmitudo seculi* aut *mundi*, quod vertimus, *quae bono publico utilia*."

32. See *Mishna*, Keritot 1:7; *Babylonian Talmud*, Pesahim 57a; *Jerusalem
Talmud*, Hagiga 2:3. To correct abuses, R. Simeon ben Gamaliel lowered the
price of a pair of doves from a golden to a silver dinar and introduced a more
lenient law regarding the number of obligatory offerings.

After Machiavelli and Hobbes:
James Harrington's Commonwealth of Israel

Gary Remer

1. Introduction

In this essay, I will analyze James Harrington's discussion of the commonwealth of Israel to show how Harrington (1611–1677) employs methods and concepts from Niccolò Machiavelli (1467–1527) and Thomas Hobbes (1588–1679) while ultimately distinguishing himself from both. Harrington highlights the importance of the commonwealth of Israel in his own thought through the attention he pays to it (invariably making examples from its functioning "the first support of every theory he brings forward, while examples from secular history come second") and by recognizing that it was the only commonwealth in history whose fabric and laws were infallible, "not fit to be altered by men," because its founder and legislator was God.[1] The Israelite commonwealth, however, is of singular importance not only in understanding Harrington's thought per se but also in elucidating the relationship between Harrington's political ideas and those of Machiavelli and Hobbes, because it is the only commonwealth that all three thinkers examine.

I argue that Harrington makes use of Machiavelli's method of historical example and adopts his republicanism while abandoning his belief that all states are mortal. From Hobbes, Harrington derives the idea that nature provides the principles for a timeless polity, but he criticizes Hobbes' political conclusions. I maintain that by selectively adapting and rejecting elements of both Machiavelli's and Hobbes' theories, Harrington arrives at a divided conception of Israel—one part historical and finite, the other ideal and immortal. In *The Commonwealth of Oceana* (hereafter referred to as *Oceana*) (1656) and, even more fully, in *The Art of Lawgiving* (1659), Harrington examines the commonwealth of Israel and how it embodies all the elements of the exemplary republic.[2] He states that the rules of the Israelite commonwealth are perfect but concedes that the Israelites never lived up to God's dictates and therefore never created for themselves a pure commonwealth. Harrington uses this division between the ideal and the reality to support, scripturally, his own model commonwealth, an idealized version of England he calls "Oceana."

Studies of Harrington have often pointed out his singularity and preeminence—for example, his near-universal acceptance as the exemplar of English republicanism—*and* the complex etiology of his thought, in that his intellectual roots are to be found among diverse thinkers and philosophical traditions.[3] Although these characteristics, originality and derivativeness, appear to be at odds with each other, I will show how they cohere in Harrington's writings. By analyzing Harrington's relationship to Machiavelli and Hobbes, two evident influences on his thinking, I hope to clarify Harrington's independence of, and debt to, these different sources. In examining Harrington's study of ancient Israel vis-à-vis Machiavelli's and Hobbes', I will attempt to demonstrate how he uses their ideas but modifies them so profoundly that, on closer inspection, that which distinguishes his thought from theirs is sometimes more significant than where they concur. Thus, to this day, Harrington inspires debate about whether he is best understood as a student of Machiavelli or as a disciple of Hobbes, which ensures that he is not viewed as the epigone of either.[4]

First, I shall examine how Harrington is intellectually indebted to, yet departs from, Machiavelli, and how Machiavelli's and Harrington's similarities and differences manifest themselves in their accounts of the politics of ancient Israel. Next, I shall consider Harrington's interest in Hobbes (and the limits of this interest) as it affects Harrington's broader political theory and his timeless ideal of the commonwealth of Israel. I shall then demonstrate how Harrington, in his inquiry into Israel, emulates Plato in that he distinguishes between the ideal or *form* of the state, on the one hand, and actual political practice, on the other.

2. Historical Example in Machiavelli and Harrington

James Harrington draws a close connection between his own thought and that of Machiavelli. As Harrington explains, Machiavelli revived ancient prudence, "first discovered unto mankind by God himself in the fabric of the commonwealth of Israel, and afterward picked out of his footsteps in nature and unanimously followed by the Greeks and Romans"; ancient prudence defines government as "an art whereby a civil society of men is instituted and preserved upon the foundation of common right and interest." Because *Oceana* was based on ancient prudence, Harrington saw Machiavelli as the work's intellectual progenitor and as "the only politician that hath gone about to retrieve" this kind of prudence. Machiavelli, whom Harrington terms "the only politician of later ages," thereby offers a yardstick against which all other political theorists should be measured.

Harrington adopts, from ancient prudence and Machiavelli, the method of historical example, in which political wisdom is sought from the practice of ancient (and sometimes modern) rulers and governments. Similarly, Harrington embraces the republicanism of ancient prudence and Machiavelli, embodied in the theory of the mixed government.[5] In applying ancient prudence specifically to Hebrew Scripture, Harrington emulates Machiavelli, who, as will be seen in the following, treats the Bible as a secular political document, inferring political precepts from its examples. In *The Prince*, Machiavelli compares the prophet Moses with the pagan leaders "Cyrus, Romulus, Theseus, and others of that stamp." And while Machiavelli prefaces his discussion of these founders by stating that "one should not discuss Moses, because he was merely an executor of what had been ordained by God," he almost immediately subverts this statement by asserting that Cyrus and others who founded kingdoms "will all be found remarkable, and if their actions and methods are considered, they will not appear very different from those of Moses, who had such a great master."[6]

Machiavelli then goes on to explain how it was necessary for Moses, as it was for other secular founders, to find his people in a vulnerable position in order to successfully gain their obedience. He writes: "It was necessary, then, for Moses to find the people of Israel in Egypt, enslaved and oppressed by the Egyptians, so that they would be disposed to follow him, in order to escape their servitude." Again, like the others, Moses had to be armed, because "all armed prophets succeed whereas unarmed fail.... If Moses, Cyrus, Theseus, and Romulus had been unarmed, the new order which each of them established would not have been obeyed for very long."[7] In *Discourses on the First Ten Books of Titus Livius* (1517), commonly referred to as *Discourses on Livy* or *Discourses*, Machiavelli elaborates on this point, noting that "whoever reads the Bible judiciously will see that since he wished his laws and his orders to go forward, Moses was forced to kill infinite men who, moved by nothing other than envy, were opposed to his plans."[8] Moses makes use of the same means, like mass killings to achieve power, as do more mundane political founders.

Harrington emulates Machiavelli's stand that biblical political precedents are comparable to their secular counterparts.[9] He almost certainly has Machiavelli in mind when he defends "politicians" who are vilified as "irreverent or atheistical" for comparing "(though but by way of illustration) legislators or politicians such as Lycurgus, Solon with Moses, or other commonwealths, as Rome and Venice, with that of Israel." Harrington accepts that scriptural examples may be intermingled with secular ones. From the fact that the advice of the heathen Jethro (Moses' father-in-law) is adopted into Scripture, Harrington finds proof that God himself does not distinguish between political wisdom gained from the Bible and that gained from nonreligious sources. As Harrington sees it, Jethro, in his capacity as king and priest of Midian, proposes to Moses a government that is Midianite, which "was of like nature with that of Melchizedek, or of the Lacedaemonian kings who were also priests."[10] Because both Israelite and pagan commonwealths can be comprehended politically, Harrington freely draws parallels between the Israelite standards of the camp and the Roman eagles; the military rolls in Israel, Athens, and Rome; and the offering of a sacrifice in both Israel and Rome before the meeting of the popular assembly.[11]

While Machiavelli focuses on the actions of biblical figures, especially Moses, Harrington looks more broadly to the structures and institutions of Israel. Harrington's reliance on institutions instead of virtue, however, is itself Machiavellian, though Machiavelli offers republican Rome's constitutional orders as his model. Machiavelli states that "as every history is full of examples, it is necessary to whoever disposes a republic and orders laws in it to presuppose that all men are bad, and that they always have to use the malignity of their spirit whenever they have a free opportunity for it"; "it is the laws," created by rightly constituted orders, "that make [men] good," that is, that "compel them to serve the common good and refrain from harming their fellow citizens, as civil and political life demands." Harrington echoes Machiavelli in writing: "'give us good orders, and they will make us good men' is the maxim of a legislator and the most infallible in the politics." Like Machiavelli, Harrington denies that a commonwealth can be based on the virtue of good men. Thus, Harrington writes: "'Give us good men and they will make us good laws' is the maxim of a demagogue."[12] As did Machiavelli, Harrington decides upon a republic of good orders as the constitutional exemplar.

Harrington uses the example of the commonwealth of Israel to show that its institutions, which are divinely planned, inform and justify the acceptance of the institutions of Oceana. The commonwealth of Israel, according to Harrington, begins with Moses and ends with Zedekiah, the last prince, "in whose reign was Judah led away captive by Nebuchadnezzar."[13] Though Harrington defines this whole period as the commonwealth of Israel, he selects his examples mainly from the period of Moses and Joshua.[14] Harrington's focus on their tenure is reasonable, as the political framework of the Israelite commonwealth was conceived during their time. In addition, Harrington can plausibly claim that neither Moses nor Joshua was a king, which buttresses his position that Israel was a commonwealth. Harrington, however, asserts that Israel was a commonwealth even during King David's reign. He supports this claim by viewing David as a limited monarch within a larger popular government: "For David was a king, who nevertheless did not otherwise make any law than by proposition unto the people, and their free suffrage thereupon." As for most other kings of Israel and Judah, Harrington does not emphasize their limited powers so much as their unstable and ineffective regimes, which he describes in just one paragraph. And, in contrast to his examination of David's rule, he shows little concern for reconciling their monarchical rule with his belief that Israel remained a commonwealth during their reign.[15]

Harrington employs Machiavelli's method of historical example to demonstrate that the commonwealth of Israel (like the Roman republic for Machiavelli) possesses contemporary relevance: the English should approve Oceana's structures based, in part, on the insights gained from an examination of Israel's institutions. In both republics, he discovers a parallel economic structure and political superstructure or constitutional arrangement. Harrington argues in *Oceana* that the stability of a republic or commonwealth, as of political forms more generally, depends on the economic structure, that is, the distribution of land: "and such... as is the proportion or balance of dominion or property in land, such is the nature of the empire." When one man possesses all or nearly all the land, an absolute monarchy exists. When the nobility holds all or almost all property, the constitution is a mixed monarchy. "And if the whole people be landlords, or hold the lands so divided among them, that no one man, or number of men, within the compass of the few or aristocracy, overbalance them, the empire (without the interposition of force) is a commonwealth."[16]

Harrington believed that a commonwealth was the proper (and stable) government for England because it had largely attained equality in landholding.[17] To maintain a stable state, Harrington suggests that the balance be fixed by law, "which is called agrarian." This agrarian law is "of such virtue that, wherever it hath held, that government hath not altered, except by consent.... But without an agrarian, government, whether monarchical, aristocratical, or popular, hath no long lease."[18]

Oceana's agrarian laws were prefigured in ancient Israel by "the division of the land of Canaan unto the whole people by lot," where the land was to be controlled by the people or, at least, with neither "one nor the few overbalanc[ing] the whole people."[19] Israel's "agrarian law, or jubilee, entailing the inheritance of each proprietor upon his heirs forever," fixed the popular balance.[20] Because all lands reverted to their original owners in the jubilee, every fiftieth year, a broad distribution of property was ensured.

The commonwealth of Israel's basic governmental superstructure also heralds that of Oceana. In outlining his model of Oceana, Harrington divides its people based on "their quality, their ages, their wealth, and the places of their residence or habitation."[21] As Harrington divides the people of Oceana for political purposes, God (and Moses) divided the people of Israel, first genealogically and then geographically.[22] In Oceana, the vote is restricted to male citizens above the age of thirty; in Israel, suffrage was limited to males who were twenty years or older. In Oceana, elections are indirect, using a complex system of lots and secret ballots in a series of stages, from "parish" through "hundred" to "tribe."[23] Similarly, in Israel, elections were performed "sometimes by the lot, without suffrage, and sometimes by the ballot, that is, by a mixture of lot and suffrage." Harrington argues that the Israelites selected both their kings ("when the people would needs have a king") and the members of the Sanhedrim, the senate consisting of seventy elders.[24] And, like Oceana's elections, Israel's were organized in a series of stages.[25]

The most significant element in the superstructure for Harrington is the distinction between debating and resolving. In Oceana's constitutional scheme, the senate (or upper chamber) debates, and the people, through their representatives in the "prerogative tribe" (or lower chamber), resolve or vote.[26] Harrington finds that God establishes a similar functional division in the commonwealth of Israel between the seventy-member senate, or Sanhedrim, and Israel's popular assembly, which consisted, at times, of the whole congregation of Israel and, at other times, of a smaller body of twenty-four thousand men.[27] Harrington's reason for separating a debating senate from a voting popular assembly is his belief that only the wisest in the commonwealth, to be housed in the senate, are intellectually capable of discovering what is best for the commonwealth and that only the people, through their representatives, are able to choose which proposals are in their common interest. In arguing that the people as a whole are unfit for political debate, Harrington presupposes the existence of a natural aristocracy of the wise. These wiser men, in contrast to "the herd," are more capable of learned debate and sagely advice.[28] But while the natural aristocrats are wiser and therefore better political debaters and policy presenters, their wisdom does not ensure that they will choose the people's common interest over their own personal interest. Therefore, the popular assembly is necessary to defend the interests of the whole. For while the people may not be sufficiently intelligent "to find out the truth of themselves," and therefore they cannot be trusted with debating and fashioning their own laws, "yet, if they be shown truth, they not only acknowledge and embrace it very suddenly, but are the most constant and faithful guardians and conservators of it."[29]

The principle of rotation is a basic institutional device of Oceana's legislature, in which annual elections and three-year term limits result in one-third of each chamber being replaced each year. In Israel, Harrington surmises, a new representative body appeared each month, with twenty-four thousand new men appearing—two thousand from each tribe—and twenty-four thousand departing. At this rate, he believes, "the rotation of the whole people came about in the space of one year."[30] Under Israel's system of rotation, more people would be involved in making decisions than in Oceana.

Harrington's delineation of Israel's political institutions reflects Machiavelli's method of distilling political prudence from ancient practice (as well as the Florentine's mixing of biblical and secular examples). But Harrington departs fundamentally from Machiavelli on whether the commonwealth of Israel (or any state) can escape the finitude of time. Machiavelli grounds his political theory in actual (or what was then accepted as actual) political facts. In *The Prince*, he explains that because he wishes to write on what will be useful, "it seems... better to concentrate on what really happens rather than on theories or speculations." Machiavelli continues: "For many have imagined republics and principalities that have never been seen or known to exist."[31] And all actual states, Machiavelli says, are temporary. "All things of men are in motion and cannot stay steady," Machiavelli writes in *Discourses*. "[T]hey must either rise or fall."[32] In contrasting Rome, a republic bent on expansion, with Venice, an inward-looking republic, Machiavelli concludes that neither type can evade mortality. Rome expanded, employing the plebeians for war and accepting foreigners, which afforded "infinite opportunities for tumult," eventually leading to its demise. Venice, too, which seeks stability over greatness, cannot maintain its stability indefinitely, Machiavelli asserts. Eventually it would be forced by circumstances to expand, which in a self-contained state like Venice "would come to take away its foundations and make it come to ruin sooner," or, "if heaven were so kind that it did not have to make war," Venice would be overtaken by idleness, resulting in effeminacy or division; "these two things together, or each by itself, would be the cause of its ruin."[33] Given that all states must succumb in the end, Machiavelli prefers the glory of Rome to the temporary tranquility of Venice.

Taking issue with Machiavelli, Harrington defends the possibility of an immortal commonwealth. Harrington believes that if the ideal ever comes into existence, it need not decay: "a commonwealth rightly ordered may for any internal causes be as immortal, or long-lived, as the world."[34] Not only does Harrington intend Oceana to be eternal, he argues (as will be seen later) that Israel, too, could have lasted forever. Unlike Machiavelli, Harrington does not identify the commonwealth of Israel so closely with other historical states as to preclude, as Machiavelli implicitly does, the possibility of its permanent survival. Harrington continues: "But if this be true, those commonwealths that are naturally fallen must have derived their ruin from the rise of them [that is, internal causes]." Harrington then observes that "Israel and Athens died not natural but violent deaths."[35] But even though Israel ultimately died a violent death, Harrington shows that it was destined to decay because the historical Israel was flawed from its inception. The perfect government instituted by Moses should not have been "by any internal cause...

broken or dissolved." The Mosaic model, though, "was never established in any such part as possibly could be holding."[36] Harrington looks beyond Machiavelli to find a conceptual framework that can make sense of a permanent commonwealth, including the conceivability of a timeless commonwealth of Israel. He turns to Hobbes for this framework.

3. Hobbes, Harrington, and the Timeless Ideal of Israel

To the degree that he extols Machiavelli, Harrington almost equally criticizes Hobbes. Harrington depicts Hobbes as a skeptic who upholds modern prudence and as such defines government as rule of one or the few in their private interest.[37] Yet, as several writers have argued recently, Harrington is intellectually indebted in no small degree to Hobbes. Jonathan Scott goes so far as to describe Harrington as "the greatest English disciple, not of Machiavelli, but of Hobbes."[38] And Harrington himself, despite his criticisms, acknowledges that "I have opposed the politics of Mr. Hobbes, to show him what he taught me." Harrington considers Hobbes "the best writer at this day in the world; and for his treatises of human nature and of liberty and necessity, they are the greatest of new lights, and those which I have followed and shall follow."[39]

What Harrington learns from Hobbes is a new metaphysics of nature. Hobbes bases this metaphysics on the assumptions that "the world, or nature, consisted of material in motion" and that "natural motion was perpetual unless arrested or diverted by pressure (motion) from a different direction: 'when a thing is in motion, it will eternally be in motion, unless somewhat els stay it.'"[40] In *Leviathan*, Hobbes expresses this vision of nature when he identifies "Voluntary Motion" as the source of all human action and thought, including that species of "Endeavor" called the passions. It is the passions that, according to Hobbes, motivate human beings to engage in a "war of all against all" in the state of nature (a condition of motion) and to accept restraints on their motion in instituting a commonwealth through covenant.[41]

Harrington thought that Hobbes' "nature" afforded him an ideal by which he might transcend the mortality of actual states. "By so copying [Hobbes' conception of] nature's perfection Harrington believed that he had harnessed for politics its very immortality."[42] Harrington paraphrases Hobbes' statement on natural motion, applying it to the commonwealth:

"For neither by reason nor by her experience is it impossible that a commonwealth should be immortal, seeing... the form, which is motion, must without opposition be endless."[43] For Harrington, the commonwealth is characterized as a whole and in its parts by motion: "for in motion consisteth life, and the motion of a commonwealth will never be current, unless it be circular." Harrington compares the government of his ideal commonwealth to "orbs and spheres," whose perfect rotation along "preconceived paths" allows these orbs and spheres to move perpetually.[44]

In *Leviathan*, Hobbes eschews, with only one exception, the study of all hitherto existing states—which he perceives as houses whose foundations have been laid on sand—for the study of nature alone, which posits "certain Rules, as doth Arithmetique and Geometry." (In contrast, Harrington studies the constitutions of several actual states to extract the principles of nature found in these constitutions.) Hobbes' sole exception is Israel, the "Kingdome of God."[45]

Hobbes, followed by Harrington, sees nature as the rational grounding of good government. They each present a secular political theory, which they describe as based on nature, standing independent of any scriptural justifications. After completing his secular theory of state in book two of *Leviathan*, Hobbes begins book three by summarizing his previous efforts: "I have derived the Rights of Sovereign Power, and the duty of Subjects hitherto, from the Principles of Nature onely;... that is to say, from the nature of Men, known to us by Experience, and from Definitions (of such words as are Essentiall to all Politicall reasoning) universally agreed on." Although Hobbes affirms these "Dictates of *Naturall Reason*" as declared by God, he understands the divine role in proclaiming natural political theory to be limited to God's vesting human beings with right reason, which does not include any beliefs based on revelation or faith.[46] Harrington attributes humankind's own uncovering of the principles of nature (separate from and subsequent to God's own revelation "unto mankind... in the fabric of the commonwealth of Israel") to the ancient Greeks and Romans, who picked ancient prudence "out of [God's] footsteps in nature."[47] Harrington also infers a "sufficient warrant, even from God himself, who confirmed [Jethro's suggestions to Moses], to make further use of humane prudence wherever I find it bearing a testimony unto itself, whether in heathen commonwealths or others." By highlighting the significance of Jethro, a heathen using human reason to help found a divine commonwealth, Harrington makes revelation superfluous.[48]

Hobbes argues that ancient Israel's government is consistent with nature. According to Hobbes, the prophetic kingdom, that is, the kingdom of Israel, is governed "*not onely by naturall Reason*, but by Positive Lawes, which he gave them by the mouths of his holy Prophets."[49]

Harrington echoes Hobbes but goes even further, emphasizing the role that nature or human reason played in the establishment of Israel: "For the courts... and the triumvirates of [Israel's] judges constituted almost in every village, which were parts of the executive magistracy," were not institutions revealed by God, but were "that part of this commonwealth which was instituted by Moses upon the advice of Jethro the priest of Midian (Exodus 18),... an heathen." For Harrington, reason (or nature) alone is sufficient to teach the principles of good government; "the commonwealth of Israel in her main orders, that is to say, the senate, the people, and the magistracy, [was]... erected by the same rules of human prudence, with other commonwealths."[50]

Hobbes is unwilling to justify Israel's government, however, on nature alone. He states his intention to base his political vision not only on the principles of nature, but "upon Supernaturall Revelations of the Will of God," that is, on Holy Writ.[51] Hobbes dedicates approximately half of *Leviathan* (part 3, "Of a Christian Commonwealth"—the longest of the four parts of *Leviathan*—and part 4, "Of the Kingdome of Darknesse") to justifying, scripturally, his main political ideas. Hobbes' analysis of the Hebrews' political condition concentrates on God's covenant with the Hebrews and the absolute power of the sovereign. God was the Hebrews' first sovereign, making his first covenant with Abraham ("by which Abraham obligeth himself and his posterity... to be subject to God's positive law") and then renewing his covenant with Moses on Mount Sinai.[52] The form of government created in this covenant was a kingship, with God as absolute sovereign and, subsequently, when renewed at Mount Sinai, with Moses as lieutenant during his lifetime and, afterward, with the high priests acting as God's vicegerents. Warren Zev Harvey calls attention to the inconsistency in Hobbes' discussion of sovereignty in ancient Israel. At times, Hobbes presents Moses, the high priest, and Samuel as no more than spokesmen who "declared God's Commandments to the people." At other times, they are submitted as de facto sovereigns under God, the de jure sovereign.[53] Hobbes' position on sovereignty, however, shows no ambiguity after the covenant was abrogated, when the people, "with the consent of God himselfe," requested of Samuel (I Samuel 8:5) to "make us a King to judge us, like all the Nations." In seeking an earthly king, Hobbes views the Israelites as "deposing the High Priest of Royall authority," and consequently deposing "the peculiar Government of God."[54] Henceforth, the people would be ruled by mortal kings, not God or his lieutenants, with "all authority, both in Religion, and in Policy," belonging to their new monarchs.[55]

Like Hobbes, Harrington seeks scriptural support for his new modes and orders. Harrington follows Hobbes' distinction between political proof based on nature alone and that supported with the direct word of God. He concludes book one of *The Art of Lawgiving* by first "observing that the principles of human prudence, being good without proof out of Scripture, are nevertheless, such as are provable out of Scripture"; then he agrees to confirm his "entire frame of popular government, in the ensuing book, by the same authority and undeniable evidence" of Holy Scripture.[56]

Harrington's mirroring of Hobbes' political use of Scripture, however, is not reflected in the political conclusions the author of *Oceana* derives from Hebrew Scripture. While Hobbes finds in ancient Israel confirmation of his secular political theory, where the people institute an absolute sovereign through a covenant, Harrington sees in the Israelite commonwealth a republic, much like Oceana, with a proper "balance of dominion or property in land" and a governmental superstructure that requires a division between debating and decision-making.[57] Hobbes is not only blind to Israel's specifically republican institutions; he ignores, thus implicitly denying the need for, any of Israel's detailed constitutional orders—and it is precisely the constitutional arrangements that are at the heart of Harrington's secular political theory in general and biblical political theory in particular. Hobbes refuses to hamstring the sovereign with the specific sort of regulations that Harrington elaborates in *Oceana*. Further, not only does Hobbes contend that the Bible places all the power in the sovereign, but he also argues that Scripture itself has no authority without the order of the present sovereign. Hobbes states that without any personal supernatural revelations, we are not obliged to obey God's written laws "by any Authority, but his, whose Commands have already the force of Laws; that is to say, by any other Authority, than that of the Common-wealth, residing in the Soveraign."[58] For Hobbes, Scripture's force and meaning derive from the sovereign's word. Harrington, though he subordinates church to state (which I do not discuss in this essay), never negates the independent validity of Scripture.[59]

Although Harrington disagrees with Hobbes on the political character of ancient Israel, he discovers in Hobbes a conception of nature that
allows him to imagine an immortal commonwealth which Harrington
claims the commonwealth of Israel could have been. The possibility of a
commonwealth based on the ideal principles of nature enables Harrington
to distinguish between the historic Israel, which fell short of nature's perfection, and the imaginary Israel, a timeless commonwealth in accord
with nature, laid down in God's laws. By speaking of "Hobbesian" nature
in relation to Israel (and not only regarding secular states),[60] Harrington
implicitly extends nature's characteristic of "perpetual motion" to Israel.
But Harrington reserves the language, especially the metaphors, of nature
mostly for Oceana.[61]

In analyzing the commonwealth of Israel, Harrington seeks a nomen-
clature that will capture Israel's special status as both historical *and* ideal.
(Oceana is only imaginary; it never was an actual state.) Plato's doctrine
of forms provides Harrington with the appropriate language.[62] Like Plato
in *The Republic*, Harrington differentiates theory from practice.[63] In Plato's
Republic, theory is linked to the doctrine of Forms, "the doctrine that
what we should call universals has a permanent and substantial existence
independent of our minds and the particulars which are called by the
same names."[64] Theory—thought concerning the Forms—is contemplation about ideas separate from, and unattainable in, the material world.
Harrington's language echoes Plato's doctrine of the Forms. He characterizes his ideal government as "a notional account of the whole frame,"
and he contrasts this notional account, which exists in the realm of ideas,
with a practical account, which is based on past examples. Responding
to a critic who compares *Oceana* to "a fiction the several members [be-
ing] so contrived," where "the whole remain without the least syllable of
truth," Harrington states: "For the model is not proposed to show the
truth of fact, or that there hath been any such exactly in practice." He
concedes that his proposed government has never existed.[65]

Because theory and practice are forever separate for Plato, the Athenian
philosopher recognizes, as George Klosko states, "that the ideal state as
described in theory can never exist precisely in practice. And so the reformer of an actual state must necessarily settle for some approximation
of the ideal."[66] In contrast to Plato, however, Harrington desires to show
that his "model is practicable," even if it has never existed.[67] Yet even
Plato himself shows some ambivalence about the unachievable nature of

his model when he has Socrates claim that "our plan is difficult—we have admitted as much—but not impossible."[68]

Harrington applies the Platonic doctrine of the Forms to distinguish the ideal commonwealth of Israel from the earthly Israel. He writes of the "model" of Israel, "the frame... instituted by Moses"—an ideal like the Platonic form of the republic that was never established:

> Moses died in the wilderness; and though Joshua, bringing the people into the promised land, did what he could during his life towards the *establishment of the form* [emphasis added] designed by Moses, yet the hands of the people, especially after the death of Joshua, grew slack, and they rooted not out the Canaanites, which they were so often commanded to, and without which it was impossible that their commonwealth should take any root. Nevertheless, settled as it could be, it was in parts longer lived than any other government hath yet been; as having continued in some sort from Moses unto the dispersion of the Jews in the reign of the emperor Hadrian, being about one thousand seven hundred years. *But that it was never established according unto the necessity of the form, or the true intent of Moses, is that which must be made farther apparent....* [emphasis added][69]

Harrington also differs with Plato on the question of the permanence of the ideal state. Because the republic would exist in the material world—a world of mortality and change—it could not last forever. Therefore, Plato, through Socrates, recounts the hypothetical degeneration of the republic, from ideal to timocracy, followed, in turn, by oligarchy, democracy, and despotism.[70]

Harrington specifies Israel as a commonwealth equal in its agrarian order, where the people own the preponderance of the land. This stands in contrast to Rome, which Harrington offers as an example of a commonwealth destroyed from within by inequality.[71] But while Israel's agrarian balance was equal compared to that of Rome, Harrington demonstrates that the division of land in historical Israel never met the ideal set forth by Moses. He explains that "the use of the lot in the division of the land of Canaan... [as implying the foundation, or balance, of the government] ought to have been the first in order, but happeneth here to come last, for that these orders were instituted in the wilderness, and so before the people had any lands to divide." Once the Israelites entered Canaan, however, they never fully apportioned the land by lot. Thus,

Harrington states, "It is true that in the whole, this law of Moses for the division of the land was never executed."[72]

The Israelites did not fully divide their lands by lot because they refused to dislodge the Canaanites, contrary to God's command. As Harrington writes, "Now supposing this law [of dividing the land by lot] to have been in the whole and methodically executed, the Canaanites must first have been totally rooted out of the land of Canaan." (With the Canaanites still remaining in areas that God promised to the Israelites, there was less land to be divided than envisioned in the Mosaic law). Although the Canaanites' continued occupation of parts of the land prevented the agrarian ideal from being fully realized, it did not totally negate the division of the land: "in the parts" that the Israelites conquered from the Canaanites, "some like course," similar to Moses' law for the division of the land, was taken, "for example, in the division unto seven tribes."[73] Sparing the Canaanites, however, also undermined Israel's political institutions.

Harrington describes Israel "during the life of Joshua, and the elders of the Sanhedrim that outlived him," as "without any sufficient root for the possible support of it... or with such roots as were full of worms." The source for this groundlessness, he explains, was "the Canaanites not being destroyed."[74] Harrington supports this claim by citing the Jewish historian Josephus Flavius (ca. 37–95 C.E.). Josephus recounts that after the Israelites had settled in the land of Canaan, "God, being moved unto anger, admonished them by a prophet that in sparing the Canaanites they had disobeyed him." The Israelites, however, "both because they were bribed by the Canaanites and through luxury," did not heed God's word. The result was that their commonwealth became "depraved"; institutions like the senate or Sanhedrim, which were once popularly elected, were now "neglected by the people." Commenting on Josephus, Harrington states that "this commonwealth which, through the not rooting out of the Canaanites, had never any foundation, came now also to fail in her superstructures."[75] Presumably, Harrington's comment about the lack of any foundation in Israel refers to the incomplete agrarian; the observation about Israel's failed superstructures refers to the demise of the Sanhedrim. Deprived of "her natural superstructures" and "her necessary foundation," Israel declined further. Under the judges, the Israelites, when weak, "served the Philistines.... Which, as it was contrary unto the command of God, so was it point-blank against all prudence." The

Israelites at the time neither made friends "nor ruined they their enemies; which proceeding, as it fared with this commonwealth…, is to the certain perdition of a people."[76]

When Harrington turns to the period of the kings, he emphasizes the concrete commonwealth's still-greater distance from the Mosaic ideal. Kingship was not God's desired government; popular rule was. As seen in Samuel, God perceived the people's request for a king as a rejection of his "personal" rule. Harrington quotes God's words to Samuel: "They have not rejected thee, but they have rejected me, that I should not reign over them."[77] Although in calling for a king, the Israelites rejected not only God but also their republican government, Harrington contends that, paradoxically, the establishment of the Israelite monarchy confirms the unique legitimacy God accords popular government. For while God "deservedly blame[s] the ingratitude of the people" for deposing him in favor of a human king, he commands Samuel, "being next under himself supreme magistrate," to listen to the people. God and Samuel must obey the popular decision, even when that decision is in favor of monarchy.[78]

Kingship distanced Israel even further from the agrarian balance. While Moses' law dictated an equal division of land, the "balance necessary unto kingly government, even where it was regulated or not absolute," required that property be taken from the people for [the king] and "his servants or creatures." To create a stable monarchy, which requires that a preponderance of the land be in the hands of the king and nobility, David was compelled to take "part of the land given unto the people by God, and which was by the law of Moses to have been divided by lot unto them." And even though the land had not yet been divided fully, so that David "took not from the people anything whereof they were in actual possession, yet, as to their legal right, took he from them" the lands that were properly theirs and gave them to the nobility.[79] David's successors, though given short shrift in Harrington's discussion, only moved the historical Israel further from the model Israelite commonwealth. Instead of a single commonwealth, Israel was rent (during the reign of Rehoboam, David's grandson) into two monarchies, Judah and Israel. "For which time this people, thus divided, had little or no rest from the flame of that civil war which, once kindled between two realms or factions, could never be extinguished but in the destruction of both."[80] The two monarchies continued on a downward spiral until first Israel was destroyed when the Assyrians took its people into captivity, and later Judah was led away captive to Babylonia.

The destruction of the two monarchies, for Harrington, was only the coup de grâce for a commonwealth that was flawed from its earthly inception. Because Harrington has clearly divorced the historical polity from its Form, he can defend his position without dealing with the parts of Scripture that would appear to weaken his argument. For example, he can judge the Israelite monarchy as a deviation from true Mosaic law. Thus, that Scripture sometimes tells a story different from Harrington's political theory does not diminish Scripture or his plan in any way; it only diminishes the commonwealth of Israel as it had actually developed.

4. Conclusion

In this essay, I have argued that James Harrington finds in Machiavelli the method of historical example by which the latter seeks to distill the practical wisdom to be gained from classical, particularly Roman, and contemporary political experience. Harrington follows suit in studying the commonwealth of Israel as a political exemplar, which both he and Machiavelli analyze in secular terms, and as a prototype of Harrington's own ideal, Oceana. Harrington also follows Machiavelli's republicanism, which Harrington reflects in his analysis of Israel as a kind of republic. He parts company with Machiavelli, however, on the question of whether states can last forever. Machiavelli contends all political communities must eventually perish. In contrast, Harrington affirms the possibility of an immortal commonwealth in his ideal Oceana. Harrington also claims that, while the actual commonwealth of Israel was not immortal, Israel's constitution, if it had been faithfully followed, would have granted eternal life to the divinely ordained republic.

Harrington takes from Hobbes a conception of nature as material in perpetual motion. Harrington believes that this view of nature, when applied to politics, demonstrates the ability of states (constructed according to nature) to themselves remain in perpetual motion. But while he believes that nature is the foundation of all good governments, he offers only two examples of immortal commonwealths—the imaginary Oceana and the commonwealth of Israel as God intended it to be. Israel is unique, however, in that it was not only grounded in nature, but divinely confirmed in the laws of Hebrew Scripture. First Hobbes, then Harrington, identifies the fundamentals of his secular political theories in Scripture. However, they derive opposing conclusions from Scripture, with Hobbes finding support for absolute monarchy and Harrington corroborating the agrarian balance and republican political institutions he delineates in *Oceana*. These political differences, however, do not diminish Harrington's need for Hobbesian "nature" to justify the idea of a perpetual commonwealth. Harrington relies more directly on Plato than Hobbes, though, in choosing a language to express the difference between the historical Israelite commonwealth and the ideal Israelite commonwealth, as laid down in Mosaic law. Plato, in explicating his doctrine of the Forms, distinguishes between the ideal world of theory and the transitory world of practice. Harrington echoes this Platonic usage when referring to the Mosaic ideal of Israel as "the form" that "was never established" and the historic Israel as the commonwealth "that was never established according to the necessity of the form."

Harrington has been analyzed both for his originality—referred to as "idiosyncratic" and "atypical"—and his intellectual provenance, especially found in the ideas of Machiavelli and Hobbes.[81] I have endeavored to demonstrate that Harrington is indebted to Machiavelli and Hobbes, but not so much that he should be defined as either Machiavellian or Hobbesian. My examination of Harrington in relation to Machiavelli and Hobbes, particularly in relation to their views on ancient Israel, shows that Harrington is indebted to both but not reducible to either.

Notes

1. J.W. Gough, "Harrington and Contemporary Thought," *Political Science Quarterly* 45 (1930), p. 398. See also Jonathan Scott, *Commonwealth Principles: Republican Writing of the English Revolution* (Cambridge: Cambridge University Press, 2004), p. 290: "*Oceana* makes extensive use of the Old Testament. It is neither Athens nor Rome which is Harrington's constitutional exemplar among the ancients... but the commonwealth of Israel..."; James Harrington, *The Political Works of James Harrington*, ed. J.G.A. Pocock (Cambridge: Cambridge University Press, 1977), pp. 161, 176.

2. Harrington's program in *The Art of Lawgiving* and his magnum opus, *Oceana*, published three years earlier, are the same, except for two things. Harrington acknowledges in *The Art of Lawgiving* that he omits there his

JAMES HARRINGTON'S COMMONWEALTH OF ISRAEL   225

complex balloting system and makes "some alteration in [his] former method."
See Harrington, *Political Works*, p. 662.

3. Scott, *Commonwealth Principles*, pp. 3, 5. John Toland, in "The Life of
James Harrington," first published in 1700, eulogizes Harrington as a man "whose
Name is sure to live so long as Learning and Liberty bear any Reputation in
England." See Toland, "The Life of James Harrington," in Luc Borot, ed., *James
Harrington and the Notion of Commonwealth* (Montpellier, France: Université
Paul-Valéry, 1998), p. 73. George Sabine, author of (at least a once) commonly
used college text on political theory, writes that Harrington "proved himself to
be a political philosopher of first-rate originality, not the equal of Hobbes in the
bold sweep of his reasoning but much his superior in the grasp of political reali-
ties." See George H. Sabine, *A History of Political Theory* (New York: Henry Holt
and Co., 1937), p. 497.

Felix Raab has "detected the presence of fourteen different Harringtons
in the scholarly literature." See Felix Raab, *The English Face of Machiavelli: A
Changing Interpretation, 1500–1700* (London: Routledge & K. Paul, 1965),
p. 187. Harrington has been depicted as Platonic, Aristotelian, neo-Roman,
"Virgilanized," Machiavellian, or a synthesis of several of these elements medi-
ated by Polybian constitutionalism. "For others Harrington's principal intellectual
debt was to Hobbes, the nature of which engagement has been vigorously disput-
ed together with its impact upon his claimed classical republicanism. Still others
have depicted Harrington as a Utopian, a Stoic, a natural philosopher, and the
author of a civic religion." Scott, *Commonwealth Principles*, p. 3.

4. Best known for linking the author of *The Commonwealth of Oceana* to
Machiavelli is J.G.A. Pocock, *The Machiavellian Moment: Florentine Political
Thought and the Atlantic Republican Tradition* (Princeton: Princeton University
Press, 1975). Other authors, however, have emphasized Harrington's intellectual
debt to Hobbes. Paul Rahe writes: "Indeed, if truth be told, James Harrington
owes far, far less to the many thinkers of classical antiquity than to Thomas
Hobbes." Paul A. Rahe, *Republics Ancient and Modern*, 3 vols. (Chapel Hill:
University of North Carolina Press, 1994), vol. 2, p. 181. Jonathan Scott describes
Harrington as "the greatest English disciple, not of Machiavelli, but of Hobbes,"
and contends that Harrington adopts Hobbes' metaphysical assumptions.
Jonathan Scott, "The Rapture of Motion: James Harrington's Republicanism,"
in Nicholas Phillipson and Quentin Skinner, eds., *Political Discourse in Early
Modern Britain* (Cambridge: Cambridge University Press, 1993), pp. 154–163.
See also Gary Remer, "James Harrington's New Deliberative Rhetoric: Reflection
of an Anticlassical Republicanism," *History of Political Thought* 16:4, pp. 548–
555; Vickie B. Sullivan, *Machiavelli, Hobbes, and the Formation of a Liberal
Republicanism in England* (Cambridge: Cambridge University Press, 2004),
pp. 165–169.

5. Harrington, *Political Works*, p. 162.

6. Niccolò Machiavelli, *The Prince*, ed. Quentin Skinner and Russell Price
(Cambridge: Cambridge University Press, 1988), p. 20.

7. Ibid., pp. 20–21.

8. Niccolò Machiavelli, *Discourses on Livy*, trans. Harvey C. Mansfield and Nathan Tarcov (Chicago: University of Chicago Press, 1996), III 30.1.

9. Harrington, *Political Works*, pp. 79–80.

10. Ibid., pp. 617, 629.

11. Ibid., pp. 623, 624, 627.

12. Machiavelli, *Discourses* I 3.1–2; Maurizio Viroli, *Machiavelli* (Oxford: Oxford University Press, 1998), p. 122; Harrington, *Political Works*, p. 205.

13. Harrington, *Political Works*, p. 643. Harrington refers to "the government restored by Zorobabel, Ezra, and Nehemiah," who returned from the Babylonian exile, as "the Jewish or cabalistical commonwealth." He considers this commonwealth a corruption of Mosaic rule, as it created laws (like banishment and the confiscation of property) that did not exist in Mosaic law. Under this government, "the word of a scribe or doctor was avowedly held to be of more validity than the Scripture." Ibid., pp. 644–645, 649.

14. Ibid., p. 176.

15. Ibid., pp. 642–643. Earlier, in part 2 of *The Art of Lawgiving*, Harrington defines a commonwealth in such a way that would make place for some kings: "Now where there is no king, or no king in a distinct capacity from the senate, and the senate hath no farther power in lawmaking than to propose unto the free suffrage of the people, the government is a commonwealth."

16. Ibid., pp. 163–164.

17. Ibid., p. 660. See Charles Blitzer, *An Immortal Commonwealth: The Political Thought of James Harrington* (New Haven: Yale University Press, 1960), p. 215.

18. Harrington, *Political Works*, p. 164. For details of the agrarian laws of Oceana, see p. 231; Blitzer, *An Immortal Commonwealth*, pp. 227–228.

19. Harrington, *Political Works*, pp. 604–605. See also pp. 174–175.

20. Ibid., pp. 233, 634.

21. Ibid., pp. 212–214; Blitzer, *An Immortal Commonwealth*, pp. 217–218.

22. Harrington, *Political Works*, pp. 621–625.

23. Ibid., pp. 223–226, 235–238.

24. Ibid., pp. 623–628.

25. Ibid., pp. 522, 625–628.

26. Ibid., pp. 174, 248, 255–257, 281–283, 596, 674–675; David Wootton, "Ulysses Bound? Venice and the Idea of Liberty from Howell to Hume," in Wootton, *Republicanism, Liberty, and Commercial Society, 1649–1776* (Stanford: Stanford University Press, 1994), pp. 346–347.

27. Harrington concedes that Israel's senate did not normally propose laws, as most other senates do, "in regard that the legislator of Israel was infallible,

and the laws given by God... were not fit to be altered by men." Nonetheless, he states that "it is not to be thought that the Sanhedrim had not always that right... of proposing unto the people, but that they forbear it in regard of the fullness and infallibility of the law already made, whereby it was needless." Israel's Sanhedrim was a law-advising senate in theory but not in practice. Harrington, *Political Works*, p. 176.

"The church or congregation of the people of Israel... had the result of the commonwealth, or the power of confirming all their laws, though proposed even by God himself, as where they make him [that is, God] king (Exodus 19). And where they reject or depose him as civil magistrate and elect Saul (I Samuel 8:8)." Because all the laws of Israel, after having been submitted by God, "were no otherwise enacted than by covenant with the people, then that only which was resolved by the people of Israel was their law; and so the result of that common-wealth was in the people." Ibid., pp. 175–176. Harrington contends that even in a divinely ordained commonwealth, the people's right of approval was guaran-teed by God. Harrington also speaks not only of God, but of Moses, as the one proposing laws. See ibid., pp. 619–620. While the popular assembly consisted at times of the whole body of the people, Harrington believes that Scripture recog-nizes a smaller "representative of the people," composed of twenty-four thousand men. His textual source for this assembly is I Chronicles 27:1, which calculates the number of Israelites—chiefs of clans, officers of thousands and hundreds, and their clerks—who served King David as twenty-four thousand. Harrington inter-prets this verse as referring to the people's representative, "which gave the vote of the people at the creation of their laws or election of their magistrates." Ibid., pp. 474, 636–637. When the verse describes these assistants to the king as "work-ing in monthly shifts during all the months of the year," Harrington construes these monthly shifts as pertaining to a monthly rotation.

28. Ibid., pp. 172–173, 268–269, 416–417.

29. Ibid., pp. 284, 172.

30. See ibid., p. 475.

31. Machiavelli, *Prince*, p. 54.

32. Machiavelli, *Discourses* I 6.4.

33. Machiavelli, *Discourses* I 6.

34. Harrington, *Political Works*, p. 321.

35. Ibid.: "Look well unto it, my lords, for if there be a contradiction or in-equality in your commonwealth, it must fall; but if it have neither of these, it hath no principle of mortality."

36. Ibid., p. 635.

37. Ibid., pp. 161–163, 165.

38. Scott, "Rapture of Motion," p. 162.

39. Harrington, *Political Works*, p. 423.

40. Scott, "Rapture of Motion," pp. 155–156; Thomas Hobbes, *Leviathan* (1651), ed. C.B. Macpherson (Harmondsworth, England: Penguin, 1968), p. 87.

41. Hobbes, *Leviathan*, pp. 118–119. For a fuller discussion of motion in Hobbes' political theory, see Scott, "Rapture of Motion," pp. 155–156; and Scott, *Commonwealth Principles*, pp. 163–164.

42. Scott, "Rapture of Motion," p. 160.

43. Harrington, *Political Works*, p. 229.

44. Ibid., p. 248; Scott, "Rapture of Motion," pp. 159–161.

45. Hobbes contends that his political conclusions are based on science, which is "the knowledge of consequences" and infallible. He contrasts his political science with what he terms "prudence," which is "a praesumtion of the future, contracted from the experience of time past," which includes the study of past commonwealths; prudence, however, is but conjecture and, therefore, fallible. Hobbes, *Leviathan*, ch. 3, pp. 97–98; ch. 5, pp. 115–117; ch. 21, p. 261. As a Christian, albeit an unorthodox one, Hobbes sees the continuation of Israel in the eventual kingdom of Christ. Israel, however, remains the only historical state that Hobbes examines in *Leviathan*.

46. Hobbes, *Leviathan*, ch. 31, p. 397; ch. 32, p. 409. See also Warren Zev Harvey, "The Israelite Kingdom of God in Hobbes' Political Thought," *Hebraic Political Studies* 1:3 (2006), pp. 311–312.

47. Harrington, *Political Works*, pp. 161–162.

48. Ibid., p. 177. See also pp. 47, 91–92.

49. Hobbes, *Leviathan*, ch. 31, p. 397. Emphasis mine.

50. Harrington, *Political Works*, pp. 496, 614–615.

51. Hobbes, *Leviathan*, ch. 32, p. 409.

52. Hobbes, *Leviathan*; David Johnston, *Rhetoric of Leviathan: Thomas Hobbes and the Politics of Cultural Transformation* (Princeton: Princeton University Press, 1986), pp. 165–166.

53. Hobbes, *Leviathan*, ch. 32, p. 413; ch. 35, pp. 446, 448; ch. 36, pp. 467–468; ch. 38, p. 482; ch. 40, pp. 499–506. Harvey, "Israelite Kingdom of God," pp. 319–320.

54. Hobbes, *Leviathan*, ch. 40, p. 508.

55. Ibid., ch. 40, p. 507.

56. Harrington, *Political Works*, pp. 613–614; see also p. 174.

57. Ibid., pp. 163, 172; introduction, pp. 78–81.

58. Hobbes, *Leviathan*, p. 426.

59. On Harrington's subordination of church to state, see Harrington, *Political Works*, introduction, pp. 77–99.

60. Harrington connects Israel to nature, for example, when discussing Israel's foundations in ancient prudence and Jethro's reason-based contributions to Israel's constitution.

61. He speaks of "the resemblance of... [its] government to orbs and spheres" in circular motion. Similarly, he describes the founder-legislator of Oceana, the Lord Archon, abdicating his magistracy after beholding "not only the rapture of motion, but of joy and harmony, in which his spheres without any manner of obstruction or interfering, but as it had been naturally, were cast." Harrington again joins nature and motion when depicting Oceana's "parliament [as] the heart, which, consisting of two ventricles, the one greater and replenished with a grosser store, the other less and full of a purer, sucketh in and gusheth forth the life blood of Oceana by a perpetual motion." Harrington, *Political Works*, pp. 248, 287, 342.

62. Although Israel is the only example of a commonwealth that existed as a concrete state and as an ideal, Harrington sometimes contrasts the ideal, immortal Oceana with actual, mortal states of the past. In this distinction, Harrington also uses Platonic language.

63. "Can theory ever be fully realized in practice? Is it not in the nature of things that action should come less close to truth than thought?" Plato, *Republic* 6:472.

64. W.K.C. Guthrie, *A History of Greek Philosophy*, vol. 4, *Plato the Man and His Dialogues: Earlier Period* (Cambridge: Cambridge University Press, 1975), p. 4.

65. Harrington, *Political Works*, p. 181. Harrington illustrates how the classical commonwealths, as well as Venice, were all imperfect. See ibid., pp. 62–63, 68–70, 161, 164, 168, 181, 206, 238–239, 260, 438; Blitzer, *An Immortal Commonwealth*, pp. 299–300.

66. George Klosko, "Implementing the Ideal State," *The Journal of Politics* 43 (1981), p. 380. Klosko acknowledges that the kalipolis can never be fully realized, even though he defends Plato against the charges (of those he terms "revisionists") that he was never serious about implementing the ideal state sketched in his *Republic*.

67. Harrington, *Political Works*, pp. 661–662, 693–694.

68. Plato, *Republic* 6:499.

69. Harrington, *Political Works*, pp. 635–636. Harrington's use of the concept "form" is discussed in Luc Borot, "Form Is the Life of the Commonwealth," in Borot, ed., *James Harrington and the Notion of Commonwealth*, pp. 151–174. Borot, however, does not link Harrington's discussion of form to the Platonic doctrine of Forms, analyzing instead how "form" is to be understood in biological terms as "life." In addition, Borot does not discuss form in its connection to the commonwealth of Israel.

70. Plato, *Republic* 8:543–9:576b.

71. Harrington, *Political Works*, pp. 184, 321, 604–605.

72. Ibid., pp. 631–632.

73. Ibid., p. 632.

74. Ibid., p. 637.

75. Ibid., p. 638; Josephus, *Jewish Antiquities*, v, ii, 7.

76. Harrington, *Political Works*, p. 639.

77. I Samuel 8:7.

78. Harrington, *Political Works*, p. 175.

79. Ibid., p. 640.

80. Ibid., p. 642.

81. Scott, "Rapture of Motion," p. 141; Scott, *Commonwealth Principles*, p. x.

The Political Thought of John Locke and the Significance of Political Hebraism: Then and Now

Fania Oz-Salzberger

I.

In recent years, for the first time, modern scholarship has begun to acknowledge the distinctive character of the Hebrew and Jewish sources of early modern political thought in Western Europe, presented in recent research as political Hebraism.[1] This term, recently put into currency, relates to the European fascination with what John Locke called "the People whose Law, Constitution, and History is chiefly contained in the Scripture."[2] Scripture, prominently the Hebrew Bible—which, for several advanced Hebraists, is buttressed by the Talmud, Josephus, and Maimonides—tells the true story of an ancient polity once created by God's chosen people. It survived for several centuries, struggled with external and internal challenges, and shaped an evolving governmental structure that included, over time, both republican and monarchical elements. It was marked by a unique, God-given, and humanly developed legal codex. Its well-documented history featured strong and memorable men and women, leaders and commoners, priests and laymen. Significantly, the fascination with the "Law, Constitution, and History" of that ancient polity went beyond its belonging to God's chosen people. Early modern thinkers found the ancient Hebrew polity interesting for historical, political, and philosophical reasons. Many of them mobilized its records for their own contemporary purposes. It spoke to their own state of affairs.

Political Hebraism flourished in European thought for about a century and a half, roughly between Bodin and Locke, with Machiavelli as a significant predecessor. The great tide of political and legal-minded Hebraism emerged in mid-seventeenth-century England, when jurist John Selden built his excellent scholarly reputation upon it, and republican theorists John Milton and James Harrington endowed it with hands-on political significance. Its ebb began in the early eighteenth century, when the Enlightenment threw out the political baby along with the theological bathwater. By the nineteenth century no major political thinker read the Old Testament politically. Only in the last three decades of the twentieth century did scholars begin to unearth political Hebraism as a particular story line—what John Pocock would call a "tunnel"—in the history of political thought.[3] Today we are far from completing the excavations, or even mapping the site. This conference is a wonderful early step in that direction.

The history of ideas is fraught with ironies, ancient and modern. We owe much of the current awakening in the study of early modern political Hebraism to the so-called Cambridge school in the history of political thought and its greatest inspiration, Pocock's modern classic *The Machiavellian Moment* (1975). Yet neither Pocock nor the current Regius professor of history Quentin Skinner has devoted much attention to the Hebraic sources of the *political* thinking of their seventeenth-century protagonists. Skinner, in his most recent work, has put great onus on the "neo-Roman" element of early modern republicanism. His programmatic monograph, *Liberty Before Liberalism*, leaves the Bible out of seventeenth-century republicanism altogether. Other significant recent studies tend to obscure or disregard the political aspects of Hebraic sources. In the indices of several such studies, Athens appears but not Jerusalem (although it is mentioned in the text); Solon and Lycurgus appear—and thus count as figures, historical or mythical, that left their mark on ancient and modern political theorists—but Moses and Solomon, although mentioned in sources and scholarly discussion, are left out of the indices.[4] They do not count as reference points for early modern political sources, not even in Solon's vague league. Similarly, while Aristotle's *Politics* and Cicero's *On Duties* are of course indexed, Deuteronomy and Leviticus are not. In several recent studies, the Bible, or the Hebrew Bible, or the Old Testament, fails to appear in indices although it is mentioned and quoted in numerous locations in the text.[5] In other words, the Bible in seventeenth-century scholarship is like the clean air we breathe: so self-evident that one needn't bother to give it credit. Or else, biblical quotations are set aside as theological icings unworthy of proper listing. The Book of Books is a non-book when it comes to many modern assessments of the early modern political bookcase.

This lack of engagement with biblical political ideas as viable source material for early modern thinkers on the part of historians of political thought, most notably of the Cambridge school, is reflected in a parallel lacuna in recent scholarship on the ancient Israelite polity. Work on the history of Jewish political thought has mostly neglected to treat its interaction with, and impact on, modern political philosophy as a whole.[6] Biblical studies, within the full range of exegesis to philology, have similarly ignored the Bible's Christian readers insofar as they used Scripture to inspire their own political theory.[7]

The recent surge of scholarly interest in political Hebraism is a timely outgrowth, therefore, of two highly energized spheres of contemporary study: the history of early modern political thought and the history of Jewish political practices and ideas. Significantly, both these fields are consciously, if cautiously, conversing with present-day political philosophy. As Quentin Skinner recently put it,

> There must be some deeper level at which our present values and the seemingly alien assumptions of our forebears to some degree match up.... Intellectual historians can hope to produce something of far more than antiquarian interest if they simply ply their trade. It is enough for them to uncover the often neglected riches of our intellectual heritage and display them once more to view.[8]

II.

John Locke, the focus of this essay, is a difficult client for students of political Hebraism. Unlike John Selden and James Harrington, Locke was not a Hebraist in the strict sense of the term: if he had a rudimentary knowledge of Hebrew vocabulary or grammar, he did not employ it in his writing. Nevertheless, Locke's command of the Hebrew Bible, especially the Pentateuch, Joshua, Judges, and Kings, was impressive. Locke's greatest contribution to political philosophy, *Two Treatises of Government* (1690), is saturated with biblical references.

Locke was partially acquainted with the Bible-minded republicans of mid-seventeenth-century England. He may have known Harrington, and surely knew Algernon Sidney. Both of these thinkers wrote in response to Robert Filmer, and Sidney met a bad end for his political efforts. For our purposes, the most important thinker with whom Locke was acquainted was likely John Selden, the full-fledged political and legal Hebraist and possibly the best English reader of Hebrew in his day. Locke owned some of Selden's books and referred to others, including *Mare Clausum*, in his response to Filmer.[9] No one who has read Selden can plead ignorance of serious, historically minded political Hebraism.

Locke spent four formative years in France, and five in the Dutch Republic. He entered the domains of French and Dutch Hebraism, in which Jewish scholars had some part, but we do not know of any of his particular encounters with Jews or Hebraists in this period. Locke claimed not to have been "well-read in Spinoza," but he did read Grotius, of course, and may have come across Petrus Cunaeus. This would suffice to bring him deep into the realm of continental Hebraism.

Whether Locke's copious biblical references testify to a deeper dimension in his political theory, especially in the *Second Treatise*, is debatable. Whether Locke's biblicism is essential rather than ornamental is an open question in current Locke scholarship. Was Locke a political Hebraist, in the sense that reading and using the Hebrew Bible were conceptually germane to his (distinctly modern) political thought? This essay will assess the evidence for responding in the affirmative. I will suggest that Locke's engagement with the Hebrew Bible was more than rhetorical, more than decorative, and extended beyond contemporary Protestant bon ton.

In the past three decades, several major works reexamining Locke have transformed his previous image as a theorist of "thin" or "negative" liberalism, as the spiritual father of capitalism, and as the herald of secular political rationalism.[10] Locke held that promises would not be kept without God, and that no social contract and no civil society would be maintained without keeping promises. He believed not only that the state must guarantee its citizens' rights to life, liberty, and property, but that its citizens also have duties toward the state, and particularly toward their fellow men, who partake in the image of God.

Locke argued for these principles with reference to both the New Testament and the tradition of natural law. But the key to the link between

Locke's theory of political obligation and his idea of social obligation lay in the Hebrew Bible. Robert Filmer, against whose ideas Locke's *First Treatise of Government* was principally directed, had argued that the king rules by the grace of God and, being a direct heir of Adam, is exempt from human control. Locke summoned all his biblical expertise in order to refute the argument that God gave Adam absolute sovereignty, or that this sovereignty was passed on, first to Noah and then by lines of legitimate patrimony all the way to James II of England. Rule is not an absolute possession, Locke asserted, and it is not passed on through lineal inheritance.[11] The right to rule depends on the ruler's commitment to the rights of the ruled, and it may be annulled and transferred when the violation of the subjects' rights exceeds tolerable limits.

For many modern interpreters, Locke's political theory, and his underlying philosophy of natural law, is independent of scriptural reliance on divine revelation. C.B. Macpherson's classical—and lately much-disputed—reading of Locke as a "theorist of appropriation" and champion of the anchoring of private property rights neatly disregarded his religious engagement and obliterated any mention of his biblical reading.[12] Leo Strauss, who took Locke for a closet Hobbesian, argued that Locke did not maintain his own presumption, stated in *The Reasonableness of Christianity* of 1695, to anchor natural right in the New Testament alone. Instead of formulating a "Politics Drawn from the Very Words of Holy Scripture," as Jacques Bénigne Bossuet would name his 1709 tome, Locke's *Two Treatises* draws on a non-Christian tradition of natural law. His method is anthropological, as Locke readily admitted in a statement Strauss took to be his working motto: "I have always thought the actions of men the best interpreters of their thoughts."[13]

Strauss ardently opposed any claim that the Old Testament was germane to Locke's theory of natural right or, indeed, to his politics. The Straussian line of argument in favor of Locke's "secularism" has been pursued by several recent scholars, mostly relying on his basic epistemological assumption, developed in *An Essay Concerning Human Understanding*, that neither faith nor worship is an innate idea. Consequently, so the argument runs, basing a moral theory on any aspect of divine revelation is by Locke's own lights rationally inadmissible; it is intellectually unworthy of Locke, and anyhow, as far as Lockean politics is concerned, it is a road not taken.[14]

By contrast, a weighty section of recent scholarship has steered Locke back into his Christian origins, his specific Protestant contexts, and his theologico-political epistemology. New scholarship stemming from the Cambridge school's emphasis on contextual history has juxtaposed Locke's *Two Treatises* with his minor works, including his Christian writings, most notably *The Reasonableness of Christianity* and the posthumously published *Paraphrases and Notes on the Epistles of St. Paul* (1706), along-side discussions of faith in *An Essay Concerning Human Understanding* and the *Letter Concerning Toleration*, both of 1690.

A memorable statement to this effect was made by John Dunn in 1980:

> The duty of mankind, as God's creatures, to obey [its] divine creator was the central axiom of John Locke's thought. The entire frame-work of his thinking was "theocentric," and the key commitment of his intellectual life as a whole was the epistemological vindication of this framework.[15]

Jeremy Waldron's *God, Locke, and Equality* of 2002 makes a strong argument for Locke's profound reliance on the New Testament for his philosophy of equality. The concept of equality, Waldron claims, is the mainstay of Locke's political thought and cannot be philosophically jus-tified without accepting his essentially Christian justification of it. The equality and dignity of all human beings, without which the founding fa-ther of liberalism stands to naught, cannot (and, in Waldron's view, need not) survive a secularization of his philosophy.

In the next section I shall review several key arguments for Locke's "New Testamentism," from Dunn to Waldron, and consider their respec-tive implications for the role, if any, of the Old Testament in his thought. My purpose in this overview is twofold: first, to examine the range of current scholarly argumentation for Locke's Scriptural anchor in general; and second, to inquire whether this Scriptural anchor is Christian alone, to find out whether the Hebrew Bible is excluded or marginalized by the emphasis on Locke's "theocentrism," and why.

The concluding two parts of this essay will develop two arguments lo-cating Locke's reading of the Old Testament at the root of this political thought. It is important to stress that these two arguments can work to-gether or as alternatives: (1) that the Hebrew Bible as a holy scripture was essential for the theological basis of Locke's politics; and (2) by contrast or complement, that parts of the Hebrew Bible were of primary impor-tance, qua man-made political, historical, and philosophical texts, for the configuration of Locke's political thought.

III.

The fundamental assumption shared by proponents of Locke's "New Testamentism" is, in Dunn's words again, that "What Locke trusted in was the Christian God and his own intelligence; and when it came to the crunch and the two parted company, what he proved to trust in more deeply was the God and not the intelligence."[16] Human cognition is God-given; human morality makes sense only within the normative contours of divine revelation formulated in holy scripture; and politics ought to provide, as best as humanly possible, for the ends of man as conceived by his Maker. In Dunn's reading of Locke, as in Waldron's, the New Testament is the ultimate source for the metapolitical values that inform all normative social behavior.[17]

Locke himself made a clear declaration in his work *A Second Vindication of the Reasonableness of Christianity* (1697):

> A Christian I am sure I am, because I believe *Jesus* to be the *Messiah*, the King and Saviour promised, and sent by God: And as a Subject of his Kingdom, I take the rule of my Faith, and Life, from his Will declar'd and left upon Record in the inspired Writings of the Apostles and Evangelists in the New Testament: which I endeavour to the most of my power, as is my duty, to understand in their true sense and meaning. To lead me into their true meaning, I know no infallible Guide, but the same Holy Spirit, from whom these Writings at first came.[18]

Despite his mellow portrait of the state of nature, which contradicted Hobbesian brutalism, Locke held a comparatively pessimistic view of human nature. According to Dunn's interpretation, Locke parted ways with Hobbes by insisting that divine beneficence is a sole guarantor of the moral value of human life, as well as for human social arrangements. Unlike the key thinkers of the Scottish Enlightenment in the generation to follow, David Hume and Adam Smith, Locke put no trust in arbitrarily cumulating social relations and constructions. In his view, such human creations could not supply a foundation for moral value, and they could not be rational in themselves. In Dunn's words, "For Locke the duties of most human beings towards terrestrial political authority are in the first instance altruistically prudential specifications of their duties, as common creatures of God, towards their fellow men." Put succinctly, "Political duty was a theoretical derivative of natural theology."[19]

This theological reading of Locke's concept of duty, however, does not single out the New Testament God from the Old Testament God. Quite apart from Locke's own confession of Christian faith and devotion, there is little that is intrinsically "New Testamentist" in his account of political duty in his major political opus. As I will argue below, it is a notion more openly reliant on Old Testament legalism.

The role of God as guarantor of human morality, which for Dunn was the crux of Locke's crucial reliance on Christian faith in all social association, is stated by Locke, in a handwritten note of ca. 1693 quoted by Dunn, in theistic terms that do not include any reference to revelation from either the New or Old Testament:

> If man were independent he could have no law but his own will, no end but himself. He would be a god to himself and the satisfaction of his own will the sole measure and end of all his actions.[20]

Locke stipulated this possibility not as a proto-Nietzschean exercise in political atheism, but as an unthinkable alternative to faith-based public morality. Yet this statement, just like the more famous rejection of an atheist's vow and hence his eligibility to sign the social contract in the *Epistle on Tolerance*, is theist rather than Christian.

In this respect, Waldron presents a clearer Christian angle on Locke's political theory when he attempts to place the idea of equality between human beings, derived from Christian theism, at its heart. According to Waldron, human equality is the common denominator, the concept providing the underlying conceptual unity, of Locke's "arguments about property, family, slavery, government, politics, and toleration."[21] Waldron directly addresses and justifies his notion of the pivotal role of the New Testament, as opposed to the Hebrew Bible, in Locke's idea of equality:

> Why "Christian"? Why not just "*religious* foundations of equality"?... The historical answer is obvious enough. Locke's mature philosophy comprised *The Reasonableness of Christianity* as well as the *Essay [Concerning Human Understanding]*, the *Letters on Toleration*, the *Two Treatises*, and the *Thoughts Concerning Education*.... As a philosopher, Locke was intensely interested in Christian doctrine, and in the *Reasonableness* he insisted that most men could not hope to understand the detailed requirements of the law of nature without the teachings and example of Jesus.[22]

Juxtaposed with *The Reasonableness of Christianity*, Locke's political theory as laid out in the *Two Treatises* bears a strong Christian mark. Waldron makes this juxtaposition a focus of his argument both for Locke's theoretical consistency and for Locke's profound conceptual reliance on the Christian God. Yet, whereas Dunn had claimed outright that the *Two Treatises* is steeped in Christian ideas, Waldron does pause to consider the difficult fact that in Locke's greatest political work citations from the Old Testament far outnumber those from the New Testament.

We remain, then, with the initial query: What is "Christian," rather than theist or, indeed, "Old Testamentist," about the *Two Treatises*, and particularly about Locke's positive statement of political morality, his account of the good polity in the *Second Treatise?*

This, I believe, is a problem not yet addressed by Dunn. Waldron takes it on board by arguing for interdependence between *The Reasonableness of Christianity* and the *Two Treatises*. Presumably, *The Reasonableness* provides the New Testament *sine qua non* for the *Two Treatises*, in which Locke felt he could ignore the direct role of Jesus in the moral justification of the good polity. [23]

Waldron's contextual treatment of the *Two Treatises* does not, of course, preclude either treatise from being considered a book in its own right, and neither does it preclude the two treatises together from being treated as such. Waldron's contextual approach, different from that of the Cambridge school, yields insights that are of great scholarly value. Yet Waldron, like Dunn and many other recent interpreters of the *Two Treatises*, fails to treat Genesis as a book in its own right, and neither Waldron nor Dunn considers the book of Judges, or indeed the whole narrative ("historical") span of the Hebrew Bible, as a work worthy of inquiry as a self-sufficient account of history and social and political theory. The Hebrew Bible was written by many hands, yet its substantial historical part, the Deuteronomist part, arguably lends itself to persuasive integral reading, indeed to several such readings, from both "secular" and "religious" vantage points and—more poignantly—from both literary and scholarly vantage points.[24]

In the following sections I argue that Locke, unlike some of his important recent interpreters, based the *Two Treatises* on a broad array of Old Testament citations not because he trusted his readers to follow up the *Two Treatises* with *The Reasonableness of Christianity* and its two *Vindications*, published between five and seven years later, but because he considered the Old Testament—just as his opponent Robert Filmer did—to be a corpus of both divine and human wisdom in its own right, a history book by its own merit, and a work where unique political and legal ideas were broached and explored.

IV.

The *Two Treatises* treats its readers to a rich and lively Old Testament tapestry of episodes and figures in direct quotes and indirect allusions. By contrast, the New Testament's appearance is meager. A perusal of the comprehensive index in Peter Laslett's edition of the *Two Treatises* should drive the point home: Locke's *Two Treatises* makes *no single mention* of Jesus or of Paul. It does mention (and often discusses at length) Aaron, Abel, Abimelech, Abraham, Absalom, Adam, Adonitsedek, Ahaz, Cain, Esau, Eve, Isaac, Ishmael, Jacob, Jeptah (in a particularly interesting way), Joshua, Judah (not Iscariot), Moses, Noah and his sons, Rebecca, Saul, and Solomon.[25]

Locke's copious use of such citations and allusions is not limited to the *First Treatise*, the polemic against Robert Filmer's Bible-based *Patriarcha*, where Locke presumably wished to strike his opponent with his own rod. It is remarkable that the *Second Treatise*, Locke's groundbreaking discourse of modern political liberty, remains heavily reliant on Old Testament references.[26] The book of Genesis alone is mentioned, referred to, and quoted dozens of times in both treatises.

And yet, Locke's extensive use of the Hebrew Bible in his most original and effective treatise of political philosophy is still generally attributed to his rhetorical battlefield with Filmer. Alternatively, it is seen as mere residue from the *First Treatise*, and more generally as contextual cliché in line with the literary habits and connotative frame of reference of seventeenth-century intellectual discourse. For advocates of Locke's "Christianity," as we have seen above, this Old Testament exclusivity is not easily explicable. For "secular" interpreters, it is little more than theological icing on an essentially irreligious cake.

This begs the question: if Locke's main rationale for using biblical quotations was to refute Robert Filmer's Bible-based endorsement of monarchical paternalism, why did Locke bother with numerous biblical allusions in the *Second Treatise*, which no longer targets Filmer? If

Locke's purpose in this work was to steer clear of Genesis-style patriarchalism, and indeed to present an essentially modern theory of political right, why bother deflecting his readers with such a rich array of biblical allusions far beyond the minimum requirements of contemporaneous rhetorical bon ton?

I will offer two distinct, though possibly commensurable, answers. First, I will argue that the God of the *Two Treatises* is God the Lawmaker, and as such he is theologically grounded in the Old Testament, and almost solely there. Second, I will refer to Locke's deep intimacy with the Bible as a historical and political source-text. That intimacy was obviously Christian in its motivation, but it allowed the Hebrew Bible to work in Locke's mind alongside the other books that made their mark on him, from Aristotle to Grotius. It affected his imagination no less than the travel literature on America did, and it provided him with moral and political problems, and a set of responses, of no lesser importance than Bodin or Hobbes did.

In the present paper, these two arguments cannot be fully developed. What follows is an analysis of some key evidence to substantiate my two main contentions: (1) that the deity guaranteeing Locke's good polity, insofar as it is a legislative deity, is closer to Jehovah than to God the Father; and (2) that the Hebrew Bible was a freestanding history book, enriched by deeply inspiring political materials, on Locke's most cherished bookshelf.

V.

For Locke, Genesis and Deuteronomy and Judges and Kings consisted of a political history worth working with. They came from an ancient civilization to be reckoned with. To be sure, the Israelites were "God's own people" and hence a special case compared with the Athenians and Spartans and Romans. But the crucial point is that they made a polity in history, a constitution in legal history. Thus, the Israelites offer a case study among others and subject matter for theoretical comparison and analysis.

Locke was not the first to historicize the Old Testament for the purposes of political theory. Niccolò Machiavelli may be credited with the first substantial historical reading of the Bible, and Jean Bodin followed suit with a detailed analysis. It is especially interesting that the natural lawyers who had a historical tale to tell, Hugo Grotius and Samuel Pufendorf, took the Old Testament seriously as a historical textbook. Locke belongs firmly in this tradition. Like Pufendorf, he treated the pre-Mosaic era as the early part of a historical phase theory of economic advance and political progress. The discussion of primitive society in terms of the post-Eden generations, or the premonarchical civil society identified with the era of the Judges, is an exercise common to Locke and to the natural jurists.

"Thus in the beginning all the World was *America*," Locke famously wrote.[27] Yet, as this pointed paraphrase of the first line of the Hebrew Bible indicates, Locke's America, throughout the *Two Treatises*, is almost always a Genesis-like America.

Textual scrutiny reveals that almost every appearance of America in the *Two Treatises* dovetails with a similar, often more detailed account from the early chapters of the Hebrew Bible. It would not be a great exaggeration to suggest that whenever Locke rhetorically crosses the Atlantic, Adam and Eve are lurking in the foliage, no more than a paragraph away.[28]

In the *First Treatise*, America's tribal and linguistic plurality is made to flow directly from the biblical pre-Babelian dispersion of nations and languages. Paragraphs 144–145 are crucial, insofar as they include America *among* (rather than descending from, or reflecting, or echoing) the primeval tribal polities described in the early chapters of Genesis. Locke's anti-Filmer argument here is clear and cutting, and his use of the Old Testament is essential: no "Fatherly Authority" and no "Adamite Lordship" were conferred on tribal chieftains, in Carolina or in Shinar. For "we know not who were their Governors, nor what their Form of Government, but only that they were divided into little Independent Societies, speaking different Languages."[29] From this state of multifarious political vagueness, Locke tells Filmer, no unilinear chain of political authority can possibly lead to James II of England and Scotland.

The argument is well known to Locke scholars. But it is seldom noted how Locke then repeats it almost verbatim, and we must pay attention to his telling use of pronoun: "The Scripture says not a word of *their* [my emphasis: i.e., the Americans,' among all primeval societies'] Rulers or Forms of Government, but only gives an account, how Mankind came to be divided into distinct Languages and Nations."[30] This is much more than a refutation of Filmer on his own scriptural ground. Scripture, specifically Genesis, describes the American tribal system. In other words, Genesis lays down the principles of every primitive polity. It may be vague about their governors and forms of government, but it provides a universal concept of primeval human society that has at least three essential components: (1) it is multinational; (2) it is multilingual; and (3) its form(s) of government and the nature of its leadership(s), whatever they were, are not on record.

The last component of the scriptural concept of primeval society is of special interest, because Locke says in the *Second Treatise* that "Government is everywhere antecedent to records."[31] Does this mean that the Old Testament is not a "record"? On the contrary, it is the one exception to the rule. "And those [records] that we have," Locke writes in the same paragraph, "of the beginning of any Polities in the World, excepting that of the *Jews*, where God himself immediately interpos'd, and which favours not at all Paternal Dominion, are all either plain instances of such a beginning, as I have mentioned, or at least have manifest footsteps of it."[32]

Genesis is clearly a historical record, then, albeit (and perhaps even enhanced by its being) God-given. Furthermore, the *Second Treatise* goes further than the *First Treatise* by stating clearly that this record may be vague about primeval forms of government, but it is clear enough, and political enough, to "favour not at all Paternal Dominion" in the Filmerite vein, meaning that no primitive leader inherited either God's paternal or Adam's lordly rights. Taken together, the passages from the two treatises are my *quod erat demonstrandum*: the Hebrew Bible is legitimate historical-political record for Locke, and even a unique and essential one. Far more than a sophisticated turning of the scriptural table on Filmer, it is a positive gleaning of a crucial category of political analysis, a viable account of the first phase of political history from the book of Genesis.

There is a fascinating parallel, to which I will return, between Locke's view of American and post-Adamite political multiplicity, and his assertion in the *Second Treatise* that in "the first Ages of the World" men owned only as much land as they could till. Here, too, Adam and Noah keep company with American tribesmen:

> The measure of Property, Nature has well set, by the Extent of Mens *Labour, and the Conveniency of Life*; No Mans Labour could subdue, or appropriate all;... This *measure* did confine every Man's *Possession*, to a very moderate Proportion, and such as he might appropriate to himself.... And the same *measure* may be allowed

still, without prejudice to any Body, as full as the World seems. For supposing a Man, or a Family, in the state they were, at first peopling of the World by the Children of *Adam*, or *Noah*; let him plant in some in-land, vacant places of *America*, we shall find that the *Possessions* he could make himself upon the *measures* we have given, would not be very large, nor, even to this day, prejudice the rest of Mankind.

Beyond the first chapters of Genesis, Locke followed John Selden, Algernon Sidney, and possibly John Milton in using the premonarchical history of the Jews in order to contradict, and even lampoon, Filmer's biblical monarchism. Again targeting his rival's reliance on the tribal throngs in the New World, he ridicules Filmer's "confused account of a multitude of little Kings in the *West-Indies*, of our *Ferdinando Soto*, or any of our late Histories of the *Northern America*... as by any thing he brings out of Scripture, in that Multitude of Kings he has reckon'd up."[33]

Locke's America, then, can be folded back into the scriptural category of primeval premonarchical society. I do not suggest, of course, applying such reductionism to the recent debate, ignited by James Tully, of Locke's alleged protocolonialist, "Eurocentrist" view of America as a real estate free-for-all.[34] This fascinating issue is beyond my present scope.

What I do argue is that anyone looking for a theory of government rooted in a historical conception of early polities need look no further, according to Locke, than the historical books of the Hebrew Bible up until I Samuel 8 and the establishment of the Israelite monarchy, a late political development (and, to Locke's republican predecessors, a lamentable one) ending a long and distinguished nonmonarchical political history.

Locke made the Hebrew Bible backfire on Filmer, but at the same time he mustered this part of Scripture to present a well-founded alternative story, a rich political history wholly devoid of kings sporting paternal rights to authority. In Locke's own words:

> ...I thought he [Filmer] had been giving us out of Scripture, Proofs and Examples of Monarchical Government, founded on Paternal Authority, descending from *Adam*; and not an History of the *Jews*: amongst whom yet we find no Kings, till many Years after they were a People.[35]

The textual proximity between America and Genesis as models of early human societies is one example of the constant Lockean interplay between "anthropological" and biblical props for basic arguments. Beyond the quote-juggling Filmer-bashing that most scholars have seen in this final section of the *First Treatise*, Locke goes on to present a firm positive political reading of the Hebrew Bible. In the *Second Treatise*, free of Filmer, Locke uses the Hebrew Bible profusely in his most pivotal discussions of the state of nature, the state of war, property, the beginnings of political society, and conquest.[36] What, then, does Locke suggest that the Hebrew Bible positively teaches of the good government?

VI.

That men left the state of nature and established civil society out of necessity is a lesson Locke drew from Hobbes but chose to establish on the historical testimony of the Old Testament. Locke's state of nature is occasionally conflictual, demanding temporal leadership and justice. Appealing to divine intervention may prove insufficient in such prepolitical quarrels: Otherwise, why would the children of Israel and the Ammonites take up arms after the judge Jeptah explicitly called upon God to judge between the two?[37]

Locke did not pick up the Jeptah story, or any other of his references from the book of Judges, in an arbitrary manner. St. Augustine had read the same biblical text politically, and like Pierre Jurieu and several other Protestant thinkers, Locke saw in the period of the Judges a transitional stage between the state of nature and civil society, and discerned in its failings a proof of the necessity of the state for resolving disputes.[38] It was the Bible, Locke argued, that documented the particular moment that "puts men out of a state of nature into that of a commonwealth, by setting up a Judge on Earth" and establishing "a political, or civil, society."[39] What modern Locke scholars have failed to note is the intrinsically political character of the book of Judges, which has a strong claim for a dominant position in a cohesive political worldview underpinning the Hebrew Bible's early historical narrative.[40]

Locke, unlike many of his modern readers, did record the legalist and limited-government essence of biblical history. The Israelites, he maintained, founded a state that was not only unique and divinely ordained, but that "favours not at all paternal dominion."[41] The Pentateuch furnishes the detailed legal basis for what Locke had called in an earlier work "national Jewish liberty."[42] This liberty was based entirely upon obedience to the laws given at Mount Sinai. It was abandoned, as Locke pointed out, both by the Pharisees, who were haughty enough to think that they "sat on Moses' chair,"[43] and by Jesus, founder of "Christian liberty," whose essential purpose was "not to submit to legal injunctions."[44] Thus, "the Scriptures being utterly silent" about everything that pertains to *other* governments, and the Bible "speaks very little of polities,"[45] indeed; but this silence is with regard to other nations and not to the manifest political logic of the Israelite state.

The presence of God in the ancient Jewish constitution, as in a modern, well-governed state, is for Locke the sole guarantee for any political transaction. Yet no ruler can arrogantly assume absolute dominion while at the same time relying on God's grace. If a ruler is tyrannical, the divine right flows through those who would rebel against him—as Locke found in the assistance God rendered to Hezekiah in rebelling against the king of Assyria in the book of Kings.[46] Once again, biblical history underscored the most fundamental of Lockean assertions, continuing the line of argument broached by the monarchomachs a century earlier.

Let us take a step further. There is a telling parallel between Locke's rejection of an alleged legacy of Adam's patrimony in governmental affairs, and his refutation of a post-Adamite claim to Adam's dominion of the world in terms of rights to property. If no king can claim an unreserved birthright dating from Adam, no owner can claim property rights going back to the same primogenitor. For just as Adam was not absolute sovereign of the earth, neither was he its owner. He received no *dominium* from his Creator over the land beneath his feet. By extension, neither did Noah or his sons. In both cases, the political and the economic, God reserved the ultimate authority, or dominion, for himself. This double limitation, on government and on possession, brings together Locke's theory of limited government with his "moral economy," delimiting single ownership in favor of human solidarity. In the beginning, said Locke, all the world belonged to all human beings.[47] Here was the subtle link between Locke's theory of government—the limitation of political dominium—and his moral economy, which was based on the limitation of material dominium. The link lay in the second and third chapters of the book of Genesis.

As we have seen, Locke directly connects his theme of small-polity pluralism, both in America and in the biblical era of the patriarchs, to his parallel claim that "every Man's possession" was confined "to a very moderate Proportion" in both these primeval societies.[48] The chapter "On Property" in the *Second Treatise* sheds light on the growth from small properties to large enclosures as a biblical timeline.[49] Estates, just like polities, grew and consolidated with the passage of time. Just as Adam did not exercise political patriarchal rights over the world, he enjoyed no private dominion over it, and thus could not pass on either legacy to any descendant:

> And thus, without supposing any private Dominion, and property in *Adam* over all the World, exclusive of all other Men, which can no way be proved, nor any ones Property can be made out from it; but supposing the *World* given as it was to the Children of Men *in common*, we see how *labour* could make Men distinct titles to several parcels of it, for their private uses; wherein there could be no doubt of Right, no room for quarrel.[50]

This statement formally parallels Locke's greatest political principle, that no single heir and no great king can claim to be the heir to Adam's lordship, let alone to a right of patrimonial authority, which even Adam himself could not claim. In strikingly similar terms, the *Two Treatises* thus denies any biblical proof for one-man patriarchy and for one-man dominion, asserting instead that both political and property rights were parceled out to numerous individuals.

More research is required to single out the Hebraic strains in Locke's "moral economy." Most of Locke's interpreters today agree that he viewed the historical phase prior to the enclosure of property, a phase identified with the early part of Genesis, as a "negative community," from which people took for themselves private property over the course of time, and not as a "positive community," according to which all of the land belongs to all human beings in perpetuity.[51]

Locke took a republican stance on the importance of private property as the sole basis for civic participation in the political community. Property is the footing of civic involvement, which in turn is the condition of liberty. Hence, the property confiscated by Charles II and James II deprived their opponents, among them radical Puritans of Locke's own milieu, of their civic standing. Despite the fact that Locke's mature political model was a limited monarchic one, some important republican elements may be discerned in his thought. He found elements of a federal republic in England, with its decentralized government, strong local rule, and lively civic participation.[52] Locke's intense interest in the multifarious smallholdings characterizing early societies, from biblical to American, falls in line with this idea of property as the prop for widespread civic rights.[53]

To be sure, the famous account of economic evolution in the chapter "On Property" of the *Second Treatise* explains why the limited self-tilling agrarian economies of the distant past were transformed by the invention of money. That necessary development greatly increased the possibility of accumulating wealth and property.[54] But if a fellow man is starving, his right to life overrules our right to property, and men are obligated to feed him at their expense. Locke's words in the *First Treatise* are well worth quoting here, although they seldom are:

> But we know that God hath not left one Man so to the Mercy of an-other, that he may starve him if he please: God the Lord and Father of all, has given no one of his Children such a Property, in his pe-culiar Portion of the things of this World, but that he has given his needy Brother a Right to the Surplusage of his Goods; so that it can-not justly be denied him, when his pressing Wants call for it.[55]

Peter Laslett, in his editor's note on this paragraph in the *First Treatise*, suggested Locke had Luke 11:41 in mind.[56] I disagree. The words of Jesus against the Pharisees in Luke are a distinct statement of voluntary char-ity: "But rather give alms of such things as ye have; and, behold, all things are clean unto you." By contrast, Locke's text puts justice before mercy and coins the term "right to surplusage," strongly reflecting the social leg-islation of the Pentateuch. There, landowners are subject by law to hand over their surplusage—the precise kinds of leftover field crop known as *leket, pe'a,* and *shicheha*—to the needy, leaving nothing to goodwill. Locke himself does not give a New Testament reference for his "right to surplu-sage" passage, but surrounds it by a refutation of Adam's claim to private dominion. "The Sovereignty of Adam, built upon his Private Dominion, must fall, not having any Foundation to support it."[57]

Absolute ownership is thus as unacceptable as absolute rule. The right to property—which Locke of course maintained—was partly offset by the hungry man's "right to surplusage." Only the Hebrew Bible, not the New Testament, could support this legalist, nonvoluntary approach to the re-lation between the wealthy and the starving, thanks to its unique model of an altruistic community rooted in law.

In an early essay written in 1663 or 1664, Locke wrote that mate-rial possessions "are never so much ours that they cease to be God's." Is it possible, Locke asked in that context, that God's words in matters of property might contradict natural law? Was the exodus from Egypt, carrying off Egyptian goods, at the command of the Lord—here Locke directs his readers toward Exodus 12:35—tantamount to a violation of the natural property rights of the Egyptians to retain their Hebrew slaves? He answered in the negative, for God may transfer property from one to another without violating the natural right of the previous owners, because all property is given to us as a "loan" from God.[58]

While I do not suggest that this early opinion remained unchanged in the *Two Treatises*, I do suggest that it echoes in the "right to surplusage" that we have seen in the *First Treatise*, as well as in the chapter "On Property" in the *Second Treatise*. Individual property, parceled out from the original community, may well enjoy "no doubt of Right, no room for quarrel"; but Adam's heirs are mutually committed to human preservation and to rightfulness in the eyes of God. In this respect, it is God who retains the ultimate *auctoritas* and the ultimate *dominium*, those that Adam never had and his heirs can never rightfully claim. Political as well as economic powers never "cease to be God's."

VII.

I now address a question that may well overturn my argument. Does Locke's resort to natural reason render his biblical quotations conceptually redundant? Is Old Testament wisdom merely a byword for natural law? Does Locke simply ornament his quintessentially modern contribution to the contemporary tradition of natural jurisprudence with biblical patterns?

Several scholars have indeed asserted that he did. I offer a recent example almost at random. "Locke," Stephen Buckle writes, "supports his argument at crucial stages by appeal to biblical quotations: God commanded us to labour, on a world he had given to us in common, and to do so because he 'has given us all things richly to enjoy'. The presence of such quotations is not enough to establish the charge, however, because he also insists that these claims are in accord with natural reason."[59]

In order to take issue with this view, I would like to focus on "God the Lawmaker," the foundation of Christian natural-law tradition. As Knud Haakonssen succinctly put it in his analysis of Locke's *Essay Concerning Human Understanding*, "In order for a rule to be a law, it has to issue from a lawmaker," and three such sets of laws and lawmakers can exist: "the divine or natural law, stemming from God; the civil law, imposed by governments; and the law of opinion or reputation, arising in a given social group."[60]

Could Locke prove rationally that natural law was enacted by God? For Haakonssen, "the central question is whether Locke did, or could, deliver something which, by his own standards, would be considered a rational argument for the proposition that God is a lawmaker for humanity..., or whether he relied, or had to rely, on revelation at this point."[61] This, I suggest, is a Christian rather than a Hebraic or Jewish dichotomy.

In Haakonssen's terms, Locke maintained that "Christ in fact re-promulgated the law of nature, which had previously been known only partially by natural reason or through God's word to Moses, and taught it and its attendant sanctions more perspicuously than these other sources could."[62] This observation, which I would not directly contest, helps bring out the irreplaceable role of the Hebrew Bible in Locke's mature political philosophy: it provided the prototype for a *law-based culture*, rather than for a legal corpus in the abstract. It offered historical evidence for an early society with a complex legalist-moral code, divinely ordained by its own lights, which worked rather well, and for rather a long time.

John Selden taught, and quite likely taught Locke, that Israelite civil law was tantamount to natural law itself. Revelation was surely at work on Mount Sinai, when Moses delivered the words of God as a ready-made constitutional text to a nation at its birth. But this was a revelation different from Christ's. It enacted a detailed and evolving legal corpus and launched legal and social institutions within a dynamic and evolving polity. Numerous workaday examples attested to a broad historical experience of enacting the laws. In at least one crucial moral sense, which I have explored, this legal tradition differed from the teachings of Christ: Locke, like Selden, took on board the Jewish *legal* and *procedural* approach to economic equity, which was quite different from the Christian voluntary appeal to *caritas*.

Precisely because, in the words of the early Locke, the purpose of Christ was "not to submit to legal injunctions,"[63] the *Two Treatises* could not rely on the New Testament. Locke's mature idea of a Bible-supported natural law, his paradigm of "God the lawmaker," and his insistence on the divine retaining of the ultimate fatherly authority and the ultimate dominion over property, made the Old Testament an indispensable political source.

I have argued that the Hebrew Bible gave Locke a solid foundation for his argument for the limitation of government as well as for the limitation of private ownership. Like Harrington and Sidney, Locke took heed of the biblical, not the Christian, economics of political stability: manifold smallholdings are the backbone of a commonwealth, and the limitation of property breeds stability. This was neither Christ's denunciation of property nor the Levelers' extreme redistribution; it was a fine-tuning of social differences, laid out in legal detail in the Mosaic law. A final advantage of revisiting Locke's Hebraic-biblical sources is that the rich fabric of legal-political thinking they convey cannot all be folded into what John Dunn has famously dubbed "what is dead" in Locke.[64]

VIII.

The case of Locke may support the proposition that political Hebraism cannot be properly addressed by scholars today unless the biblical narratives of ancient Israel are placed on par with *The Constitution of the Athenians* and *The Twelve Caesars*. They ought to be placed on the same shelf as other important sources of early modern political thought. After all, hath a (biblical) Jew no polis, legal organs, constitution, rulers, political language? Faced with the same crises, does he not respond politically? Failed by his form of government, does he not reform it? Hit by a drought, does he not exercise distributive justice? Locke scholars today would not skip Grotius, whom Locke read attentively. They ought not skip Genesis, Deuteronomy, and Leviticus, Judges and Samuel and Kings, which Locke read even more attentively. These books make a good political read. At the very least, they merit the detailed respect Locke himself gave them.

Notes

1. For recent assessments, see Arthur Eyffinger and Gordon Schochet, "From the Editors," *Hebraic Political Studies* 1:1 (2005), pp. 3–6; Fania Oz-Salzberger, "The Jewish Roots of Western Freedom," *Azure* 13 (2002). For substantial recent research into modern Hebraism in the context of political thought, see Frank

E. Manuel, *The Broken Staff: Judaism Through Christian Eyes* (Cambridge, Mass.: Harvard University Press, 1992), and Daniel J. Elazar's four-volume opus *The Covenant Tradition in Politics* (New Brunswick: Transaction, 1995–1998). See also Adam Sutcliffe, *Judaism and Enlightenment* (Cambridge: Cambridge University Press, 2003), esp. chs. 2 and 10.

2. John Locke, "First Treatise," in Locke, *Two Treatises of Government (1690)*, ed. Peter Laslett (Cambridge: Cambridge University Press, 1988), 169, p. 263.

3. Ian Hampsher-Monk, "Political Languages in Time—The Work of J.G.A. Pocock," *British Journal of Political Science* 14 (1984), p. 89.

4. See, for example, Anthony Pagden, ed., *Languages of Political Theory in Early Modern Europe* (Cambridge: Cambridge University Press, 1987). In other respects this is a most valuable volume.

5. Thus, Peter Laslett's immensely popular and impressively thorough edition of Locke's *Two Treatises of Government*, published in *Cambridge Texts in the History of Political Thought* (Cambridge: Cambridge University Press, 1960 and numerous later editions and amended reprints), has no "Bible," "Hebrew Bible," or "Old Testament," or indeed "New Testament," in its bibliography or index. Individual biblical tomes are similarly absent; the book of Genesis, the focal point of the present essay, is thus nonexistent as a source of Locke's thought. By contrast, all authors known to Locke, from Aristotle to Tyrell, are duly listed and indexed.

6. This absence is particularly conspicuous in Michael Walzer et al., *The Jewish Political Tradition*, vols. 1–2 (New Haven: Yale University Press, 2000, 2003).

7. Cf. Norman K. Gottwald, *The Politics of Ancient Israel* (Westminster: John Knox, 2001).

8. Quentin Skinner, *Liberty Before Liberalism* (Cambridge: Cambridge University Press, 1998), pp. 117–119.

9. See Locke, "First Treatise," 21, p. 156, and the editor's note there.

10. It was understood thus by C.B. Macpherson in his well-known book *The Political Theory of Possessive Individualism: Hobbes to Locke* (Oxford: Clarendon, 1962). Some of the more significant reassessments that have appeared recently are mentioned in subsequent footnotes.

11. Locke dedicated the first of his treatises on government to this subject. His refutation of the hypothesis of lineal inheritance, making extensive use of the Bible, appears in Locke, "First Treatise," 9, pp. 218–236.

12. Macpherson, *Political Theory of Possessive Individualism*, part 5.

13. John Locke, *An Essay Concerning Human Understanding* (London, 1690), ed. P.H. Nidditch (Oxford: Oxford University Press, 1975), book 1, ch. 2, 3. See Leo Strauss, *Natural Right and History* (Chicago: University of Chicago Press, 1950).

14. A recent example is Michael P. Zuckert, *Launching Liberalism: On Lockean Political Philosophy* (Lawrence, Kans.: University Press of Kansas, 2002), part 2.

"It is Locke's view," Zuckert writes, "that reason is not in possession of such rational knowledge of the existence of a revealing God.... Since Locke lacks rational knowledge of a revealing God, he knows of no authentic revelation, including of course the Hebrew and Christian Scriptures."

15. John Dunn, "From Applied Theology to Social Analysis: The Break Between John Locke and the Scottish Enlightenment," paper presented at a symposium sponsored by the Conference for the Study of Political Thought and the Folger Institute for Renaissance and Eighteenth-Century Studies, Folger Shakespeare Library, Washington, D.C., March 21–23, 1980; published in Istvan Hont and Michael Ignatieff, eds., *Wealth and Virtue* (Cambridge: Cambridge University Press, 1983), pp. 119–135, here p. 119. Cf. John Dunn, *The Political Thought of John Locke* (Cambridge: Cambridge University Press, 1969).

16. John Dunn, *Western Political Theory in the Face of the Future* (Cambridge: Cambridge University Press, 1979), p. 40.

17. Dunn, *Western Political Theory*, pp. 41–42. Jeremy Waldron, *God, Locke, and Equality: Christian Foundations in Locke's Political Thought* (Cambridge: Cambridge University Press, 2002). Cf. Victor Nuovo, "Locke's Christology as a Key to Understanding His Philosophy," in Peter A. Anstey, ed., *The Philosophy of John Locke: New Perspectives* (London: Routledge, 2003), pp. 129–153.

18. John Locke, *A Second Vindication of the Reasonableness of Christianity* (London, 1697), in Locke, *The Works of John Locke in Nine Volumes* (London: Rivington, 1824), 12th ed., vol. 6, ch. 47, p. 359.

19. Dunn, "From Applied Theology," pp. 128–129.

20. Bodleian Library MS, Locke c. 28, fol. 141, quoted in Dunn, *Political Thought of John Locke*, p. 1.

21. Waldron, *God, Locke, and Equality*, p. 151.

22. Ibid., p. 12.

23. Another line of defense is offered by Victor Nuovo in his review of Waldron's book, where he rightly claims that "Waldron never makes clear just what kind of Christianity Locke adhered to, except a vaguely Protestant sort." In Nuovo's view, Locke's Christianity was "messianic," in the sense that he took the whole scriptural narrative to form "a sacred history" from the Garden of Eden to the Last Judgment. Locke's political thought leans against the early part of this eschatological narrative, "prior to the Mosaic theocracy"; hence his dense use of the book of Genesis in the *Two Treatises*. I doubt whether this line of explanation accounts for Locke's significant use of the book of Judges, which I will analyze in the next section. See Victor Nuovo, review of *God, Locke, and Equality*, by Jeremy Waldron, *Notre Dame Philosophical Reviews*, May 4, 2003, http://ndpr.nd.edu/review.cfm?id=1267.

24. The recent history of political thought, including most of the scholarship on Locke, has not caught up with new scholarly readings of the Hebrew Bible, which treat it (or some of its components) with an exegetical respect more similar to that of Locke himself. Outstanding examples include Robert Alter's interpretative introduction to his edition of *The Five Books of Moses* (New York: W.W.

Norton and Company, 2004); Leon R. Kass, *The Beginning of Wisdom: Reading Genesis* (New York: Free Press, 2003); and Yoram Hazony, "Does the Bible Have a Political Teaching?" *Hebraic Political Studies* 1:2 (2006).

25. This is a partial list of Hebrew Bible names in the index of the Laslett/ Cambridge edition; see *Two Treatises*, pp. 451–464.

26. For an exceptionally comprehensive, book-length analysis, see Kim Ian Parker, *The Biblical Politics of John Locke* (Waterloo, Ontario: Wilfrid Laurier University Press, 2004).

27. Locke, "Second Treatise," 49, p. 301.

28. Locke, "First Treatise," 144, 153; Locke, "Second Treatise," 36–38, 65, 101–102, 108–109.

29. Locke, "Second Treatise," 144, p. 247.

30. Locke, "Second Treatise," 145, p. 247.

31. Locke, "Second Treatise," 101, p. 334.

32. Ibid.

33. Locke, "First Treatise," 153, pp. 254–255.

34. James Tully, "Rediscovering America: The *Two Treatises* and Aboriginal Rights," in G.A.J. Rogers, ed., *Locke's Philosophy: Content and Context* (Oxford: Clarendon, 1994), pp. 165–196; Tully, *An Approach to Political Philosophy: Locke in Contexts* (Cambridge: Cambridge University Press, 1993), pp. 137–176. For a representative counterargument, see Stephen Buckle, "Tully, Locke, and America," *British Journal for the History of Philosophy* 9:2 (2001), pp. 245–281.

35. Locke, "First Treatise," 153, p. 253. Locke's argument on the nonpatriarchal nature of authority in the premonarchical biblical polity goes on until 158, p. 257.

36. Significant instances include "Second Treatise," 11, 21, 25–26, 36, 101, 109, and 196.

37. Judges 11:27. Jeptah went as far as confronting the Ammonites with legalistic arguments regarding the right of the Israelites to their land. The crucial role of this story for Locke is apparent in his "Second Treatise," 21, p. 282; cf. Locke, "First Treatise," 163, p. 260, and "Second Treatise," 109, p. 340, and 176, p. 376. In an editor's note, Laslett maintains that "Locke evidently regarded the story of Jeptah as crucial to the scriptural foundations of his case about civil society and justice" (Locke, "Second Treatise," p. 282).

38. Laslett, editor's note, Locke, "Second Treatise," p. 282.

39. Locke, "Second Treatise," 89, p. 325.

40. For a recent, and in my mind persuasive, reconstruction of this worldview as focusing on limited monarchy with moderate republican elements, see Hazony, "Does the Bible Have a Political Teaching?"

41. Locke, "Second Treatise," 101, p. 334.

42. John Locke, "First Tract on Government" (1660), in Locke, *Political Essays* (Cambridge: Cambridge University Press, 1997), pp. 26–27.

43. Matthew 23:2.

44. Locke, "First Tract on Government," pp. 26–27.

45. Locke, *Political Essays*, p. 51. If the holy scriptures had been a complete constitution for all human concerns, argued Locke, then any new civil legislation would be considered blasphemy. See his "Second Tract on Government" (ca. 1662), in Locke, *Political Essays*, p. 72.

46. "And the Eternal was with him; wherever he went forth he prospered; and he rebelled against the king of Assyria and would not serve him" (II Kings 18:7). In this context Locke highlighted the biblical use of the verb "rebel," indicating explicit divine sanction for political rebellion. Locke, "Second Treatise," 196, p. 396.

47. In the "First Treatise," Locke argues that neither Genesis 1:28 nor any other source makes reference to "Adam's monarchy or private dominion, but quite the contrary.... To conclude, this text is so far from proving Adam sole proprietor, that on the contrary, it is a confirmation of the original community of all things amongst the sons of men, which appearing from this donation of God, as well as other places of Scripture; the sovereignty of Adam, built upon his private dominion, must fall, not having any foundation to support it." Locke, "First Treatise," 40, p. 169. Cf. Peter Laslett, "Introduction," in Locke, *Two Treatises*, p. 101.

48. Locke, "Second Treatise," 36, p. 292. Cf. editor's note on p. 292.

49. Locke, "Second Treatise," 38, pp. 295–296.

50. Locke, "Second Treatise," p. 296.

51. See especially Richard Tuck, *Natural Rights Theories* (Cambridge and New York: Cambridge University, 1979); James Tully, *A Discourse on Property: John Locke and His Adversaries* (Cambridge: Cambridge University Press, 1980); Dunn, *Political Thought of John Locke*. Tully, who argues that Locke employs the principle of "positive community," is in disagreement on this point with Tuck and Dunn (as well as with Hont and Ignatieff), who attribute to Locke the model of "negative community."

52. In these political qualities Locke found a mixture of good Christianity and Roman republicanism. The primary sources for the study of morals, according to his work "Concerning Reading," were Cicero's *De Officiis* and the New Testament. On this point I follow the interpretation of Mark Goldie, "Introduction," in Locke, *Political Essays*, esp. p. xxvi.

53. A particularly interesting interpretation of Locke's use of Genesis is offered by George M. Gross, "Notes for Reading the Bible with John Locke," *Jewish Political Studies Review* 9:3–4 (1997), pp. 5–18. Gross suggests that Locke's engagement, in the *Two Treatises*, with the divine blessing ("Be fruitful and multiply, and replenish the earth") is republican in essence, and aimed against the population-limiting consequences of absolute monarchy. I intend to grapple with this interpretation in an expanded version of this essay.

54. Locke, "Second Treatise," 36, pp. 292–293, and the editor's note to this paragraph on p. 292. Several pivotal aspects of early modern natural jurisprudence remain beyond the present discussion, notably the distinction between "perfect right" and "imperfect right," as well as the dispute between Filmer and Locke over the kind of consent involved in the original division of property. Locke took pains to emphasize, with the aid of the Bible, that the state of nature was an era of great abundance, and hence universal agreement was not required when some individuals began to appropriate land.

55. Locke, "First Treatise," 42, p. 170.

56. Ibid., editor's note.

57. Ibid., 40, p. 169. And again, immediately following the "right to surplusage" passage and concluding the *First Treatise* chapter on "Adam's Title by Donation": "From all which it is clear, that tho' God should have given *Adam Private Dominion*, yet that *Private Dominion* could give him no *Sovereignty*; But we have already sufficiently proved, that God gave him no *Private Dominion*."

58. John Locke, "Essays on the Law of Nature VII" (ca. 1663–1664), in Locke, *Political Essays*, p. 126.

59. Buckle, "Tully, Locke, and America," p. 275, referring to Locke, "Second Treatise," 25, 31.

60. Knud Haakonssen, *Natural Law and Moral Philosophy from Grotius to the Scottish Enlightenment* (Cambridge: Cambridge University Press, 1996), p. 53, referring to John Locke, *An Essay Concerning Human Understanding*, book 1, ch. 2, 3, book 2, ch. 28, 5–10.

61. Haakonssen, *Natural Law*, p. 54.

62. Ibid., p. 57.

63. Locke, "First Tract on Government," n. 42 above.

64. John Dunn, "What Is Living and What Is Dead in the Political Theory of John Locke," in Dunn, *Interpreting Political Responsibility, Essays: 1981–1989* (Oxford: Polity, 1990), pp. 9–25.

V. THE STATE OF THE FIELD

The Judeo-Christian Tradition as Imposition:
Present at the Creation?

Gordon Schochet

1. Of Traditions: Judaic, Hebraic, and Judeo-Christian

Is there a Jewish, or Judaic,[1] *political* tradition? The late Daniel Elazar, who was a pioneer in the field, would probably have answered yes,[2] as would, in all likelihood, David Novak and L.E. Goodman, among others. Michael Walzer and his colleagues, in their monumental *The Jewish Political Tradition*, have given a qualified but positive response as well,[3] and it is reasonable to presume that the contributors to their collaborative effort would agree. Ultimately, of course, the response to the question depends on what is meant by *tradition*, a notion that is fraught with ambiguity and imprecision.[4]

The two parts of this essay are much revised versions of very different but closely related presentations at the 2004 conference. Both deal with the uses of Judaism and Judaic writings—their *appropriation* and attempted absorption—by Christianity and what is here called "Christianized" western culture. Part 1 is the more conventionally academic and scholarly of the two. Part 2, on the other hand, is largely autobiographical narrative. But the points of both parts are identical: to highlight the cultural (and conceptual) impositions that are at the roots of so-called Judeo-Christianity, to take back those parts that properly belong to Judaism, and to continue an argument that goes back at least to the beginnings of "exilic" or diaspora Judaism's self-consciousness for the autonomy, growth, and continuing vitality of a Judaic tradition that can comfortably exist both within and alongside a Christian world.

In the "strong" or "robust" and etymologically literal sense, tradition is a "handing down" from the past that is accomplished with a discernible persistence or continuity and somewhat intentionally and contains an overarching coherence; and from that perspective, the answer to my question is probably an equally qualified No. While it is possible to find political meanings in Jewish texts—the comments about monarchy in Deuteronomy and Samuel come immediately to mind—and to infer principled bases for the political arrangements that appear in the Hebrew Bible, self-conscious theorizing about politics was not a characteristic feature of historical Judaism the way it was and continues to be of cultures that confront the relationships among overlapping but conflicting normative systems, such as law, religion, and morality.

This essay examines the issues surrounding the question of a Jewish political tradition, moves on to consider what we have come to call "political Hebraism," and from there to a discussion of the "Judeo-Christian tradition," and concludes that that tradition represents an *appropriation* from Judaism, not, as alleged, its *incorporation* into the folkways of the modern world. That incorporation, I argue, begins with the primitive Christian claim to have *succeeded* biblical Judaism. The consequent re-rendering of the Hebrew Bible into the Old Testament[5] is a reduction of the fundamental text of Judaism to the exemplary—sometimes positive, sometimes negative—prehistory of Christianity, and the process is in full force in the early modern period.

There is, to be sure, a Jewish religious and *theological* tradition—several of them, in fact, the evidence suggests, which makes the larger tradition itself complex and subject to varying interpretations—that satisfies all the requirements. It is in the nature of religious traditions that they be continuously handed down and actively received, and that reception often takes the form of commentary and amendment. In the case of Judaism, the self-conscious theological tradition and the biblical history from which it springs are the necessary starting points for all analyses.

But what is missing is an equally persistent tradition of what is called political discourse. It is possible to *extract from*, and even *impose upon*, theological and historical Judaism political contents or set of meanings and implications. Even though there is no body of specifically political writing that we can point to—nothing (directly) comparable to, say, *The Republic*, *Leviathan*, or *On Liberty*—there are embedded in Judaic writings pervasive and continuing concerns with and observations on questions of membership, authority, obedience, law, justice, social and economic exchanges, and suchlike—the issues that are inherent in political systems and which inspire the reflective commentary that is conventionally known as "political theory." They are a series of not at all consistent injunctions to Jews about how they should live with one another and respond to secular authority. For rhetorical and therefore political purposes, these concerns and observations can be abstracted, strung together, commented on, and thereby understood as a tradition of Judaic political discourse, but that would be a relatively loose way of speaking and relies on a considerably weaker sense of tradition than the etymology calls for. Short of "inventing" it, as Eric Hobsbawm and Terrence Ranger famously put it,[6] it is very difficult to find a self-contained political tradition within these injunctions and more difficult yet to uncover a tradition of political discourse.[7]

It is a near commonplace of recent historical scholarship that political meanings can be found in "texts" and writings[8] from genres that are not overtly political: literature, religion, and even art and architecture all, in different ways, are bearers of political aspects of the cultures within and/or for which they were created. They can reinforce, attempt to undermine, or simply reflect the ideologies or power structures of their societies as they address more abstract issues or depict the commonplaces of life (and satisfy the overt criteria of their genres). Wittingly or no, texts enter into and broaden their cultures' self-descriptions, contribute to social and political discourse, and become intellectual fodder for latter-day commentators. Such analysts will readily *find* political ideas and political thought *in* the Hebrew Bible, *in* rabbinic commentaries, and *in* the Talmud. And to the extent that they also find continuities and coherences, they might well be inclined to speak of a Hebraic political tradition.

Such claims, however contentious, would assert that there is a characteristically Jewish conception of politics, but in order to be understood, this conception must be extracted from sources that students of the history of political thought might regard as unconventional. While this is not the same as saying that there are functional equivalents within Judaism to *The Republic*, *The Two Treatises*, and all the rest, it does suggest that Judaism has a place in the history of political thought. Even though we do not encounter references to *a*—let alone *the*—biblical political theory or tradition, it is certainly arguable, at a further remove, that Judaic writings have rightful places in the canon of western political thought.

And the uses of biblical teachings and historical examples to support contemporary political injunctions underscore the notion, perhaps most contentiously, that Judaism has contributed to what we call the western political tradition. But the substance of that contribution remains at issue: just as scholars and commentators disagree about the meanings of Plato, Hobbes, and others, they will disagree about the direction and the content of political Judaism.

The "invented traditions" of Hobsbawm and Ranger are of little help here, for they are *practices*[9] and the roots of *institutions*—as in "We've long or always done or had that"—not the traditions of transgenerational *discourse* that are the grails of historians of political thought. The establishment of practical and institutional traditions calls for historical "cherry picking" of a retrospective sort that purports to explain to the present where it has "come from" and why it is important to retain its venerable practices and values. The difficulty presented by appeals to traditions is evident from the debates that surround reliance on precedent in common law adjudication and interpretation. The rich body of phenomena that constitutes the past supports multiple and conflicting sides of debates about whether precedents govern specific situations and, if so, which one rules. And the law in this respect is a more rigidly structured and precise instancing of what is always involved in an appeal to a justifying and ruling past, to a tradition. It is necessary to demonstrate both that the tradition or precedent exists and that it actually covers a case at hand. As binding norms, precedent and tradition are important means of regulating complex and diverse societies. In Judaism, where so much of the tradition and practice is contained in juridical fiat, as in the societies that are heirs to the English common law tradition, the law is one of the primary carriers of the governing tradition, and the law must be *interpreted* in order to determine its applicability.[10]

A cobbled-together—"invented"—conceptual and intellectual *tradition of discourse* is difficult to sustain, for the putative participants might not recognize it as it is deployed in the present. Nonetheless, we string together assertively similar writings with great frequency and, without full regard for conceptual niceties, call them traditions. The claims are that bodies of people engage in continuing, one-way "conversations" in the form of commentaries on their predecessors, and that the records of those conversations constitute traditions of discourse. As I said, these commentary conversations are the very stuff of theology, and there is no question but that there are theological and religious traditions of discourse.

"Judeo-Christianity," variously described as a "tradition," a "heritage," a "culture," or even a "way of life," is widely regarded as the basis of western culture. The "Judeo-Christian tradition" is proclaimed to be the sacred and shared heritage of the West; it purports to remind us that our foundational beliefs and practices—equality, liberty, justice, toleration—are rooted in "The Bible," which is itself conceived as a harmonious composite of its *old* and *new* Testaments. This "tradition" speaks of the kindredness of humankind—at least of western humanity—telling us that we are all members of the same, encompassing family. It is something of a "totalizing" ideology, a means—much like the old self-understanding of America as a "melting pot"—of appreciating that our differences, whatever they may be, are overshadowed and absorbed by what we have in common, which is contained within the tradition. And like most ideology-based traditions, it rests on a set of spiritual or suprahuman claims both about itself and about the kinds of ties it establishes among its adherents.

The Judeo-Christian tradition appears to have begun to acquire its cachet as a self-conscious response to Nazism and the anti-Semitism it encouraged.[11] The subsequent popularity of the concept in the period immediately after World War II was due to the attempt of much of western Christianity to understand and confront the factors that led to the Shoa. And in that respect, the invention of Judeo-Christianity was probably as much an embarrassed response as it was, rather like the rainbow that God placed in the sky after the flood, a mark of western civilization's commitment to see to it that nothing like this would ever again occur.[12] Mass extermination, so the implicit mantra would run, is contrary to all that defines us.

Despite the relatively recent appearance of the name, the roots of the modern Judeo-Christian tradition can be traced back to the foundational moments of Christianity and the resolution of questions about its doctrinal relationship to Judaism. Christianity presents one of the clearest and most interesting instances of doctrinal appropriation by absorption in the history of thought. Paul, the unknown author of the Epistle to the Hebrews, and the compilers of the New Testament simultaneously retained and superseded Old Testament revelation. The relatively narrow and almost "national" divine law of the Hebrews, when it was not replaced, was complemented by the faith of Christians and the universal grace of salvation. It was doctrinally and practically a brilliant move that separated Christianity from the need for a territorial base.

The "Europeanized" world—more conventionally known as "the West"—has long borne the yoke of the "Judeo-Christian tradition," long before it was given a name and often without knowing that it is a burden to be endured. This longer tradition, the one that extends back to the birth of Christ, is ultimately an invention of Christianity and did not need the Nazi horrors to summon it to life. It asserts a continuity between Judaism and Christianity and, indeed, claims that they are basically compatible on fundamental issues, but without specifying what those issues are other than a commitment to monotheism. It does not necessarily require that this "Judeo-Christian" God be omniscient, omnipotent, or even universal, only that it (or "He") be singular. Implicitly, this tradition asserts, along with Christianity itself, that Judaism is continued by Christianity, or at least that what was vital in biblical or prophetic Judaism was incorporated into and thereby perpetuated by Christianity. And embedded in that assertion is the notion that Judaism was succeeded and supplanted by Christianity, which, of course, is the story that Christianity alone tells about itself.

The difficulty with this story is that Judaism continued to exist after the advent of Christianity, and from the perspective of that living, postbiblical Judaism, any talk of a Judeo-Christian tradition has to be deeply offensive. There is a softer but even more problematic version of the story that holds that the values of Judaism and Christianity together are foundational to modernity. But what could those values possibly be, given both the substantial differences between Christianity and Judaism and the fact that Christian dogma is dependent upon the phoenix-like emergence of Christianity from the dying remnants of biblical Judaism? In the history that Christianity has here conceived, something called "Judaism" managed to hold on to its institutional life and to insinuate itself into the Christianized world, but the *true* Judaism, the pre-Christian Judaism, has been absorbed into and perfected by Christianity. There is simply no room for that older Judaism in the world made by Christianity.

In another sense, however, the *notion* of a Judeo-Christian tradition seems to suggest something different, precisely because of its vague imprecision. It seems to be an invitation to modern Judaism to recognize or to enter into a partnership with Christianity on the grounds that they share enough that is important to permit them to dissolve their differences.

Like all traditions, it is an incorporating story that brings in outsiders by sanitizing them, by *assigning* them a role in a story that is probably not their own but which they are encouraged to adopt. It seems almost to suggest a two-way affection, but it is ultimately deceivingly Machiavellian in that the basis of the proffered love is fear: accept and participate in the story, or be destroyed by exclusion; these are the terms of the new social covenant.

Among the advantages of participation is the prospect of being permitted to have one's own space, but on problematic and sometimes difficult terms:

> We know that there are differences between us; that's part of what makes life interesting. But those differences are tolerable only in the context of general agreement and sameness.

This offer has to be oppressive, but it is often the only viable option for members of minority groups. In this respect, it ceases to be exclusively about Jews in a world of Christian hegemony but is about all who retain "identities" that differ from those of the dominant culture. And it may be that the offer, in the end, is relatively generous in a world of intense anxiety and cultural insecurity.

But there is a different worldview that begins with a celebration of "difference" and "diversity" and presumes that they are desirable (and perhaps ineliminable, which carries the further implication that we should make the most of what we cannot avoid). While this begs the questions of how much pluralism a society can tolerate without jeopardizing its existence and whether the minority or divergent groups can actually be trusted not to attempt to overthrow the society, these are empirical *and* psychological questions, and both are questions to which we have no definitive answers. Nonetheless, the *model* of toleration and forbearance, "recognition" and liberty, and rights and trust is a preferable alternative to *practices* that are rooted in superiority and anxiety.

While I do not mean to suggest that all uses of the Judeo-Christian tradition are intentionally oppressive and mean-spirited—it is often invoked innocently and with the best of explanatory motives and intentions—the notion itself certainly is. But from the outside, it functions as a coded imposition of what can only be called hegemonic Christianity that works most effectively when it is not cited by name.

The failure of attempts to add references to God to the preamble to the constitution for the European Union in order to retain an awareness of Europe's "Christian heritage" is a case in point. And the way that they played out is illustrative of my claims. First, there were complaints about obscuring the "Jewish contributions" to that heritage, and then about the missing Muslims. Subsequently, with the prospect of Turkish member-ship, Pope Benedict XVI, then Cardinal Joseph Ratzinger, a major Vatican spokesperson on matters of faith, argued that Muslim Turkey stands "in permanent contrast to Europe." At that point, the self-important *New York Times* replied editorially that the values the cardinal wished to pre-serve "are universal, not a Judeo-Christian monopoly."[13]

According to the story it tells about itself—which, for present purpos-es, will be taken as a true story—Christianity begins its conceptual and structural lives as an extension of biblical Judaism. From its own internal perspective, it was a "reforming" movement, but unlike the Reformation Protestant sects with which we are familiar, Christianity did not originate in the need to correct the "errors" of the established religion. Its far less modest goal was derived from a new revelation, not the discovery of mis-take or corruption; and its vantage was the future, not the past. In these terms and from the perspective of the Judaism that it sought to amend, Christianity was heretical and ultimately "schismatic," in the almost soci-ological vocabulary that Christianity itself was to use in the early modern period to condemn breakaway sects: heretical because it advocated doc-trines that were contrary to those of Judaism; schismatic because while it did not succeed in taking over and/or destroying the parent (Judaism, in this case)—which is the goal of any reformist sect—it did become strong enough to exist on its own.[14]

I do not intend to suggest that Judaism, in whatever state of organi-zation it was when confronted by emergent Christianity, systematically treated the new sect as heretical. However, it is important to understand that the representatives of Christianity soon behaved in the strident man-ner of the reformer imbued with a new truth, a truth so all-encompassing and striking that, if adopted, would undo the whole of biblical Judaism. One of the first goals of these Christians was to convert the Jews who had not yet "accepted Christ" as the Messiah and "son of God." The ba-sic claim, as enunciated in the Epistle to the Hebrews and Paul's Epistle to the Galatians, among other places, was two-pronged: that Christianity was continuous with and a legitimate extension of Judaism and that those who rejected Christ would be denied admission to heaven and the bless-ings of eternal salvation.

This notion of continuity, of course, is the germ of what moderns call the Judeo-Christian tradition: that there is a distinct set of values that is the joint and presumably evolved legacy of historic Judaism and Christianity, that this legacy is shared and kept alive by Jews and Christians, and that it provides the way of understanding and acting in the world that is characteristic of the West, a "cultural tradition" that, according to J.H. Hexter, is "the oldest in the world."[15] The core of that tradition is a moral and spiritual universalism anchored by a monotheistic conception of the deity. And in those terms, it sounds like a version of Christianity filtered through and sanitized by the Kantian Enlightenment. But beyond this, it is difficult to identify what this tradition contains. It is much easier, however, to see it relied upon as a legitimating concept.

"Tradition," as I suggested above, is an inherently political notion. A substantial part of the link it makes between past and present is irreducibly political. The "handing down" or "over" from the past to the present *functions* as a "reaching back" from the present to the—perhaps better thought of as *a*—past. To identify something as a tradition, or traditional, is to assert and in some instances to establish that link and to embed a specific present in an equally specific (although not necessarily specified and however general) past. Placing a text, a practice, a rule, a fashion, or even a mode of understanding within or declaring it to be part of a tradition is interpretatively to constitute that practice or rule and functionally to police it: to establish backward-looking controls over what it is, what it requires, and what can be said within and about it. The invocation of tradition prescribes standards for behavior and establishes the borders of permissibility against rival claimants; in short, it establishes what Friedrich Carl von Savigny, the founder of German historical jurisprudence, described as "the vital connection that ties the present to the past."[16]

The Judeo-Christian tradition serves precisely this set of functions: it constitutes, it polices, and it legitimates—all by invoking the past. At the same time, in its modern form, it is "invented." Invented traditions are self-consciously political; they are brought into being to lend the status of natural social growth to an institutional contrivance. To call something a tradition is to attempt to clothe it with an authority that is virtually unassailable.[17] The invention of the Judeo-Christian tradition by that name,[18] probably in the period following World War II, was a way of making Jews and the post-Nazi world safe for each other. But the ingredients of that "tradition"—the presuppositions on which it rests and the historical claims it makes—are far older than the name. They go back at least to the Christian Hebraists of the early modern period.

Even without the name "Judeo-Christian tradition," the appeal to authority of venerated Hebrew writings served precisely this function. Use of the Hebrew Bible—as the so-called Old Testament—as a valid historical text was a well-established practice in early modern Europe, rendered all the more important because of the claimed inheritance of the Hebrew past, which had been transformed into the prologue to the Christian present and future. Because Christianity completed and ultimately superseded it, the Hebrew Bible was not a significant source of doctrine. Whatever it contained of God's plan for humankind had been amplified and clarified by the new revelation. It is easy to understand that an age that was increasingly obsessed with history and historical justification on the one hand and with religion and theology on the other would look to biblical history.

One of the hallmarks of early modernity was its response to political and religious upheavals. Overcoming crisis required roots, continuities, and, most important, guidance. Machiavelli's combing of Roman history in search of solutions to what he saw as the instability of Florence is well known. The hand-in-glove development of English historiography and common law jurisprudence is perhaps a somewhat less familiar instance of the same sort of behavior. They were parts of a more general movement from a humanist to a "juridical" worldview,[19] to a perspective that would come to value "interests" and "order" more than it would "civic virtue," that, beset by multiple religious denominations, would eventually have to find room for non-adherents within confessional states.

The Hebrew Bible was one—albeit perhaps the most important—text to which early modern political theorists and theologians turned, but the *meaning* of its historical narrative was hardly straightforward. To take only one example, Samuel's response to the demand for a king by the Children of Israel and the fearsome picture he drew of monarchical powers was taken by Sir Robert Filmer as an endorsement of absolutism, whereas other commentators saw it as a warning. And the appeal to the God-given power of Adam in the book of Genesis by that same Filmer to justify patriarchal kingship was used by John Locke to an altogether opposite end, to fortify the claim that familial and other kinds of authority were fundamentally distinct from political power.

But why, beyond the use of the Hebrew Bible as a historical source, was there a turn to post-biblical and rabbinic Hebrew texts in this period? What was the politics of this move? What was at stake, and why? In an age that, with some notable exceptions, was hardly friendly to its own Jews, why were the Hebrew forebears of Christianity often treated as just another ancient civilization like the Greeks and Romans? To be sure, the Hebrew Bible enjoyed a special status as being inspired by God, an account of God's originally chosen people, and the initial working out of God's plan, but that is not sufficient to explain its relatively newfound political popularity. I'm not persuaded that we yet know the answers to these questions, but I want to suggest that looking at them from the general perspective of the anomalous Judeo-Christian tradition might help.

Functionally and politically, the use of rabbinic and other Hebrew writings was a way for early modern Christian polemicists to solidify the incorporation of Hebrew history into their own. It was a continuation of the Pauline argument for Christianity as a necessary completion of that history, a capturing of the "chosenness" of the Children of Israel for early modern and especially Protestant Europe,[20] and a condemnation of those who did not embrace the new revelation. Interestingly enough, as I have noted, it was not the doctrines or religious practices of the ancient Hebrews that were invoked but their history and political practices. The expulsion of Adam and Eve from Eden and the flood story—both pre-Hebrew—were put to significant doctrinal use with little or no overt recognition that they came from the Old Testament. Even granting the important exceptions, we should keep in mind that this early modern Hebraism existed in a Europe that had little fondness for the Jews of its own day, unless, of course, they were willing to convert to Christianity. The operational story is something like the following:

> We are the legitimate heirs to the promises of the Old Testament. To be sure, your ancestors were the original bearers of that promise, and even among the rabbinic commentators, there were those who understood and could interpret it. But it is now our story, and if you want to participate in it, you must join us; you must redeem the failure of your ancestors to accept the Word. Those who do not join us will be separated and persecuted.

But the Christian interpolations were not an extension and perfection of the original revelation; they were its subversion. Universality and salvation, the foundations of biblical Christianity, are antithetical to biblical Judaism. The first gives rise to proselytizing and intolerance, tempered by other-regardingness and charity; the second is immanent and knowable. Together, they provide a Christian mission to "bring the Word" to and to convert the world in order to save it. The Christian world is a particularly unpleasant place for those who have been offered grace but have rejected it; Jews are especially hated because, according to some accounts, they initially attempted to destroy Christian truth and subsequently refused to embrace it. Since biblical Judaism is also the wellspring of Christianity, there is a special mission to convert them.

The history of political thought, whatever else it is, is the history of inspiration and appropriation: it is a series of accounts of "authors," in the larger sense, who have reached conclusions in their thinking and writing *because of* the "texts"—also conceived expansively—of others. In the case of "inspiration," it is not necessary that the later and "inspired" authors have read or interpreted the prior "texts" *correctly* or in ways that the earlier, "original" authors would have approved or even recognized; only that there be a demonstrable if not conscious dependence on the original text.[21] "Appropriation," as the direct use and incorporation of someone else's arguments, is somewhat more problematic. Unless the later author acknowledges the appropriation and identifies the sources from which he or she is appropriating, it is often up to the scholar-interpreter to discover similarities between texts and somehow to establish that one set of claims has been lifted from an earlier source, sometimes in so crude a formulation as "That sounds very much like what X said 300 years earlier; *therefore*, it is likely that it was inspired by or even lifted from X."[22] The stock in trade of historians of political thought has long been the delineation of continuity through similarity.

Both inspiration and appropriation fall under the general rubric of "influence," a category that was famously rendered suspect by what has come to be called "Cambridge historicism," that is, the methodological work of Quentin Skinner and John Dunn[23] and their students.[24] Too much of what had passed for the "history of political thought," they demonstrated, consisted of invented influences and concocted "traditions of discourse" that ultimately revealed more about the so-called historians of political thought than about the authors they studied. But without some showing of continuity—some demonstration that authors responded to and incorporated the work of others—the history of political thought is not a proper history at all but is a mere chronological string of beads. The challenge was not to forgo the (false) history of political thought and to replace it with a deeply contextualized and historicist approach to political thought but to work harder and to uncover proper influences, which Skinner certainly did in his masterful *The Foundations of Modern Political Thought*[25] (without using the dreaded term); which Dunn accomplished in his studies of trust, political obligation, and the development of "democratic" political ideas;[26] and which was richly done in the various collaborative histories of philosophy and political thought published by Cambridge University Press.

What we increasingly think of the "Hebraic political tradition"—that is, the uses of biblical, rabbinic, and talmudic Judaic writings in politics and the history of political thought—is considerably less problematic as a mine of inspiration and appropriation than is the broader history of political thought. The resort to Hebraic texts, however, has long been hidden from view—obscured by the absorption, re-naming, and derogation of the Hebrew Bible by Christianity, by the social and political marginalization of Judaism in Europe, and by the fact that the Jews were long without a political state of their own. On the whole, it was presumed that Jews did not make identifiable contributions to political thought. The interpretative practice of seeing a growing separation of politics from theology for the period after the Renaissance and the Enlightenment-bred suspicion of religion—manifesting itself equally if differently in constitutionalist liberalism and Marxism—made recognition of a Hebraic political tradition that much less likely.

The relatively small handful of recognized Jewish thinkers and philosophers (and theologians)—including Philo, Josephus, various rabbinic commentators, Maimonides, Spinoza, Mendelsohn, Herzl, Buber—have not generally been conceived as constituting a "tradition," and certainly not a *political* tradition. And so long as a "tradition" is regarded as possessing a certain coherence and consisting of people with compatible interests and needs talking with and appropriating from one another over time, it remains difficult, as I argued above, to make a case for a persistent Jewish political tradition that could reasonably take its place in the company of the "liberal," "Christian," or even "American" political traditions. But once we broaden our perspective and look to the *uses* of Hebraic writings by all sorts of people—not just fellow Jews—who were *inspired* by them and/or *appropriated* some of their claims, and, further, once we disentangle the Hebrew Bible/Old Testament from its appropriation by Christianity and conceptual absorption into *the* Bible, we can begin to appreciate the existence of a genuine Hebraic political tradition.

In the end, early modern Hebraism, like the Judeo-Christian tradition to which it is related, is reflective of a deeply rooted intolerance despite the appearance of openness and accord. What seems to be at work here is an inability or unwillingness to accept the pluralistic "diversity" and "difference" that were coming to characterize Protestant Europe. Assimilation—absorption—rather than tolerance remains the first response, and if we cannot make you sufficiently like us, we will have to exclude you. This, I think, is the dark side of Hebraism, that is, of the uses to which Hebraic writings and conceptualizations were put by early modern European (Christian) theorists. But it is far from the whole of the story; it details one of what turned out to be the necessary steps on the path to true tolerance and liberty, a path along which the world still haltingly stumbles.

2. Of Lives: Judaic, Hebraic, and Judeo-Christian

When I was very young, more than sixty years ago—I was seven or eight—my mother gave me a book entitled *One God: The Ways We Worship Him*. For a Jewish kid who had acquired a substantial part of his self-consciousness in the terrifying world of the Shoa and who lived in partial fear of the anti-Semitism of his neighbors, it had a soothing effect, making me feel that there were people who valued me and my family. But it also had a homogenizing quality that I found somewhat offensive even then: *One God* was divided into three sections, one each on "The Jewish Way," "The Catholic Way," and "The Protestant Way." Its message was that despite differences in practices and rituals, we are all the same and we all believe in the same, singular God.

It was undoubtedly a book born of World War II and the Nazi horror, manifesting a rather typically American Enlightenment universalism. Its implicit message seems to have been "We would never treat Jews—or anyone else—the way the Nazis did; after all, we are all brothers." While I do not claim to know what my mother was up to in giving me that book—she was my mother, after all, and her mysterious ways could never be fully comprehended—I am fairly certain that something like what might be thought of as "assimilation" was at work. She sought to make me fit to live and function in the Christian society that the United States was and remains.

Despite the fact that the War was over—but just barely—and despite the appearance of the collective guilt that followed in its terrifying wake, it was not easy or comfortable being Jewish in middle-Atlantic America in that period. On more than one occasion, I had my hat pulled off so that people could see my exposed horns; I was often called "Christ killer" and, some years later, occasionally attacked on my way to bar mitzva lessons; my parents and I were once accosted by a drunk who declared that "Hitler was right; you all should have been killed" (that was the only time I saw my father about to strike someone other than me); and I was educated in a public school system in which we said Christian prayers every morning and in December sang Christmas carols (which to this day I detest; I cannot go into a shopping mall in December without experiencing inordinate revulsion, which can lead to serious limitations in New Jersey, where I live).

On the other side were probably the best of intentions: both to make Jews comfortable and to make us acceptable to Christians, tasks that were all the more vital after we learned about Nazism. And it was probably part of a rote assertion of brotherhood. But the motives of the conscious purveyors of the Judeo-Christian tradition were far more suspect, for that notion bespoke a triumphant and self-justifying certainty that was to be feared and resisted. I am reminded in this context of a very frightening line in Maurice Sendak's wonderfully wicked children's book, *Where the Wild Things Are*: "We love you so much we could eat you up," that is, as I saw it, consume you so that you will no longer exist except as part of us.[27]

Let me return to the book, *One God*.[28] It seems to have been about what, many years later, I learned to call *adiaphora*, religious practices and modes that are deemed to be unessential to religion because God was silent about them. Thus, they are optional and may safely be done or ignored without offense to the central doctrines. The early modern Church of England designated them as "things indifferent," because they were not *necessary* to salvation. Indifference looks like the basis of a doctrine of toleration, but as it was worked out in the early modern period, it was the ground of persecution and imposition: if it is not essential, you can do it our way with no loss, the dominant religious power claimed. The difficulty, as John Locke observed in his *Letter Concerning Toleration*, is that in religion "nothing is indifferent." That is, to paraphrase, your saying that God does not require it cannot trump my belief to the contrary; by your lights, I am being stubborn; by mine, you are being oppressive.

What struck me about the book at the time was that it simplified everything and elided the differences between Christianity and what I had been taught to believe. And I knew a fair amount about Christianity, too, for some of my best friends, as it were, were Christians; indeed, my only friends were Christians. And what I had learned from them, on the contrary, was that we were *very different* but that it really did not matter. Indeed, our differences were an important part of what made our interactions interesting.

What I knew and retained—and what the very idea of my mother's *One God* and subsequently of a Judeo-Christian tradition attempted to obscure—were that the central and ineliminable "fact" of Christianity is the Crucifixion; that the point of Christianity is salvation, which was made necessary by the Fall of humankind; that these two or three (Crucifixion, salvation, and the Fall) are fundamentally, deeply, and inextricably linked but *meant absolutely nothing to me*. And if I knew the story of the Fall, it was not because I had learned it in Hebrew school or even from my grandmother, but because it is an ineliminable part of the story that the Christianized West tells about itself to explain that most perplexing of problems, the existence of evil in a divinely-created and inspired world.[29]

As I said, I was then seven or eight. Today, more than sixty years later, I am hard-pressed to find any comparably central features of Judaism, except, perhaps, the covenantal giving and accepting of the law. But I do not want to engage—or engage in—theology here other than to note that it would be exceedingly difficult for a Jew to participate in a series of practices or to subscribe to a worldview in which the Crucifixion and salvation were central.

True, I speak as an outsider, but I fail to see how theological Christianity can be anything other than, to quote the title of a popular seventeenth-century text, "a doctrine of the cross."[30] But if non-religious, non-theological humanism that is not overtly derived from monotheistic divinity is what is meant by the Judeo-Christian tradition, then, it seems to me, that it is not necessarily either Judeo or Christian, although it may share social and moral injunctions with both.

It is certainly a matter of prudence in the classical sense—practical knowledge derived from experience and, in this case, knowledge that marks one of those rare places where self-interest and virtue intersect—that a world of other-regardingness is simply better—preferable—to one in which people *always* maximize personal advantage. At some point—I don't know how many generations or how much experience it would take—this practical knowledge can become or give rise to a general rule- or norm-system that would include cooperation, forbearance, toleration, and liberty among its primary components.

Figuring out that these things, these practices, are good, that they may even be good in and of themselves—intrinsically good, as they might be called by Kantians and others who accept that category (which I obviously do not)—is undoubtedly difficult. It is more likely that we come to value cooperation and the rest because they sustain and improve our lives. It may take rules that are followed out of some combination of fear and respect for authority to teach us that, and it may be that the original sources of our understanding that cooperation and the rest are desirable are to found in compulsion.

But Christianity insists that its rules be followed because of autonomous acceptance of something that is known to be right and good and is not imposed and because of the love of God; neither self-interest nor prudence can be substituted for faith and acceptance. Much of the energy of Christianity is devoted to the inculcating of the love of Christ. But faith cannot be the basis for politics, unless the political order—state, nation, call it what you will at this point—is the striking arm of the church: obedience to the rulers and following the rules are parts of one's duty to obey God, which, of course, the faithful do without flinching.

The characteristically early modern notion of the divine right of kings was designed to show the faithful that political disobedience was sinful in the fullest sense. This doctrine functioned as an "explanatory threat" and provided a religious justification for punishing the politically disobedient. It was a nice, neat package. To the extent that it was a Calvinist theory—and for these purposes, the two dragons of divine right absolutism, Filmer and Bossuet, must be understood as having used a Calvinist-derived doctrine, even though one was Anglican, and the other Roman Catholic—it was also the consequence of a political Hebraism. For the early Calvinists, the touchstone of that political Hebraism was rooted in an understanding of the Hebrew "theocracy," to which Filmer added interpretations of the first chapter of Genesis, of God's response to the building of the Tower of Babel, and of the powers and entitlements of Moses and the Sanhedrin. But there was another, non-absolutist ways to understand these same examples from the Hebrew Bible: Althusius' way, Selden's way, Locke's way—as models of the *limited*, constitutional political order. (Incidentally—to enter the lists in an extraneous but otherwise important fray—it is nothing short of interpretative mayhem to lump Hobbes and Locke together as "liberals." Whatever it is or is not, liberalism is concerned at its core with the rule of law, limited government, and constitutionalism, none of which is Hobbesian, all of which is Lockean, and some of which is Hebraic.)

In politics, especially the politics that have evolved since the Renaissance era, it is often necessary to do that which is practical rather than that which is *good*. Politics, modern politics most especially, is about conflicting interests and divergent conceptions of the good, about situations in which government-based conflict resolution means the imposition of someone's understanding of that good on someone else. These impositions are in the name of righteousness, to be sure, but they are possible and generally successful precisely because the state is *strong enough* to impose. The good cannot be compromised; the "right," however, is precisely about the forbearance that characterizes compromise.

This is a *non-perfectionist* politics that is altogether at variance with any view of the state as serving substantive moral or religious ends. The job of the state in these terms is not to perfect people, not to make them moral, and not to provide them with the vehicle through which they achieve their true and proper ends, be those ends "virtue" or salvation. This is the "juridical" or rule-of-law, territorial, and ultimately secular state that is codified in 1648 in the Peace of Westphalia. Many of its features had already been celebrated by Machiavelli, demarcated by Bodin, and circumscribed by Althusius, often, so we have been told, with the help of biblical Hebraism. This is the state that is already moving away from the traditional "nation," because the *political* accomplishment of the Reformation—but certainly not the aim of its progenitors—was the irreducible and ineliminable pluralism and heterodoxy that would call forth persecution and toleration, in sequence.

The daunting task facing this state was to find some way of uniting its members once it was realized that they no longer had their traditional bonds of unity, and one of the initial instances of this ideological re-unification was the movement toward what can be seen as a notion of cooperative Christianity despite important sectarian differences. That is not part of our story, but the various practices that we loosely identify with the rule of law and the rest were the preconditions of this eventually-to-emerge modern, tolerant state.

Christianity as we encounter it in the early modern period is incapable of enduring an imperfectionist politics. Christianity is *perfectionist*. The Crucifixion-salvation stories require that it be. Christian politics, therefore, is necessarily perfectionist. Early Christians happily became martyrs to their principles when necessary, because they knew that a perfected next life awaited them. But these early Christians were members of a minority and often persecuted sect, not the commanders of political orders. By the early modern period, when perfectionist Christians had been in political control in the West for more than a millennium, the Reformation presented the world with rival perfectionisms. Asceticism had long since given way to politics and power and was not to be restored to its earlier, ethereal status. True, there were millennial ascetics and other self-denying enthusiasts, but they were on the fringes of mainstream Christianity.

By contrast, biblical and rabbinic Judaism and political Judaism in particular, perhaps because of their relative indifference to an afterlife, were starkly imperfectionist. This imperfectionism was not based on an inherently pessimistic view of human nature but was more the result of an understanding of the world in terms of ever-changing contingencies. And it was precisely the worldview that early modern politics needed.

Appendix

I have borrowed the general notion of *practice* from Michael Oakeshott, and my usage is derived from his, as I understand it. See the essays collected in his *Rationalism in Politics and Other Essays*, new ed., foreword by Timothy Fuller (Indianapolis: Liberty Fund, 1991), esp. "Rationalism in Politics," "Rational Conduct," and "The Tower of Babel"; and his *On Human Conduct* (Oxford: Clarendon Press, 1975), ch. 1.

I agree with Oakeshott that "practices" emerge and grow up more or less "on their own," as it were, and that they are closely tied to what is generally meant by *tradition*. Bundles of practices that persist and somehow "cohere" can be thought of as traditions. (It should be noted, however, that a *practice* by its very nature has already persisted, so the relationships are much more complex than this account suggests.) I do not accept what often appears to be Oakeshott's wholesale rejection of reason and rationality as part of the process. I would argue, on the contrary, that reason can play important roles in shaping and modifying practices and enables them to be accommodated to new or changing conditions.

Oakeshott certainly agreed that practices and traditions were "alive"—which is a way of characterizing their persistence—but had little to say beyond that. For the most part, his *descriptive* accounts were a kind of cultural anthropology, written from the perspective of the outsider, but in the essays commended above, he also wrote *persuasively*, urging those who participated in practices and traditions—and especially those with whom he shared them—to preserve them by recognizing that they could not be reduced to reason and rational rules.

Implicitly relying on H.L.A. Hart's *Concept of Law* and Ludwig Wittgenstein's *Philosophical Investigations*, I would argue that there is a profound separation between *external* accounts of practices and traditions and *internal* participation in them. Oakeshott seems to argue that such participation is best if it is unconscious, but the consciousness he downplays is an unavoidable part of contemporary society, all the more so in societies that are "diverse" or "pluralistic" and in which multiple practices and traditions conflict. The need to defend or *justify* practices—which often is initially done simply by calling them "traditions"—makes those who *participate* in them *conscious* of their existence and function and suggests that they are "constructs" that can be manipulated and not functional, organic, and semi-mysterious growths. But when we have reached that stage, which bears affinities to Max Weber's movement from "traditional" to "rational-legal" societies, we have entered a different conceptual dimension, one in which reason and rationality play substantial roles. Now it is possible for participants to assert their entitlements and/or abilities to alter or even to abandon practices or to persuade others to adopt, honor, or jettison them.

Notes

1. I am distinguishing here between *Jewish* and *Judaic*, on the one hand, to refer to things directly about or internal to Judaism itself, and *Hebraic*, on the other, to refer to things about or external to Judaism and/or the uses of Judaic "things"—Judaic language, history, sacred writings, practices—for purposes that are not necessarily Jewish.

2. See, among other works, Elazar's four-volume series, *The Covenant Tradition in Politics* (New Brunswick, N.J.: Transaction, 1995–1998); and his edited volume, *Kinship & Consent: The Jewish Political Tradition and Its Contemporary Uses*, 2nd. ed. (New Brunswick, N.J.: Transaction, 1997).

3. Four volumes projected, two published to date (New Haven: Yale University Press, 2000–). For the comments about the existence and nature of the tradition, see vol. 1, *Authority*, pp. xxi–xxiv.

4. There is a huge literature on this subject. For recent commentary, see Mark Phillips, "What Is a Tradition When It Is Not 'Invented'? A Historiographical Introduction," in Phillips and Gordon Schochet, eds., *Questions of Tradition* (Toronto: University of Toronto Press, 2004), pp. 3–29.

5. See, for instance, the essays in part 1 of Roger Brooks and John L. Collins, eds., *Hebrew Bible or Old Testament? Studying the Bible in Judaism and Christianity* (Notre Dame, Ind.: University of Notre Dame Press, 1997).

6. In Eric Hobsbawm and Terrence Ranger, eds., *The Invention of Tradition* (Cambridge: Cambridge University Press, 1983).

7. Walzer et al. note that one of their goals is "*retrieval*: we want to make its [i.e., the Jewish political tradition's] central texts and arguments available to new generations of students and potential participants." *Authority*, p. xxiii.

8. Generally, I use the notion of "texts" and "writings" in the expansive senses made familiar by the anthropologists Clifford Geertz and James Clifford to include "culture" and its artifacts—in short, things that, like literal "texts," can and often need to be interpreted. But cultural artifacts, unlike literal texts, do not necessarily have *authors* whose intentions may be important to their meanings. Overt political theory, on the other hand, begins with such literal texts, and its scholarly and historical interpretation often cannot escape the issues that surround authorship. Labeling something as a "tradition" is generally a movement to "persuasion" and avoids many of these attendant problems.

9. By *practice* I mean identifiable social and cultural activity or "conduct" that is more than an unwitting habit but less than coerced behavior and can be seen to have endured over time. In these respects, an enduring practice is similar to a tradition. For further discussion of the notion of "practice" and its relationship to "tradition," see below, Appendix.

10. For discussion of relationships between Judaic and common law, see Robert M. Cover, "The Supreme Court, 1982 Term—Forward: Nomos and Narrative," *Harvard Law Review* 97 (1983/4), pp. 4–68; Suzanne Last Stone, "In Pursuit of the Counter-Text: The Turn to the Jewish Model in American Legal Theory," *Harvard Law Review* 106 (1993/4), pp. 813–894; and Samuel J. Levine,

"*Halacha* and *Aggada*: Translating Robert Cover's Nomos and Narrative," *Utah Law Review*, 1998, pp. 465–504. All three articles contain many useful references that push this topic further.

But there is at least one major theoretical difference: the body of common law remains open and subject to expansion and change through the interpretative process, whereas Judaic law, because it is presumptively based upon divine dictates, is unchanging. For a related analysis, see Aharon Lichtenstein, "Does Jewish Tradition Recognize an Ethic Independent of Halakhah?" in Martin Fox, ed., *Modern Jewish Ethics* (Columbus, Ohio: Ohio State University Press, 1975), pp. 62–78.

11. See Mark Silk, "Notes on the Judeo-Christian Tradition in America," *American Quarterly* 36 (1984), pp. 65–85.

12. Something like that is probably the source of the more recent attempts to include Islam under the same umbrella by appealing to the lineage of Abraham. See, for instance, F.E. Peters, *The Children of Abraham: Judaism, Christianity, Islam,* 2nd ed. (Princeton: Princeton University Press, 2004), and Paul Peachey, George F. McLean, John Kromkowski, eds., *Abrahamic Faiths, Ethnicity, and Ethnic Conflicts* (Washington, D.C.: Council for Research in Values and Philosophy, 1997).

13. "Saying No to Turkey," *New York Times*, August 15, 2004.

14. The aim of orthodoxy, of course, is to destroy heresies and to re-absorb their adherents; when that is done, the former heresy is reduced to an historical curiosity, if it is remembered at all. But when re-absorption attempts fail and heretical groups establish themselves as independent sects that have caused ruptures in the church, they are regarded as "schismatic" or, if the differences are not perceived as being so great, merely "separatist."

15. J.H. Hexter, *The Judaeo-Christian Tradition,* 2nd ed. (New Haven: Yale University Press, 1995), p. xv.

16. As translated from von Savigny's *System des heutigen römanischen Rechts,* 1, p. xv, in Richard Zimmerman, *Roman Law, Contemporary Law, European Law: The Civilian Tradition Today* (Oxford: Oxford University Press, 2001), p. 188. For further development of this understanding of tradition, see my "Tradition as Politics and the Politics of Tradition," in Phillips and Schochet, *Questions of Tradition.*

17. See Hobsbawm and Ranger, *Invention of Tradition.* This should not be taken as an endorsement of that notion; indeed, my essay cited in the previous note and all the other essays in the volume to which it is the conclusion are addressed to the general question, What are traditions when they are not invented?

18. See, for instance, Arthur A. Cohen, *The Myth of the Judeo-Christian Tradition and Other Dissenting Essays* (New York: Schocken, 1970).

19. This shift has been a persistent theme in the writings of J.G.A. Pocock and Richard Tuck. I have discussed it in several places, especially in my "Why Should History Matter? Political Theory and the History of Political Discourse," in J.G.A. Pocock, Gordon Schochet, and Lois G. Schwoerer, eds., *The Varieties of*

British Political Thought (Cambridge: Cambridge University Press, 1994); and in my forthcoming *Rights in Contexts: The Historical and Political Construction of Moral and Legal Entitlements.*

20. Divine providence—the notion that God took a special interest in the individual nations of Protestant Europe, protecting them from their enemies and punishing them when they transgressed—was frequently invoked in the pre-Enlightenment period, especially in England and its American colonies. This was not just a Calvinist view, but it may have had its roots in Calvinist determinism, which itself claimed a descent from biblical Judaism.

21. Among the best-known examples of such conscious inspiration is Kant's assertion that it was his reading of Hume that "interrupted my dogmatic slumber," even though Kant's awakening led him to conclusions that Hume would have rejected. Kant, *Prolegomenon to Any Future Metaphysics* (1783), introduction, 280, Library of Liberal Arts edition, ed. Lewis White Beck (Indianapolis: Bobbs-Merrill, 1950), p. 8. Indeed, any work that comments on—negatively or favorably—another work would fall into this category, such as John Locke's attack on Sir Robert Filmer in his *Two Treatises*. The simple but not-often-enough-appreciated point is that the conclusions of one text are demonstrable consequences of something found in another.

22. A more subtle (and perverse) rendering would be "That's probably a disguised version of X's claims, which suggests that this author is ultimately X but is unwilling to reveal their agreement."

23. Skinner's methodological writings are conveniently gathered—albeit sometimes revised—in his *Visions of Politics*, 3 vols. (Cambridge: Cambridge University Press, 2002), vol. 1, *Regarding Method*. The best known of them is "Meaning and Understanding in the History of Ideas," *History and Theory* 8 (1969), pp. 3–53, revised and reprinted in *Regarding Method* as ch. 4.

Many of Dunn's relevant writings have been collected in his *History of Political Theory and Other Essays* (Cambridge: Cambridge University Press, 1996), but his central contribution to the subject, "The Identity of the History of Ideas," *Philosophy* 43 (1968), pp. 85–116, is not included. It is reprinted in his *Political Obligation in Historical Context: Essays in Political Theory* (Cambridge: Cambridge University Press, 1980), ch. 1; and in Peter Laslett, W.G. Runciman, and Quentin Skinner, eds., *Philosophy, Politics, and Society*, 4th ser., (Oxford: Blackwell, 1972), ch. 7.

24. J.G.A. Pocock is often included with Skinner and Dunn. As important as his work was for the development of Cambridge historicism, he contributed little to the attacks on "influence," but, on the contrary, has continued to insist on distinction between historical and philosophic readings and interpretations. See, in particular, Pocock, " The History of Political Thought: A Methodological Inquiry," in Peter Laslett and W.G. Runciman, eds., *Philosophy, Politics, and Society*, 3rd series (Oxford: Blackwell, 1962), pp. 183–202.

25. 2 vols. (Cambridge: Cambridge University Press, 1978).

26. See the previously cited collections of his essays.

27. In a recent radio interview, Sendak, who is Jewish, said that many of the images in and the larger motivation behind *Wild Things* came from the Second World War.

28. Which I found on the Internet for $1.50 (plus $3.50 postage).

29. I sometimes claim that Jewish accounts of the Garden of Eden story as a "fall" of some sort are a manifestation of "evil envy," attempts to solve the perplexities of the book of Job. For a historical and text-based discussion of the entrance of "incarnate" evil into the world of Judaism, see Elijah J. Schochet, *Amalek: The Enemy Within* (Los Angeles: Mimetav Press, 1991).

30. John Kettlewell, *Christianity, A Doctrine of the Cross: or, Passive Obedience Under Any Pretended Invasion of Legal Rights and Liberties* (London, 1691).

Contributors

Miriam Bodian is a professor of Jewish history at the Graduate School for Jewish Studies of Touro College. Her first book, *Hebrews of the Portuguese Nation* (Indiana University, 1997), received both a National Jewish Book Award and the first Koret Book Award in History. Her second book, *Dying in the Law of Moses: Crypto-Jewish Martyrdom and the Iberian Inquisitions*, was published by Indiana University Press in 2007.

Arthur Eyffinger holds a Ph.D. in classics from Amsterdam University. From 1970 to 1985 he was a research fellow of the Grotius Institute of the Netherlands Academy of Arts and Sciences; subsequently, he became head librarian of the International Court of Justice of the UN in The Hague. Upon his retirement in 2002, he launched Judicap, a center for publications and presentations in the domains of international law and peace studies. Dr. Eyffinger is a cofounder of the Grotiana Foundation and has published extensively on the life and works of Hugo Grotius, on seventeenth-century Dutch issues, and on the history of internationalism and the international courts in The Hague. He is the editor of *The Hebrew Republic* by Petrus Cunaeus (Shalem Press, 2006) and coeditor of *Hebraic Political Studies*. His current projects include a biography of the Russian internationalist F.F. Martens and an edition of Latin poetry by Hugo Grotius on behalf of the Huygens Institute in The Hague.

Meirav Jones is an associate fellow in the Institute for Philosophy, Politics, and Religion, and directs the Shalem Center's Project on Jewish Ideas in the West. She is also associate editor of *Hebraic Political Studies*. In August 2004, Jones organized Shalem's first international academic conference, entitled "Political Hebraism: Judaic Sources in Early Modern Political Thought." In December 2006 she ran an additional conference exploring political Hebraism from biblical times to the present, which was attended by over 100 scholars and graduate students from 10 countries. Jones holds a B.A. in political science and philosophy and an M.A. in political science from the Hebrew University of Jerusalem. She is writing a doctoral dissertation on "The Image of Israel and the Development of Political Ideas in England, 1640–1660."

Menachem Lorberbaum is chair of the department of Hebrew culture studies at Tel Aviv University and a research associate at the Shalom Hartman Institute in Jerusalem. He is the author of *Politics and the Limits of Law: Secularizing the Political in Medieval Jewish Thought* (Stanford, 2001), and coeditor with Michael Walzer and Noam Zohar of *The Jewish Political Tradition*, vol. 1, *Authority* (Yale University Press, 2000), and vol. 2, *Membership* (Yale University Press, 2003).

Christopher Lynch is program director of Great Ideas: Intellectual Foundations of the West and professor of political science at Carthage College. His first book, a translation of Machiavelli's *Art of War* with an introduction, notes, and commentary, was published by the University of Chicago Press in 2003, and he is currently writing a book on war in the works of Machiavelli.

Alan Mittleman is the director of the Louis Finkelstein Institute for Religious and Social Studies and a professor of Jewish philosophy at the Jewish Theological Seminary. He is the author of three books: *Between Kant and Kabbalah* (SUNY Press, 1990); *The Politics of Torah* (SUNY Press, 1996); and *The Scepter Shall Not Depart from Judah* (Rowman & Littlefield, 2000). He is also the editor of *Jewish Polity and American Civil Society* (Rowman & Littlefield, 2002); *Jews and the American Public Square* (Rowman & Littlefield, 2002); and *Religion as a Public Good* (Rowman & Littlefield, 2003). His many articles, essays, and reviews have appeared in such journals as *Harvard Theological Review*, *Modern Judaism*, *The Jewish*

Political Studies Review, The Journal of Religion, First Things, and *The Notre Dame Journal of Law, Ethics and Public Policy.* He is a contributor to *The Cambridge Companion to American Judaism* and is writing a book on politics and hope under contract with Oxford University Press.

Kalman Neuman holds a Ph.D. in history from the Hebrew University of Jerusalem. His dissertation, written under the supervision of Professor Michael Heyd, was on "The Literature of the *Respublica Hebraeorum*: Depictions of the Ancient Israelite State in Early Modern Europe." He is an ordained rabbi and an alumnus of the Mandel Jerusalem Fellows program. In addition to early modern political Hebraism, his interests include questions of philosophy of halacha as well as the religious Zionist application of halacha to contemporary political questions.

Fania Oz-Salzberger is a senior lecturer in history at the University of Haifa and the director of its Posen Research Forum for Jewish European and Israeli Political Thought at the Faculty of Law. Professor Oz-Salzberger is Leon Liberman Chair of Modern Israel Studies at Monash University in Melbourne. Her books include *Translating the Enlightenment: Scottish Civic Discourse in Eighteenth-Century Germany* (Oxford: Clarendon Press, 1995) and *Israelis in Berlin* (Jerusalem: Keter, 2001 [Hebrew]; Frankfurt am Main: Suhrkamp, 2001 [German]). She recently coedited, with Eveline Goodman-Thau, *Das jüdische Erbe Europas* (German and English, Berlin: Philo, 2005). Professor Oz-Salzberger has published essays on the Scottish and the German Enlightenments, on the history of political thought, and on the role of history in current Israeli-European Relations.

Emile Perreau-Saussine received his *diplôme* (B.A.) from L'Institut d'Études Politiques in Paris, and then studied for his Ph.D. at L'École des Hautes Études en Sciences Sociales (Centre Raymond Aron), spending time as a visiting scholar at King's College, Cambridge, and as an Olin Fellow at the University of Chicago (Committee on Social Thought). Since 2001, he has been a fellow of Fitzwilliam College, lecturing at the University of Cambridge on the history of political thought. His two latest articles—the first on Raymond Aron and Carl von Clausewitz, the second on liberals and revolutions—were published in *Commentaire.* His first book, *Alasdair MacIntyre, une biographie intellectuelle. Introduction* *aux critiques contemporaines du libéralisme*, with a foreword by Pierre Manent, was published in September 2005 by Presses Universitaires de France.

Gary Remer is an associate professor of political science at Tulane University and was a visiting scholar at the Center for American Politics and Citizenship at the University of Maryland in the fall of 2005. He is the author of *Humanism and the Rhetoric of Toleration* (Pennsylvania State University Press, 1996) and coeditor of *Talking Democracy: Historical Perspectives on Rhetoric and Democracy* (Pennsylvania State University Press, 2004). He has published numerous articles in journals such as *Political Theory*, *History of Political Thought*, *Journal of Political Philosophy*, *Review of Politics*, and *Polity*.

Jason P. Rosenblatt is a professor of English at Georgetown University. He has also taught at Brown University, the University of Pennsylvania, and Swarthmore College. His publications include *Torah and Law in 'Paradise Lost'* (Princeton, 1994); *Renaissance England's Chief Rabbi: John Selden* (Oxford, 2006); and, as coeditor, *"Not in Heaven": Coherence and Complexity in Biblical Narrative* (Indiana University Press, 1991). He is preparing a critical edition of *Milton's Selected Poetry and Prose* for W.W. Norton. Professor Rosenblatt's awards include fellowships from the John Simon Guggenheim Foundation, the Folger Shakespeare Library, and the National Endowment for the Humanities. He is a past president of the Milton Society of America (1999) and recipient of its Hanford Award (1989).

Wilhelm Schmidt-Biggemann is a professor at the Institute for Philosophy of the Free University of Berlin, and a founding member of the International Society for Intellectual History. His many publications include *Topica universalis* (Meiner, 1983); *Theodizee und Tatsachen* (Suhrkamp, 1988); *Geschichte als absoluter Begriff* (Suhrkamp, 1991); *Blaise Pascal* (C.H. Beck, 1999); *Sinn-Welten, Welten-Sinn* (Suhrkamp, 1992); *Philosophia perennis* (Suhrkamp 1998; English version, Kluever/Springer, 2004); and *Politische Theologie der Gegenaufklärung* (Akademie-Verlag, 2004).

Political Thought at the Folger Shakespeare Library. He is the author of *Patriarchalism in Political Thought* (Blackwell, 1975; 2nd ed., 1988), *Rights in Contexts* (forthcoming), *From Reformation to Revolution: Western Political Thought in the Early Modern Period* (forthcoming), and numerous articles on political philosophy and its history and is coeditor of *Hebraic Political Studies*. His current research and writing deals with the political thought of Hobbes, Locke, Filmer, and Mandeville, politics and patriarchy, religious liberty, Western concepts of conscience, and Hebraism in early modern political and legal philosophy.